While Dangers Gather

While Dangers Gather

Congressional Checks
on Presidential War Powers

*William G. Howell
and Jon C. Pevehouse*

PRINCETON UNIVERSITY PRESS

PRINCETON AND OXFORD

Copyright © 2007 by Princeton University Press

Published by Princeton University Press, 41 William Street,
Princeton, New Jersey 08540
In the United Kingdom: Princeton University Press, 3 Market Place,
Woodstock, Oxfordshire OX20 1SY

LIBRARY OF CONGRESS CATALOGING-IN-PUBLICATION DATA
Howell, William G.
   While dangers gather : congressional checks on presidential war powers / William G.
Howell and Jon C. Pevehouse.
      p.   cm.
   Includes bibliographical references and index.
   ISBN 978-0-691-12515-2 (alk. paper) — ISBN 978-0-691-13462-8 (pbk. : alk. paper)
1. Executive power—United States. 2. Legislative power—United States. 3. Terrorism—
Government policy—United States. 4. War and emergency powers—United States.
I. Pevehouse, Jon C. II. Title.
   JK516.H68 2007
   328.73'07456—dc22   2007013194

British Library Cataloging-in-Publication Data is available

This book has been composed in Sabon

Printed on acid-free paper. ∞

press.princeton.edu

Printed in the United States of America

10   9   8   7   6   5   4   3   2   1

Contents

List of Figures   vii

List of Tables   ix

Preface   xi

Acknowledgments   xxv

PART One
Background and Theory   1

CHAPTER 1
Possibilities of Congressional Influence   3

CHAPTER 2
Conditions that Abet Congressional Influence   33

PART Two
Testing Claims about Congressional Influence   51

CHAPTER 3
Trends in Military Deployments   53

CHAPTER 4
Responding to "Opportunities" to Use Military Force
(with Douglas L. Kriner)   75

CHAPTER 5
Studies in Domestic Politics and the Use of Force   114

PART Three
One Causal Pathway   153

CHAPTER 6
Congress and the Media (with Douglas L. Kriner)   155

CHAPTER 7
The Media and Public Opinion   192

CHAPTER 8
Conclusion   222

APPENDIX A
Tables Relating to Chapter 3   243

APPENDIX B
Text and Tables Relating to Chapter 4   245

APPENDIX C
Table Relating to Chapter 6   259

APPENDIX D
Table Relating to Chapter 7   260

Notes   263

References   307

Index   323

Figures

FIGURE 3.1: Examples of Uses of Force   60

FIGURE 3.2: Time Series of U.S. Uses of Force, 1945–2000   61

FIGURE 3.3: Time Series of U.S. Militarized Interstate
Disputes, 1945–2000   69

FIGURE 4.1: Geographic Distribution of Opportunities
to Use Military Force, 1945–2000   82

FIGURE 4.2: Time Series of Opportunities, Worldwide   83

FIGURE 4.3: Time Series of Opportunities, by Region   84

FIGURE 4.4: Trade, Capabilities, and the Incidence
of Opportunities   88

FIGURE 4.5: Strategic Avoidance and the Incidence
of Opportunities   91

FIGURE 6.1: Media Exposure of Washington Politicians   174

FIGURE 6.2: Production of Arguments for and against
a War against Iraq   179

Tables

TABLE 3.1: Frequency of Uses of Force by the United States 64

TABLE 3.2: Frequency of Minor Uses of Force, Including Background Controls 65

TABLE 3.3: Frequency of Major Uses of Force, Including Background Controls 66

TABLE 3.4: Frequency of Major Uses of Force, with Period Effects 68

TABLE 3.5: Frequency of U.S. Militarized Interstate Disputes (MIDS) 70

TABLE 3.6: Frequency of Uses of Force and MIDS, Congressional Parties and Veterans 71

TABLE 4.1: Probability of a Military Response 96

TABLE 4.2: Probability of a Military Response, Including Background Controls 97

TABLE 4.3: Probability of a Military Response, Adjusting for Strategic Avoidance Behavior 102

TABLE 4.4: Timing of a Military Response, Including Background Controls 106

TABLE 4.5: Timing of a Military Response for Selected Subsamples of Countries 109

TABLE 4.6: Timing of a Military Response, with Period Effects 110

TABLE 4.7: Timing of a Military Response, Congressional Parties and Veterans 111

TABLE 6.1: Who Appears in Stories on Iraq 173

TABLE 6.2: Arguments on Iraq Made in Congress and the Media 176

TABLE 6.3: Volume of Arguments on Iraq Presented in News Stories 183

TABLE 6.4: Volume of Arguments on Iraq Presented in News Stories, with Background Controls 185

TABLE 6.5: Balance of Arguments for and against a War against Iraq 186

TABLE 7.1: Impact of Local News Coverage on Public Support for a War against Iraq 198

TABLE 7.2: Impact of Local News Coverage on Republicans', Democrats', and Independents' Support for a War against Iraq 203

TABLE 7.3: Impact of Local News Coverage on Public
  Concerns about a War against Iraq   204
TABLE 7.4: Experimental Manipulations of Congressional
  Position Taking   209
TABLE 7.5: Public Belief in and Support for the President,
  Including Background Controls   212
TABLE A.1: Descriptive Statistics for Chapter 3 Analyses   243
TABLE A.2: Frequency of All Uses of Force, Including
  Background Controls   244
TABLE B.1: Opportunities to Use Military Force,
  1945–2000   256
TABLE B.2: Descriptive Statistics for Chapter 4 Analyses   257
TABLE B.3: Results from the First Stage of Models
  Presented in Table 4.3   258
TABLE C.1: Descriptive Statistics for Chapter 6 Analyses   259
TABLE D.1: Descriptive Statistics for Chapter 7 Analyses   260

Preface

Which branch of government takes us to war? The executive? Legislative? Or some combination of the two?

The question runs deep. And for centuries scholars have sought answers: beginning perhaps most explicitly with Immanuel Kant and Charles-Louis de Secondat, Baron de Montesquieu; carrying through the *Federalist Papers;* preoccupying the imaginations of the greatest legal scholars of the eighteenth and nineteenth centuries, including the likes of William Blackstone and John Bassett Moore; transfixing the Supreme Court justices in the "Prize Cases"; motivating Edward Corwin's famous observation that the Constitution "is an invitation to struggle for the privilege of directing American foreign policy";[1] and attracting the attention of some of our nation's most famous political historians, from Arthur Schlesinger, Jr., to John Lewis Gaddis.

Among scholars, then, we are hardly the first to sort through the domestic politics of war. Nor are we even among relatives. In 1928, William Howell's great-grandfather, then a faculty member at Yale University's political science department and the director of research at the Council on Foreign Relations, produced a volume that documented congressional efforts to influence U.S. foreign policy in conflicts between the War of 1812 and the "Great War." Reflecting on this history, Charles P. Howland wrote that "Congress and the Senate have sometimes objected to presidential war making . . . and have attempted, especially since the war, to control the President's discretion in such matters, with the result . . . that 'the conduct of foreign relations will be almost impossible of satisfactory direction if the Senate shall continue in future to interfere with and hamper the executive as it has done the last four years.'"[2]

Three-quarters of a century hence, Howland's insights resonate still. During the lead-up to a military venture, the discretion to use force obviously remains with a president who enjoys extraordinary powers, not least of which is the ability to act unilaterally. But the president's war powers also have limits, as Congress occasionally "interferes" and "hampers the executive" in ways that make the successful prosecution of a war immensely difficult. Congress matters, and matters greatly: to a nation's ability to credibly convey resolve to enemies and allies alike, to campaigns for public support, to the president's discretion over military decision making, and to the ultimate conduct of a military venture. Does the president or Congress ultimately decide whether we go to war? Obviously, they both do.

What possibly is left to say? A fair bit, we think. Scholars have accumulated only partial answers to vital questions about how our system of governance approaches issues involving war. During the lead-up to a military operation, who within Congress is most likely to oppose the president? And under what conditions are presidents likely to abide their concerns? How, for instance, do uncertainty about a military operation's execution and the partisan composition of Congress jointly influence the president's willingness to deploy young men and women abroad in the service of some national objective? And how can Congress possibly influence executive decision making, when presidents have at their disposal such vast informational and tactical advantages? The questions get to the heart of how our system of checks and balances functions in the most perilous and uncertain of times—namely, when our elected leaders contemplate the prospects of war.

In several ways, this book advances our understanding of the domestic politics of war. For starters, it considers many more manifestations of congressional influence than previous scholars have recognized. Interbranch struggles do not typically resemble duels wherein the president and Congress mark ten strides and fire, leaving the victor standing and the vanquished bleeding in the dirt. In politics, both often end up wounded, just as both can claim a measure of success. The trick, we think, is to account for a fuller range of possible outcomes when two branches of government, with opposing objectives and different resources at their disposal, square off against one another. This book does more than identify instances when Congress, with one carefully fired shot, fells a president. It documents those occasions when it maims him, when it grazes a limb, and perhaps most importantly, when a president walks away from a fight he feared losing. If we hold as our standard of proof the obliteration of White House military planning, we overlook the copious ways in which Congress influences presidential decisions about how often to use force, which kinds of foreign crises warrant actions and which kinds do not, the timing of a deployment, and its scope. The counterfactual to a world of congressional irrelevance does not require the elimination of the largest and most vital deployments from the historical record. Instead, the correct counterfactual may be a delayed deployment in some instances, a shorter one in others, or the reassignment of national priorities in others still.

This book also pays careful attention to the mechanisms by which Congress manages to influence presidential decision making on the use of force. Sometimes Congress intervenes directly, establishing reporting requirements, setting budgets, holding hearings, or passing laws that restrict the scope or duration of a military deployment, and in these instances, the connection between the actions that Congress takes and the decisions that presidents make are more easily discerned. In other instances, though, congressional influence follows a more circuitous route. When members of Congress proclaim their reluctance to use force abroad, they may encourage U.S. adversaries who then fight longer and harder, just as they may influence the public's willingness to back their president. In either case, the president may have cause to scale back or even abandon a military venture, even though Congress has not passed a single bill or resolution that formally curtails his war powers. He does so, though, not so much because Congress itself matters, but rather because the actions that members take set in motion forces that materially impact his capacity to wage war successfully.

Additionally, this book assembles and analyzes a tremendous amount of data. Some datasets allow us to systematically examine Congress's influence over the frequency with which presidents deploy troops abroad; others allow us to examine whether Congress affects the probability that presidents respond militarily to different kinds of foreign crises. We introduce another dataset—the only of its kind—that allows us to trace congressional deliberation about an impending military venture through a wide variety of local and national print and television media outlets; we then compile other observational and experimental public opinion data that allow us to examine whether congressional influence over the media extends to influence over public's willingness to support a war. We know of no other book on the domestic politics of war that compiles so many or so diverse a set of original databases.

Throughout, this book takes a decidedly positive—contra normative—perspective. We do not consider who ought to declare war. We do not ruminate on the constitutionality of recent presidential uses of force. Nor do we consider whether careful deliberations (which, presumably, Congress can best deliver) or energy and dispatch (mainstays of executive leadership) contribute more to a successful foreign policy. Instead, we set our sights on how the federal government works in practice, how powers are asserted, how institutional advantages are advanced, how perceived weaknesses are exploited, and ultimately, which decisions are rendered. We scrutinize how, and under what conditions, one branch of government goes about checking the war powers of another. And we leave it to others to decide whether the findings uncovered would please the nation's Founders, or anyone else.

The objective here is plain enough: to identify how and when Congress checks presidential war powers, and then to reflect on its consequences for both U.S. foreign policy and the overall balance of powers within the federal government. The journey, though, is fraught with peril. There are, after all, reasons why scholars have not yet produced the definitive treatment of congressional-presidential relations on matters involving war.

(And we make no pretenses for having done so ourselves.) Above all, it is extremely difficult to identify which branch of government influences which, when both simultaneously anticipate the actions that the other is likely to take. When a president foregoes military action, is it because he fears a congressional uprising, or is it because he himself would prefer an alternative foreign policy? Is the fact that Congress rarely rebukes the president evidence of congressional weakness (as its members obviously have failed to come together and advance their interests in use-of-force decisions) or strength (as presidents, wary of offending key members, dare not do anything that would evoke a formal legislative response)? And how do we begin to distill the influence that Congress wields from the in-dependent influence of interest groups or foreign nations or members of the president's own administration? These are nettlesome issues, and no single dataset or statistical model is likely to solve them, once and for all. And so instead, in the pages that follow, we remain attuned to ambiguities in the evidentiary record, we examine datasets from many different per-spectives, we suggest fixes to the various methodological problems that inevitably arise, and we remain upfront about the limitations of our find-ings.

ANALYTIC RESTRICTIONS

Moving forward, it is worth recognizing two limiting features of this book. First, we focus on just one among many domestic political constraints on the use of force—namely Congress. We make no pretense of having ex-haustively surveyed the domestic political landscape during times of war. Second, though members of Congress may deliberate about the efficacy of a venture before, during, and after troops are actually sent to battle, we focus primarily on the politics that precede military action. Below, we discuss both of these analytic restrictions and outline the implications they have for the analysis that follows.

Restrictions in Kind

Although this book exclusively examines congressional checks on presi-dential war powers, Congress is hardly the only political institution that presidents must contend with when planning a military action. The mili-tary, the courts, and international institutions all can take measures to affect presidential decision making on the use of force. And, occasionally, the influence they wield intersects with congressional efforts to restrict presidential war powers.

Rather than passively receiving orders from on high, the military often engages in use-of-force politics, raising concerns about certain ventures, prognosticating on the probable human and financial costs of an intervention, calling on Congress and the president to provide adequate support, and occasionally, pinning blame for botched military deployments on other political actors. During the modern era, no showdown between the military and the president was more public, or more consequential, than that between General Douglas MacArthur and Harry Truman during the Korean War. At every step, the two struggled against one another; and when early military advances evaporated and China entered the conflict, MacArthur was quick to denounce the president publicly for failing to support a more expansive military engagement. Smaller and quieter showdowns between presidents and the military ostensibly under their command are rather commonplace. While the nation debated the merits of using military force to respond to such crises as Formosa in 1955, Berlin in 1961, Jordan in 1970, Lebanon in 1980, Bosnia in 1995, and Iraq in 2003, current and former representatives of the armed forces came out publicly either to articulate the potential costs of military action or to oppose the intervention outright.

When the military representatives oppose a planned use of force, they can influence the public's willingness to back the president and increase the likelihood that the president will be blamed should a deployment go awry. As such, the military can readily complicate a president's war planning. Reflecting on the politicization of the armed forces during the past several decades, Robert Buzzanco concludes that "it is not hyperbolic to suggest that the military has demonstrated virtual veto power over aspects of U.S. foreign and military policy. In the aftermath of Vietnam, military leaders began to challenge openly the White House's decision-making prerogative."[3] In so doing, the armed forces—sometimes working in concert with one another, sometimes vying for benefits and control—have established themselves as key players in debates that precede military ventures. Wagering their resources and drawing on independent bases of power, generals, admirals, and their staff have found ample ways to check presidents who contemplate the use of force.

Unlike the military, courts during the past half century have wielded remarkably little influence over presidential decision making during the ongoing conduct of a military venture.[4] As Edward Keynes notes, "The contemporary record of the Federal courts suggests that the government is free to initiate and conduct undeclared wars and military hostility with very few constitutional limitations."[5] Rarely in the modern era have judges or justices intervened directly into a president's military campaign. The Supreme Court, for instance, still has not ruled on the constitutionality of the War Powers Resolution, usually finding some reason (typically lack of standing or the political questions doctrine) to deny certiorari, even though numerous plaintiffs, including members of Congress, have sought injunctions that presidents invoke the resolution before using force. During the entire Vietnam War, only two federal district courts ever challenged the president's power to oversee military operations without a formal congressional authorization; and in both instances, these decisions were overturned on appeal.[6] Not once in the modern era have the courts repudiated a military action and demanded that the president bring the troops home.

Occasionally, though, the courts do rule on matters that bear on a presidential use of force. Consider recent events during President Bush's "war on terror." On June 28, 2004, the Supreme Court released three decisions regarding individuals deemed enemy combatants and held in military custody. The first two cases, *Rumsfeld v. Padilla* and *Hamdi v. Rumsfeld,* concerned the indefinite detention of American citizens, who by virtue of their citizenship were not subject to the military tribunals that Bush established in order to try foreign nationals suspected of committing, or planning to commit, terrorist attacks against the United States.[7] The third case, *Rasul v. Bush,* bore directly on the right of the federal government to hold indefinitely noncitizens at Guantanamo Bay, Cuba. Writing for the majority, Justice John Paul Stevens struck down the military order's provision that detainees lacked recourse to civilian courts, ruling that the U.S. District Court did have jurisdictional authority to hear petitions of habeas corpus because the United States "exercises plenary and exclusive jurisdiction" if not "ultimate sovereignty" over Guantanamo Bay.[8] Though it allowed detainees to challenge the legality of their detention and could compel the administration to either try them or release them, the court ruling applied strictly to those individuals held at Guantanamo Bay.

In July 2006, the Supreme Court issued its most sweeping indictment of the president's "war on terror."[9] With Chief Justice Roberts recusing himself because he had previously participated (and found for the government) in the appeals court decision, the court by a 5–3 ruling struck down the president's military tribunal system. The majority opinion in *Hamdan v. Rumsfeld* expressly rejected the administration's claims that Article II of the Constitution, the 2002 Authorization for Use of Military Force, and the 2005 Detainee Treatment Act collectively granted the president the authority required to create a military tribunal system unilaterally.[10] Moreover, the court ruled that the president's military tribunals as constituted— specifically, the provisions refusing the accused the right to hear and contest all evidence presented against him and the admission of hearsay testimony—violated the requisite safeguards and protections laid out in the Uniform Code of Military Justice (UCMJ) and the Geneva Conventions.

Still, the high court did not close the door on military tribunals altogether. In a concurring opinion joined by Justices Kennedy, Souter, and Ginsburg, Justice Breyer conceded that the court's ruling did not forbid the use of military tribunals in principle, but only the Bush administration's legal justification for not seeking congressional authorization for their creation. "The Court's conclusion ultimately rests upon a single ground: Congress has not issued the Executive a 'blank check.'. . . Indeed, Congress has denied the President the legislative authority to create military commissions of the kind at issue here." Presciently, Breyer concluded, "Nothing prevents the President from returning to Congress to seek the authority he believes necessary." Or as Justice Kennedy recognized in his own concurring opinion, "Because Congress has prescribed these limits [on presidential power], Congress can change them."

The administration promptly accepted the justices' invitation. Immediately after the decision's announcement, the administration advertised its willingness to work with Congress on drafting military tribunal legislation.[11] Reactions on Capitol Hill predictably split along party lines, with Democrats calling for a sweeping review of the president's efforts to combat terrorism, and Republicans reciprocating the administration's newfound spirit of cooperation.[12] Finally, on October 16, Congress enacted the Military Commissions Act of 2006, with 95 percent of Republicans in both chambers voting in favor of the law, as compared to just 16 percent of Democrats in the House and 27 percent in the Senate. The Military Commissions Act validates the use of military commissions to prosecute foreign terrorism suspects and clarifies the interrogation techniques that CIA officers may use on detainees. As Bush approvingly noted in remarks made during the bill-signing ceremony, the legislation successfully passed his "one test": it allows controversial CIA detention programs to continue.[13] Still, the act rejects Bush's earlier attempt to narrowly define the Geneva Convention obligations to "unlawful enemy combatants," and it bars military commissions from considering testimony obtained through interrogation techniques involving "cruel, unusual or inhumane treatment or punishment."[14] Absent judicial (and then congressional) intervention, the nation's policies for detaining and then trying suspected terrorists would look rather different than they do today.

In addition to the military and courts, supranational organizations and their associated alliances also may figure prominently in presidential decision making on matters involving war. In the modern era, at least, they have often stood front and center in presidents' efforts to build support for a prospective military venture. Truman, for instance, claimed that U.S. obligations to the United Nations justified his decision to initiate war against North Korea without congressional authorization; Johnson pointed to the Southeast Asia Treaty Organization as justification for an expanded military engagement in Vietnam; and Clinton pointed to the North Atlantic Treaty Organization as reason for launching strikes against Kosovo. None of these claims pass constitutional muster, for in every case the international organizations required that participating nations respect their constitutional processes for launching wars. Nonetheless, in each instance the president effectively highlighted obligations to international organizations in order to add legitimacy to his claims and to rally the support of domestic political factions behind a planned military venture.

Occasionally, international organizations restrain the presidential use of force. Recall, for instance, the efforts of Bush in the fall of 2002 and winter of 2003 to secure United Nations support for military action against Iraq. Repeatedly, Bush and members of his administration called on the United Nations to condemn Saddam Hussein for building an arsenal of chemical, biological, and nuclear weapons, and then to set a firm date to demonstrate compliance with past resolutions, after which military action would justifiably follow. To the immense frustration of the Bush administration, certain members of the Security Council (notably France, Germany, and Russia) threatened to veto any new resolutions that endorsed immediate military action. In October 2002, Bush declared at a Republican rally in Denver, Colorado, that by refusing to comply with past resolutions Saddam Hussein "has made the United Nations look foolish,"[15] and Secretary of State Colin Powell claimed that "we can't continue to have a debate that never ends."[16] Making little headway, two months later Bush took umbrage at the suggestion that United Nations inspectors just needed more time to do their work: "This business about more time—how much time do we need to see clearly that he's not disarming? Surely our friends have learned lessons from the past. Surely, we have learned how this man deceives and delays. This looks like a rerun of a bad movie, and I'm not interested in watching it."[17] During this period, the United Nations did call on Saddam Hussein to reveal to its inspectors all of Iraq's stockpiles of weapons, but it never signed off on military action. As a result, Bush proceeded to war without UN endorsement. It is worth noting, though, that his efforts to persuade the United Nations (and Congress) to support military strikes turned what might have been a summer 2002 war into a spring 2003 war.

In systems of federated and divided powers, and in an increasingly interdependent world, it is difficult to identify the effect of one institution without accounting for many others. Hence, where appropriate, we recognize the influence of the military, the courts, and supranational institutions. We account for these institutions, however, only to the extent that they have consequences for legislative-executive relations. Our analytic focus steadfastly remains on Congress, for it is Congress that was intended to guide the nation through matters involving war, it is Congress that the courts regularly call on to check presidential power, and it is Congress, more than any other institution, that has been taken to task for its recent refusal to stem the tides of war.

Restrictions in Time

We focus squarely on the domestic politics that precede uses of military force, scrutinizing interbranch dynamics up until the moment when troops are in the field and the costs and benefits of a military action begin to be revealed. As much as possible, we set aside the politics that transpire during the course of a military campaign.[18] We are hardly the first to distinguish the politics that precede military deployments from those that take hold once troops are mobilized. As Bruce Russett observes, "The dynamics of dispute initiation and escalation may differ."[19] Domestic forces that encourage military action—say, a depressed economy, as the literature on diversionary war would suggest—may have little to do with how a military initiative is actually conducted. The institutional arrangements that discourage military action—say, robust elections or a viable legislature or court system—may encourage heads of state to stay in conflicts for longer periods of time. The terms of debate shift the moment that troops are put in harm's way, as the exigencies of protecting American lives drown out many of the prior reservations raised about a military action. The domestic political world changes, as it were, the instant that presidents formally decide to engage an enemy.[20]

Our analytic focus on the domestic politics that precede the use of force has two consequences for our assessments of congressional checks on presidential power. First, we do not emphasize many of the observable actions—debates, hearings, or votes—that punctuate congressional-presidential relations over the use of military force. Usually only after troops are committed to combat does Congress introduce resolutions and bills that affect daily presidential decisions about whether to stay the course, to withdraw, or to expand the scope of conflict; consider appropriations that affect the ongoing funding amounts and discretionary allocations of funding for a presidential use of force; or hold public hearings, and thereby assign meaning to the images of lives lost and families left behind that fill the evening television news. By restricting our focus to the period that precedes the use of force, a period defined by uncertainties and speculations, we miss this considerable drama.

On the other hand, by focusing on this period we stand a better chance of identifying evidence of congressional influence. If presidents consider the views of Congress before deploying troops abroad, then they ought to delay, even abandon, military actions that are likely to evoke widespread dissent. Meanwhile, when they do send troops abroad, presidents ought to do so with a certain measure of confidence that at least some members of Congress will support them. If true, and the findings presented in this book suggest so, then analyses of executive decisions during an ongoing military venture are based on censored samples, and ones in which evi-

dence of congressional influence ought to be more limited. To be sure, the
task of assessing congressional checks during the lead up to a military
venture is considerably trickier, for much of the political calculations are
anticipatory, as much of the action has yet to occur. If Congress matters,
it ought to matter most by dissuading presidents from engaging in risky,
costly military ventures abroad.

As with all analytic distinctions, the dividing line between debate and
action is not always as neat or well defined as we might prefer. Launching a military venture, after all, is not always akin to turning on a light
switch. Given the planning required and the politics involved, presidents
may opt to proceed slowly and cautiously, rather than storming the
proverbial beaches on some quiet Tuesday morning. Recall, both Bush
(41) and Bush (43) amassed hundreds of thousands of troops in the Gulf
before invading Iraq in 1991 and 2003. What would eventually become a
full-blown war in Vietnam initially consisted of a steady build-up of military personnel and political advisors. In various regions of the world—the
Philippines, South Korea, the Middle East, and Panama, among others—
the United States maintained a military presence for extended portions of
the modern era, enabling presidents to avoid much of the discussions
about whether new or additional forces should be sent abroad. Presidents
do not always remake the domestic political world when battleships and
planes leave these shores and then, moments later, troops land on distant
ones. There can be considerable stretches of time when the military stands
poised for conflict, but no shots are ever fired.

Moreover, much of what happens before an actual deployment derives
from a set of expectations about what will happen afterward. When crafting their arguments for or against a planned military venture, members of
Congress anticipate whether the venture is likely to succeed, and whether
their constituents are likely to rally behind the president or scatter. Concomitantly, when deciding whether or not to respond militarily to different foreign crises, presidents consider the likelihood that members of Congress will later throw up roadblocks, threatening to cut funding, to issue
resolutions demanding that troops return home, or to hit the airwaves
condemning the president for acting irresponsibly or, worse, unconstitu-
tionally. Politics do not occur one day at a time. Politicians perennially
keep an eye fixed on tomorrow, while simultaneously trying to discern
lessons from all that happened in the past.

In the pages that follow, we stay attuned to these complicating factors.
For some statistical tests, we develop coding rules that distinguish new
troop deployments from preexisting military commitments; for others,
we carefully assess the beginning of individual uses of force; and in the
case studies, we monitor how members of Congress craft and publicize
statements of opposition and support in expectation of events that are

likely to occur during the course of a military venture. The analytic focus of the book, however, remains fixed on congressional-presidential relations that precede actual military deployments—the domestic politics that occur while dangers gather.

WHAT AWAITS

This book is divided into three main sections: the first identifies how Congress influences presidential decision making and when its members are most likely to have success in influencing the process, the second surveys statistical and case-study evidence of Congress's influence over the use of force, and the third presents important mechanisms by which this influence is achieved.

After recognizing the extraordinary advantages that presidents enjoy in foreign policy generally, and military policy in particular, we reflect in chapter 1 on recent American history in order to identify and characterize the various formal and informal means by which Congress can constrain the presidential use of force. The prospect of Congress enacting legislation that cuts funding or restricts the scope or duration of a military operation, holding investigative hearings, and engaging in a running public debate about the efficacy of a use of force may temper the president's willingness to deploy troops abroad.

The possibility of congressional influence, however, is appropriately distinguished from the fact. Often, even in the face of abject military failure, Congress leaves the president to do as he will. In chapter 2, therefore, we outline a series of expectations about when Congress is best equipped, and most inclined, to constrain the presidential use of force. Three factors stand out. First, in order to overcome the tremendous collective action problems and transaction costs that plague the institution, large and cohesive majorities must govern in Congress if its members are to keep pace with the president. Second, the actual deployment must be sufficiently large in scope, and long in duration, to warrant congressional concern. And third, the deployment must be considered discretionary—there are plenty of occasions, we readily admit, when exigencies of the international system (for instance, binding agreements with foreign states, balance of power considerations, the possibility of Soviet involvement) effectively trump concerns about congressional opposition.

In chapter 3, we begin to test these expectations by examining a body of work found within international relations that considers the frequency with which troops are deployed abroad. This chapter revisits the event-count models used to predict uses of force, extending the time series through 2000 and adding appropriate measures of congressional support for the president. The findings are unambiguous and run directly against the notion that politics stop "at the water's edge." During the post–World War II era, partisan support within Congress serves as a significant predictor of the number of "major" (but not "minor") foreign military engagements that the United States initiates each quarter. Effects persist even when controlling for a host of other domestic and international factors. As partisan support within Congress increases, presidents engage in military initiatives more and more often; but as support within Congress wanes, so does the frequency with which presidents exercise their authority to use military force abroad.

Investigations of congressional checks on presidential war powers, however, need not be restricted to statistical analyses of the number of times that troops are sent abroad in any given quarter or year. Congress may affect the probability that presidents respond militarily to different foreign crises, the timing of the deployments, their scope, their duration, and the terms under which they eventually end. The most basic decisions that presidents face when confronting some kind of foreign crisis is whether to intervene at all. Unfortunately, most of the statistical tests conducted to date have provided little purchase on this matter. Indeed, quantitative studies of the use of force overlook the myriad domestic and international contexts in which the United States does *not* respond. By only examining actual uses of force, scholars have assembled an incomplete view of the dynamics of presidential decision making.

To address this shortcoming, in chapter 4 we introduce and analyze a dataset that consists of roughly fifteen thousand reports of "opportunities" to use force abroad. These data consist of international crises that (a) received domestic media coverage and (b) had some potential to elicit a military response from the United States. After using these data to summarize world crises between 1945 and 2000, we present statistical tests showing that the partisan composition of Congress correlates with the chances that presidents respond militarily to different kinds of events happening in different regions of the world involving nations with different levels of strategic importance to the United States. Moreover, we find that Congress's influence is greatest when conflict erupts in states that are not allies of either the United States or the Soviet Union, and that trade relatively infrequently with the United States. Analyses of these data, we believe, represent one of the most promising additions to the quantitative literature on U.S. militarized disputes since Barry Blechman and Stephen Kaplan constructed the original use-of-force time series.[21]

Obviously, and unavoidably, large-N statistical studies overlook important details about domestic politics and the use of force. To more fully account for the various ways in which Congress does (and does not) influence presidential decision making on matters involving war, we take a closer look in chapter 5 at domestic deliberations about proposed interventions into Indochina, Lebanon, Nicaragua, Panama, Bosnia, and Kosovo. Though these studies are primarily intended to illustrate the varied levels and types of congressional influence over presidential decision making in matters involving war, they also reveal instances when congressional involvement in military matters does not conform to our principal theoretical expectations.

The findings from chapters 3, 4, and 5 suggest that the partisan composition of Congress regularly, but not uniformly, influences the presidential use of force—impacts appear most pronounced when presidents contemplate larger-scale military initiatives where certain systemic imperatives are not present. In chapters 6 and 7, we examine one of the principal ways in which Congress wields this influence during the lead-up to a military deployment. Specifically, we consider how members of Congress affect both the media coverage of, and public support for, a planned use of force—elements that can critically affect the president's calculus of the risks and rewards of military action. The focal point of the empirical analyses conducted in the book's third section is the debates and congressional deliberations that preceded the 2003 Iraq War.

In chapter 6, we build on a political communications literature that examines the influence of domestic political institutions on national media coverage of planned presidential uses of force. The chapter proceeds in two parts. The first evaluates the principal arguments and evidentiary claims made by advocates of the "indexing hypothesis," which suggests that journalists rely on political elites generally, and Congress in particular, when determining the scope and content of their coverage of a planned use of force. More than an isolated literature review, this section shows how a group of scholars principally concerned with the prerequisites for a free and independent press have stumbled across one of the most important ways in which Congress constrains the president's ability to deploy troops abroad. To test and extend their claims, the chapter presents a unique database of national and local television news coverage on Iraq during the lead-up to the 2003 Iraq War. In doing so, it demonstrates that Congress influences discussions on the use of military force that occur in national *and* local television news, from which the vast majority of Americans receive their news about politics.

In chapter 7 we examine the implications of chapter 6's findings for democratic governance. Using a variety of national public opinion surveys conducted in the fall of 2002, we demonstrate that Congress's influence over the media translates into influence over public opinion. We find that citizens residing in those media markets that aired a higher proportion of arguments against using force in Iraq were as much as 20 to 25 percentage points less likely to support the war than were citizens in media markets with more favorable coverage. Then, through an experimental survey conducted in the fall of 2004, we show that congressional support for and opposition to a proposed use of force figure prominently in citizens' thinking about whether to believe the president when he says that a mounting crisis is occurring abroad and whether to endorse his proposed military solution to the crisis. Citizens of different ideological orientations, partisan affiliations, and demographic profiles all show evidence of weighing congressional support and opposition to the president in their thinking about a proposed use of force. Interestingly, though, the gains afforded the president associated with congressional support tend to be roughly half as big as the losses associated with congressional opposition.

Finally, in chapter 8 we summarize the book's arguments and evidence and then outline avenues for future research. So doing, though, we also relate the key lessons from this book to contemporary, and ongoing, military engagements in Afghanistan and Iraq and prospective ventures in Iran; we encourage American politics, international relations, and political communication scholars to engage one another in ways that go beyond the standard cursory nod and accompanying footnote; and we speculate on how the results from the 2006 midterm election will impact the current president's discretion to continue past, and perhaps launch new, military ventures abroad.

The book has high ambitions. It engages work found within international relations, American politics, and political communications. It introduces and analyzes a variety of original datasets. It presents a host of case studies, some well known, others less so. It surveys a wide swath of American political history. Through it all, though, the book has one central objective: to investigate the checks Congress intermittently places on presidents who are contemplating the use of the single most potent of government powers—namely, sending young men and women abroad to fight, kill, and die.

Acknowledgments

These days, no one writes alone. We are no exception. First, and undoubtedly foremost, we have benefited from the yeoman work of Doug Kriner who, in one way or another, contributed to the construction of just about every dataset in this book. As his involvement in two was especially important, he justifiably stands as a coauthor on chapters 4 and 6. Kathryn Ciffolillo and Jack Rummel provided superb editorial assistance. Chuck Myers at Princeton University Press lent guidance and support throughout the writing of this book. Students in Harvard University's Government 99, Domestic Politics and War, contributed to the book's conceptualization in its early stages. Subsequently, we were fortunate to enlist the able research assistance of Jason Brozek, David Coddon, Pat Cottrell, Courtney Hillebrecht, Peter Holm, Tana Johnson, Travis Nelson, Greg Ramaswamy, Ann Rivlin, Matthew Scherbarth, Ben Sedrish, Ben Srour, Amir Stepak, Kevin Warnke, and Jessica Winchell.

From this project's inception, we turned (again and again) to Ben Fordham for insight and guidance. Ken Goldstein was instrumental in generating the dataset on local and national television media coverage of the Iraq War debates. Paul Peterson read entire drafts of the manuscript and nudged us in all the right directions. Adam Berinsky, David Lewis, Ed Mansfield, Lisa Martin, Diana Mutz, and Bruce Russett each read and provided extensive comments on several chapters for an "authors-meets-critics" conference, which the Institutional Development Initiative at Harvard University sponsored during the fall of 2005. We also benefited from the feedback of Michael Barnett, Matthew Baum, Chris Berry, Nigel Bowles, Stephen Brooks, Barry Burden, Brandice Canes-Wrone, David Canon, Daniel Carpenter, Matthew Dickinson, George Edwards, Michael Fleishman, Linda Fowler, Michael Herron, Sunshine Hillygus, Eric Schickler, Alastair Smith, and Marty West. Two anonymous reviewers at Princeton University Press provided still more outstanding suggestions.

Drafts of chapters from this book have been presented at workshops and seminars at Brigham Young University, the University of Chicago, Columbia University, Dartmouth College, Emory University, George Washington University, Harvard University, the University of Iowa, the University of Minnesota, New York University, Ohio State University, the University of Pennsylvania, Princeton University, Washington University, the University of Wisconsin, and Yale University, as well as the annual meetings of the American Political Science Association and the Midwest

Political Science Association. The Weatherhead Center at Harvard University provided extensive financial support, including the funding of Howell's leave to write this book during the 2004–5 academic year. We also gratefully acknowledge the support of the Center for American Political Studies, the Institutional Development Initiative, and the Institute for Quantitative Science at Harvard University; and the Wisconsin Advertising Project and the Wisconsin Alumni Research Foundation at the University of Wisconsin.

Finally, we dedicate this book to our mentors, now friends, Ed Mansfield, Terry Moe, and Paul Peterson.

PART ONE

Background and Theory

CHAPTER 1

Possibilities of Congressional Influence

THE FEDERAL GOVERNMENT exerts no greater power than when it places American men and women in harm's way. In sending troops off to kill and die in the service of some principle, high or low, the state exhibits all of its authority, wholly displacing individual wants and interests with collective purposes and ends. Rather than acting as some benign force, state leaders in these moments consciously and deliberately reshape the world around them. By constitutional design, therefore, the Founders prudently dispersed control over the military across the various branches of government, assigning presidents the mantle of commander in chief while granting Congress the more substantial responsibilities of raising armies and declaring war.

For much of American history, the system seemed to work. From the founding of the Republic to the mid twentieth century, most major uses of force received formal sanctioning by both Congress and the president. While presidents occasionally pressed outward on the boundaries of their constitutional authority—James Polk orchestrated a series of military provocations along the Texas border that would launch the Mexican-American War, and Lincoln wielded extraordinary extra-constitutional powers during the Civil War—Congress's rightful place in deliberations over war appeared reasonably well established. With Harry Truman, however, this would change. By declaring the Korean War a "police action" that did not require a declaration of war, Truman established a precedent for subsequent presidents to strike out on their own, deploying the military on prolonged tours of duty, humanitarian ventures, and targeted strikes without ever securing Congress's formal consent.

Truman's presidency coincided with the nation's emergence as a genuine superpower. At the close of World War II, the United States stood as the world's strongest military and economic power, with new interests to protect and promote in even the most distant reaches of the globe. Isolationists no longer ruled U.S. foreign policy. Indeed, the Founders could hardly have imagined the awesome influence that America would wield in international affairs, and the pressures that this would place on the commander in chief. A dangerous new world, many would argue, required powerful, determined, and rapid responses that only a president could manufacture.

By Richard Nixon's second term, the White House war machinery seemed out of control. Presidents had long initiated military operations without a formal declaration of war, but now they were doing so without the faintest recognition of Congress's rightful authority. Faced with dubious claims about North Vietnamese attacks on U.S. ships in the Gulf of Tonkin, the conduct of a secret war in Laos, and the persistence of an illegal bombing campaign in Cambodia, political observers at the time began to cry foul. In a celebrated indictment of what he called an "imperial presidency," Arthur Schlesinger noted that "by the early 1970s the American President had become on issues of war and peace the most absolute monarch (with the possible exception of Mao Tse-tung of China) among the great powers of the world."[1] Plainly, something needed to be done.

The 1973 War Powers Resolution was supposed to rein in a presidency run amok and to reassert congressional prerogatives over foreign policy making. It required that presidents "in every possible instance" consult with Congress before introducing military forces into foreign hostilities, secure formal authorization within sixty to ninety days or withdraw troops, and if the military engagement was approved by Congress, submit regular reports to that body. The resolution, its advocates claimed, would correct the decades-long presidential incursions into congressional war powers and put members of Congress back in charge of deliberations involving the use of military force, as the Framers intended them to be. At its signing, cosponsor senator Jacob Javits (R-NY) announced that "never in the history of this country has an effort been made to restrain the war powers in the hands of the president . . . [This bill] will make history in this country such as has never been made before."[2] With this resolution, congressional aspirations to reclaim lost ground in an age-old struggle over who has the right to declare war had peaked.

Instead of firmly reasserting congressional prerogatives, however, the resolution brought disappointment. Every president since Nixon, Democrat and Republican, has refused to recognize its constitutionality. In the last three decades, presidents have launched one military initiative after another—in Grenada and Haiti and Lebanon and Panama and Kosovo and Liberia—without ever securing congressional authorization. Only once, for Lebanon in 1983, has the War Powers clock even been started, and then the president was granted an eighteen-month grace period. And when launching smaller-scale military operations, presidents frequently have dodged the resolution's reporting requirements. Rather than correcting for gross imbalances in the nation's system of separated powers, the War Powers Resolution, astonishingly, turned bad to worse.

On this, almost everyone agrees. According to Robert Katzman, "A growing consensus maintains that the War Powers Resolution has not worked as Congress envisioned. Presidents have refused to invoke the law in ways that could limit their freedoms of action; indeed, they have not even conceded its constitutionality. Congress, for its part, has been reluctant to challenge the president."[3] According to John Hart Ely, "Thanks to a combination of presidential defiance, congressional irresolution, and judicial abstention, the War Powers Resolution has not worked."[4] Observes Peter Irons, "Every president since Nixon has disregarded—and in some cases flatly disobeyed—the provisions of what has become a monument to legislative futility."[5] The resolution, says Louis Fisher, "was a sellout, a surrender."[6]

As Congress's best effort to reclaim control over military affairs, the resolution's failings would seem to reflect all of the inadequacies of the institution that enacted it. According to Stephen Weissman, in matters involving war, Congress is infected by a "culture of deference: a distinct set of norms and beliefs, customs and institutions, that confine it to the margins of power."[7] And this culture of deference—if indeed it is a "culture"—sabotages the machinery of government more generally. Ely rails against "the disappearance of the separation of powers, the system of checks and balances, as it applies to decisions to go to war."[8] Claiming that "legislative abdication is the reigning modus operandi" in foreign affairs, and that Congress's involvement in decisions involving war has been "decimated," Neal Katyal suggests that we abandon our focus on Congress and instead look to independent executive agencies to check presidential war powers.[9] According to Joanne Gowa on matters involving war, Congress and the president adhere "to a tacit truce [as] a means to escape rather than a reflection of accountability," the result of which is "a subversion of a checks-and-balance system."[10] In their indictment of Congress's failures to oversee the president's prosecution of foreign wars, Norman Ornstein and Thomas Mann conclude that, "In the past six years . . . congressional oversight of the executive across a range of policies, but especially on foreign and national security policy, has virtually collapsed."[11]

With the erosion of congressional checks on presidential war powers, these scholars note, comes the erosion of our system of separated powers. There emerges, then, an unconstrained president who launches military forces at will, perhaps attentive to his place in history or to the international balance of powers, but liberated from the congressional interference that so often foils his domestic policy initiatives. As Louis Fisher characterizes the post-Truman presidency, "On matters of war, we have what the framers thought they had put behind them: a monarchy. Checks and balances? Try to find them."[12]

This book accepts Fisher's challenge. It searches for congressional efforts to constrain presidential war powers during the post–World War II era, and in so doing, it discovers considerable evidence that checks and balances, though diminished, persist nonetheless. There is no denying that Congress has abdicated considerable responsibilities over war making, or that presidents have stepped into the fray and claimed powers and rights that the Framers never intended them to hold. But a closer look reveals more activity and more influence than scholars have been willing to admit. By broadening the scope of inquiry, and by distinguishing what is from what should be, one discovers evidence that Congress—imperfectly, intermittently, but remarkably predictably—continues to monitor the presidential use of force. More than occasionally, its members do things, or threaten to do things, that materially affect presidential decisions about war. And perhaps not surprisingly, those members who do the most to check presidential war powers consistently come from the ranks of the opposition party.

Using a variety of original datasets and drawing from diverse literatures within political science, this book demonstrates that Congress continues to play an important role in shaping the domestic politics that precede military action, and in influencing the willingness of presidents to embark on new ventures abroad. While the power its members wield may not satisfy every interested party, Congress's mark is readily detectible. By staying attuned to partisan divisions between the legislative and executive branches, the efforts of each to anticipate and accommodate the other's future actions, the challenges of coordinating a military venture, and the uncertainty and devastation wrought by war, we find considerable evidence of congressional influence. After exploring the roots and dimensions of presidential dominance in matters of war, the remainder of this chapter characterizes the various means by which members of Congress influence presidential decisions regarding military action; the subsequent chapter, then, identifies the conditions under which Congress most effectively employs them.

THE EXECUTIVE *Is* CHIEF

Scholars who argue that presidents dominate the politics of war do so with good reason. In political struggles over military deployments during the past half century, Congress has ceded to the president considerable ground—so much, in fact, that its members no longer meet even basic standards of responsibility set by the Constitution.[13] Before we examine the influence Congress continues to wield, we must recognize the historical trends and institutional advantages that have catapulted the president to the forefront of decisions involving the use of force. This section briefly outlines some of the more important reasons presidents predominate in debates over war and in the making of foreign policy more generally.

There is, at present, a burgeoning body of work within American politics that documents the strategic advantages presidents enjoy when they exercise their unilateral powers, or what elsewhere we have called "power without persuasion," which very much embodies the deployment of troops abroad.[14] Two features of this unilateral politics literature are worth noting. The first concerns sequence. When presidents act unilaterally, they stand at the front end of the policy-making process and thereby place on Congress and the courts the burden of revising a new political landscape. If adjoining branches of government choose not to retaliate, either by passing a law or ruling against the president, then the president's order stands. Only by taking (or credibly threatening to take) positive action can either adjoining institution limit the president's unilateral powers.

Members of Congress often do confront presidents when their military orders prove misguided or ill-informed. They do so, however, under less than ideal circumstances. For starters, when debating the merits of an ongoing military venture, members of Congress are vulnerable to the accusation that they are undermining troop morale and catering to the enemy. As James Lindsay recognizes, members often avoid putting themselves in "the politically and morally difficult position of allowing funds to be cut off to troops who may be fighting for their lives."[15] By way of example, recall Clinton's deployment of troops to Haiti in 1994. Before the action, a majority of senators opposed the plan, but once troops were deployed, Congress did not attempt to force their immediate return. One political commentator surmised, "There's bipartisan criticism of going into Haiti. There's also bipartisan support, at least, in supporting the troops now that they're there."[16] Though members can, and do, take on the president during the ongoing course of a military venture, they do so under conditions that hardly foster open and critical debate.[17] Instead, members proceed cautiously, ever aware of how their actions and words are likely to be interpreted by a public wary of any criticism directed at troops who have willingly placed their lives on the line.

Some military actions, meanwhile, are sufficiently limited in scope and duration that Congress has little if any opportunity to coordinate an effective response, either before or during the actual intervention. In the spring of 1986, for instance, Reagan "consulted" with congressional party leaders on planned air strikes against Libya while U.S. planes were en route to Northern Africa. Obviously, there was little that these members could do to curb these attacks. As one Democrat attending the meeting noted, "What could we have done? . . . Told [the president] to turn the planes around?"[18] The military completed its bombing campaign long before members of Congress could possibly have resolved their differences and enacted authorizing legislation. Though Congress might have passed leg-islation either supporting or condemning the president's action after the fact, its members could do precious little to redirect the course of this particular targeted military strike. By seizing the initiative and unilater-ally deploying the military to perform short and small attacks, presidents often elude the checks that Congress might otherwise place on them.

The second feature of unilateral powers that deserves attention is that when the president acts, he acts alone. Of course, he relies on numerous advisors to formulate the policy, to devise ways of protecting it against congressional or judicial encroachment, and to oversee its implementation. But to issue the actual policy, as either an executive order or memorandum or any other kind of directive, the president need not rally majorities, com-promise with adversaries, or wait for some interest group to bring a case to court. The president, instead, can strike out on his own, placing on others the onus of coordinating an effective response. Doing so, the modern president is in a unique position to lead, break through the stasis that pervades the federal government, and impose his will in more and more areas of governance.

In foreign policy making generally, and on issues involving the use of force in particular, this feature of unilateral powers reaps special rewards. If presidents had to build broad-based consensus behind every deployment before any military planning could be executed, most ventures would never get off the ground. Imagine having to explain to members of Congress why events in Liberia this month or Ethiopia the next demand military action, and then having to secure the formal consent of a supermajority before any action could be taken. The federal government could not possibly keep pace with an increasingly interdependent world in which every region holds strategic interests for the United States. Because presidents, as a practical matter, can unilaterally launch ventures into distant locales without ever having to guide a proposal through a circuitous and uncertain legislative process, they can more effectively manage these responsibilities and take action when congressional deliberations often result in gridlock. It is no wonder, then, that in virtually every system of governance, executives (not legislatures or courts) mobilize their nations through wars and for-eign crises. Ultimately, it is their ability to act unilaterally that enables them to do so. In sum, the advantages of unilateral action are significant: they allow the president to move first and move alone.

All of the institutional features of Congress that impede consensus building around a military venture ex ante also make it equally if not more difficult, later, to dismantle an operation that is up and running. This is what makes the president's unilateral powers so potent. Multiple veto points, high transaction costs, and collective action problems regu-larly conspire against the president when he tries to guide his legislative agenda through Congress. Each, though, works to his advantage when he issues a unilateral directive, as each cripples Congress's capacity to muster an effective response. To be sure, congressional checks on presidential war powers do not disappear entirely—this book is based on the premise that under well-specified conditions (see chapter 2) they remain operative. But in an era when presidents unilaterally deploy troops with greater and greater frequency, Congress often trips over the same institutional features that undermine its capacity to govern more generally.

Beyond the strategic advantages that unilateral powers impart, presidents also benefit from the substantial information imbalance that characterizes executive-legislative relations. When a conflict erupts abroad, more often than not the president is the first to know, has access to the most acurate and current information about it, and is best situated to evaluate the relative costs and benefits of different courses of action. A massive network of national security advisors, an entire intelligence community, and diplomats and ambassadors stationed all over the globe report more or less directly to the president. Nothing comparable supports members of Congress. For the most part, they count on the president and those within his administration to share information that might bear on contemporary foreign policy debates. When the president refuses to disclose all relevant information, or he tailors the presentation of facts to suit his own strategic interests, members have a difficult time prying from the administration the information they claim to need.[19]

Should the president decide that it is in the nation's best interest to send troops into Grenada, Lebanon, Haiti, or Somalia, at least initially Congress often lacks the information required to offer a substantive objection. Instead its members are left to raise questions about the potential costs of a military venture, to worry aloud about the potential loss of human life, or to criticize the president for not having made his case to the American people. As Robert Dahl recognized over a half century ago, "Of all the alternative methods of dealing with a given crisis in foreign affairs, the executive-administrative selects that one which appears soundest to it, and henceforth its pressures are mobilized behind that alternative. What this really means is that the executive, by and large, determines the scope and nature of the debate. Congressmen may support, or they may oppose the executive proposals. But they are rarely in a position to examine the full range of alternatives that may be open to them."[20]

Strong informational advantages coupled with the unique ability to act unilaterally in the international arena make the president, by Paul Peterson's account, "the most potent political force in the making of foreign policy," while Congress remains "a secondary political player."[21] There is no escaping this fact. The primary questions that this book intends to answer are not whether congressional power effectively matches presidential power, or whether Congress has met its constitutional obligations over foreign policy making. On both of these fronts, answers obviously assume the negative. Rather, the interesting questions are uncovered when we examine those interbranch struggles that persist, when we try to determine whether Congress, in any material fashion, constrains the presidential use of force.

CONGRESS, STILL RELEVANT

Endowed with powers of unilateral action and immense informational advantages, why should the president worry about Congress? What can its members really do that has any bearing on his assessments of the potential risks and rewards of military action? A fair amount, we think. Its actions will not convince every president, every time, to change course. But through both legislative enactments and public appeals, Congress can increase the likely costs, financial and otherwise, of a planned military venture. The bills Congress introduces, the resolutions it passes, the hearings it holds, and the public declarations its members make can establish legal constraints on presidential war powers and increase the political costs of battlefield failures. In this section, we summarize past congressional efforts to influence presidential decision making through both legislative processes and public appeals: We then offer some lessons about how these activities shape the larger politics that precede military action.

OPPOSITION THROUGH LEGISLATION/APPROPRIATIONS

Should the president embark on a misguided or unexpectedly costly military venture, members of Congress can actively work against him, by either restricting the scope or duration of a conflict or by establishing firm reporting requirements. Members also oversee the appropriations process, which, according to James Lindsay, "gives Congress tremendous say over the budgets, structures, and duties of the armed forces."[22] Though no specific remedy negates the vast arsenal of powers available to the president during times of war, each goes some distance toward checking presidential war powers—and collectively, they may materially affect the course of a military campaign, and the probability that the American public and international allies continue to support the president along the way. Surveying the past seventy years of American history, one discovers numerous instances when Congress asserted its prerogatives over matters involving war, and presidents promptly, though to varying degrees, adjusted their behavior.

Few stronger examples of congressional influence on foreign policy exist than the period preceding American entry into World War II. Advancing the long-standing tradition of American isolationism, as well as a preoccupation with depression-related economic policies, Congress passed Neutrality Acts in 1935 and 1937 that restricted the president's ability to direct military or financial aid to Allied powers engaged in war. Although he staunchly opposed legislative efforts to keep America out of European hostilities, Roosevelt also recognized the extent to which congressional views resonated in the public, and he feared that Congress might derail his domestic agenda if he pushed for American involvement.[23] Hence, in the late 1930s and early 1940s, Roosevelt moved haltingly—from Winston Churchill's perspective, perilously so—to provide vital aid needed to stall the Nazi expansion.

Nearly two years would pass before Roosevelt formally attempted to repeal aspects of the 1937 Neutrality Act. These efforts had an inauspicious start when it was revealed that a French officer had been allowed to fly in a newly designed American fighter plane, which subsequently crashed. Undeterred, Roosevelt called secret congressional hearings on French attempts to purchase American-built advanced fighters. By mid March 1939, in response to Hitler's annexation of Czechoslovakia, Roosevelt publicly appealed for the lifting of the Neutrality Act's mandatory arms embargo to belligerents. Hitler's subsequent invasion of Poland then assured some congressional concession. Still, though, isolationist sentiments remained strong. Charles Lindbergh, Father Charles Coughlin, and a number of senators publicly denounced Roosevelt's request and thereby unleashed "a torrent of letters and telegrams . . . in Washington" counseling against lifting the arms embargo.[24] As a compromise, Congress did agree to repeal the arms embargo later that year, but it also insisted that cash alone be paid for war materials and that foreign vessels be used to collect the shipments.

Recognizing the seemingly implacable spirit of isolationism, Roosevelt began to take the message of defending against the Axis powers directly to the public. As he wrote in a December 1939 letter, "What worries me is that public opinion over here is patting itself on the back every morning and thanking God for the Atlantic Ocean (and the Pacific Ocean). We greatly underestimate the serious implications to our future. . . . Therefore . . . my problem is to get the American people to think of conceivable consequences without scaring the American people into thinking that they are going to be dragged into this war."[25] Midwestern conservatives and left-leaning pacifists, however, worked assiduously to undermine presidential pleas, retorting at every instance that any grant of aid to Britain further guaranteed U.S. involvement in what was properly understood to be a European war.

The world itself would have to change before Roosevelt would gain any advantage over his adversaries in Congress. The fall of France, the Battle of Britain, and continued Japanese expansion in Asia all helped to whittle away at isolationist claims that Axis powers posed no threat to the United States. In March 1941, Roosevelt managed to persuade members of Congress to pass the Lend-Lease Act, which directed armaments to Britain. The fall of that same year, the president convinced Congress to repeal those parts of the Neutrality Act that forbade merchant ships from arming and traveling in hostile sea lanes. It is worth noting, though, that the president still lacked the confidence to seek outright repeal of the act, despite the fact that 70 percent of Americans then agreed that it was "more important to defeat Hitler than stay out of the war." As the *New York Times* noted, "Mr. Roosevelt is reported to be anxious to avoid a two-month debate in Congress on the Neutrality Act, and that is why modification, rather than repeal, may be decided upon."[26]

In the face of continued Italian, German, and Japanese aggression, and despite continued calls by the president and the State Department to be the "arsenal of democracy," Congress publicly repudiated presidential efforts to aid France and Britain. Not until the morning of December 7, 1941—when the Japanese struck Pearl Harbor, killing 2,335 soldiers and 68 civilians, destroying 164 U.S. planes, and sinking or disabling 19 ships—were isolationist sentiments in Congress and the public finally quashed, and did the president secure the domestic political support needed to lead the nation headlong into war.

Though future congresses, and future historians, would soon renounce this era of isolationism, members continued to challenge the presidential use of force. Within a decade, in fact, the two branches of government would once again square off against one another. According to many historians, the Korean War ushered in the modern presidential era, one wherein presidents regularly deploy troops abroad without first acquiring any kind of congressional authorization. By calling the deployment a police action rather than a war, Truman effectively abjured constitutional requirements and established precedent for all subsequent presidents to circumvent Congress when sending the military abroad. What is often forgotten, though, is that Congress hounded Truman throughout the Korean War, driving his approval ratings down into the twenties and paving the way for a 1952 Republican electoral victory. Rattling off a litany of complaints, from the president's firing of General MacArthur to his meager progress toward ending the war, Senator and then-presidential candidate Robert Taft (R-OH) announced that "the greatest failure of foreign policy is an unnecessary war, and we have been involved in such a war now for more than a year. . . . As a matter of fact, every purpose of the war has now failed. We are exactly where we were three years ago, and where we could have stayed."[27] Unfortunately for Taft, it was General Eisenhower who could credibly promise to end the war in Korea, and by so doing secure the Republican nomination and win the White House.

Taft's comments, nonetheless, reflected growing congressional and public discontent with the president's foreign policy.

During this period, Congress grew increasingly vocal, largely along partisan lines, on a variety of defense-related issues. For starters, Truman's seizure of steel mills was roundly criticized by both Democrats and Republicans within Congress. The Senate voted to withhold funds needed to run the mills, several House Republicans attempted to have Truman impeached, and a number of GOP senators extended the debate on West Germany's inclusion into NATO in an attempt to stop Truman from expanding the western alliance. Republicans also attempted to attach an amendment to the bill barring the president from using U.S. troops to defend West Germany without congressional authorization. After an extended debate over the amendment, congressional Democrats rallied in a unified front to Truman's side, defeating the amendment. The amendment can be viewed as an attempt, by Republicans, to wrestle commander in chief powers from Truman as punishment for Korea. Because the amendment would have required Congress to approve a troop deployment to defend West Germany, consultations and a vote would be needed, even during the heat of an international crisis in Europe. Finally, in 1952 Congress slashed Truman's proposed defense budget by more than 20 percent. Despite lobbying from the administration and defense officials, Congress held firm on the cuts.

During the early 1960s, tensions between the White House and Congress centered on Cuba. From the beginning, congressional Republicans chided Kennedy over the Bay of Pigs fiasco. But it was Republican senator Kenneth Keating's continued claims of Soviet nuclear expansion that led to increased surveillance of the island and, in time, to the discovery of Soviet missiles and the Cuban Missile Crisis. Even in the immediate aftermath of this nuclear brinksmanship, Republican opponents of Kennedy escalated their criticism, charging the administration with damaging U.S. prestige by showing "ineptness in foreign affairs."[28] Indeed, the *New York Times* wondered how, after what was "widely regarded as one of the most adroit uses of power and diplomacy since the last war," it came to be that "this achievement has been blurred in the last three months . . . over Republican charges that the Kennedy administration has been 'managing the news' and misleading the American people."[29] Kennedy hardly enjoyed a rally effect or a postcrisis period of calm—rather, partisan politics returned with a vengeance, buoyed by calls from Senator Barry Goldwater to reblockade Cuba and accusations from Senator Keating that the administration continued to underestimate the number of Soviet advisors that remained in Cuba.[30]

It was the Vietnam War, however, that brought congressional opposition to the presidential use of force to a fever pitch. As the war dragged on and casualties mounted, Congress and the public grew increasingly wary of the larger purposes served, and of the 1964 Gulf of Tonkin Resolution's empowerment of the president "to take all necessary steps, including the use of armed force, to assist any member or protocol state of the Southeast Asia Collective Defense Treaty requesting assistance in defense of its freedom." In 1970, with upward of 350,000 U.S. troops in the field and the war spilling over into Cambodia, Congress formally repealed that resolution. And over the next several years, legislators enacted a series of appropriations bills intended to restrict the war's scope and duration. In December 1970, for instance, Congress enacted a supplemental foreign assistance appropriations act that prohibited the use or diversion of any monies to fund either the introduction of U.S. troops into Cambodia or the provisions of U.S. "advisors" to the Cambodian army.[31] Then in June 1973, after the Treaty of Paris had been signed, Congress enacted a supplemental appropriations act that cut off all funding for additional military affairs in Indochina—including Cambodia, Laos, North Vietnam, and South Vietnam—after August 15, 1973.[32] In December 1974, Congress enacted a foreign assistance act that restricted the number of U.S. personnel allowed in Vietnam to just four thousand within six months, and three thousand within twelve.[33] Finally, when South Vietnam fell in the spring of 1975, despite desperate calls from President Gerald Ford and Secretary of State Henry Kissinger, Congress forbade American troops from enforcing the Paris peace accords.

The memoirs of Henry Kissinger exude frustration with Congress for having repeatedly sought to trim American troop levels, halt military operations within Cambodia, and end the Vietnam War prematurely. Kissinger, of course, objected to any meddling in the president's war planning. But according to the secretary of state, congressional involvement in tactical decisions about the war had other consequences. Legislative activity, Kissinger believed, fundamentally compromised the president's ability to negotiate reasonable terms for the war's resolution. As Kissinger explained, "The pattern was clear. Senate opponents of the war would introduce one amendment after another, forcing the Administration into unending rearguard actions to preserve a minimum of flexibility for negotiations. Hanoi could only be encouraged to stall, waiting to harvest the results of our domestic dissent."[34] That most of Congress's efforts to limit the continued use of force failed in one chamber or another does not negate the basic point—that is, by repeatedly trying to force the withdrawal of American troops, Congress undermined the president's bargaining position and, perhaps, inadvertently prolonged the actual conflict.

Three years later, Congress again forbade the use of funds for military actions supported by the president—this time, covert aid for non–U.S. paramilitary forces in Angola. The 1976 defense department appropriations act stipulated that no monies would be used "for any activities involving Angola other than intelligence gathering."[35] Then, four months later, Congress enacted separate legislation that made the ban permanent, noting that "no assistance of any kind may be provided for the purpose, or which would have the effect, of promoting, augmenting, directly or indirectly, the capacity of any nation, group, organization, movement, or individual to conduct military or paramilitary operation in Angola."[36] Facing such staunch congressional opposition, Ford suspended military action and aid in Angola, sniping that Congress, with regard to foreign policy, had "lost its guts."[37]

During the 1980s, no foreign policy issue captivated members of Congress as much as aid to Nicaraguan contras, a band of rebels engaged in an ongoing guerrilla war against the nation's Sandinista government. In 1984, Congress enacted a continuing appropriations bill that forbade Reagan from supporting the contras, either financially or militarily. Leaving little doubt about their position on the matter, members of Congress wrote into the law the following language: "No funds available to the Central Intelligence Agency, the Department of Defense, or any other agency or entity of the United States involved in intelligence activities may be obligated or expended for the purpose or which would have the effect of supporting, directly or indirectly, military or paramilitary operations in Nicaragua by any nation, group, organization, movement or individual."[38] Reagan appeared undeterred. Rather than abandon the project, the more prudent course of action, Reagan instead opted to divert funds from Iranian arms sales to support the contras, establishing the basis for the most serious presidential scandal since Watergate. Absent congressional opposition on this issue, Reagan might well have intervened directly, or at least directed greater, and more transparent, aid to the contra rebels fighting the communist government.

In just one instance, the case of Lebanon in 1982–83, Congress formally invoked the War Powers Resolution to influence the nation's involvement in a military venture.[39] Most scholars who call Congress to task for having failed to fulfill its constitutional responsibilities make much of the fact that it authorized the use of force for a full eighteen months, rather than the sixty days required under the resolution. What critics often overlook is that Congress simultaneously forbade the president from unilaterally altering the scope, target, or mission of the military's participation in the United Nations Multinational Force; asserted its right to terminate, at any time, the venture with a one-chamber majority vote or a joint resolution; and established firm reporting requirements as the occupation continued.[40] Thus, when marine headquarters were bombed and the president expanded the theater of operations to include Syrian antiaircraft emplacements, Congress mobilized to end the nation's involvement in the United Nations operation. Though conditions on the ground worsened, and though Lebanon subsequently rejected a formal peace treaty with Israel, congressional and public opposition helped convince Reagan to abandon the nation's military commitments. Four months after the marine-barrack bombing, Reagan ordered marines redeployed to U.S. ships in the Mediterranean Sea; one month later, the president withdrew from the operation.

A similar sequence of events played out in 1993 and 1994, when a joint United Nations humanitarian venture in Somalia devolved into urban warfare, and the grisly deaths of U.S. soldiers played out on television sets across the nation. Though Congress had publicly declared its support for the president's actions in Somalia, opposition mounted as the costs of the war escalated and the scope of the mission expanded to include the training of a civilian police force and the disarming of factions within the country.[41] When United Nations troops clashed with supporters of the Somali warlord Mahommed Farah Aideed and images of a United States soldier being dragged through the streets of Mogadishu filled nightly newscasts, Congress moved quickly to curb presidential efforts to bolster the number of troops and supplies in the region. In November 1993, legislators enacted a Department of Defense appropriations act that simultaneously authorized the use of force in Somalia to protect United Nations units and also required that forces be withdrawn by March 31, 1994.[42] In the next year's defense appropriations bill, in an amendment introduced by Dirk Kempthorne (R-ID), Congress reaffirmed its past stance by including provisions that "none of the funds appropriated by this Act may be used for the continuous presence in Somalia of United States military personnel after September 30, 1994."[43] As a result of these congressional actions and growing public opposition to the continued presence of U.S. troops in Somalia, Clinton abandoned the venture long before he was able to achieve any of the strategic or humanitarian objectives identified by Bush, who had launched the original deployment in December 1992.

In 1994, another African country witnessed killings that, by sheer volume, eclipsed those in Somalia. Over a three-month period, Hutus in Rwanda butchered roughly 800,000 Tutsis, while the United Nations and Western nations did little to stem the killings. Clinton's failure to recognize the slaughter early on, and to intervene, is well documented—and by Clinton's own account, it was his single greatest regret about his presidency.[44] Less noticed, though, is Congress's complicity in this unfortunate history. Congress slashed humanitarian assistance to Rwanda from $270 million to $170 million and sought to ensure that the United States did not become entangled in another African nation's domestic troubles—as Robert Byrd (D-VA) explained, "We had enough of that in Somalia."[45] And so, in the same 1994 defense appropriations act that forbade the ongoing presence of military personnel in Somalia, Congress declared that United States troops would not enter the region, stipulating that "no funds provided in this Act are available for United States military participation to continue Operation Support Hope in or around Rwanda after October 7, 1994, except for any action that is necessary to protect the lives of United States citizens."[46] This was preceded in May by the signing of Presidential Decision Directive (PDD) 25, which restricted the involvement of U.S. forces in peacekeeping operations. In response to congressional outrage over Somalia, Clinton took it upon himself to tie his own hands in Rwanda.

Just as Congress restricted funding for a military venture conducted under the auspices of the United Nations in 1994, it took steps to restrict the use of funds for a humanitarian crisis occurring in Kosovo under the direction of the North Atlantic Treaty Organization (NATO). Responding to the Yugoslav government's persecution of ethnic Albanians in Kosovo, on March 24, 1999, the president, in alliance with NATO, launched a massive air strike campaign. One month later, the House passed a bill that would have forbidden the use of defense department funds to introduce U.S. ground troops into the conflict,[47] at least until Congress subsequently authorized the use of force, which it never got around to doing.[48] The Senate, however, did not follow through and pass funding restrictions of its own. Instead, the more hawkish Democrats and Republicans in Congress seized on the opportunity to attach additional monies for unrelated defense programs, military personnel policies, aid to farmers, and federal relief for citizens affected by Hurricanes Mitch and Georges and passed a supplemental appropriations bill that was considerably larger than the amount requested by the president.[49] The mixed messages sent by Republicans were not lost on Clinton's Democratic allies. As Martin Frost (D-TX) noted, "I am at a loss to explain how the Republican Party can, on one hand, be so irresponsible as to abandon our troops in the midst of a military action to demonstrate its visceral hostility toward the commander in chief, and then, on the other, turn around and double his request for money for what they call 'Clinton's war.'"[50]

There is, of course, something superficial about any running count of the times that the War Powers Resolution has been invoked or that appropriations have been cut or that resolutions either authorizing a use of force or forbidding military action have been enacted. For these overt actions say very little about the strength of congressional checks on presidential war powers. Indeed, if Congress was all powerful (which it plainly is not) and the president only pursued military options that a majority of members support (which he obviously does not do), then we would never witness any bills or appropriations that were intended to rebuke or restrain the exercise of presidential power since each side could anticipate the outcome.

We are not suggesting that the absence of congressional action is appropriately interpreted as evidence of the institution's prepotency. Instead, we mean only to raise a cautionary point: the observed behaviors of either branch of government do not necessarily reveal who was in charge, or whose interests were best represented, when the military was deployed. As John Ferejohn and Frances Rosenbluth point out, "Depending on the distribution of costs and benefits associated with the use of power, heterogeneous interests might be inclined to exercise veto points built into American political institutions; *and even if their use is not often observed to block military aggression, their influence is likely to be incorporated in anticipation of their use.*"[51] When trying to gauge congressional influence over presidential war powers, it simply will not do to count the number of times that the War Powers Resolution has, or has not, been invoked. For as Ferejohn and Rosenbluth aptly note, one branch of government may wield considerable influence over another even when the historical record is quite sparse. Knowing that members of Congress will rail against what they perceive to be a seriously misguided military venture, presidents may scale back, or even abandon, their plans. In such instances, however, the proof of congressional influence is not to be found in the corpus of law that members enact. Rather, it is to be located in the silence accompanying a president who would like to respond militarily to some foreign conflagration, but who prudently abstains.

Reflecting on congressional involvement in the Vietnam War, David Mayhew noted, "Often the voicing of public opinion has policy effects without any laws being passed: presidents, bureaucrats, and judges, anticipating trouble with Congress, take action to avoid it. Thus the congressional uprising during the Tet Offensive of 1968 (no legislation was passed) was a contributing element in President Johnson's decision to stop escalating the Vietnam War."[52] A simple count of the number of times Congress intervened legislatively into the Vietnam War reveals very little about the actual influence that any branch of government ultimately wielded over the writing or implementation of foreign policy about Southeast Asia in the 1960s and 1970s. Nor does it now. And because legislative inactivity does not necessary connote congressional abdication, a resumption of congressional activity need not allay the deeper concerns that so many critics of Congress justifiably raise about the appropriate balance of policy powers across the legislative and executive branches of government.

From our vantage point, this is a vitally important point, and one that helps explain why previous scholars have overlooked evidence of congressional influence on presidential war making. When trying to discern power, analysts must look beyond actions taken and reactions made and instead infer how each reflects underlying dynamics that cannot be observed directly. That they have come out in opposition to certain military actions and have passed appropriations that cut funding for the use of force, and that they have demanded an end to certain campaigns, does suggest that members of Congress were attuned to what the president was doing.[53] In order to assess the actual checks Congress places on presidential power, however, we will need to dig deeper and construct a set of empirical tests that go beyond a mere accounting of the actions that each branch of government takes. This is the primary objective of chapters 3 through 5.

Recent congressional efforts to directly influence military operations directly nonetheless yield several important lessons about interbranch dynamics in matters involving war. For starters, Congress almost always reacted to a foreign policy agenda set by the president. For institutional reasons that we outlined previously, the president usually determined whether a military response to an observed foreign crisis was even a possibility. Criticizing Clinton's initial lack of attention to foreign affairs, Jim Hoagland of the *Washington Post* recognized that "Congress can never lead on foreign policy. It can only react, criticize and restrict when that suits congressional self-interest."[54] Though "never" is probably too strong, the basic point remains: in matters involving the use of force, Congress has been largely a reactive institution. While Congress has occasionally voted to authorize a presidential use of force, in almost every instance members have cast their support for, or opposition to, initiatives advanced by the president.

Second, Congress has usually acted to restrain, rather than stimulate, military action. By design, Congress is meant to "clog the road to combat," to slow and sometimes silence calls for military action.[55] Hence, when it has chosen to participate in decisions involving war, Congress has usually enacted legislation intended to reduce, or even terminate, offshore troop deployments. Rarely has Congress openly contradicted a president and insisted that more personnel be sent abroad, that ground troops be introduced where the president launched only an air campaign, that the scope of a venture be broadened, or its duration extended. Of course, Congress often does accede to presidential demands—authorizing certain deployments, providing funds for others, and issuing resolutions that affirm their support for the troops.[56] But not since the Spanish-American War has a unified Congress arisen to publicly advocate on behalf of a major military venture on which the president was inclined to take a pass.[57] Nor should this come as much of a surprise, for Congress typically lacks the most basic information to put before the president a firm foreign policy agenda. Members generally cannot participate in tactical decisions about the optimal course of action simply because they lack the most essential information about ground-level operations. Hence, they can articulate only the vaguest of concerns to spur presidential action. The impetus for military action almost always originates from within the executive branch.

The view that Congress principally restrains, rather than impels, the use of force is occasionally challenged. Contemplating military action, presidents may anticipate the domestic political fallout of failing to redress a mounting foreign crisis. By this account, then, Lyndon Johnson sent increasing numbers of advisors first, and troops second, to South Vietnam not because he himself felt a strong obligation to contain communism in Southeast Asia, but instead because others, including key members of Congress, did. Fearing a congressional backlash if he did not demonstrate leadership in the face of Northern Vietnamese aggression, especially a backlash against his beloved Great Society legislation, Johnson reluctantly responded militarily to a foreign crisis that he otherwise would have preferred to ignore.

Obviously, a full recounting of the lead-up to the Vietnam War is not possible here. If only to support our basic characterization of Congress, it is worth noting several important limitations to this particular historical account of Johnson's thinking about South Vietnam. For starters, the account ignores: the fact that Johnson's initial Vietnam policy was essentially a continuation of Kennedy's and Eisenhower's; the strong endorsements within the president's own administration of the "domino theory," which stipulated that Vietnamese surrender to communism would prompt the fall of Cambodia, Thailand, and Indonesia; Johnson's willingness, indeed eagerness, to pursue the North Vietnamese in the aftermath of purported attacks on the U.S.S. *Maddox* in the Gulf of Tonkin; Johnson's genuine concerns about Chinese aggression in the region; congressional divisions about the efficacy of military action in South Vietnam during the first year of Johnson's administration; and Johnson's fear of provoking domestic doves, especially from within his own party.[58] Indeed, it was not until the Gulf of Tonkin that members uniformly supported the presidential use of force; and it was the massive escalation of war with the Tet Offensive in early 1968, rather than inattention to a perceived foreign crisis, that ultimately led to Johnson's undoing. At some level, Johnson probably did fear the political costs of abandoning Vietnam to the communists. But it overstates matters considerably to claim that it was Congress, rather than concerns about his place in history, personal convictions, or counsel from members of his own administration, that ultimately convinced Johnson to launch military strikes against the North Vietnamese. In Vietnam, as in most every other use of force in the modern era, congressional influence eventually registered—when it registered most clearly—as a constraint on military action.

Our brief review of interbranch relations also suggests important lessons

concerning the timing of congressional action. With the Neutrality acts of
the 1930s and the 1976 defense department appropriations being important exceptions, Congress has rarely used legislation or appropriations to
limit presidential power before a conflict actually began. Congressional
meddling in presidential plans has usually erupted, if it erupted, after
troops were in the field. During the lead-up to a military venture, Congress has been notably silent, rarely considering legislation or appropriations that would limit the president's capacity to fulfill a stated mission.

Even after the president's launching of troops, moreover, Congress has
not always sprung to action. Typically, members only punished the president when a military venture subsequently became protracted or costly.
As long as a military initiative accomplished its objectives in short order
and with relatively little expense, presidents usually could rest assured
that Congress would remain reasonably quiet. With the president in the
limelight of success, having settled a foreign conflagration expeditiously,
and having secured American interests abroad, little could be heard from
the halls of Congress.

The trouble, of course, is that the president cannot be sure that all will
go according to plan, which raises the final, and most central, point to be
made about interbranch dynamics involving the use of force. The periods
that lead up to war are rife with uncertainty and doubt: about how
quickly the U.S. military can fulfill its objectives, about how adversaries
and allies will respond to U.S. actions, about the resilience of the enemy's
troops and the capabilities of its military command, about the willingness
of foreign civilian populations to cooperate in a protracted military venture, and about the quality of the intelligence gathered. What start out as
small-scale initiatives may rapidly escalate into larger and longer military
commitments; intelligence reports may, on further investigation, prove to
be woefully misguided; what appear to be foolproof military plans may, on
execution, fail miserably; and other travesties—the killing of civilians or
the accidental deaths of U.S. soldiers—can have devastating consequences,
both domestically and abroad.

Reflecting on Great Britain's Boer War of 1899–1902, Winton Churchill
offered the following admonition:

Let us learn our lessons. Never, never, never believe any war will be
smooth and easy, or that anyone who embarks on the strange voyage can
measure the tides and hurricanes he will encounter. The statesman who
yields to war fever must realize that once the signal is given, he is no
longer the master of policy but the slave of unforeseeable and uncon-
trollable events. Antiquated War Offices, weak, incompetent or arrogant
Commanders, untrustworthy allies, hostile neutrals, malignant Fortune,
ugly surprises, awful miscalculations all take their seat at the Council

Board on the morrow of a declaration of war. Always remember, however sure you are that you can easily win, that there would not be a war if the other man did not think he also had a chance.[59]

Or, going back even further in history, Thucydides proffered similar advice:

Think, too, of the great part that is played by the unpredictable in war: think of it now, before you are actually committed to war. The longer a war lasts, the more things tend to depend on accidents. Neither you nor we can see into them; we have to abide their outcome in the dark.[60]

Or, propelling back to the present, when reflecting on the experiences of recent American presidents at war, historian Michael Barone concluded,

Wars are chancy things. The friction of war, as the Prussian military philosopher Carl von Clausewitz wrote, is inevitable and its effects unpredictable. The responsibility for sending men to their deaths has weighed heavily on our commanders in chief . . . who, relying on imperfect information, must make and have often made, life-and-death decisions without being able to know for certain what effects they will have.[61]

Be forewarned, Churchill, Thucydides, and Barone counsel. When making that fateful decision to launch the military abroad, and to send troops into battle, the head of state unleashes forces that escape his, and his government's, mastery. For always, the possibility lingers that even the grandest, most carefully planned military strategies will collapse on execution.

And herein lies the rub. Should things go badly, some members of Congress can be expected to pile on, expressing public opposition while also taking concrete steps to curtail presidential discretion to continue to wage war. At least two presidents during the modern era (Truman and Johnson) were run out of office when initially smaller-scale military initiatives expanded in scope while showing few signs of progress.[62] No president wants a Bay of Pigs or a USS *Pueblo* or a "Black Hawk Down" or a USS *Cole* or an Abu Ghraib on his watch. Even the best laid plans, those of Robert Burns's "mice and men," can be thrown asunder—and the stakes are never higher than when the plans center on war.

Of course, when things have gone awry, Congress has not always excoriated the president or his administration. Quite the opposite, members have, in some instances, turned around and appropriated even more funds so that he could adequately address new challenges in the field. And just as important, members have gone out of their way to declare publicly their support for the president. They have explained to the American people that though losses have been incurred and missteps have been taken, the president pursues a noble cause, and one whose costs are well worth paying. In war, after all, mishaps are unavoidable, and adjustments are always required. In the face of adversity, members have insisted, the nation must gather its resources, dispense with criticism, and recommit itself to the fundamental principles and objectives that the commander in chief stands to advance.

Immersed in all of the uncertainty that precedes war, presidents struggle mightily to assess the possibility that the military's plans will fail, and to evaluate whether Congress in due course either will publicly condemn him and actively work to dismantle the engagement or will affirm its allegiance to him and give him the money and delegated authority he needs to proceed. If Congress will come to the president's aid and provide him with political cover, then he may have the assurances he needs to incur the risks involved. On the other hand, if the president looks up at Capitol Hill and sees a swarm of representatives poised to pounce at the first misstep taken, he may instead choose to abandon military options altogether. In chapter 2 of this book, we discuss in some detail how presidents make this calculation.

OPPOSITION THROUGH PUBLIC APPEALS/DISSENT

At the front end of a military venture, members of Congress usually do not enact laws that either endorse or oppose the president's plans. Instead, members more often effect change indirectly, participating in larger debates about the efficacy of military action, raising concerns about the costs involved, and expressing doubts about the plans laid before the American public. Doing so, they put the president on notice. For should a military venture subsequently go awry, the opposition party, in public appearances and electioneering and hearings, may level due criticism; and if the opposition speaks with one voice and holds large majorities in Congress, it may sway a significant number of citizens to vote against the president and his party.[63] To right the ship, the president not only must make all necessary midcourse corrections to the military venture itself, he must explain to the American public why he did not heed the early advice and warnings of Congress.[64]

Although the United States would become heavily involved in a ground war in Southeast Asia throughout much of the 1960s and early 1970s, the fact that we refer to the conflict as the Vietnam War rather than the Indochina War is, in part, testament to Congress's public appeals and vocal dissent. As its position in Indochina became precarious in the early 1950s, France began to push its stronger Western ally, the United States, for money and materiel. The requests initially fell on sympathetic ears, as the Eisenhower administration offered significant resources, especially military aid. As a part of the administration's "new look" defense policy, outlined in NSC 162/2 in October 1953, "Indochina was listed as an area of

and many Democrats rather succinctly: "As members of Congress, we have to confront the very real possibility of American soldiers being put in harm's way. . . . At this juncture, it seems appropriate that Congress take an active role in the debate."[72] This debate forced Clinton to justify continually his plans for coping with the Haiti crisis. Deployment of U.S. forces finally did come in September 1994, but only after the military junta had agreed to step aside and allow Jean-Bertrand Aristide to return to power peacefully. U.S. forces were sent to ensure a peaceful transition of power rather than to be front-line fighters for democracy. And so, with peace established on the ground, Congress acquiesced and the debate over Haiti faded.

Two features of the public debates that preceded military action deserve emphasis. First, the probability that Congress lodged complaints against a use of force depended on its perceived costs. Lower-level deployments were unlikely to attract widespread attention, but large initiatives (measured in terms of sheer manpower and financial investment) stood some chance of eliciting Congress's organized opposition—for larger deployments required the most planning, were the most difficult to execute, and involved the greatest risk. When the president launched a small-scale, retaliatory strike in the immediate aftermath of some foreign conflagration, it was unlikely that the military would become bogged down in war, and hence unlikely that Congress would have the opportunity, much less the incentive, to work against the president. It was when the stakes rose, and the scope and duration of a conflict expanded, that Congress stirred to action.

Second—and most importantly—much of the action was anticipatory. Rather than going head-to-head with Congress at the front end of a military campaign, presidents anticipated what members of Congress would do once they had a chance to observe evidence of the campaign's success or failure. When Congress appeared likely to extend sympathy and support throughout the course of a military venture, presidents usually were more willing to deploy the troops. But when early disappointments seemed likely to trigger congressional reprisals, presidents, from the beginning, appeared more risk-averse. Early congressional discussions about an impending military action sent valuable signals to the president about the reception he would likely receive when, and if, military actions did not beget immediate success.

Finally, as we approach our empirical investigation of congressional influence on use-of-force politics, it is worth reflecting on the necessary proof of congressional influence over presidential decision making. Though they may persuade a president to back down altogether, members of Congress also may exercise influence over more subtle aspects of a planned us of force. Members may affect the timing of a deployment, its size and scope, and the terms under which the president eventually executes it. The chapters that follow present a wide assortment of evidence of different congressional checks on presidential war powers.

The Importance of Congressional Appeals/Dissent

Because they are legally binding, legislation and appropriations passed by Congress directly impinge on a president's discretion to wage war. Not surprisingly, then, opponents of a president's war typically call on Congress to pass laws and cut appropriations. But the public debates that precede military actions also have important consequences for presidential power. Two stand out. By expressing dissent, members of Congress can weaken the president's ability to credibly convey resolve to foreign allies and adversaries, and they can turn public opinion against him.[73] Here, we briefly summarize both of these avenues of congressional influence.

SIGNALING RESOLVE

To the extent that congressional discontent signals domestic irresolution to other nations, the job of resolving a foreign crisis is made all the more difficult. As Kenneth Schultz shows, an "opposition party can undermine the credibility of some challenges by publicly opposing them. Since this strategy threatens to increase the probability of resistance from the rival state, it forces the government to be more selective about making threats"—and, concomitantly, more cautious about actually using military force.[74] When members of Congress openly object to a planned military operation, would-be adversaries of the United States may feel emboldened, believing that the president lacks the domestic support required to see a military venture through. Such nations, it stands to reason, will be more willing to enter conflict, and if convinced that the United States will back down once the costs of conflict are revealed, they may fight longer and make fewer concessions. Domestic political strife, as it were, weakens the ability of presidents to bargain effectively with foreign states, while increasing the chances that military entanglements abroad will become protracted and unwieldy.

A large body of work within the field of international relations supports the contention that a nation's ability to achieve strategic military objectives in short order depends, in part, on the head of state's credibility in conveying political resolve. Indeed, a substantial game theoretic literature underscores the importance of domestic political institutions and public opinion as state leaders attempt to credibly commit to war.[75] Confronting widespread and vocal domestic opposition, the president may have a difficult time signaling his willingness to see a military campaign to its end. While congressional opposition may embolden foreign enemies, the perception on the part of allies that the president lacks support may make them wary of committing any troops at all.

The dangers of domestic political dissent are not lost on presidents and members of Congress. Indeed, for Bush (43) it constituted an important reason for seeking congressional authorization to use force against Iraq in the fall of 2002. In a Rose Garden ceremony on October 2, the president noted, "The statement of support from the Congress will show to friend and enemy alike the resolve of the United States. In Baghdad, the regime will know that full compliance with all U.N. security demands is the only choice and that time remaining for that choice is limited."[76] Then, in remarks eight days later on the House's vote to authorize the use of force, the president proclaimed, "The House of Representatives has spoken clearly to the world and to the United Nations Security Council: The gathering threat of Iraq must be confronted fully and finally. Today's vote also sends a clear message to the Iraqi regime: It must disarm and comply with all existing U.N. resolutions, or it will be forced to comply. There are no other options for the Iraqi regime. There can be no negotiations. The days of Iraq acting as an outlaw state are coming to an end."[77] By securing congressional authorization, it was supposed, the president could communicate his views and intentions more effectively to the international community that Iraq's defiance of United Nations resolutions would no longer pass unnoticed.[78] In doing so, it was hoped, Saddam Hussein would finally relent to Bush's demands.

Imagine what might have happened during the lead-up to and execution of the Iraq War had Congress not authorized the use of force. Two outcomes seem plausible, even likely. First, the president would have had an even more difficult time assembling an international coalition in support of military action. Recall, after all, that the president expressly sought congressional authorization in the hopes that it would improve the chances of later securing a UN Resolution in support of military action. Second, and in a more speculative vein, had Congress not authorized the use of force, the military operation itself might not have gone so smoothly. During the early stages of the Iraq War, the U.S. military took pains to persuade the enemy to lay down its arms and surrender, rather than fight and face certain death. Accompanying these claims were regular assurances that the United States would see this war through to the end, that it would not stop until the entire Hussein regime was dismantled. To substantiate these claims, Congress's authorization was critical.

For a moment, put yourself in the place of an Iraqi field officer in the spring of 2003. On the one hand, the United States military is bearing down upon you, threatening to kill you and every one of your comrades unless you abandon the fight. On the other hand, should you surrender prematurely, and should the United States fail to depose the Hussein regime, then you can expect to face the wrath of a spurned and spiteful ruler—as the southern Shi'a did a decade prior, after they had risen up in defiance of the Hussein regime only to be persecuted the moment that U.S. troops withdrew. Which option seems preferable critically depends on the likelihood that the United States will see the campaign to its end. For if you have reason to doubt the nation's resolve, and Congress's refusal to authorize the use of force would buoy this concern, then the latter option might be the right one—producing a longer, bloodier military conflict and raising the cost to an invading army.

Similar concerns arose in subsequent years when the United States contemplated troop withdrawals from Iraq. Though the insurgency continued to take its toll on U.S. forces, the president's popularity waned, and calls for the Iraqi government to police its own state intensified, Bush nonetheless refused to set a firm timetable for troops to leave. And his reasons for doing so were plain enough. The president insisted that insurgents were watching U.S. politics closely and that a timetable would encourage the insurgents to "just go ahead and wait us out." Setting a fixed withdrawal date, Bush concluded, simply "concedes too much to the enemy."[79] Whether this prediction was accurate or not, its logic relied on the realization that others monitor U.S. politics generally, and Congress in particular, to gauge the nation's resolve.

PUBLIC OPINION

Congressional dissent also may influence the public's willingness to back the president during the lead-up to war. By regularly using the media to air arguments against military action, and by underscoring the risks involved, Congress may temper any rally effects the president would otherwise enjoy.[80] And to the extent that Congress can stoke public opposition, earlier concerns about signaling only intensify. Public discontent confirms the belief of would-be adversaries that the United States will eventually back down, thereby encouraging them to drag out a conflict and to commit and publicize atrocities intended to signal their own commitments.[81] To the extent that Congress is able to sway public opinion, it secures an important avenue of influence over presidential decision making.

In 1984, Secretary of Defense Casper Weinberger gave a major address on the uses of military power before the National Press Club in Washington, D.C. In it, he laid out the conditions under which presidents ought to deploy the military to curb a perceived foreign threat. Repeatedly, Weinberger underscored the importance of securing a united and unflappable "national will," both to buoy the morale of troops in the field and to convey to enemies and allies alike a spirited determination to see a conflict through to the end. In this view, the support of Congress and the public are prerequisites for exercising military force. As Weinberger put it, "Before the U.S. commits combat forces abroad, there must be some reasonable assurance we will have the support of the American people and their elected representatives in Congress. . . . We cannot fight a battle with the Congress at home while asking our troops to win a war overseas."[82] To be sure, Weinberger did not claim that presidents needed to secure a formal authorization before exercising military force. And he was quick to criticize Congress for "interfer[ing]" in what is at heart an executive decision, and for refusing to accept "responsibility" for the outcomes of military deployments. Still, for Weinberger the prospects of facing a hostile Congress or public during the ongoing course of a military venture warranted sufficient concern as to make "some reasonable assurance" of their support a precondition for using force at all.[83]

Weinberger's recommendations are not without foundation. Political scientists have assembled rich empirical literatures that scrutinize the influence of public opinion on foreign policy generally, and presidential deliberations about the use of force in particular.[84] Ole Holsti has conducted one of the most thorough examinations of the topic.[85] Drawing from extensive surveys on the public's foreign policy attitudes and surveying a large historical literature on uses of force, Holsti finds that the public is reasonably well informed about matters involving war, especially when the nation stands to confront the most calamitous of foreign disasters. While recognizing the temporal and structural instabilities of American public opinion, and while admitting that the public is eminently susceptible to persuasion by political elites, Holsti nonetheless finds that citizens appear reasonably competent when evaluating the military's efforts to quell foreign crises.

Moreover, the judgments that citizens formulate about foreign affairs and the use of force have important policy ramifications. Both quantitative research and case studies call into question the "impotence" thesis, which argues that public opinion is a "shapeless lump" and that "the processes by which foreign policy is made are essentially impervious to public influence."[86] Quite the contrary, during the lead-up to World Wars I and II, French military disasters at Dien Bien Phu, the nation's confrontation with China over the islands of Quemoy and Matsu, the long buildup to the Vietnam War, the insurgencies in Nicaragua in the 1980s, and the Balkan crises of the 1990s, public opinion's imprint—in particular, its aversion to casualties, its isolationist tendencies, and its insistence that force be used only when vital national interests are at stake—on U.S. foreign policy is readily detectible.[87] According to John Aldrich and his colleagues, "A mounting body of evidence suggests that the foreign policies of

American presidents—and democratic leaders more generally—have been influenced by their understanding of the public's foreign policy views."[88] Though public opinion is not always coherent or well informed, public support for (or opposition to) a planned military action would appear to be a prize well worth capturing.

In his detailed study of public opinion and foreign policy during the post-Vietnam era, Richard Sobel demonstrates that presidents regularly heeded public opinion when formulating policy on Nicaragua during the 1980s, the Persian Gulf War in 1991, and the Bosnia conflict in the 1990s.[89] By Sobel's account, public opinion acts as an "intervention constraint"—and one that presidents ought to mind when contemplating the use of military force. The way in which the public influences presidential decision making has much in common with Congress's efforts to do so—that is, by reacting to, rather than leading, a set of initiatives that come out of the White House. As Sobel puts it, "Public opinion constrained but did not set American foreign intervention policy. . . . The public's attitudes set the parameters within which policymakers operated."[90] As public opinion defines boundaries to permissive conduct, it invites congressional attention. For if members of Congress can shape public opinion, they gain an important foothold in affecting presidential decision making.

In a similar vein, Matthew Baum argues that public scrutiny raises the potential costs of a military venture and thereby exerts considerable influence over use-of-force decisions.[91] When missteps occur, they are advertised widely and the "domestic audience costs"—code words for electoral retribution and other kinds of political punishment—that are featured in the diplomacy literature rise, often significantly. Public attentiveness, as such, can dissuade presidents from engaging in particularly risky military ventures. As Baum puts it, "Unless a president is highly confident of success, an attentive public can, when the strategic stakes are relatively modest, inhibit him from undertaking risky foreign policy initiatives, including using military force."[92] Baum differentiates between current public opinion, which is volatile and often disengaged, and the more stable and informed future public opinion, which "creates politically relevant domestic audience costs" and figures prominently in presidential decision making.[93] Then, in an extensive case study of the 1993–94 Somalia intervention, Baum details the ways in which the Clinton administration struggled to maintain public support for the operation and adjusted its strategic decision making to minimize public backlash.

Much of the literature on foreign policy and public opinion attempts, in various ways, to dissemble an undifferentiated "public" into different groupings and then assess the variable influence of each group. In a recent paper, Lawrence Jacobs and Benjamin Page compare the relative influence of average citizens, business leaders, labor leaders, and "experts" on the expressed foreign policy preferences of members of Congress and presidential administrations.[94] Perhaps not surprisingly, Jacobs and Page find that business and labor leaders and experts exert more influence than do average citizens on the full range of government officials' foreign policy views. Still, the authors suggest that on the specific issue of war, as compared to more arcane matters of trade and foreign aid, the views of average citizens might well matter greatly. As they put it, "The public may play a substantial part in the highly salient questions of war and peace."[95] Still, for our purposes, their analysis serves as a useful reminder that the views of all citizens, on all foreign policy issues, may not always matter. Indeed, when the profile of a military deployment declines, so may the engagement of average citizens and the influence their views have on political elites.

Because the president speaks with one voice while Congress chimes in with many, because of the profound informational asymmetries that define executive-legislative relations, and because the ability to act unilaterally yields significant agenda-setting powers, presidents obviously have the advantage in campaigns to mobilize public support for a planned military venture. Just because the president dominates these proceedings, however, does not mean that Congress is wholly irrelevant. Quite the contrary, there is considerable cause for believing that Congress can be a major player in public debates over foreign policy initiatives. And to the extent that congressional views determine the tone and content of media coverage and thereby influence public opinion—and in chapters 6 and 7, we demonstrate that they can—it gains an important entrée into executive decision making on matters involving war.

Collectively, then, congressional dissent may matter greatly. To the extent that it reduces the president's capacity to signal resolve to allies and enemies and influences the content of public opinion, opposition from Capitol Hill constitutes something more than idle chatter. In the next chapter, we identify the political conditions and types of foreign conflicts that are most likely to engender congressional dissent, and the implications this dissent may have for the president's discretion to wage war.

CHAPTER 2

Conditions that Abet Congressional Influence

WHILE THE NATION contemplates war abroad, members of Congress wield weapons of their own. Its members can enact legislation and appropriations that restrict the size, scope, or duration of a military venture. They also can publicly rail against what they believe to be an ill-advised use of force. There are, moreover, ample reasons to expect that both courses of action will increase the costs of a military venture, and hence influence presidential decision making at the precipice of war.

That Congress can act, however, does not require that it always will. The possibility of influence must not be confused with its realization. Indeed, the primary function of a theory of interbranch relations during the lead-up to war is to identify those factors that abet congressional influence, and those factors that impede it. For the fact of the matter is that Congress does not always take on the president, either through formal or informal means, even when there is objective cause for doing so. Often, Congress lacks the institutional wherewithal and public will to mount an effective campaign against the president, and even when Congress is capable of challenging the president, its members regularly choose not to. Disappointment awaits any observer who, on reviewing the historical record, anticipates Congress's active and consistent involvement in the domestic deliberations leading up to war.

This chapter outlines three conditions under which congressional opposition to a prospective military venture is most likely to emerge—one having to do with Congress itself, another with the proposed deployment, and another with the military's intended target. Evidence of opposition, and by extension influence, should mount as (1) the opposing party to the president's retains larger and more cohesive governing majorities within Congress; (2) military operations grow in size; and (3) operations focus on nations that are less strategically important to the United States. These three conditions, we suggest, go some distance toward specifying Congress's capacity and willingness to intervene in presidential deliberations about the use of force. As such, they establish the focal point of the empirical tests that subsequent chapters present.

The Partisan Composition of Congress

To begin, we make a simple, but all too often neglected, observation: Congress does not have intentions, or aspirations, or preferences; rather, people do. As a consequence, Congress does not check presidential power; individuals within it do. As an institution, Congress merely sets rules and procedures that define the relationships among elected legislators and the steps required for them to perform specific tasks. It makes little sense to conceive of congressional interests or motivations outside of the members who work within the institution. In the bills they introduce, the laws they enact, the appropriations they pass, the hearings they hold, and the public statements they release, members influence presidential decisions about the use of force. Congress merely denotes the institution within which these activities occur.

Because members of Congress act purposively—rather than Congress itself—it is nonsensical to treat the legislative branch as a unitary actor.[1] Congress, instead, consists of 535 voting members from almost as many districts and states who work in two chambers and on plenty more committees and subcommittees. While parties provide a modicum of order, the institution itself is remarkably decentralized, with individuals given broad latitude to pursue those policies and those activities that bear most heavily on their reelection prospects. The perennial challenge is to build and sustain coalitions that are sufficiently large to overcome the multiple veto points that are scattered across the House and Senate and sufficiently enthusiastic about a particular policy to devote the considerable resources required to effect change. To accomplish anything at all, legislators must coordinate their activities and direct their resources toward goals on which a majority, and in some cases a supermajority, can agree. When doing so, they confront all of the problems that plague collective decision-making bodies, most especially transaction costs (which refer to the costs of retrieving information required for exchange, negotiating the terms of the exchange, and then developing mechanisms for enforcing deals between legislators) and collective action problems (which reduce the chances that any individual will pay such costs).

If Congress is properly understood as a collective decision-making body with diverse and often conflicting interests, rather than as a unitary actor with singular preferences, then the probability that Congress takes steps to limit presidential power critically depends on the members who, at any given moment, inhabit the institution. When divisions run deep within its ranks, members have an exceedingly difficult time enacting laws, holding hearings, and affirming nominations, among other things—activities that affect the content of public policy and check the assertion of presidential power. When the membership is relatively unified and strong, however, policy entrepreneurs find it considerably easier to affirm or challenge the president.

None of this is news to congressional scholars, who have amassed an impressive body of theory and evidence about how different structures (e.g., committees) and different procedures (e.g., the filibuster) raise or reduce transaction costs and thereby influence the chances that a bill will be enacted or a budget approved.[2] Scholars have demonstrated that the production of laws critically depends on the heterogeneity of preferences within Congress and the divisions between the legislative and executive branches.[3] Too often, though, the realities that Congress is not a unitary actor and that its ability to operate effectively varies according to the latest election results are overlooked by scholars with considerably wider analytic frameworks. Congress is presumed weak in military politics because *it* refuses to fulfill its constitutional obligations, or because *it* denies any responsibility for overseeing world affairs, or because *it* is incapable of responding with speed and conviction to foreign crises. The institution, of course, matters greatly. It does so, however, because it structures incentives and provides resources for different members, each serving different constituencies with different preferences and commitments, to check presidential power in this and every other policy domain.

If Congress is best characterized as a "they" rather than an "it," a simple, but vital, question arises. At the front end of a military campaign, who within Congress is likely to back the president, and who is likely to oppose him? On reflection, this proves to be a remarkably nettlesome question, not least because the probability that members of Congress will take on the president surely depends on the particulars of each individual crisis and the impact members see it having on their constituents, and by extension, the prospects for their reelection. Moreover, different members of Congress probably draw on different principles and different notions of the national interest when thinking about the pros and cons of military action. For some members, genocide may constitute reason enough to intervene militarily into some region of the globe; for others, the nation's strategic interests must be imperiled before they will lend their support. Much, as it were, depends on a host of contextual factors. When trying to generalize across a wide range of crises, we can hope only to generate probabilistic statements about members' proclivities that turn out to be right more often than not.

Are there any general indicators that Congress as a whole will be more or less inclined to limit the presidential use of force? We suggest the following, which constitutes our second point about how to characterize Congress: on average, members of a president's own party are likely to support military action, while those who appear more skeptical fall disproportionately from the ranks of the opposition party. To generate a rough indicator of the likelihood that Congress will object to a wide range of uses of military force, one ought to focus on the level of partisan support that the president enjoys on Capitol Hill. As his party's numbers grow, the president ought to enjoy greater discretion to exercise military force when and as he pleases; as they dwindle, the president should proceed with considerably more caution.

There are a variety of reasons to expect Democratic members of Congress to back Democratic presidents, just as Republican members back Republican presidents. Here, we sketch out four:

(1)   Common Worldviews: First, and perhaps most obviously, Democratic presidents and Democratic members of Congress may simply agree on the conditions under which military action is warranted, just as Republican presidents and Republican members of Congress do. Within each party, politicians may have distinct views about the nation's priorities, the specific countries and regions that bear on these priorities, and the kinds of crises (human rights violations, threats to national trade interests, large numbers of U.S. casualties, etc.) that rightfully call for action. Presidents, therefore, are likely to propose interventions that appeal most to members of their own parties. If the worldviews of Democrats and Republicans differ markedly from one another, then the president may well evoke pointed criticism from members of the opposition party when he embarks on any specific venture.

(2)   The Content and Credibility of Signals: While presidents and members of Congress may share a worldview, they do not share an equivalent amount of information about crises occurring abroad. As we noted in chapter 1, presidents have at their disposal considerable amounts of private information about developments abroad and their impacts on the nation's strategic interests. Congress, meanwhile, has few formal mechanisms for corroborating this information. When a president makes a case for deploying troops abroad, Congress often must decide whether or not to take him at his word.[4]

A number of game theoretic models demonstrate that the credibility of signals sent between political actors improves as their preferences converge.[6] For instance, the first principle of Keith Krehbiel's information theory of congressional committees states that "the more extreme are the preferences of a committee specialist relative to preferences of a nonspecialist in the legislature, the less informative is the committee."[7] When senders and receivers in incomplete information games share a common worldview, the signals conveyed can readily be trusted and hence are more informative; conversely, as preferences diverge, signals are less trustworthy, and hence less informative. If the president is to make an effective case for deploying troops, members of Congress must believe the information he transmits. If shared ideological orientations facilitate belief, as the game theory suggests, then presidents should garner trust from members of his party, and suspicion from the opposition party. As his party grows in size and strength, the president ought to benefit from greater legislative discretion to exercise force abroad.

As just one example, recall the reluctance of Republicans to authorize the use of force against Kosovo in 1999. Robert Dole (R-KS), then retired from the Senate but a stalwart supporter of military action to curb Serbian aggression against Kosovo's ethnic Albanians, had an extraordinarily difficult time convincing his fellow Republicans to sign on to the military venture. As he explained, "I don't think that most Republicans are isolationist. There is a lot of mistrust of Clinton." To wit, Senator Don Nickles (R-OK), in an appearance on the ABC News program "This Week," claimed that he did "not really" trust Clinton, and hence could not back military action.[5] Concerned that Clinton was being less than straightforward about conditions in Kosovo and that his administration lacked the skills needed to effectively diffuse the Balkan crisis, Republicans in Congress refused to authorize the use of force, even though the president had the support of a broad international coalition at the time.

(3) Shared Electoral Fortunes: One might posit that Democratic members of Congress will tend to back Democratic presidents, and that Republican members of Congress will back Republican presidents, without ever conceding that congressional members from either party have a clear vision about foreign policy or the desire to collect the information required to assess the president's claims. Instead, support or opposition may derive entirely from members' expectations about how presidents will impact future congressional elections.

Consider the following: because their electoral fortunes are linked to the president, congressional members of the president's party have a vested interest in the president's success, just as members of the opposition party do in his failure. If presidential approval ratings increase when presidents exercise force abroad (as the rally-around-the-flag literature suggests),[8] and if high presidential approval ratings boost members' electoral prospects (as the literature on coattails suggests),[9] then, all else equal, members' willingness to grant the president broad discretion to exercise force abroad should critically depend on his partisan identification. Presidential uses of force redound to the electoral benefit of members of the president's own party and, by implication, to the detriment of the opposition party. Members of the president's party, all else equal, ought to actively support the president's plans to exercise force abroad, as members of the opposition party either reserve judgment or voice opposition.

(4) Currying Presidential Favor: The fourth reason why we should expect the locus of congressional support for the president to be among

members of his own party is a straightforward extension of the third. Presidents have considerable means by which to influence the electoral prospects of members of Congress. By visiting their districts, appearing in their television advertisements, or introducing them to potential funders, presidents can significantly affect members' electoral returns. Of course, presidents work on behalf of members of their own party. Republican members of Congress rarely have anything to gain from currying the favor of Democratic presidents. Similarly, Democratic members have little reason to go out of their way to support Republican presidents. Precisely because constituents pay more attention to domestic than foreign policy matters when deciding how to vote, members of Congress often have little to lose, and often much to gain, from actively supporting a president interested in exercising force abroad. To the extent that broad grants of authority in foreign affairs help members remain in a president's good graces, Democratic members have cause to support Democratic presidents when they consider using force abroad, just as Republican members have cause to support Republican presidents.

Each of these four arguments rests on separate, and not always compatible, first principles. But they all lead to the same conclusion: congressional members of the president's party ought to line up behind the president during times of international crisis, while either because they disagree with him, they do not believe him, they see themselves as in competition with him, or they have nothing to gain from courting his approval, members of the opposition party may not. For the most part, these expectations appear to be consistent with members' actual behavior. In the only three nonunanimous use-of-force authorization votes to occur before troops were deployed into the field in the last twenty-five years, members of the president's party consistently fell behind the commander in chief, while dissenting voices disproportionately came from the opposition party.[10] In 1991, a Republican held the presidency, and Congress debated what would become the Persian Gulf War.[11] In the House, 164 of 167 Republicans supported the war, as compared to 86 of 265 Democrats;[12] and in the Senate, 42 of 43 Republicans supported the war, while just 10 of 56 Democrats did.[13] In 1999, when a Democrat resided in the White House, Republicans opposed the use of force in Kosovo. In the House authorization vote, 174 of 192 Democrats supported the president, as compared to 44 of 217 Republicans;[14] and in the Senate, 32 of 35 Democrats supported the president, while only 16 of 48 Republicans did.[15] These trends once again reversed themselves. In the 2002 Iraq authorization vote in the House, 215 of 221 voting Republicans supported the use of force, as compared to 81 of 207 Democrats; and in the Senate, 48 of 49 Republicans supported the use of force, as compared to 21 of 50 Democrats.[16]

Party voting is hardly isolated to authorization votes that precede actual deployments. Indeed, once a military venture is up and running, partisan divisions continue to run deep. When troops are in the field, congressional voting patterns on bills that concern the authorization to use force, the appropriation of funds, and the delineation of a conflict's scope or duration continue to break down along party lines. When Clinton assumed office in 1993 and expressed his support for the Somali mission that Bush had launched just two months prior, Democrats came rallying to his side, just as Republicans fled in droves, even though only a few months prior many Democrats had expressed skepticism of the venture, and Republicans had lent support.[17] In a May 25 authorization vote, 239 of 248 House Democrats backed the president, as compared to just 3 of the 173 Republicans.[18] Later, when Congress considered a series of measures to restrict funding for the military venture and to set firm dates on which troops would have to return, Democrats overwhelmingly supported the president, while Republicans opposed him.

So it went in almost every military use of force during the past several decades. When Republican presidents exercised military force in Lebanon (1982–83), Grenada (1983), and Panama (1989), Republican members of Congress came out in support, while many Democrats dissented. When Democratic presidents exercised force in Haiti (1993–96) and Bosnia (1992–98), allegiances shifted, and Democratic members of Congress came out in support, while Republicans expressed disapproval.[19] To be sure, members of Congress often choose not to vote on uses of force; and when roll call votes do occur, victories can be quite lopsided. Consistently, though, where opposition to a presidential use of force surfaces, it comes from the ranks of the opposing party. When trying to assess the levels of interbranch conflict that a military deployment is likely to engender, one would do well to monitor the levels of partisan support that the president enjoys within Congress.

Given the extant theory on congressional-presidential relations, these voting patterns, and the reasons why presidents should care about Congress outlined in chapter 1, there is considerable reason to expect that the president's discretion to exercise force abroad ought to covary with the relative size and unity of his party's membership in Congress. Nevertheless, two alternative possibilities linger, each of which casts doubt on these claims. First, in addition to having fixed (and divergent) preferences about the kinds of crises that warrant military action, Democrats and Republicans may have independent views about the frequency with which force is appropriately used. If, for instance, Democrats essentially are doves and Republicans are hawks, then congressional support for the presidential use of force ought to increase as the number of Republicans, as opposed to the number of copartisans, increases. Alternatively, partisan divisions may be a rather recent phenomenon. If both parties shared the same outlook on foreign policy matters during the period between World War II and the Vietnam War, as a number of scholars have argued, then measures of congressional support for the president may be time-dependent.[20] In the empirical tests that follow, we explore both of these possibilities.

It also is possible that congressional influence depends not only on the levels of partisan opposition to the president, but also the distribution of Democrats and Republicans across two chambers and multiple committees and subcommittees. The overall percentage of seats held by one party or another, of course, is not the only way to characterize Congress. But as the partisan composition of committees reflects the partisan composition of their chambers, as the public prestige of key committees (Armed Services in the House and Foreign Relations in the Senate) depends on the size of the governing majority,[21] and as parties typically win and lose seats in the House and Senate in roughly equal proportions, we prefer to keep things as simple as possible and to focus on the overall seat advantages that one party holds over the other. We leave to future research the tasks of assessing the relevance of, say, a ranking Democrat holding a chairmanship on the Foreign Affairs Committee, or a class of freshmen Republicans storming the Armed Services Committee, or the Rules Committee insisting that the floors of the House or Senate consider bills involving the use of force on an up or down basis.

Ultimately, though, the best way to characterize congressional support for the president and to determine whether such characterizations covary with presidential uses of force are subjects for empirical investigation. In subsequent chapters we explore alternative measures. For now, though, we take some comfort in the fact that the vast majority of scholars in American politics who have studied the conditions under which Congress supports presidential initiatives, broadly defined, call attention to the partisan composition of the legislative branch.[22] As George Edwards counsels, "Members of the president's party almost always form the core of the president's support in Congress."[23] Still, in the empirical tests that follow, we present a variety of statistical models to ensure that the effects we do observe do not depend on any particular time period, model specification, or measurement strategy.

THE SIZE OF A DEPLOYMENT

See the world, for a moment, as a typical member of Congress does. You have a short period of time—two years in the House, six in the Senate—

to establish a record of accomplishments to present to your constituents. Your job responsibilities range across every conceivable issue, from farm subsidies to immigration to health care to roads to jobs. And given the multiple veto points that align the legislative process, the collective action problems that pervade your institution, and the transaction costs associated with assembling a legislative coalition, your chances of enacting a rich collection of important laws in time to satisfy a sizable portion of your district or state are slim.

Given a limited time horizon, sprawling expectations, the immense challenges associated with enacting legislation, and the resulting opportunity costs of pursuing any specific policy agenda, how should you devote scarce resources while in office? The short answer is simple enough: selectively. You should do those things that matter most to your constituents, those things for which you can claim credit, and those things that stand a reasonable chance of success. And you should leave it to others, be they in the legislative or executive branches, to do the rest. Prudently, you refuse to scrutinize those issues that do not immediately bear on your electoral fortunes, either because they do not address the particular interests of the people who elected you or because they attract little public attention. To do otherwise would be foolish. Frittering away precious time and resources on ancillary issues invites disaster at the next election.

To any observer of American politics, none of this comes as news. The travails of the legislative process, members' incessant efforts to shore up their electoral fortunes, and the selective attention afforded different public policies are all amply documented, and require no further review here.[24] These observations, however, have obvious and important implications for our expectations about congressional checks on presidential war powers. The electoral fortunes of most members most of the time do not ride exclusively, or even primarily, on their capacity to formulate and implement coherent foreign policy. Other competing issues and impending crises—plenty of which are purely domestic in nature—continually vie for their attention. Every day, members must choose whether to tackle education, welfare, health care, the presidential use of force, and dozens of other policies besides. And in a moment's notice, a member's attention may shift from matters involving war to the more pressing exigencies of a summer drought, industry foreclosure, announced job losses, or hurricane.

When, then, can we expect members of Congress to mobilize against a presidential use of force? At a minimum, the deployment's stakes need to reach some basic threshold of importance. Minor excursions—be they symbolic shows of force, discrete strikes against a foreign enemy, or short expeditions conducted abroad—are unlikely to attract much notice within the halls of Congress. When launching a few missiles into a suspected terrorist's encampment or performing a twenty-one-gun salute off the coast of an ally's shores or cooperating with another state on some routine training expedition, there is not much chance that American lives will be lost or that the mission will derail. In these instances, members have few incentives to get involved, leaving the president plenty of discretion to deploy troops, or not, when and where he pleases.

Calculations change, however, when the size and scope of a mission expands. When committing sizable troops and force, presidents confront the possibilities of a protracted mission yielding American casualties, alienating key allies, or disrupting foreign trade. Given such risks, members of Congress have greater cause to stand up, take notice, and devote the time and resources needed to formulate an opinion and, possibly, a response. As David Auerswald and Peter Cowhey observe:

> Congress has implemented restraints or threatened to restrain the president using the [the War Powers Resolution] or similar legislation when U.S. deployments lead to the long-term and large-scale use of force. Congress has acquiesced to the use of force so long as the administration's action is swift or small scale. Such deployments raise little likelihood of future Vietnam-style conflicts and do not necessitate congressional action. Without exception, however, long-term conflicts were met with either congressional threats or legislative action with the potential to start the war powers clock.[25]

Congress tends to pay attention when the expected costs of a military venture escalate. For with the escalation of a deployment's size comes the escalation of risk, giving members of Congress cause to weigh in on the debates that precede military action.

THE IMPORTANCE OF THE INTERNATIONAL SYSTEM

Even when presidents face a relatively large contingent of partisan opponents, and when presidents are considering a larger military deployment, Congress as an institution may still demur. International relations theorists, especially those aligned with the realist school of thought, have long emphasized the importance of international factors in shaping states' foreign policy behavior.[26] This section borrows from this literature to identify a variety of international conditions that may mediate the relative influence that Congress wields over presidential decision making on matters involving war.

Despite their differences, both realists and neorealists hold that important systemic factors (the global distribution of power, networks of alliances, the power of a hegemon, global trade flows, among other things) limit or compel state action apart from domestic politics.[27] At their core, these systemic theories of international relations insist that states in similar situations (defined by some set of structural characteristics) will behave similarly, regardless of the domestic politics within each state. By extension, decision makers ought to behave similarly over time if placed in a similarly structured situation, regardless of the domestic politics at the time.

Plainly, realists and neorealists maintain an analytic focus very different from this book's. And we continue to maintain that structural approaches to international relations give short shrift to the influence of domestic politics on interstate relations. Nonetheless, we fully admit the possibility that in certain situations, structural factors will condition the effect of domestic politics on foreign policy. For example, when dealing with an ally or when confronting an opportunity in a strategically important state, Congress may not inform decisions regarding the use of force. The reverse, however, may also be true. When opportunities arise in nations that do not hold much strategic importance to the United States, presidents operate outside the constraints of powerful international forces; and in such instances, the partisan composition of Congress may matter greatly. Interbranch politics, as such, should intensify when decisions about the use of force are appropriately deemed matters of volition.

No scholar makes a clearer case for structural theory than Kenneth Waltz. For Waltz, though, structural theory does not and should not reduce to a theory of foreign policy. Structural variables (e.g., balance of power considerations) yield clear and broad predictions about state behavior, but the particulars of that behavior are left unexplained (and unexplored). As Waltz insists, "The clear perception of constraints provides many clues to the expected reactions of states, but by itself the [balance of power] theory cannot explain those reactions."[28] Thus, leaders react to international constraints in well established ways, but these same constraints provide little insight into which specific policies are chosen. For example, in the case of presidential uses of force, one might argue that some international factors make intervention a foregone conclusion, erasing partisan dynamics that could discourage a deployment. The theory, however, lends little insight into whether the use of force is large or small, or when, exactly, it is likely to materialize; and, of course, the theory says even less about an adjoining branch of government's say over the matter.

Though structural factors ought to attenuate congressional influence over presidential decision making, structural theories still posit probabilistic predictions. As Waltz himself points out, rarely will structural forces completely determine foreign policy. Whether leaders respond to a particular crisis is, in the end, still a matter of an individual's choice, and an individual who is embedded in a particular system of government and who confronts a specific contingent of political supporters and opponents. In his own study of comparative British and American foreign policy, Waltz reminds us that "[foreign] policy should ideally be responsive, in fine balance, both to internal constituents and external conditions."[29] Note the language that Waltz employs. It is not simply that states respond to both internal constituents and external conditions, but that the relevance of each would appear to depend on the other—presidents, after all, seek a "fine balance" between the two.

When confronting an international opportunity to use force, what external conditions ought to weigh most heavily on presidents' thinking? For traditional neorealist thinkers such as Waltz, the distribution of military capabilities plays the most important role in constraining foreign policy decisions.[30] Indeed, a long debate has raged as to what distribution of power has the biggest constraining effect on state conflict behavior.[31] For our analysis, however, this question is moot. Over the time period covered by our study, there is relatively little variation in the distribution of power, given that a bipolar system dominated world politics. Although in our empirical tests, we do check for changes in the post–Cold War period, we hesitate to place too much emphasis on a paltry few years of data where the structure of the international system was in flux.[32] Thus, it is difficult to determine what influence the distribution of power might have on choices concerning the use of force.

Realist and neoclassical realist thinkers also suggest that the balance of power between states reasonably predicts conflict behavior.[33] When states confront a more powerful nemesis, realists argue, deterrence is likely; after all, rational states tend not to act aggressively when they are at a military disadvantage. Conversely, states will appear relatively unconstrained in their behavior towards smaller, less powerful states. Again, though, for our purposes the balance of power affords little opportunity to advance our analyses. With *very few* exceptions during the postwar period, the United States maintained an overwhelming military advantage over all potential targets. Indeed, the only exception to this would be the Soviet Union, a case to which we return below. Thus, we should not expect marked variation in the balance-of-power constraints faced by presidents when considering the use of force.

Though we lack variation in the distribution and balance of power, considerable variation persists in the levels of economic trade and types of military alliances that the United States has maintained during the postwar period. Scholars have long argued that military alliances are crucial elements of the international system, in particular the functioning of a balance-of-power system.[34] To be sure, alliances come in a variety of forms, be they mutual defense pacts (e.g., NATO), ententes, or nonaggression pacts; and the commitment of signatories in each of these cases varies significantly. On the whole, though, all of these alliances discourage states, either because of shared interests or contractual obligations, from attacking fellow signatories.

Presidents should feel especially constrained when confronting states that are allied militarily with the United States. Presumably, the similarities in interests that come with formal alliances, not to mention the reputational costs of attacking one's own ally, sharply restrict the latitude that a president has in dealing with a crisis emerging from an allied state. Signaling and informational models of war also suggest that as the quantity and quality of information exchanged between states rises, the incentive to fight declines.[35] If alliances can facilitate this exchange of information (as argued by many institutional theorists), then we should expect fewer conflicts between members. As Russett and Oneal argue, "The institutional bonds of military alliances make war among their members less likely."[36]

Of course, the logic could work to compel action too—formal alliances often have strict provisions about lending military support when third parties attack any signatory. In either case, external factors may overshadow domestic political concerns and the potential threats posed by Congress. Whether the effect itself is positive or negative is immaterial to our argument—the point, rather, is that presidents will respond more readily to this important international concern than to domestic political calculations.

Another related international variable may also condition the effect of Congress. For reasons previously identified, one might expect external constraints to be particularly important in cases where the potential target is an ally of the Soviet Union, especially during the Cold War. Much scholarship in international relations has attempted to determine whether alliances assist in extended deterrence—that is, whether states considering the use of force against a target examine whether that state is an ally of a strong, rival state. Initial answers were occasionally supportive, but mostly inconclusive.[37] More recent work by Brett Leeds, however, suggests that alliances do enhance extended deterrence, and that defensive alliances reduce the propensity of states to attack.[38]

With respect to U.S. foreign policy, Soviet involvement in some foreign crises may discourage military action, if only to avoid an escalation to major power warfare. In other instances, though, low-level conflicts that involve the Soviet Union may spur action by the United States, which appears intent on checking Soviet influence in the zero-sum Cold War. Again, no matter which way the relationship works, Soviet involvement in a foreign crisis may overwhelm any influence that Congress wields at the forefront of military action.

Finally, we consider the possibility that interstate economic relations condition the influence of domestic politics on matters involving war.

Recently, a large body of empirical research has suggested that trade and investment levels between states heavily influence the probability of war erupting between them.[39] Consistently, these studies have shown that increasing levels of trade or investment lower the propensity of states to engage in military conflicts. And it is easy to see why. State leaders will feel pressured to limit hostilities with trading partners, since conflict threatens to scuttle the economic activity of both private traders and consumers on which politicians' electoral fortunes often depend.[40]

Scholars engaging the rationalist war literature have proffered another explanation that links states' trade patterns with their conflict behavior.[41] According to their line of reasoning, states that are involved in a dispute can use trade as a credible signal to convey resolve to an adversary. States with few economic linkages have fewer levers to pull during a negotiating process and must resort to military force sooner in the process. States with high levels of trade, meanwhile, can communicate in ways that do not strictly involve cheap talk—in this instance, by threatening to disrupt trade rather than succumb to bargaining pressure. In our case, this suggests that high levels of trade with the United States will provide presidents with another policy lever to pull before even considering a more costly policy such as military force.

Whichever causal logic one relies on, the same prediction emerges: states engaged in high levels of trade have large incentives to keep their swords sheathed. Economic factors are likely to be key components in the decision-making process of a president. Hence, when the United States confronts a crisis in which a valuable trading partner is involved, concerns over Congress may recede in the president's decision calculus. Again, this is true whether one accepts the logic of the commercial liberal point of view or whether one adopts the more cynical view of traditional economic imperialist logic, where economic exchange serves as an *impetus* for intervention.[42] In either case, an international factor pushes a president toward a particular outcome, making domestic concerns less important.

We thus examine three systemic variables that may limit the relevance of domestic politics in presidential decision making involving war: whether a crisis involves an allied nation, the Soviet Union, or an important trading partner. Some may object that we mix levels of analysis too lightly. Our general approach on this matter is consistent with that of Bueno de Mesquita (1981). In his model, state leaders may or may not initiate war due to personal risk propensities. Yet, key for Bueno de Mesquita are structural conditions that are perceived by state leaders. Conflict is thus the outcome of variables such as the distribution of power as well as individual risk propensity. While our own theory does not rely on risk propensity, in this section we have suggested that conditions that abet military action depend on both structural factors (alliances and trade) as well as contextual factors (a president's political party's control in Congress).

We also note that Waltz explicitly rejects attempts to bridge structural and domestic theories of foreign policy, arguing that the number of factors and variables required to conduct such work necessarily become unwieldy. We disagree. Indeed, if the goal is to explain each and every foreign policy behavior of the United States (or any other state), a theorist will always be disappointed. Yet, we have identified a set of conditions at the domestic and international level that should produce consistent behavior over time. Our approach also heeds calls by scholars such as James Fearon to use structural theories to establish "baseline expectations to ground and motivate a next round of empirical and theoretical inquiry."[43] That is, we have deduced factors from structural theories that should condition (probabilistically) whether Congress informs use-of-force politics.

SUMMARIZING THE THEORY

The theoretical expectations laid out in this chapter derive, in large part, from our previous work on unilateral powers.[44] There, we examined the conditions under which presidents issued a variety of domestic and foreign policy directives, either in the form of executive orders, executive agreements, national security directives, or proclamations. There, as here, we argued that constraints on presidential action depend on the partisan composition of Congress, the importance of the policies being considered, and the choice set made available to the president.

When presidents use executive orders, proclamations, and other unilateral directives to advance their policy agendas, their initiatives are not fixed in stone. Congress, after all, has subsequent opportunity to amend and overturn them and, more easily still, to restrict their funding. Hence, when contemplating action, presidents have considerable cause to account for congressional preferences and, when necessary, to adjust course accordingly. The core function of a theory of unilateral action is to identify when adjustments are, in fact, necessary. To wit, the existing American politics literature on the topic pays particular attention to the partisan composition of Congress. When strong majorities stand in opposition to the president, Congress is best equipped and most prone to overturn especially controversial directives. Hence, as we show elsewhere, during such periods presidents prudently issue fewer executive orders.[45] And they are right to do so. Should they press their luck and aggressively issue a bevy of orders, presidents can well expect Congress to amend them, if not strike them down. Only when presidents anticipate that governing majorities within Congress will pretermit his orders will they venture onward.[46]

Within any given congressional session, however, not all policy changes bear equal chance of evoking a legislative response. As long as they remain off Congress's radar screen, presidents can basically do as they choose, and the easiest way to ensure as much is by issuing minor policy changes. It is little wonder, then, that during his tenure in office Bill Clinton issued directives that accomplished such modest tasks as monitoring the smoking habits of teenagers, reforming health care programs' appeals processes, and requiring trigger safety locks on guns purchased for law enforcement agencies, while Bush (43) issued orders designed to extend federal funds to faith-based organizations, revamp environmental laws, and relax industry regulations. To be sure, collectively these policy initiatives, in combination with many others, accomplished a fair amount. Individually, though, they were less exceptional, and they thereby managed to avoid congressional scrutiny.

Finally, presidents can only issue domestic and foreign policy initiatives when they have statutory and/or constitutional authority for doing so. Clinton might have liked to unilaterally raise the minimum wage, entirely revamp the nation's health care system, and impose new taxes on tobacco consumption, just as Bush might have liked to unilaterally institute a ban on same-sex marriages, extend additional tax relief to citizens, or begin the process of privatizing aspects of Social Security accounts. In all instances, though, the two presidents lacked the needed authority for taking such actions unilaterally; and in every instance, therefore, they relented. And so it is with all presidents. The policy options available to presidents depend on more than their imagination today and the possibility of defeat tomorrow. Vitally, the larger constitutional framework and the corpus of statutory law that presidents inherit also define their ability to unilaterally launch new policy initiatives.

Parallels between these observations about unilateral directives generally and those that concern the use of force specifically are readily apparent. With minor modifications, the constraints on presidential powers identified by the existing literature on unilateral action reappear when the topic turns to the use of force. In both instances, the partisan composition of Congress affects the underlying probability that members will be able to overcome the multiple veto points and transaction costs that regularly confound legislative efforts. In both instances, interbranch dynamics are likely to ease when the subject turns to less significant actions, be they smaller troop deployments or policy changes. And in both instances, larger regimes, whether international or constitutional in nature, structure the choice set put before the president.

In summary, we identify three key factors that ought to augment the chances that Congress will constrain the presidential use of force: large and cohesive majorities opposed to the president holding office; deployments of larger-scale initiatives; and instances when the international environment does not bind the president to a particular course of action to resolve a specified foreign crisis. Drawing from a variety of original datasets and case studies, the next section tests these claims.

PART TWO

Testing Claims about Congressional Influence

Trends in Military Deployments

WAR POWERS have shifted, perhaps irrevocably, from Congress to the president.[1] When foreign crises erupt, the domestic political constraints that wreak havoc on White House plans to reform welfare or scale back farm subsidies or cut discretionary programs suddenly slacken, leaving the president newfound latitude to navigate the international environment. Whether by reference to the influence they wield in domestic policy today, or the influence they wielded over foreign policy a century ago, modern presidents' war powers are astounding.

The widespread notion, however, that domestic political constraints entirely evaporate when presidents contemplate war exaggerates matters. In this chapter, we discuss and evaluate those domestic factors that shape military deployment trends in the postwar era. We argue that existing literatures in international relations are largely bereft of meaningful discussions of Congress and the influence it continues to wield. Through a series of quantitative evaluations, we then demonstrate Congress's persisting relevance to decisions involving military deployments.

THE QUANTITATIVE USE-OF-FORCE LITERATURE

During the past thirty years, an impressive quantitative literature on the use of force has emerged within international relations studies. Scholars have introduced, extended, and modified a series of datasets that track troop deployments over time. They have considered the impacts of numerous foreign and domestic political forces on presidential decision making. Moreover, a number of scholars have paid careful attention to the ways in which different political influences change over time and interact with one another. By all indications, this is a vibrant area of research.

The literature finds its origin in Barry Blechman and Stephen Kaplan's seminal 1978 book, *Force without War*.[2] Blechman and Kaplan scoured military records and media reports for incidences of military force "short of war." By these, Blechman and Kaplan mean discrete, nonroutine military operations that serve political purposes such as demonstrating national resolve, communicating the government's interests, expressing solidarity with foreign nations, or altering the strategic considerations of other nations

interacting with one another.[3] Ultimately, they found 226 instances between 1946 and 1976, the vast majority of which involved naval forces
as the entirety of the deployment or as a supplement to land-based air
units and ground combat forces. The bulk of their book is devoted to analyzing a random sample of 33 deployments to see when, and whether,
U.S. presidents actually achieve their strategic objectives over the short
and long terms. While this particular issue received little attention in subsequent research, the original dataset Blechman and Kaplan constructed
laid the groundwork for virtually every quantitatively oriented scholar interested in the use of force.

Beginning in the mid 1980s, scholars built on Blechman and Kaplan's
database to test a variety of international relations theories about interstate conflict and political psychology insights into executive decision
making. Two such scholars, Charles Ostrom and Brian Job, argued that
U.S. presidents use simple decision rules to balance the competing demands placed before them.[4] As commander in chief, chief executive, and
"political leader," presidents "monitor salient dimensions in the domestic,
international, and political arenas" before committing U.S. forces abroad.
Domestic politics, however, retain special significance. In Ostrom and Job's
empirical analysis, the substantive impacts of domestic variables (weighted
economic misery index, presidential approval, and national elections) on
the frequency with which presidents exercise military force consistently
match or exceed those of their international counterparts.[5]

Most studies that followed Ostrom and Job examined how the economy, public opinion, and electoral cycles influence a president's decision
to deploy troops abroad. Patrick James and John Oneal introduced a new
variable tapping international threats to U.S. interests, yet still found the
domestic political factors that Ostrom and Job identified to be largely responsible for the use of force.[6] Benjamin Fordham subsequently argued
that economic factors and public opinion do not directly shape presidential
choices, but instead influence how the president views his external environment.[7] The president, according to Fordham, tends to "see" opportunities to use force when the domestic economy is poor: when inflation is
low and employment high, presidents have few incentives to imperil their
reelection prospects with foreign military ventures. By Richard Stoll's account, the president's proclivity to launch new military ventures abroad
systematically varies according to the election cycle and the presence of
war.[8] Specifically, Stoll found that during wartime election years, presidential uses of force peak, while during peacetime election years, they drop.

The notion that domestic politics inform presidential decisions to exercise force abroad is not without controversy. According to realists, neorealists, and their various offshoots, heads of state do not weigh the likely
impact of an economic downturn or a shift in public approval ratings when

contemplating military action; instead, they keep their eyes squarely on considerations of the nation's standing in an anarchic international system. In his classic formulation of the claim more than a quarter century ago, Kenneth Waltz argued, "It is not possible to understand world politics simply by looking inside of states."[9] Balance of powers, hegemony, the involvement of the Soviet Union, and foreign threats to perceived national interests loom largest when presidents contemplate military action abroad. Domestic politics, by contrast, appear rather muted.

Following Waltz, a number of scholars contributing to the quantitative use-of-force literature have documented evidence that underscores the vital importance of international factors in shaping presidential decision making. James Meernik, for instance, found that domestic economic forces played little to no role in predicting American use of military force in response to foreign crises between 1948 and 1988.[10] Instead, threats to the nation's overseas defense commitments and the possibility of confronting the Soviet Union appear preeminent. By his own account, Meernik's results "would seem to indicate that when balancing domestic and international conditions, presidents' decisions are more often motivated by national interest than personal political gain."[11] Using a different dataset on uses of force, Joanne Gowa discovered that neither the partisan nature of Congress, nor electoral cycles, nor the state of the economy predicts the regularity with which presidents exercise military force.[12] Similarly, Will Moore and David Lanoue found that presidential approval ratings are unrelated to the use of force between 1953 and 1978, concluding that "international politics, not domestic politics, [must be] the primary determinant of conflictual U.S. foreign policy behavior."[13]

Though controversies about the relative importance of domestic and foreign politics persist, two commonalities within the quantitative use-of-force literature deserve recognition. The first is methodological in nature. Virtually all statistical models on the use of force analyze quarterly (sometimes annual) event counts of military deployments.[14] Though scholars have continually refined the statistical procedures used to analyze such data,[15] all have always agreed on the intended objective—namely, to identify those forces that contribute to the frequency with which president exercise military force abroad.[16] Nothing about these data allows one to isolate those factors that critically affect the choice of foreign crises to which presidents respond or the timing of these responses. The data, and hence the analyses, are stripped of all the particular features and contingencies that preoccupy presidents, Congress, and their respective constituents. All that we can say, in the end, is that certain factors positively (or negatively) contribute to rates of foreign military deployments, while others yield no discernible impact at all.[17]

The second characteristic of the existing quantitative use-of-force literature is more substantive, and more consequential for this book's central thesis. Though international relations scholars disagree about the relative importance of domestic and international forces in contributing to presidential decisions over military deployments, they generally agree that the institution of Congress is weak.[18] Rarely are measures of congressional relations with the president included in statistical models on the use of force, and when they are included, they are crudely specified, typically as nothing more than indicator variables for divided government,[19] the postwar Powers Resolution era,[20] or periods of "cold war consensus."[21] An assumption of legislative impotence has achieved the status of conventional wisdom. As Meernik contends:

> The literature on U.S. foreign policymaking unambiguously demonstrates that because of his constitutional prerogatives and political incentives as well as congressional weaknesses in foreign policy, it is the president who exercises supreme control over the nation's military actions. Thus, I consider the president as the "ultimate decider" who determines when and how military force is to be used for political purposes.[22]

Domestic institutional constraints, as such, play no part in his analysis. They do, however, in Gowa's, which provides one of the few systematic tests of Congress's influence on the use of force. Nonetheless, Gowa also claims that "the use of force abroad is invariant to both the domestic political calendar and the partisan composition of government. . . . The use of U.S. military power abroad responds only to changes in national power and to the advent of the world wars."[23] Developments abroad, as it were, captivate presidents and their staff, while domestic politics are relegated to the most distant peripheries of decision making on the use of force.

The claim is straightforward enough. Because the president is commander in chief, Congress cannot (or will not) encroach on his freedom to decide when and how to use the military. While Congress may direct domestic policy making, its hold over foreign policy is quite tenuous. When the president decides to exercise military force abroad, members of Congress can only complain amongst themselves. For the most part, the president's authority over military matters would appear undisputed.

Consider, by way of additional examples, the scholarship on two of the more prominent topics concerning domestic politics and the use of force: diversionary war and "rally-around-the-flag" effects. The diversionary war hypothesis suggests that heads of state deploy troops abroad in an effort to deflect attention away from domestic strife, most commonly poor economic indicators.[24] Many advocates of the theory assume that Congress, the bureaucracy, and the public are blind to a leader's true intentions and, as a consequence, regularly accept—on faith—proffered justifications for conflicts.[25] By sending troops abroad, it is supposed, presidents can shift public attention away from a failing economy and rally widespread support,[26] as members of Congress, including those of the opposition party, naturally and automatically fall behind their chief executive.

"Rally-around-the-flag" effects occur when citizens express their patriotism and national unity in the aftermath of an observed crisis by rewarding their head of state with higher approval ratings. What makes these bounces in approval ratings distinctive is that they have nothing to do with the president's actual job performance. Such jumps, instead, are brought on by a threatening event, and not any kind of realization about the president or his policy accomplishments. Lest you doubt that rally effects exist, answer the following: Did Bush do anything to deserve the thirty-five-point increase in his approval ratings between September 10 and September 15, 2001, except hold office on the 11?[27]

To be fair, the September 2001 jump in Bush's job approval ratings was unprecedented. Most other swings are more modest, and it is not always easy to figure out what, if anything, caused them. Consequently, there is an ongoing debate among scholars about which kinds of crises can be expected to generate rally effects, and how we might differentiate rally effects from rewards for actual accomplishments.[28] Most quantitative tests of rally effects, however, wholly disregard the role of political elites generally, and Congress in particular. Congress's stance on military ventures conducted abroad, it is assumed, does not mediate the size or direction of changes in the president's public approval ratings.[29] While "aggressive foreign behavior [may be] a useful tool for dealing with domestic political problems," domestic political institutions do not hinder the president's ability to engage in aggressive foreign behavior.[30] Quite the contrary, members of Congress are just as susceptible to the rally phenomenon as is the general public.[31] As Barbara Hinckley argues, "The use of force shows the clearest conventional pattern: presidents are active and Congress accedes to what the presidents request. On these occasions both Congress and the public rally around the President and the flag."[32]

By our account, this claim is overstated. To be sure, presidents are not empty vessels held captive to any legislator's passing whims. As noted in Chapter 1, presidents retain profound informational and tactical advantages over Congress that make them the most powerful actors in U.S. foreign policy. Nonetheless, we question the "unambiguous demonstration" that domestic political institutions do not, or cannot, depress the propensity of presidents to use force abroad. "By discarding Congress in the use of force decision calculus," Jeffrey Peake observes, "scholars pay scant attention to the branch of government with which the Founders, by most accounts, meant the war power to lie. Scholars should refocus their attention on congressional factors in explaining decisions to use force, much as they have expanded their examination of other domestic explanations, such as public opinion and the media."[33] Sensitive to the fact that presidents cannot easily and automatically dupe their political opponents, especially when doing so entails putting American troops in danger and when the risks of a military venture prove substantial, both this chapter and this book heed Peake's advice. Congress, as it were, is given its due.

In revisiting the event-count models used to predict the frequency with which presidents launch military ventures abroad, we now take the existing quantitative use-of-force literature on its own terms. These data permit tests of two of the three hypotheses that were laid out in the previous chapter:

Congress's Composition: *All else equal, presidents should use force more often when their copartisans retain large and cohesive majorities within Congress, and less often when the opposition party controls Congress.*

Deployment's Size: *All else equal, Congress's composition should exert more influence over presidential decisions regarding major uses of force, and less influence over presidential decisions regarding minor uses of force.*

The first hypothesis draws our attention to how changes in the partisan composition of Congress can influence the frequency of troop deployments. The second hypothesis, meanwhile, suggests that evidence of the first may depend on the size of the deployments themselves. Unfortunately, given the aggregate nature of these data, we cannot yet examine whether Congress's influence also is conditional on features of the conflict itself, as theories of realism emphasize. Tests of this third hypothesis await the next chapter.

MODELING THE FREQUENCY OF TROOP DEPLOYMENTS

To test whether congressional politics play a role in the president's calculus to deploy military troops abroad, we conduct several statistical examinations of the use of force by the United States between 1945 and 2000. To extend through 2000 the original Blechman and Kaplan time series, which ended in 1976, our data draw from the work of Benjamin Fordham and others.[34] The dependent variable is a count of the number of times each quarter that the president initiates military force abroad.

Blechman and Kaplan ranked uses of force on a five-point severity scale. Many scholars use only the most severe uses of force in their analyses—that is, instances that involved the deployment of nuclear capabilities or the mobilization of multiple aircraft carrier task groups, battalions, or combat wings.[35] Smaller uses of force, by contrast, would include neither strategic nuclear units nor anything more than one battalion, aircraft carrier, or combat squadron. We estimate separate models for all uses, major uses (1–3 on the severity scale), and minor uses (4–5).[36] We expect, however, that Congress exerts the most influence on major uses of force.

To convey some sense of what these data represent, figure 3.1 provides examples of military ventures included in the major and minor time series. All of the major uses of force involved large military deployments in response to very serious, and very public, foreign crises: in Berlin in 1959, Cuba in 1962 and 1984, North Korea in 1968 and 1975, and the Middle East in 1970 and 1980. Though minor uses also spanned the globe, they involved smaller deployments whose objectives were typically less pressing: a "friendly port" visit in 1946 to affirm our nation's solidarity with and commitments to Greece, surveillance exercises in Panama and the Middle East, the deployment of a company of advisors to Saigon in the lead-up to the Vietnam War, and the stationing of a transport aircraft in Africa.

Figure 3.2 traces use-of-force trends in U.S. foreign policy.[37] As shown in the three panels, between 1945 and 2000 presidents exercised force a total of 383 times, or an average of 1.7 times per quarter. Of these, 141 uses were major (averaging 0.6 per quarter) and 242 were minor (1.1 per quarter). Note in all three of these panels the two major peaks in the early 1960s and mid 1980s. The first reflects increased pre-Vietnam War activity in Southeast Asia, multiple crises in the Middle East, as well as the recurrent Berlin crises of the early Kennedy administration. The second represents U.S. deployments to the Middle East after the Israeli invasion of Lebanon and increased activity in Central America.

KEY EXPLANATORY VARIABLES

Consistent with the previous chapter's observations regarding the partisan composition of Congress, we construct three measures of congressional support for the president. The first, *Unified Government*, simply indicates whether the congressional majority party is the same as the president's party in both the House and Senate.[38] To obtain a more nuanced assessment of the level of congressional support for the president, we also compute the average percentage of seats held by the president's party in the House and Senate and label this variable *Percent President Party*.

Southern Democrats present obvious problems for partisan-based measures of presidential support. While Democrats enjoyed large majorities in the House and Senate in the 1960s, they also faced strong divisions

Major Uses

East/West Germany, 1959. Mobilization of troops in Western Europe in response to Berlin Deadline Crisis.

Cuba, 1962. Naval blockade in response to Soviet nuclear weapons deployment to Cuba.

North Korea, 1968. Deployment of three aircraft carrier groups in response to seizure of Pueblo.

Jordan, 1970. Three aircraft carriers sent to eastern Mediterranean to warn Syria against intervention in Jordanian civil conflict.

South/North Korea, 1975. Mobilization and deployment of U.S. troops in response to increase in North Korea–South Korea border clashes.

Egypt/Saudi Arabia, 1980. Forward deployment of rapid reaction forces, including naval and air force personnel. Stationing of SR-71, AWACs, and F-4Es to Egypt and Saudi Arabia in aftermath of Soviet invasion of Afghanistan.

Cuba, 1984. Major increases in scale and length of war games conducted off coast of Cuba, all originating at Guantanamo Bay. Nuclear-capable forces are "showcased."

Minor Uses

Greece, 1946. Battleship makes "friendly visit" to port.

Morocco, 1956. Stationing of marine company and transport aircraft in Morocco.

Panama, 1959. Use of surveillance aircraft to monitor civil strife and canal area.

South Vietnam, 1962. Deployment of company of army advisors with helicopters to Saigon.

Israel/Egypt, 1970. Small deployment of surveillance aircraft to monitor Egypt-Israeli ceasefire.

Persian Gulf, 1974. Unscheduled exercises in Persian Gulf.

Poland, 1980. During height of tensions between labor opposition and government forces, naval forces were increased and several American AWACs planes were sent to West Germany.

Gulf of Suez, 1984. Mine-sweeping and surveillance equipment is sent to Egypt after several mines are found in the Red Sea and Egypt accuses Syria of involvement.

Figure 3.1. Examples of Uses of Force.

within their ranks. To address this shortcoming, David Brady, Joseph Cooper, and Patricia Hurley constructed "legislative potential for policy change" scores.[39] They base LPPC scores on four factors: (1) the size of the majority party; (2) the majority party's internal cohesiveness; (3) the size of the minority party; and (4) its cohesiveness.[40] To generate our third measure of congressional support for the president, we modify these scores only slightly, substituting the president's and opposition parties for

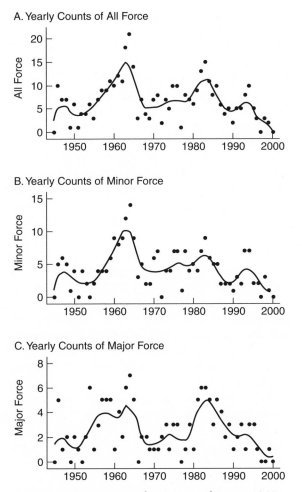

Figure 3.2. Time Series of U.S. Uses of Force, 1945–2000. Graphs use annual counts and present a nonlinear smoother for visual coherence.

the majority and minority parties respectively.[40a] When the president's party is relatively large and unified, and confronts a relatively small and divided opposition party, the president should be able to use force more freely. Conversely, when the president's party is relatively small and divided, and the opposition party is larger and more unified, the president's freedom to use force abroad should decline. We label this variable *President Party Power.*

BACKGROUND CONTROLS

In most of the statistical models we estimate, we incorporate controls for many of the hypothesized alternative influences on the use of force. From the beginning, though, it is worth highlighting that none of the main results presented below depend on the inclusion of any particular set of background controls. The observed relationships between congressional support for the president and use-of-force frequencies appear robust to numerous alternative model specifications.

A burgeoning literature on the political economy of the use of force suggests that poor economic performance is likely to generate incentives for the president to act aggressively in foreign policy affairs.[41] As such, we incorporate the quarterly unemployment rate (*Unemployment*) and the inflation rate (*CPI*), both of which were taken from the Bureau of Labor Statistics.

Because much of the literature on the use of force draws on diversionary war theory, we control for the president's public approval rating (*Public Approval*). The impetus for much of the original quantitative work on the subject was Ostrom and Job's finding that approval ratings were a highly significant determinant of the use of force,[42] though, as we note, subsequent research has proven less definitive on the matter. To mitigate concerns that public opinion derives from, and does not itself induce, government actions, we measure the first Gallup approval rating for the president in each quarter.[43]

A related body of work examines whether upcoming elections usher in additional uses of force.[44] This research contends that "rally-around-the-flag" effects establish incentives for presidents to use force during the months immediately preceding an election. Thus, we introduce *Election Year*, which identifies the first three quarters of a presidential election year.[45]

The next four variables capture facets of the international environment that may impinge on the president's autonomy in foreign policy. Due to contemporary military commitments, there should be a tendency for presidents to employ force for bargaining purposes less often during times of full-blown war. Thus, we create a variable labeled *Ongoing War*, which identifies periods of international wars in which the United States was involved (here, Korea, Vietnam, and the 1991 Gulf War). The Cold War was also a period of unprecedented concern about international engagement of U.S. forces. To control for its influence, we include *Cold War* which identifies the 1945–89 period.

To account for systemic forces that have been linked to the onset of both interstate wars and disputes,[46] we include a measure of U.S. hegemony during the period of analysis (*Hegemony*). The measure is the percentage of international military capabilities held by the United States and derives from the Correlates of War Capabilities dataset.[47] With hegemonic power may come responsibilities (and incentives) to monitor and intervene into conflicts worldwide. Thus, hegemony ought to be positively associated with the use of force. Finally, we include a measure of the number of world (i.e., non-U.S.) military conflicts beginning in each quarter of observation. Presumably, a higher number of world conflicts provides more opportunities for the United States to respond with the use of force.[48] We use counts of non-U.S. militarized interstate disputes (MIDs) over the period of observation, labeled *World Disputes*.[49]

Finally, to account for baseline differences in each president's leadership style, military experience, conception of the national interest, and policy agenda, all of which may have some bearing on his willingness to exercise force, we always include intercept variables for each administration.[50] Descriptive statistics for all dependent and explanatory variables are reported in table A.1 in appendix A.

MAIN RESULTS

We first estimate simple event-count regressions that posit the use of force as a function of only the partisan composition of Congress and presidential fixed-effects.[51] The results, presented in table 3.1, are strikingly consistent. We note initially that when we rely on all and only minor uses of force as the dependent variable, columns 1, 2, 4, 5, 7, and 8, none of the key explanatory variables are statistically significant. Thus, it would seem, interbranch relations do not play a strong role in defining the president's decisions to exercise military force abroad. But examining columns 3, 6, and 9, major uses of force *are* affected by domestic political factors, as significant effects are consistently observed; the positive coefficients suggest that as the size of the president's party grows, the president's propensity to use the military for significant purposes also increases.

Perhaps more important, the influence of partisanship on the predicted number of deployments per quarter is substantively large. Based on the estimates using the *Unified Government* measure, the predicted number of quarterly uses of force rises by more than 30 percent. Raising the *Percent President Party* variable by one standard deviation from the mean, while holding all the fixed effects at zero, yields a predicted increase of more than 20 percent, while a similar increase in *President Party Power* scores a predicted rise of nearly 25 percent in the frequency of force.[52]

Obviously, decisions about the use of force hinge on many more factors than the identity of a presidential administration and the partisan composition of Congress. Subsequent models, therefore, include controls for those variables deemed important to the use of force: the unemployment rate, the consumer price index, the president's approval rating, indicator

TABLE 3.1
Frequency of Uses of Force by the United States

	All Force		Minor		Major	
	(1)		(2)		(3)	
Unified Government	0.02	[0.56]	−0.13	[0.83]	0.27*	[0.18]
Constant	−0.04	[0.15]	−0.34*	[0.21]	−1.34***	[0.05]
	(4)		(5)		(6)	
Percent President Party	−0.07	[3.27]	−1.33	[4.74]	2.10**	[1.25]
Constant	0.00	[1.62]	0.28	[2.24]	−2.31***	[0.63]
	(7)		(8)		(9)	
President Party Power	0.55	[2.10]	−0.06	[2.97]	1.53**	[0.84]
Constant	−0.03	[0.02]	−0.38***	[0.03]	−1.26***	[0.00][1]
(N)	224		224		224	

Negative binomial regressions estimated. Quarterly number of uses of force analyzed from 1945 to 2000. *** = $p < 0.01$, one-tailed test; ** $p < 0.05$; * $p < 0.10$. Huber/White/sandwich standard errors clustered on presidential administrations reported in brackets. Though not reported, models also contain fixed effect terms for each presidential administration.

[1] This, plainly, is an unreasonably small standard error. When dropping from the model the Truman dummy variable (Clinton is the excluded category), the constant term is −1.18 with an estimated standard error of 0.06, and the estimated impact of *President Party Power* remains unaffected.

variables that identify election years, periods of war, and the Cold War, level of U.S. hegemony, and the number of non-U.S. world disputes. As before, the key variables of interest concern congressional support, and all of the statistical models include presidential fixed effects.[53]

The next two tables present the estimated regression results from the more fully specified models for each measure of congressional support—*Unified Government, Percent President Party,* and *President Party Power*—on minor and major uses of force, respectively.[54] The main results appear quite comparable to those recovered from the simpler fixed-effects models. When minor uses of force serve as the dependent variable, as shown in table 3.2, none of the key explanatory variables are statistically significant. But major uses of force, shown in table 3.3, *are* affected by domestic political factors. The partisan composition of Congress appears to play a significant role in shaping the president's willingness to deploy troops abroad.[55] As in the previous estimations, the positive coefficients suggest that as the size of the president's party grows, the president's use of the military for significant purposes also increases.

TABLE 3.2
Frequency of Minor Uses of Force, Including Background Controls

	(1)		(2)		(3)	
Unified Government	0.17	[0.54]	—		—	
Percent President Party	—		−0.03	[3.04]	—	
President Party Power	—		—		0.57	[1.78]
Unemployment	0.24***	[0.06]	0.25***	[0.06]	0.24***	[0.06]
CPI	0.07***	[0.03]	0.06***	[0.02]	0.06***	[0.02]
Public Approval	−0.00	[0.01]	−0.00	[0.01]	−0.00	[0.01]
Election Year	0.16	[0.16]	0.15	[0.13]	0.17	[0.13]
Ongoing War	−0.66***	[0.21]	−0.63***	[0.21]	−0.65***	[0.21]
Cold War	0.25***	[0.10]	0.27***	[0.10]	0.25***	[0.10]
Hegemony	−2.75	[3.77]	−1.91	[3.56]	−2.69	[3.74]
World Disputes	0.03	[0.03]	0.03	[0.03]	0.03	[0.03]
Constant	−1.20	[1.20]	−1.36	[2.12]	−1.12	[1.12]
(N)	224		224		224	

Negative binomial regressions estimated. Quarterly number of uses of force analyzed from 1945 to 2000. For all table entries: *** = $p < 0.01$, one-tailed test; ** = $p < 0.05$; * = $p < 0.10$. Huber/White/sandwich standard errors clustered on presidential administrations reported in brackets. Though not reported, models also contain fixed effect terms for each presidential administration.

Every measure of congressional support for the president serves as a significant predictor of the quarterly number of major military deployments. Presidents exercise major force roughly 45 percent more often during periods of unified government than during periods of divided government. A one standard deviation increase from the mean of *Percent President Power* corresponds with a 17 percent increase in the use of force by the United States. Conversely, a one standard deviation drop leads to a 16 percent decline in the number of uses of force. When shifting from the mean to the maximum value of *Percent President Party* (68 percent), the model predicts a 36 percent increase in the incident rate.

Similar results arise when using the *Presidential Party Power* scores. A one standard deviation increase in the relative size and cohesiveness of the president's party yields a predicted 19 percent increase in the number of uses of force, while evaluating the variable at its maximum generates a predicted increase of 39 percent. The substantive meaning of these results

TABLE 3.3
Frequency of Major Uses of Force, Including Background Controls

	(1)		(2)		(3)	
Unified Government	0.40***	[0.09]	—		—	
Percent President Party	—		1.71**	[0.84]	—	
President Party Power	—		—		1.17**	[0.80]
Unemployment	0.22***	[0.08]	0.22***	[0.09]	0.21***	[0.09]
CPI	0.04	[0.03]	0.03	[0.03]	0.03	[0.04]
Public Approval	−0.00	[0.01]	−0.00	[0.01]	−0.00	[0.01]
Election Year	0.09	[0.21]	0.10	[0.23]	0.10	[0.22]
Ongoing War	−0.42*	[0.26]	−0.36	[0.28]	−0.39*	[0.28]
Cold War	0.65***	[0.14]	0.66***	[0.14]	0.65***	[0.14]
Hegemony	3.12	[2.91]	3.86	[3.24]	3.52	[3.50]
World Disputes	−0.01	[0.02]	−0.01	[0.02]	−0.01	[0.02]
Constant	−3.37***	[1.11]	−4.19***	[1.28]	−3.20***	[1.33]
(N)	224		224		224	

Negative binomial regressions estimated. Quarterly number of uses of force analyzed from 1945 to 2000. *** = $p < 0.01$, one-tailed test; ** = $p < 0.05$; * = $p < 0.10$. Huber/White/sandwich standard errors clustered on presidential administrations reported in brackets. Though not reported, models also contain fixed effect terms for each presidential administration.

is unambiguous: the level of partisan support for the president within Congress stands out as a major determinant of the U.S. propensity to use force abroad.

For the most part, estimates of the control variables correspond with findings from prior research. For instance, estimates for unemployment mirror the original Ostrom and Job findings that higher levels of "economic misery" correspond with higher levels of military activity.[56] Inflation rates also contribute positively to minor deployments, but do not influence major uses of force. Similar to those scholars who do not differentiate wartime and peace-time elections,[57] we find no statistical relationship between the election cycle and the use of force. In addition, the approval variable never attains statistical significance in any of our estimates.[58] Other variables are of the predicted sign. During the Cold War, the expected number of uses of force more than doubles. Ongoing wars depress the propensity of presidents to deploy U.S. troops, yet their statistical significance varies based on whether minor or major uses of force serve as the dependent variable. The level of military hostility in the world and the level of U.S. hegemony appear to have no consistent or statistically significant influence on the propensity of the United States to engage the military.[59]

Do congressional effects hold for the entire postwar era? A number of scholars have observed that during the 1950s and early 1960s, a broad consensus about the proper role of the United States (and its military) transcended party lines in American politics. In attempting to explain Dwight Eisenhower's high legislative success rates on foreign policy, for instance, a number of scholars working on the "two presidencies" thesis (one presidential role for domestic policy and another for foreign policy) have argued that political elites at the time generally agreed on the principal objectives of foreign policy and the best means of achieving them.[60] This era of good feeling, however, ended with the Vietnam War, which quickly reestablished partisan cleavages. According to Barry Blechman:

> The Congress was slow to wake to the transformation of U.S. defense policy following World War II. Throughout the 1950s and early 1960s, the legislature was content to go along with presidential initiatives, ceding authority and post-dating its approval of military actions from Korea through the Middle-East to the Gulf of Tonkin. It was the Vietnam War, of course, that changes all of this.[61]

Rising partisan conflicts regarding foreign policy should have immediate implications for interbranch relations regarding the use of force. If these temporal dynamics are strong, we should observe sharp period effects. Although the partisan composition of Congress might profoundly affect the presidential use of force during the post-Vietnam years, it should have a negligible impact before. But if the conventional view overstates congressional acquiescence during the early stages of the Cold War, as some scholars now suggest, then we may not find any evidence of period effects at all.[62]

Table 3.4 examines whether presidents were particularly sensitive to the composition of Congress following the passage of the War Powers Resolution (1974).[63] This resolution makes for a useful dividing line, as it stood as the centerpiece of the congressional resurgence of the early 1970s and, according to many scholars, marked Congress's reassertion of its constitutional prerogatives over foreign policy making.[64] Hence, in addition to all of the other background controls, these models include each measure of congressional support, an indicator variable for the period following the enactment of the War Powers Resolution, and an interaction term between the two. If the War Powers Resolution ushered in an altogether new

TABLE 3.4
Frequency of Major Uses of Force, with Period Effects

	(1)		(2)		(3)	
Congressional Support						
Unified Government	0.36***	[0.10]	—		—	
Percent President Party	—		2.34**	[1.08]	—	
President Party Power	—		—		1.58***	[0.67]
Post-War Powers						
Resolution	−1.09***	[0.40]	0.23	[1.30]	−1.26**	[0.68]
CongressSupport ×						
Post-WPR	0.12	[0.18]	−3.20	[3.62]	−1.48	[1.90]
Constant	−2.52***	[0.95]	−3.34***	[1.07]	−2.18**	[1.07]
(N)	224		224		224	

Negative binomial regressions estimated. Quarterly number of uses of force analyzed from 1945 to 2000. *** = p < 0.01, one-tailed test; ** = p < 0.05; * = p < 0.10. Huber/White/sandwich standard errors clustered on presidential administrations reported in brackets. Though not reported, models also include all variables in table 3.2.

era of congressional dominance, then the main effect associated with congressional support should attenuate, and the estimated effect for the interaction term should be large, positive, and statistically significant.

Though it may have altered the nature of congressional-presidential relations in other ways, the War Powers Resolution does not appear to have enhanced Congress's influence over the regularity with which presidents deploy troops abroad. We do not find any evidence that Congress's impact on the quarterly number of major uses of force is confined to the second half of the time series.[65] Quite the contrary, whether using *Unified Government, Percent President Party,* or *President Party Power,* the main effects remain large and statistically significant, and the interaction terms never even approach standard thresholds of statistical significance. Two of the models in Table 3.4 do suggest that the frequency of troop deployments declined somewhat following the resolution's passage. None, however, support the contention that Congress, with the War Powers Resolution, secured a more prominent place in presidential decision making about matters involving war.

Another concern is that these findings are peculiar to the particular dataset analyzed. As previously noted, virtually all quantitative work on the use of force in U.S. foreign policy relies on the original Blechman and Kaplan data. Indeed, these data were designed especially for this kind of investigation, and various updates have kept them current. Traditionally, however, cross-national studies of military conflict use the Militarized In-

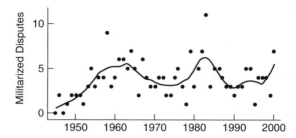

Figure 3.3. Time Series of U.S. Militarized Interstate Disputes, 1945–2000. Graph uses annual counts and presents a nonlinear smoother for visual coherence.

terstate Dispute (MID) data.[66] Though they arrive at very different conclusions about the relevance of Congress, Joanne Gowa and David Clark both use the MID data in their contributions to the use-of-force literature. (Figure 3.3 presents the MID time series of the post–World War II era.)

For several reasons, we prefer the Blechman and Kaplan data over the MID. First, this choice facilitates comparison with a larger body of past statistical work that uses the Blechman/Kaplan data. Second, as Fordham and Sarver have shown, the MID data do a poor job of coding many uses of force included in the Blechman/Kaplan data.[67] Whereas the Blechman/Kaplan series includes deployments involving a change in the location or alert status of American forces ordered by national authorities, many U.S. MIDs relate to actions that resulted from military officials but not national authorities. Plainly, as we are trying to model decisions that presidents make, we ought to focus on those military actions to which they were party. Our third objection relates to the second. The MID data contain a disproportionate number of violent events.[68] The resulting bias leaves MID with far fewer threat-level deployments, exactly the sorts of events that our research seeks to explain. This is not meant to be a general criticism of the MID data. Like all datasets, the MID was coded with a specific purpose in mind. As one strays from that purpose, however, the applicability of the data wanes.

These objections aside, as a robustness check we substitute a quarterly count of MIDs involving the United States. Recall that Gowa's findings (using MID data) rejected the idea that partisan politics play a role in decisions to use force abroad. Finding an insignificant effect for divided government on MIDs counts for the period between 1870 and 1992, Gowa concluded that with regard to the use of military force, "partisan politics has . . . remained muted."[69] Using the same data but limiting the analysis to the post-1945 era, Clark found consistent and large congressional effects on both the frequency and duration of MIDs. From his analyses, Clark

TABLE 3.5
Frequency of U.S. Militarized Interstate Disputes (MIDS)

	(1)		(2)		(3)	
Unified Government	0.22*	[0.14]	—		—	
Percent President Party	—		1.86*	[1.32]	—	
President Party Power	—		—		0.88**	[0.53]
Constant	0.42	[1.16]	−0.19	[0.98]	0.66	[1.03]
(N)	224		224		224	

Negative binomial regressions estimated. Quarterly number of uses of force analyzed from 1945 to 2000. *** = $p < 0.01$, one-tailed test; ** = $p < 0.05$; * = $p < 0.10$. Huber/White/sandwich standard errors clustered on presidential administrations reported in brackets. Though not reported, models also contain all variables in table 3.2.

concluded that "institutional incongruence, represented by divided government, a recurrent pox upon efficient governing, actually serves to restrain American presidents as they contemplate entering international conflict and as they decide when to exit international disputes."[70]

We are able to replicate Gowa's null finding when restricting the analysis to the 1945 to 1992 period. But when more properly specifying the statistical model using more informative measures of partisan dynamics and extending the MID time series through 2000, very different findings emerge, and they are much more consistent with Clark's. As the results in table 3.5 indicate, *Unified Government, Percent President Party,* and *President Party Power* all serve as significant predictors of the frequency of MIDs involving the United States.[71] During periods of unified government, military interventions increase by nearly 25 percent, and a one standard deviation jump from the mean values of *Percent President Party* and *President Party Power* generates a 19 and 13 percent increase in military involvements, respectively. If these relationships measure the health of our system of separated powers, as Gowa suggests, then there is more cause for optimism than previously recognized.

CONGRESS: A BODY OF PARTIES OR VETERANS?

Every one of the tests presented thus far assumes that congressional constraints on presidential war powers are best characterized by the partisan composition of the House and Senate. In a recent book, however, Christopher Gelpi and Peter Feaver assert the importance of congressional members' prior military experience, while downplaying the significance of their partisanship.[72] Examining U.S. MIDs, Gelpi and Feaver argue that presidents exercise force with lower frequency when higher proportions of veterans reside in the House and cabinet. They conclude that the well-documented divide between civilians and military personnel translates, at the elite level, into "substantively large" differences in beliefs about military deployments—differences, presumably, that challenge our assessments of the most salient dimensions of congressional-presidential relations during the lead-up to a planned use of force.[73]

None of Gelpi and Feaver's statistical models include any measures of the partisan composition of Congress. By considering only the House and cabinet, they also overlook ways in which the Senate contributes to foreign policy decision making. Moreover, for reasons never explained, Gelpi and Feaver limit their analysis to only male members of Congress; though they do consider the percentage of male and female veterans in the cabinet. To address these issues, we reestimate the fully specified models for the various use-of-force time series, while adding a measure of the percentage of all House and Senate seats held by veterans. Table 3.6 presents the findings for *Percent Veteran* and *Percent President Party*.[74]

Though we find some evidence that the proportion of veterans holding seats within Congress does figure into presidential decision making, the findings appear much weaker than those that Gelpi and Feaver present. We do not find any evidence that the proportion of veterans within Congress has any bearing on the number of "all," "minor," or "major" uses of force.[75] The effects for the MID data, meanwhile, are marginally significant and in the expected direction. Moving from one standard deviation below the mean of percent veteran to one standard deviation above,

TABLE 3.6
Frequency of Uses of Force and MIDs, Congressional Parties and Veterans

	All Uses of Force	Minor Uses of Force	Major Uses of Force	MIDS
Percent President Party	0.14 [1.89]	−1.29 [2.58]	2.52** [1.17]	2.95* [2.19]
Percent Veteran	2.01 [4.01]	4.83 [4.49]	−3.05 [3.98]	−3.11* [2.23]
Constant	−2.66 [2.42]	−3.24 [2.90]	−2.97 [2.04]	0.62 [0.91]
(N)	224	224	224	224

Negative binomial regressions estimated. Quarterly number of uses of force analyzed from 1945 to 2000. *** = p < 0.01, one-tailed test; ** = p < 0.05; * = p < 0.10. Huber/White/sandwich standard errors clustered on presidential administrations reported in brackets. "Percent Veteran" refers to the percentage of members in the House and Senate who were veterans. Though not reported, models also include all variables in table 3.2.

while keeping all other variables at their means and discreet variables at their mode, translates into a roughly 45 percent decrease in the quarterly number of MIDs.

Consequentially, our estimates for *Percent President Party* appear unaffected by the inclusion of *Percent Veteran*. Large, positive, and statistically significant effects are again observed for the major use-of-force and MID time series, while null effects are observed for minor and all uses of force. Though not reported, findings of comparable magnitude are observed when substituting for *Percent President Party* our other measures of congressional support. Assuredly, members' party identifications are not the only feature of Congress that affects presidential decisions about military deployments. It does not appear, however, that our various estimates of congressional support depend on the exclusion of another potentially important determinant of members' preferences and behaviors.

REPUBLICAN AND DEMOCRATIC PRESIDENTS

When contemplating military action, do Republican presidents systematically differ from Democratic presidents? Unfortunately, the data presented in this chapter do not permit us to investigate all aspects of the question. It is possible, for instance, that crises that evoke a military response from Republican presidents differ systematically from those that catch the attention of Democratic presidents. Democrats may be more apt to exercise military force when confronting human rights abuses or national calamities, while Republicans may be especially prone to exercise force when material U.S. interests are threatened. Not until chapter 4, when we introduce the "opportunities" data, can we address these matters.

All else equal, though, are Republican presidents more (or less) hawkish than Democratic presidents? If Gowa is correct that "foreign policy preferences vary across parties," and if these preferences inform not only when presidents deploy the military, but how often, then significant partisan effects across presidential administrations ought to mark the use-of-force time series.[76]

We revisited the data to explore these possibilities. In three of four comparisons, small and statistically insignificant differences are observed. In the all force, minor force, and MID time series, Republican and Democrats appear to exercise force with roughly equal frequency. In the major time series, however, where Congress's influence appears most pronounced, substantial differences arise. During the postwar era, Republican presidents initiated major uses of force, on average, 0.79 times per quarter, as compared to Democratic presidents who did so 0.47 instances per quarter. This pattern also substantiates some older survey research on citizens' views of party differences on foreign policy.[77] Moreover, these differences appear significant in both simple bivariate comparisons and in the multivariate models previously examined.[78] These data provide modest support for contemporary conceptions of conservatives as hawks and liberals as doves.[79]

SUMMARIZING THE EVIDENCE

The analyses presented in this chapter demonstrate that Congress critically affects the frequency with which presidents initiate military ventures abroad. When we consider all deployments of troops between 1945 and 2000, we do not observe any correlation between the composition of Congress and the quarterly frequency with which presidents use force abroad. Nor are effects observed when isolating minor uses of force. But, consistent with the theory laid out in chapter 2, when presidents consider a major use of force abroad, the level of partisan support within the Congress appears to matter greatly. This finding is robust across various model specifications, datasets, and time periods, and using multiple measures of congressional support.

In two ways, these findings challenge existing quantitative work on the use of force. First, few studies control for potential congressional involvement in foreign policy; nearly all, in fact, assume away its importance. Meanwhile, the only models that incorporate measures of congressional preferences—typically, by controlling for periods of divided government—usually do not find substantial effects. Second, when incorporating the influence of Congress in shaping use-of-force dynamics, some traditionally important variables (e.g., public opinion and inflation rates) cease to hold much explanatory power. Jointly, these facts suggest that international relations scholars have done a rather poor job of conceptualizing domestic political constraints on presidential power. Instead of a distant public or a fickle economy independently preoccupying presidential decision making, the partisan composition of Congress appears to hold considerable sway—a basic fact long recognized by scholars within American politics.

Up to this point, we have engaged the quantitative use-of-force literature where it currently stands. Indeed, all we have done here is insert measures of congressional-presidential relations into reasonably well established use-of-force models. For a variety of reasons, there is reason not to suspend the analysis here. After all, the partisan composition of Congress may affect more than just the quarterly frequency with which presidents deploy troops abroad. Mobilized opposition within the institution's ranks may stall some deployments (recall the delays Bush experienced between the summer of 2002 and spring of 2003 as he attempted to rally the nation in support of a war in Iraq); scale back the size of others (recall Bush's tepid response to crises erupting in Liberia and Haiti in 2003); and completely undermine others (recall the Bush administration's flirtations with confronting Iran *and* Syria, prominent adversaries in the war on terror, which thus far have come to naught). Little in the existing count models permits the analyst to examine such possibilities.

To conduct such analyses, two adjustments must be made to the statistical models that we estimate. First, if we are to assess Congress's influence over the timing or scope of a military deployment, we must account for differences in types of military deployments. Rather than using the quarterly number of troop deployments as our dependent variable, as this chapter does, individual uses of force must become the unit of analysis. Second, we need to account for the many instances when presidents consider using force abroad, but decide against it. The quantitative use-of-force literature has gone to considerable lengths to explain when presidents use force, but with only one exception,[80] scholars have ignored those occasions when presidents opted to keep troops ashore.

The next chapter explores these concerns. By introducing the "opportunities" database, which allows us to recast the statistical models around individual decisions to deploy troops abroad, chapter 4 examines how members of Congress influence the probability that presidents respond militarily to specific crises happening across the globe. And because the empirical analyses account for features of the events themselves—where they were happening, whether the Soviet Union was involved, whether an ally or trading partner of the United States was involved, and other factors—the chapter presents a considerably richer set of findings than those recovered from simpler event-count models.

CHAPTER 4

Responding to "Opportunities" to Use Military Force

WHEN FACING STRONG and unified congressional opposition, presidents appear leery of exercising military force abroad. By our calculations, the quarterly number of military deployments declines, on average, by roughly one-fifth when the opposition party picks up 10 percent of the seats in the House and Senate. Findings of comparable magnitude hold up when using a wide variety of measures of congressional opposition, two distinct datasets on the use of force, and multiple model specifications.

There remain, however, important features of politics that event-count models cannot address. For starters, by focusing on the regularity with which troops are deployed, rather than the actual missions embarked on, the models overlook many of the contextual features that surround military ventures. Such models tell us next to nothing about where troops were sent, what objectives they sought to fulfill, how serious the precipitating crisis was, the extent of U.S. interest in the region, whether the targets were nonstate actors, or whether targets that were actual states were democracies or authoritarian regimes. The models deliberately set aside all sorts of details about these deployments, even though such particulars figure prominently in presidential decision making.

Furthermore, quarterly counts of troop deployments are not the only litmus test of whether Congress, or any other institution, influences presidential decision making about matters involving war. Beyond the regularity with which presidents send troops abroad, Congress might affect the speed with which presidents respond to different foreign crises, the size of the deployments, the duration of the deployments, the propensity of adversaries to fight longer and harder, and the willingness of allies to fight alongside American troops. Most important, perhaps, Congress may affect the willingness of presidents to use military force at all. Past research provides little purchase on the myriad domestic and international contexts in which the United States does *not* respond militarily.[1] There is reason to expect, however, that in such "nonevents" lie important clues of Congress's influence. Facing vocal opposition from legislators and the media, and anticipating congressional reprisals at the first sign of failure, presidents may decide to take passes on especially risky military ventures—

preferring, instead, to admonish foreign leaders publicly, initiate economic sanctions, call for the involvement of the United Nations, or perhaps, sit quietly and allow the crisis to run its course. Military action, after all, does not exhaust the possible solutions to foreign crises. Moreover, during any given period, presidents have more than just one opportunity to deploy troops abroad. Beyond influencing the number of missions that presidents initiate within quarters (or years, or administrations), Congress may also affect the president's selection of foreign crises that warrant a military response. Which crises evoke a military response and which do not may very much depend on congressional interests and priorities.

MODELING THE PROBABILITY OF A DEPLOYMENT

Imagine the following:

Scenario #1: Sporadic fighting breaks out along the border of two South American nations. Neither country suffers extensive casualties, and the fighting remains fairly localized. The dispute, however, threatens to disrupt the flow of U.S. exports to the region. In the previous three months, similar crises erupted in Central America, prompting a U.S. military response. While the public expresses high levels of support for the president, members of the opposition party hold majorities in both chambers in Congress.

Scenario #2: A full-blown civil war erupts in an African nation with which the United States has few economic or political ties. Casualties soon number in the thousands, although the lives of U.S. citizens in the region do not appear threatened. The rest of the globe remains relatively calm, with few standing U.S. deployments. At home, the domestic economy is strong, the president enjoys widespread popular support, and members of his own party retain large majorities in Congress.

What are the chances that the president will use the military to intervene in these two scenarios? In the first, the strategic importance of South America, the threat posed to U.S. trade, and the public's support for the president all would seem to enhance the probability of a U.S. deployment. Yet the conflict's small scale, the engagement of U.S. troops in Central America, and the paucity of congressional support would seem to weigh against a new deployment. In the second scenario, the warring nation holds little strategic importance to the United States and the U.S. economy remains relatively strong; these factors would appear to reduce the chances of military intervention. But the crisis itself is intense, the U.S. military is not preoccupied by other missions, and the president retains strong support both from the public and Congress, all factors that ought to enhance the probability of military intervention. Depending on the importance that he assigns to each of these considerations, the president might decide to respond in any number of ways.

Every time presidents confront foreign crises like those described above, they weigh a host of competing considerations. Rarely is the optimal course obvious. Some factors encourage military action, while others militate against it. Rather than recount in detail individual decisions about particular uses of force, this chapter presents a variety of statistical models that simultaneously estimate the relative influence of different factors on presidential responses to the thousands of crises that have arisen in the modern era. This chapter scrutinizes how aspects of the crises themselves influence the president's willingness to exercise military action. This examination reveals yet another means by which Congress checks presidential power on matters involving war.

To estimate the probability that presidents respond militarily to particular crises occurring about the globe, one basic adjustment must be made to the statistical models introduced in chapter 3: we must identify those occasions when presidents might have exercised military force but decided against it. Foreign crises that evoked a military response must be recognized as a subset of a larger class of events. It is our job to identify this class in ways that are transparent and replicable. Shortly, we will have a lot to say about what constitutes an "opportunity." For now, though, we simply recognize that the unit of observation for the data is an opportunity rather than a use of force, allowing us to assess when the United States does and does not deploy troops abroad.

A database of "opportunities" to use force should yield considerable payoff. While trying to assess Congress's influence on presidential decision making, we will be able to control for features of precipitating events themselves—where they occur, the economic and political relations between the United States and the targeted nation, and whether it is an isolated or repeated occurrence. Does it matter, for instance, whether the opportunity to use force occurs in Africa or Central America? Whether the United States has strong trade relations with the foreign government? Whether the government is a democracy or an authoritarian regime? Whether the Soviet Union is a party to the crisis? Precisely because the phenomenon now requiring explanation is the nation's response to an observed foreign crisis, we can account for these and many other factors, all the while assessing Congress's influence over presidential decision making.

These data have many advantages, foremost among them being their attention to the foreign crises that actually precipitated a military response. They are not well suited, however, to test for differences between major and minor deployments abroad, the second hypothesis laid out in chapter 2. Although the event-count models in chapter 3 could readily trace the independent commission of major and minor deployments, opportunities identified in this chapter could readily provoke either—indeed, whether the president uses a major or minor deployment might itself depend on the composition of Congress, a possibility we explore later in this chapter. The main statistical tests in this chapter therefore focus on the following two hypotheses:

Congress's Composition: *All else equal, the probability and celerity of a military response to a perceived foreign crisis should increase when the president's copartisans retain large and cohesive majorities within Congress, and decrease when the opposition party controls Congress.*

The International System: *All else equal, Congress's composition should exert more influence over presidential decisions regarding uses of force that target strategically less important nations, and less influence over uses of force that target strategically more important nations.*

The first claim, you may notice, takes a slightly different form. Whereas in chapter 3, we related Congress's composition to the frequency with which troops are sent abroad, we now relate it to the probability and timing of a military response to a perceived foreign crisis. And, at last, with data on individual crises we also can test the possibility that realpolitik considerations occasionally trump domestic partisan politics.

OPPORTUNITIES TO USE MILITARY FORCE

To identify foreign events that stood a nontrivial chance of provoking a U.S. military intervention, we scoured the *New York Times* for front-page mentions of violent acts perpetrated against the United States government, threats to the stability of foreign regimes, gross violations of international law, and nuclear proliferation.[2] While we make no pretenses of having captured every single event that might have precipitated a military venture abroad, we do claim to have identified the vast majority of those events that fall within specified categories and that received prominent domestic media coverage. Appendix B outlines a variety of analytic and measurement challenges associated with building the opportunities database, and the solutions we propose for each. In the following pages, we briefly summarize the most important features of the data.

Focusing on the period between 1945 and 2000, we searched the *New York Times* for reports about any of the following types of occurrences: attacks on United States embassies and consulates; instances when United States ambassadors, consuls, or military personnel were killed; hijackings that included human casualties; stateside attacks perpetrated by foreign groups; civil wars; interstate armed clashes; coups and attempts coups; assassinations (or attempts thereof) of heads of state; declarations of states of emergency or martial law; downing of aircraft by a foreign military; hostile claims to international waters; attacks on United Nations personnel; crimes against humanity on a mass scale; military violations of United Nations territorial mandates; nuclear proliferation; and violations of agreements to dismantle weapons of mass destruction. In the modern era, almost all military deployments captured in our use-of-force data were in response to events that fell within at least one of these categories. By systematically cataloging all such events that received domestic media attention, we can compare those that elicited a military response from the United States with those that did not, and then assess whether differences in the domestic political arena corresponded with the president's decisions on the matters.

Focusing on newspaper stories solves three problems inherent in building the dataset. First, it relieves us of the responsibility of figuring out what constitutes a crisis, of deciding whether atrocities committed by a government against its citizens are one big event or lots of smaller events, of setting arbitrary rules about how much time should pass or how many lives must be lost before one event becomes two, rather than being two developments in one larger event. Instead, we need only capture all of the relevant stories on these occurrences. Second, we do not need to figure out when an event starts and when it ends, a truly vexing issue given the ebb and flow of international relations and the probability that any event could elicit a military response at any time. Instead, we need only monitor the daily flow of reports on qualifying events. An opportunity to exercise force abroad is considered alive as long as the *New York Times* continues reporting on it.[3] Finally, by focusing on *Times* stories, we have a built-in solution to the problem of discerning more and less pressing opportunities to exercise force abroad. As more important crises attract greater media coverage, and as less important crises receive more abbreviated notice, we can reliably discern the relative importance of different crises. Of course, observations in the dataset cannot be considered independent of one another, requiring a variety of adjustments to the statistical models that we subsequently estimate. Nevertheless, we have, at least, some way of assessing the relative urgency of different crises occurring in different parts of the world.

Judgment calls are unavoidable when constructing a dataset of this kind. In appendix B, again we describe in considerable detail the protocols used to construct these data and the specific classes of foreign crises that qualified as opportunities to use military force. Several features of the coding rules, however, deserve special emphasis. First, to count as an opportunity to initiate a new military venture, past ventures in that location must have ended.[4] Because we are interested in identifying opportunities to launch new military operations abroad, and not the factors that contribute to dispute escalation and deescalation, reports about qualifying foreign crises must concern countries that are not already the target of U.S. military operations.[5] Second, the unit of observation is an individual state's involvement in a qualifying foreign crisis that received coverage on the front page of the *Times*. Each qualifying *Times* story is dissembled into separate observations for each state that is identified as a direct participant.[6] A story about a border clash between Ecuador and Peru will generate two opportunities to use force, while another story about a civil war in Uganda will only generate one. And because the *Times* often writes multiple stories about ongoing conflicts, there may be many opportunities generated by a single conflict.[7] The resulting dataset consists entirely of state-by-report observations.

Before proceeding to the analysis, we note two additional features of the data. First, we do not model who within a particular state initiated a conflict. Whether a crisis was due to the actions of a foreign government or a rebel faction lies beyond the scope of these data. Second, observational units do not include nonstate actors.[8] Basque rebels in Spain, Marxist guerillas in Central and South America, and (notably) Palestinians are not identified as potential targets of a military intervention. Again, it is not that events involving nonstate actors were excluded by definition, but rather the nonstate actors themselves were not identified as a potential target for U.S. military action.

Having sorted through well over 100,000 articles, we identified 15,004 opportunities to use force that occurred in nations where, and when, there was not a contemporaneous U.S. military engagement. Examples of opportunities include reports of the Cuban Missile Crisis on October 23, 1962; Libyan claims to the Gulf of Sidra on March 27, 1986; attacks by Bosnian Serbs on the United Nations safe havens of Goradze and Srebrenica on July 23, 1995; the bombing of a U.S. military housing complex in Saudi Arabia on June 27, 1996; and border clashes in Kashmir on August 27, 1997. Overall, the most common types of events in the dataset consisted of interstate clashes (43 percent) and civil wars (32 percent).[9] Less frequently observed were coups (7 percent), downed aircraft (6 percent), states of emergency (3 percent), and assassination attempts (2 percent). The remaining nine categories of events each contributed less than 1 percent of cases in the database, and combined they accounted for less than 8 percent of the overall total. It is perhaps not surprising, given this distribution of event types, that the number of opportunities involving any deaths of Americans is low, slightly more than 4 percent.[10]

GEOGRAPHIC DISTRIBUTION OF OPPORTUNITIES

Figure 4.1 depicts graphically the distribution of observations across the globe. In the map, the shading of each country reflects the number of opportunities that it contributed for the United States to use military force.[11] Those regions that produced more opportunities are darker, while those that produced fewer are lighter.[12] Most every region generated events to which the United States might have responded militarily; some constituted genuine hot beds of activity. The Middle East generated far and away the most opportunities, yielding more than 35 percent of cases in the database. Europe and the Asian-Pacific region each added 24 percent, the Americas generated over 10 percent, while Africa generated a mere 6 percent of the opportunities.

During this fifty-five-year period, fully 147 different countries produced at least one opportunity for military action; 57 countries produced 50 or more; 35 produced 100 or more; and 7 produced 500 or more. This final group, which contributed more than 40 percent of all the opportunities in the database, includes Israel, France, Egypt, Russia/USSR, Syria, Lebanon, and the United Kingdom. Twenty-three countries, including places such as Canada, Jamaica, Latvia, Bhutan, Australia, Fiji, Suriname, Niger, Maldives, and Malta, provided just one or two opportunities. A handful of additional nations yielded no opportunities, with Finland, Belarus, Norway, and New Zealand being among the more prominent examples. (See table B.1 of appendix B for a complete listing by country.)

In figure 4.2, we plot the annual number of opportunities to use force around the globe. The first thing to notice is the considerable variation, both from decade to decade and year to year. While each year produced an average of 268 opportunities, six generated fewer than 100 and seven generated more than 500. Peak years were 1982 and 1956, when 676 and 662 opportunities to use force emerged, respectively. In contrast, 1997 and 2000 were low points, generating just 34 and 41 opportunities, respectively.

The first spike in opportunities observed in figure 4.2 coincides with the 1948 Arab-Israeli War. Immediately after the state's creation, Israel was simultaneously attacked by its Arab neighbors, with Jewish settlers and Palestine's Arab inhabitants being central actors in the struggle. Not surprisingly, the Middle East continued to dominate the high frequency years of the aggregate time series. Events in the region proliferated in 1956 and

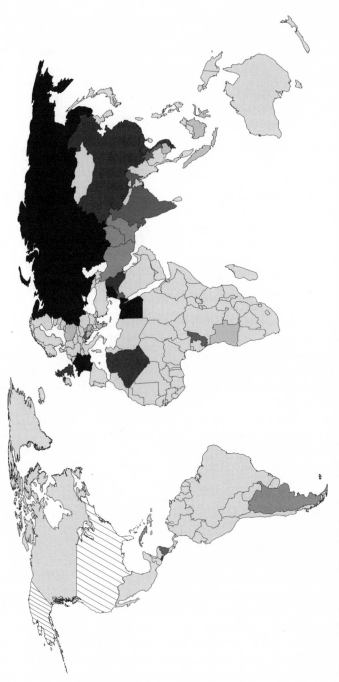

Figure 4.1. Geographic Distribution of Opportunities to Use Military Force, 1945–2000. For purposes of shading, the Soviet Union, Czechoslovakia, Yugoslavia, and Vietnam are each treated as unified nations. See table B.1 of Appendix B for a complete listing. Darker shadings imply more opportunities.

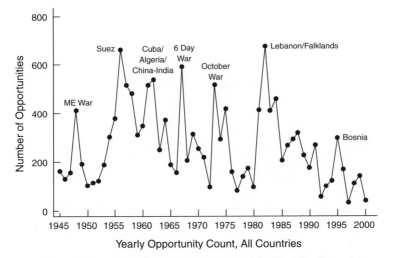

Figure 4.2. Time Series of Opportunities, Worldwide. The figure identifies some of the crises that contributed many of the opportunities counted at peaks in the time series.

1957. By nationalizing the Suez Canal in 1956 and then forbidding Israeli shipping through it, Egypt's leader, Gamal Abdel Nasser, attracted considerable attention. The 1957 events include the aftermath of Suez, such as controversy over control of Aqaba, but also Egyptian moves against British and Saudi allies in Yemen. In addition, the anticolonial Algerian War began to heat up, spawning rising tensions between radical French colonists, Algerians, and Paris-oriented French colonists.

Three events contributed to the high number of opportunities witnessed in 1962: continuing controversy over Cuba, culminating in the October Cuban Missile Crisis; escalating colonial violence in Algeria; and an intense militarized dispute between India and China over a mountainous region on the border known as the Aksai Chin. The Middle East again produced numerous events, reflected in the next three major spikes of opportunities—1967, 1973, and 1982. In 1967, the Six Day War erupted, which resulted in the Israeli capture of the Sinai Peninsula, Gaza Strip, West Bank, and Golan Heights. In October 1973, Egypt launched a surprise attack on Israel in what would come to be known as the Yom Kippur War. Finally, in 1982, the year with the highest number of opportunities, Israel invaded Lebanon as that country's civil war escalated, and Britain waged war against Argentina over the Falkland/Malvinas Islands. With the end of the Cold War in the late 1980s, the overall number of opportunities declined significantly. The final remaining uptick in the data coincides with the rise in violence in the Balkans.

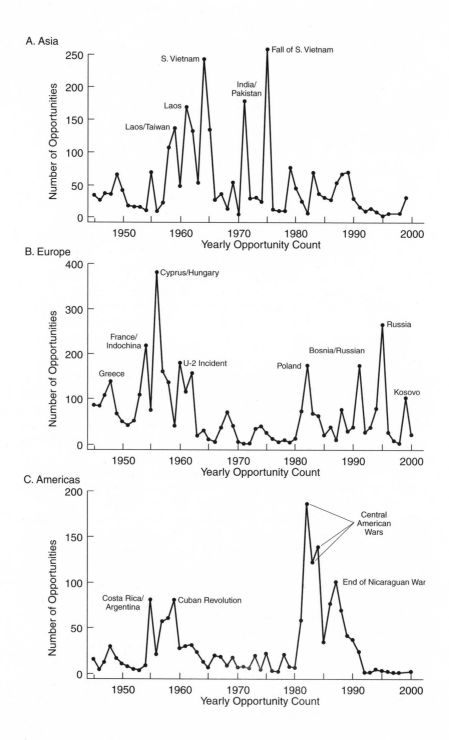

A. Asia

Number of Opportunities

250 — Fall of S. Vietnam
S. Vietnam
200 — India/Pakistan
Laos
150 — Laos/Taiwan
100 —
50 —
0 —

1950   1960   1970   1980   1990   2000
Yearly Opportunity Count

B. Europe

Number of Opportunities

400 —
Cyprus/Hungary
300 —
Russia
France/Indochina
200 — Bosnia/Russian
Greece   U-2 Incident   Poland
100 — Kosovo
0 —

1950   1960   1970   1980   1990   2000
Yearly Opportunity Count

C. Americas

Number of Opportunities

200 —
Central American Wars
150 —
End of Nicaraguan War
100 —
Costa Rica/Argentina   Cuban Revolution
50 —
0 —

1950   1960   1970   1980   1990   2000
Yearly Opportunity Count

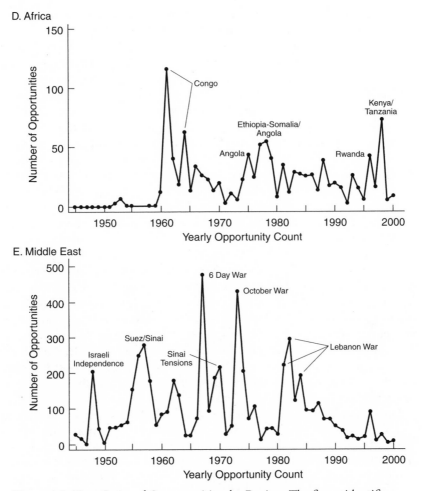

Figure 4.3. Time Series of Opportunities, by Region. The figure identifies some of the crises that contributed many of the opportunities counted at peaks in the time series.

Figure 4.3 plots the annual number of opportunities to use force for each region of the world. Panel A, to begin, focuses on Asia. The 1959 Taiwan Straits Crisis as well as rising tensions in Laos mark the first major set of opportunities, followed closely by civil war in Laos in 1961. Increasing strife between North and South Vietnam account for the rise in 1964.[13] Both 1965 and 1971 are dominated by conflicts between India and Pakistan. The 1965 fighting over the border area around the Rann of Kutch, accompanied by the threat of Chinese intervention, provides a significant number of opportunities. The 1971 war, which began between West and East Pakistan and ended with East Pakistani independence (Bangladesh), precipitated continued fighting between Pakistani and Indian forces, again largely in Kashmir. Opportunities in 1975 largely arise from the fall of South Vietnam after the 1973 exit of U.S. troops.

Panel B presents the time series for Europe. Though a substantial number of the opportunities in this time series concern French and British involvement in colonial territories (especially in Africa), plenty of others identify crises within Europe itself. The Greek Civil War provides many of the opportunities observed in 1948, including controversies involving increasing U.S. military aid and support for communist fighters from neighboring Yugoslavia and Bulgaria. French fighting in Indochina and the fall of Dien Bien Phu account for the escalation of opportunities in 1954. In 1956, Cyprus's civil war (fighting British colonial control) and the Soviet invasion of Hungary (in response to moves toward democracy and independence from the Warsaw Pact) yield a number of opportunities. The U-2 spy plane incident and other Soviet attacks on Western military aircraft account for the rise in opportunities in 1960. Despite the relative quiet during the period of détente, the Soviet Union's crackdown and imposition of martial law on Polish labor unions in 1982 brings a return of opportunities. The Russian coup attempt against Gorbachev and the beginning of violence in the former Yugoslav republics lead a significant increase in opportunities in 1991, and the civil war in Bosnia generates the time series' final significant spike in 1995. Finally, the Kosovo conflict coincides with the surge in 1999.

Panel C reveals the opportunity trends in the Western Hemisphere. The civil war in Costa Rica and emerging civil conflict in Argentina under Juan Peron generated the spike in opportunities in 1955. The next three upticks reflect Cuba, with civil violence in 1958 giving rise to the overthrow of the Batista regime in 1959. The late 1960s and 1970s proved to be a period of relative calm, especially by comparison to the outbreak of the 1980s. Increasing civil strife in Nicaragua, El Salvador, and Guatemala dominate the 1981–87 period, with a brief respite in 1985. The century's final decade proved to be relatively quiet in the Western Hemisphere, with just a handful of opportunities arising in different South and Central American countries.

Panel D focuses on Africa. War in the Congo (Zaire) dominates the early 1960s in the African time series. The war of independence against Belgium and the civil war between the central government and Katanga provide the bulk of opportunities reported up until 1964. Though little activity registers during the latter 1960s and 1970s, the 1975 war of Angolan independence and ensuing civil war accelerate the production of opportunities that decade. The 1978 Ogaden War between Ethiopia and

Somalia as well as continued strife in Angola drive the series upward in the late 1970s. The Rwandan civil war and genocide partially explain the surge observed in 1996. Finally, al-Qaeda attacks on U.S. embassies in Kenya and Tanzania in 1998 constitute the last flash of activity in the region before the century's close.

Panel E presents the opportunities in the Middle East region. Two observations are worth noting. First, the scale of the Y-axis is larger here than any of the other regional time-series graphs. Second, the major spikes on this graph parallel those observed in figure 4.2, which plotted the global time series. The 1948 war over Israeli independence aligns with the first spike, while the Suez crisis and subsequent controversy of the Sinai Peninsula produce additional bumps in 1956 and 1957. The 1967 Six Day War yields the highest yearly number of opportunities for the Middle East series, while saber-rattling by Egypt and Israel over control of the Sinai creates a small rise in the time series in 1970. The 1973 October War produces another large spike, while the expansion of the Lebanese civil war, Israeli intervention, expulsion of the Palestinian Liberation Organization, and Syrian and Israeli reactions to Western (French and American) intervention yield a consistent flow of opportunities in the early to mid 1980s.

ECONOMICS AND POLITICS, AT HOME AND ABROAD

Just as the geographic distribution of opportunities varied considerably, so did the United States' political and economic relationships with possible target nations. Twenty-seven percent of opportunities for military action involved countries that were direct allies of the United States.[14] Another 15 percent involved nations that were allies of the Soviet Union (or, in the 1990s, Russia). Interestingly, opportunities typically arose in small and nondemocratic states; major powers contributed only 19 percent of the opportunities in the database,[15] and democratic states were involved in just 26 percent of the cases.[16] These findings are especially surprising, given the media's predisposition to monitor those nations that have closer political and economic ties to the United States: a coup that occurs in Burundi, for example, is not likely to receive as much attention as a coup in Saudi Arabia, just as an assassination attempt in Chad is unlikely to garner as much coverage as one occurring in Mexico.[17] It is especially noteworthy, then, that the typical opportunity arose in a small, nondemocratic state that was an ally to neither the United States nor the Soviet Union.

Figure 4.4 reveals the power and economic relationships that the United States maintains with countries where opportunities have arisen. The top panel shows the distribution of trade levels between the United States and targeted nations.[18] (The dark bell curve in the graph represents the nor-

A. Trade and Opportunities

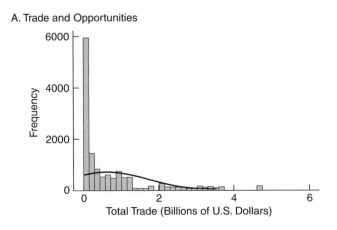

B. Capability Ratios and Opportunities

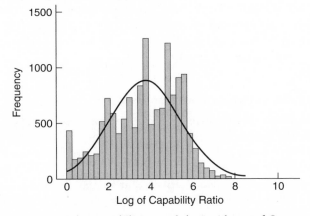

Figure 4.4. Trade, Capabilities, and the Incidence of Opportunities.

mal distribution, given the variable's mean and standard deviation.) Levels of trade with targeted nations appear quite high. In the opportunities dataset, the mean level of trade between the United States and targeted nations is $1.46 billion, as compared to $3.3 billion worldwide.[19] Many of the states generating high numbers of opportunities averaged $1 billion or more per year, including Israel, the United Kingdom, Russia/USSR, France, Iraq, Argentina, and South Africa.

The bottom panel of figure 4.4 shows the distribution of opportunities across different levels of capability ratios between the United States and potential targets. We measure a state's capabilities by averaging its share of the international system's total population, urban population, military expenditures, military personnel, iron and steel production, and energy consumption. The capability variable, then, is the ratio of these capabilities for the United States divided by these capabilities for the potential target state.[20] Because the spread of the capabilities ratio variable is quite large, the graph in figure 4.4 presents the logarithmic transformation. Three things are worth noting here. First, all (unlogged) values are greater than zero, indicating that in every instance the United States has greater capabilities (as measured by this operationalization) than the countries that present the opportunities. Second, a few major powers—most prominently China and the Soviet Union—presented many opportunities to use force, and consequently, those cases populate the lower left end of the distribution. Finally, in numerous instances the capabilities of the United States eclipse those observed for potential targets. Values of 2 indicate that the United States has roughly 7.5 times more capabilities; values of 3 indicate a ratio of 20 to 1. Taken together, these simple descriptors suggest that the United States confronts opportunities to use force in nations that, militarily, are relatively weak.

STRATEGIC AVOIDANCE BEHAVIOR

Imagine, for a moment, that leaders of a political faction within a South or Central American nation are considering launching a coup to topple the sitting government. In addition to gauging the levels of support such a coup would enjoy domestically, the likelihood of its success, as well as the benefits and costs of the effort, these leaders might well consider the probability that the United States would interfere. Anticipating that the moment protests erupted on the street American helicopters would come swooping down to suppress the insurrection, the would-be instigators might not initiate the coup at all; by their passing on the option, the opportunity for the United States to exercise military force would not appear in our database. By contrast, if they thought that the United States would not interfere in their plot, then these leaders might be more willing to proceed; in this case, they would contribute additional opportunities to the database.[21]

Before initiating a border clash, hostile takeover of international waters, or terrorist act, do foreign governments, factions, rebels, or parties consider the probability that the United States will interfere in either their domestic affairs or their conflicts with other nations? The prospect is intriguing. Surely, some states (and the individuals within them) pay little mind to the United States before instigating a civil war or coup or assassination attempt. Others—those, perhaps, with better information about U.S. foreign policy or closer ties to the United States, or who are least capable of repelling a U.S. intervention—might well worry about the possibility of U.S. interference in their political designs. To the extent that they do, the number, location, and type of opportunities that are generated over time are not, from the vantage point of the United States, exogenously determined.

If at least some parties to the kinds of opportunities we are monitoring intermittently anticipate the possibility of U.S. involvement in their affairs, how do they do it? Most obviously, they would reflect on their government's political and economic relationship with the United States, the strategic importance of their country to the United States, as well as its history with the White House and its allies. One additional possibility, though, bears directly on the empirical investigations of this book—namely, domestic politics. If either public opinion, the state of the economy, the president's party identification, or the partisan composition of Congress affects the occurrence of military deployments, then foreign states might monitor these politics before initiating conflict either within their own borders or with one another. And if so, then the key domestic factors that we highlight as contributors to presidential decision making might also affect the incidence of opportunities to use force that the president confronts at any moment. By this logic, the opportunities database's very existence could itself be the product of domestic politics.

Examining how opportunities are distributed across different political and economic conditions may shed some light on the possible existence of what Benjamin Fordham and others refer to as "strategic avoidance behavior"—that is, instances when foreign states wait until the United States is in a bad situation economically or politically before they themselves behave "badly."[22] Figure 4.5 begins to address the question. The graph in panel A shows the distribution of inflation rates during opportunities in the data.[23] While opportunities are observed across the full range of inflation values, the density of the graph is higher at lower ends of the spectrum. Recall that in chapter 2 we found that inflationary pressures tended to increase the propensity of presidents to deploy troops abroad. It would seem, then, that instigators of opportunities were engaging in risk avoidance strategies, acting aggressively when domestic political forces depressed the likelihood of a U.S. military response.[24] In actuality, though, the data do not support this contention, as the inflation rate remained static and low from 1945 to the latter 1970s, and then steadily climbed upward. The fact that opportunities are clustered at the bottom end of the inflationary scale simply reflects the fact that inflation was low for much of the postwar era. Indeed, when focusing on the period between 1978 and 2000, when the incidence of different inflationary values appeared more uniform, we do not witness any bunching of opportunities at the low end of the scale; there are, however, a fair number of observations at the scale's high end, which runs directly contrary to expectations about strategic avoidance.

If not inflationary trends, might opportunities peak during periods of relatively low unemployment rates?[25] Take a look at panel B of figure 4.5. It is the case that slightly more opportunities occur when unemployment

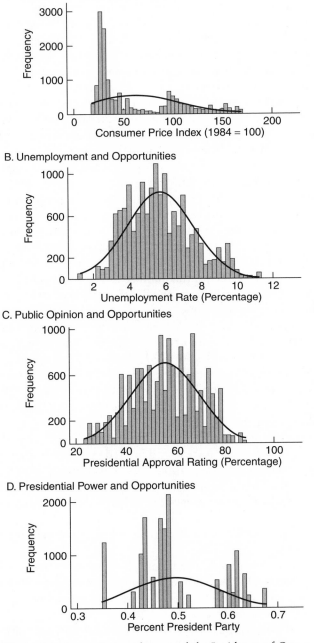

Figure 4.5. Strategic Avoidance and the Incidence of Opportunities.

rates rest below the approximate mean of 6 percent. As unemployment rates also induce military action, these findings too would comport with our expectations about strategic avoidance. Again, though, during most of the period under investigation—specifically, 60 percent of the time—the unemployment rate was lower than 5.9 percent. We see more opportunities when unemployment is low only because unemployment is low most of the time. Moreover, the cluster of opportunities that occur around the 9 to 10 percent range fly directly in the face of expectations about avoidance behavior. When accounting for temporal trends in the economy, we do not observe any clear indications that the incidence of opportunities increases at either the lowest or highest unemployment levels.

Panel C shows the distribution of opportunities across different presidential approval ratings. If strategic avoidance is prevalent, we would expect to see concentrations of opportunities when presidential approval ratings are high—for during these periods, presidents supposedly have little cause to imperil their public support with risky foreign entanglements. The observed distribution of opportunities provides only slight evidence that avoidance behavior takes place. While there are more opportunities above the mean (56 percent), the number is not overwhelming. Nonetheless, this graph suggests that we consider the notion of strategic avoidance more fully, which we do below.

Finally, in panel D, we consider the production of opportunities across different partisan alignments of the presidency and Congress. Initially, average yearly opportunities for Republican and Democratic presidents appear to be quite different. During Republican administrations, the average number of opportunities arising is approximately 330 per year, while under Democratic administrations the number is 205 per year. Conventional arguments about strategic avoidance, however, cannot readily account for these findings. If Republicans are generally considered more hawkish (a claim for which we found limited evidence in chapter 3), then presumably, states concerned about U.S. intervention would time their conflicts when a dovish administration and/or Congress held power. This appears not to be the case, suggesting either (a) Republicans are not perceived internationally to be hawkish, or (b) states (and nonstate actors) pay little heed to U.S. domestic politics when contemplating their own foreign policies.

Some evidence to support arguments about strategic avoidance emerges when examining the breakdown of unified (defined by Republican *or* Democratic control of the House, Senate, and presidency) and divided government. In the thirty-four years of divided government, the annual rate of opportunities is 221, while the annual rate during twenty-two years of unified government is 322.[26] Though this could suggest that states time their aggressive behavior to coincide with periods of divided government (hoping then for a muted U.S. response), the balance of evidence suggests that there are few such strategic calculations occurring. The bottom panel of figure 4.5 shows the number of opportunities to arise when the president enjoys lower and higher levels of partisan support within Congress. While a fair number of opportunities emerge across the spectrum, for values less than 0.4 there does appear to be a spike, for which temporal dynamics cannot account. These opportunities arose during the last two years of Eisenhower's administration and generally consisted of reports surrounding the Soviet's downing of a U.S. U-2 spy plane, the Cuban revolution, a civil war in Congo, and the Algerian revolution. We cannot know whether the protagonists in these struggles purposefully ratcheted up their activities when the president faced staunch opposition within Congress, when the probability of a U.S. use of force was small, or whether the occurrences were mere coincidence. This one spike in the time series, however, is the only observation that supports the theory of strategic avoidance behavior.

On the whole, we find very limited support for the proposition that foreign states systematically monitor political and economic indicators that reduce the probability of U.S. intervention. Rather than focusing on the hegemon, states may simply respond to their own local or regional conditions or the status of domestic politics and economics within their own borders. Just as we argue that U.S. decision makers focus on their own economic conditions and the strategic situation vis-à-vis their direct adversary, there is little reason to believe that other states behave in fundamentally different ways. In the sections that follow, we explore these issues further and report findings from some more advanced statistical models that account for the possibility that foreign states reveal strategic avoidance behavior on the basis of factors other than those considered here. For now, though, we recognize a more basic point—the observed features of the economy and domestic politics of the United States do not obviously correlate with the annual yield of opportunities, suggesting that arguments about strategic avoidance probably apply under fairly restrictive conditions. We return to this question later in this chapter.

MODELING DEPLOYMENT DECISIONS

The opportunities database consists of roughly fifteen thousand media reports of violent acts perpetrated against the U.S. government, threats to the stability of foreign regimes, gross violations of international law, and nuclear proliferation that occurred between 1945 and 2000. In slightly more than 9 percent of cases, the United States sent troops to nations involved in these conflicts within one month of their reporting.[27] In this section, we estimate a series of statistical models that are designed to predict the probability that an opportunity evoked a military response.[28]

KEY EXPLANATORY VARIABLES

To estimate the effects of partisan alignments across the branches of government on the president's willingness to deploy troops abroad, we reconsider all three versions of congressional support for the president, including *Unified Government, Percent President Party,* and *President Party Power.*[29] The first measure, as defined in chapter 3, simply identifies whether the president's party holds majorities in both the House and Senate. The latter two account for both the size of the president's party and the relative cohesion of its preferences. As they obviously contain more information about the magnitude and strength of congressional support for the president, a priori we have reason to place more stock in their results.

BACKGROUND CONTROLS

All of the factors that purportedly influence the regularity with which presidents deploy troops abroad might also influence the probability that the president uses military force in response to any particular foreign crisis. Therefore, in the statistical models that follow, we include measures of public approval for the president,[30] inflation and unemployment trends,[31] the extent of U.S. hegemony in the international arena, the number of concurrent military disputes taking place, and identifiers for election years and each presidential administration—that is, all of the controls used in chapter 3.[32] The two exceptions concern *Cold War* and *Ongoing War.* Rather than including a simple indicator variable for the period between 1945 and 1989, we identify those opportunities during the Cold War in which the Soviet Union was either a direct participant or an ally to those nations involved in the crisis.[33] Rather than note the occurrence of ongoing wars (Korea, Vietnam, and Persian Gulf), we identify the number of U.S. troops in a targeted country at the time that an opportunity arises. Because they focus on particular features of a targeted nation, both of these new variables take fuller advantage of the opportunities database.

Because the unit of observation here is a report of a state's involvement in an individual foreign crisis, rather than a quarterly count of U.S. troop deployments, we also can account for characteristics of the conflicts and targeted nations themselves. First, we introduce *Alliances* to differentiate nations that have a political-military alliance with the United States. This variable counts the number of alliances between the United States and the state in question and is based on the Correlates of War Alliances database.[34] Similarly, a large literature in international relations on the democratic peace claims that democracies rarely, if ever, use military force against one another.[35] We thus include an indicator variable, *Democracy*, to code whether the potential target is a democracy.[36]

Power relationships also may affect decisions concerning the use of force, as argued by realist scholars in international relations. We introduce a number of variables to tap this dimension of interstate relations. First, *Major Power* identifies states that the Correlates of War project considers to be major powers.[37] Second, as previously discussed, *Capability Ratio* gauges the relative military strength of the United States and a targeted country. Third, liberal scholars of international relations have long argued that economic concerns figure prominently in decisions about the use of military force. To this end, we add a variable (*Trade*) that measures the value of the potential target's trade with the United States.[38]

Finally, we account for the density of past and present opportunities to arise within a targeted country and around the world. To account for the number of competing opportunities that invite U.S. military action, we introduce *Contemporaneous Opportunities*, which counts the number of opportunities from around the world that are ongoing on the day of a particular opportunity's reporting. Then, to differentiate opportunities that come on the heels of ongoing crises from those that appear more aberrational, we include *Previous Opportunities*, which counts the number of opportunities produced by a country during the previous thirty days. Descriptive statistics for all variables included in this chapter's analyses are presented in table B.2 of appendix B.

MAIN RESULTS

We first estimate standard maximum likelihood regressions that posit the use of force as a function of the three measures of Congress's partisan composition and presidential fixed-effects.[39] Each model predicts the probability that the United States employed the use of military force against a targeted country within one month of an opportunity.[40] It is worth emphasizing, however, that there is nothing special about the choice of a one-month cutoff. Statistical models that set deadlines for a military response at ten, twenty, forty, fifty, or sixty days generate comparable results.

Table 4.1 presents the results. The first thing to notice is that two of the three measures of congressional support yield estimates that are statistically significant and in the expected direction. Although the estimated effect of *Unified Government* is not statistically significant, both *Percent President Party* and *President Party Power* powerfully predict U.S. military decision making. In each case, moving from one standard deviation below the mean of these variables to one standard deviation above, while holding the continuous variables at their means and discrete variables at their modes, more than doubles the probability that the United States sends the military to a targeted nation within one month of an opportunity.

TABLE 4.1
Probability of a Military Response

	(1)		(2)		(3)	
Congressional Support						
Unified Government	−0.31	[0.46]	—		—	
Percent President Party	—		4.18*	[3.11]	—	
President Party Power	—		—		2.91**	[1.77]
Constant	−3.19***	[0.63]	−5.55***	[1.64]	−3.42***	[0.66]
(N)	15,004		15,004		15,004	
Pseudo-R^2	.03		.03		.03	

Logistic regressions estimated. The dependent variable is coded 1 when the United States responds militarily within 30 days to an opportunity between 1945 and 2000, and zero otherwise. *** = p < 0.01; ** = p < 0.05; * = p < 0.10; one-tailed tests. Huber/White/sandwich clustered standard errors on country-president combinations reported in brackets. Though not reported, models also contain fixed effect terms for each presidential administration. Models that estimate the probability of a military response within 10, 20, 40, 50, and 60 days generate comparable results.

Presidents appear more willing to incur the risks associated with military action when they enjoy strong partisan support within Congress.

We do not know why in these models the results associated with *Unified Government* appear so different than our other measures. It is worth noting, however, that among the measures of presidential support within Congress, *Unified Government* contains the least amount of information. Rather than assess the relative size and cohesion of the president's party, the variable merely denotes whether it retains majorities in the House and Senate. When deciding how to respond to an observed foreign crisis, however, presidents have ample reasons to consider more than just their party's majority status. Marginal increases in the number of seats held by their party, whether from 44 to 48 percent or from 54 to 58 percent, may be enough to derail congressional efforts to tie the president's hands if and when things go poorly on the battlefield—and hence, such marginal increases may positively contribute, ex ante, to the probability that presidents respond militarily to the kinds of foreign crises in the opportunities database. As they contain more information about the likelihood that Congress will stand by the president during the course of an ongoing military venture, it is not especially surprising that *Percent President Party* and *President Party Power* generate estimates that are statistically significant and in the expected direction, while *Unified Government* does not.

Table 4.2 presents the results from statistical models that include a richer array of control variables that account for domestic politics and the economy, characteristics of the targeted nation, the nature of U.S. relations with the targeted nations, the number of prior and ongoing opportunities

TABLE 4.2
Probability of a Military Response, Including Background Controls

	(1)		(2)		(3)	
Congressional Support						
Unified Government	−0.28	[0.64]	—		—	
Percent President Party	—		8.44***	[3.22]	—	
President Party Power	—		—		5.79***	[1.97]
Standard Background Controls						
Unemployment	0.49***	[0.11]	0.44***	[0.11]	0.43***	[0.11]
CPI	0.02	[0.02]	0.03	[0.02]	0.04*	[0.02]
Public Approval	0.00	[0.02]	−0.00	[0.02]	−0.00	[0.02]
Election Year	0.04	[0.31]	0.23	[0.32]	0.21	[0.32]
Hegemony	1.93	[11.96]	−8.71	[8.73]	−10.83	[8.66]
World Disputes	−0.07*	[0.06]	−0.07*	[0.05]	−0.07*	[0.05]
Targeted Nation						
Major Power	−0.77	[0.70]	−0.68	[0.71]	−0.67	[0.71]
Democracy	0.17	[0.31]	0.19	[0.32]	0.17	[0.32]
U.S. Relations with Targeted Nation						
Alliances	−0.18	[0.41]	−0.19	[0.41]	−0.20	[0.41]
Trade (billions)	0.01	[0.02]	0.01	[0.02]	0.01	[0.02]
Soviet Involvement	−0.18	[0.34]	−0.21	[0.35]	−0.22	[0.35]
Capability Ratio (log)	−0.34**	[0.15]	−0.35***	[0.15]	−0.35***	[0.15]
Prior, Ongoing Opportunities and Commitments						
Prev. Opportunities	0.01*	[0.01]	0.01*	[0.01]	0.01*	[0.01]
Contemp. Opportunities	−0.35***	[0.14]	−0.35***	[0.14]	−0.35***	[0.14]
Troops Deployed (log)	−0.11**	[0.07]	−0.12**	[0.07]	−0.12**	[0.07]
Regional Fixed Effects						
North, Central America	1.20**	[0.72]	1.33**	[0.69]	1.32**	[0.69]
South America	0.80	[0.79]	0.84	[0.78]	0.85	[0.77]
Middle East	0.91**	[0.52]	0.99**	[0.49]	0.97**	[0.49]
Asia, Pacific	1.07**	[0.54]	1.11**	[0.51]	1.09**	[0.51]
Western Europe	0.18	[1.12]	0.13	[1.15]	0.09	[1.16]
Eastern Europe	0.46	[0.83]	0.48	[0.82]	0.44	[0.83]
Constant	−6.07*	[3.71]	−7.78**	[3.18]	−3.14	[2.82]
(N)	13,327		13,327		13,327	
Pseudo-R^2	.12		.13		.13	

Logistic regressions estimated. The dependent variable is coded 1 when the United States responds militarily within 30 days to an opportunity between 1945 and 2000, and zero otherwise. *** = $p < 0.01$; ** = $p < 0.05$; * = $p < 0.10$; one-tailed tests. Huber/White/sandwich clustered standard errors on country-president combinations reported in brackets. Though not reported, models also contain fixed effect terms for each presidential administration. For regional fixed effects, Africa is the reference category. Models that estimate the probability of a military response within 10, 20, 40, 50, and 60 days generate comparable results.

to use force and actual military commitments, and regional and presidential fixed effects.[41] If anything, the main results are strengthened.[42] Though the estimated effect of unified government remains insignificant, the effects for both *Percent President Party* and *President Party Power* are positive, large, and highly significant.

The results for the standard background controls, for the most part, are intuitive. Just as high unemployment rates correlate positively with the number of troop deployments presidents engage each quarter, so too do they positively contribute to the probability that presidents respond militarily to specified foreign crises. Moving from one standard deviation below the mean of *Unemployment* to one standard deviation above, again keeping all other continuous variables at their means and discrete variables at their modes, increases the marginal probability of a military response fivefold. Additionally, we find some evidence that foreign military engagements are not independent of one another. The higher the number of ongoing non-U.S. militarized interstate disputes (*World Disputes*) that occur on the day of an opportunity, the less likely it is that the president responds militarily. Finally, as previously observed, *CPI*, *Public Approval*, *Election Year*, and the levels of *U.S. Hegemony* appear unrelated to presidential decisions involving the use of force.

How do features of the opportunity itself influence presidential decision making? Only *Capability Ratio* registers a statistically significant effect. The United States appears less likely to respond militarily to countries with relatively smaller militaries and more likely to respond militarily to countries with larger militaries. Other characteristics (*Alliances*, *Major Power*, or *Democracy*) and U.S. relations with the targeted nation (*Trade* and *Soviet Involvement*) appear unrelated to use-of-force decisions, at least in the models. Interestingly, though, inventories of past and present opportunities and deployments (*Previous Opportunities*, *Contemporary Opportunities*, and *Troop Deployments*) generate results that are both in the expected direction and that consistently surpass standard thresholds of statistical significance. The logic of these collective findings is straightforward enough: the higher the number of previous opportunities to emerge from a targeted country, the more likely it is the United States will respond militarily, while the greater the number of competing opportunities in other nations, and the higher the level of ongoing U.S. troop commitments in the targeted country, the less likely it is the United States will launch a new deployment.[42a]

What of the regional and presidential fixed effects? A number of the regional fixed effects appear statistically significant. The United States is more likely to respond militarily to countries in North or Central America, the Middle East, Asia, or the Pacific region than it is to countries in Africa, the reference category. Null effects are observed for nations in Europe and South America. Additionally, in chapter 3 we found limited evidence that Republican presidents exercise major force with greater regularity than do Democratic presidents. These findings do not appear to extend to statistical models that estimate the probability that presidents respond militarily to different opportunities. Though not reported, all of the models in table 4.1 contain fixed effects for each presidential administration. While these fixed effects are jointly significant, we do not find any evidence that the estimated coefficients for Democratic presidents are ever smaller than those for Republican presidents.[43]

MAJOR VERSUS MINOR DEPLOYMENTS

Our second hypothesis, which received strong support in chapter 3, was that the domestic politics of troop deployments would be more important for major uses of force. Interestingly, though, all of the previous results relied on a combination of major and minor uses. Indeed, the results remain roughly consistent when only major *or* minor uses of force are analyzed.[44] This suggests that when the dynamics of decision making concerning the use of force are modeled as choices concerning individual opportunities, rather than aggregate deployments, domestic partisan politics are always important.

On one hand, this finding, and the ones below combining major and minor uses, does not lend support to an important hypothesis developed in chapter 2. Regardless of the size of deployment, evidence of congressional interference can be detected in those models that include the full bevy of control variables.[45] One explanation for the variation in results could lie in the difference in specification—in chapter 3, we purported to know nothing about the potential target, or the nature of the crisis. When information regarding either is incorporated, partisan dynamics appear ubiquitous regardless of the size of deployment.

Still, this finding supports the book's general argument that Congress can and does involve itself in foreign policy. We would also reemphasize that we believe the empirical models in this chapter are superior to the event-count models that characterize the world in ways decision makers do not necessarily see it. We therefore continue to use both major and minor deployments to measure the use of force in the remaining two sets of models.

STRATEGIC AVOIDANCE

Strategic avoidance behavior, we have noted, could complicate our statistical analyses. If some states regularly refuse to carry out attacks on others because they anticipate a U.S. intervention, and if their assessments of a U.S. intervention occurring depend on factors not included in our statistical models, then we confront what econometricians refer to as a selection effect that can complicate our analyses. If strategic avoidance behavior is widespread—though up until now, we have little reason to believe that it is—simple regression models may generate estimates from which we cannot reliably draw inferences.

To remedy this potential problem, we turn to more advanced statistical techniques—specifically, Heckman selection models, named after a Nobel Prize–winning economist at the University of Chicago. These models are designed to account for systematic variation on who enters a sample and who does not. Early work on these models focused on questions of wages and gender, examining the relative earnings of comparable women and men. Simple comparisons of individuals who appear equivalent to one another in all respects save their gender will not do, as many women (especially mothers) opt out of the workforce, and these women differ systematically from those who are employed. Consequently, to estimate the effect of gender on earnings one must first account for who "selects" into the workforce, and hence has an observable wage, and who "selects" out, and hence does not. For our purposes, some states may choose to engage in aggressive behaviors, and hence enter the opportunities database, while others choose not to, and hence are excluded. If their choices relate to unobserved features of U.S. domestic politics or to other unobserved factors that influence the probability of U.S. military action, the estimated effects in tables 4.1 and 4.2 are potentially biased.

Preliminary analyses conducted earlier in this chapter did not reveal strong relationships between the production of opportunities and either domestic politics or economic conditions, which should mitigate our concerns about strategic avoidance behavior. Nonetheless, to investigate the matter more thoroughly we reconfigured the opportunities database to estimate these Heckman selection models, which consist of two equations: the first predicts whether a state produces an opportunity on any given day between 1945 and 2000; the second estimates the probability, conditional on there being an opportunity, that the United States responds militarily.[46] Our revised dataset, which consists of country-by-day observations, identifies whether a given country participated in an opportunity on a given day, and then whether the United States responded militarily to that country within 30 days.

The model's second stage, which generates the results of substantive interest, relies on the same predictors used in table 4.2.[47] In order to correctly estimate the two equations simultaneously, we need additional identifying variables that in the first stage predict when opportunities actually arise. To this end, we introduce a new variable that identifies the size of the target nation's per-capita GDP.[48] The logic here is straightforward. We have little reason to expect that the material welfare of a targeted nation's citizens will influence the presidential use-of-force decisions, and certainly not after having controlled for its military capabilities, economic and political relations, and type of government. There is good reason to expect, however, that the welfare of a nation's citizens will influence the outbreak of crises within its borders and its willingness to intervene in other crises occurring beyond them. As such, *PerCapGDP* satisfies the key statistical properties required to identify the first stage of this system of equations.[49] We also incorporate in the first stage other variables from stage two, including measures of congressional support, *World Disputes, Hegemony, Major Power, Democracy, Troop Deployments, Previous Opportunities,* and regional fixed effects.[50]

Table 4.3 presents the main estimates from these selection models.[51] Again, we find that two of the three measures of congressional support show a strong relationship with decisions to use force, even while accounting for the possibility of strategic avoidance behavior. *President Party Support* and *President Party Power* are both statistically significant predictors of the use of military force, though the magnitudes of these effects are somewhat smaller than in our previous models. Moving each of these variables from one standard deviation below their means to one standard deviation above, while holding all other continuous variables at their means and discrete variables at their modes, yields a roughly 60 percent increase in the probability of a use of force. The observed relationship between *Unified Government* and troop deployments continues to be statistically insignificant. Overall, though, these new models provide strong support for our argument that the partisan composition of Congress correlates with the use of force.

A number of differences are observed between the estimated effects of our control variables and those observed in previous models. In fact, among the most important predictors of troop deployment decisions observed in the prior regressions, only *Unemployment* and *North/Central America* continue to register statistically significant effects. The estimated effects of *World Disputes, Capability Ratio, Previous Opportunities, Contemporary Opportunities, Troop Deployments, Middle East,* and *Asia Pacific* now are all statistically indistinguishable from zero. Interestingly, though, *Public Approval* and *Soviet Involvement* are significant, whereas before they were not. Consistent with diversionary war theory, presidents appear to be especially likely to respond militarily to foreign crises when their public approval ratings languish. Additionally, the chances that presidents will intervene militarily in foreign crises diminish when either the Soviet Union or an ally of the Soviet Union is involved.

We are particularly interested in the estimate of an additional parameter of the model, rho, which gauges the strength of the relationship between the error terms of the model's two equations. A significant estimate of rho suggests that a selection process is at work, while an insignificant estimate suggests that each stage is appropriately modeled independently. In this in-

TABLE 4.3
Probability of a Military Response, Adjusting for Strategic Avoidance Behavior

	(1)		(2)		(3)	
Congressional Support						
Unified Government	−0.13	[0.29]	—		—	
Percent President Party	—		2.01*	[1.36]	—	
President Party Power	—		—		1.61**	[0.90]
Standard Background Controls						
Unemployment	0.14***	[0.05]	0.13***	[0.05]	0.12***	[0.05]
CPI	−0.00	[0.01]	0.00	[0.01]	0.00	[0.01]
Public Approval	−0.01*	[0.01]	−0.01*	[0.01]	−0.01*	[0.01]
Election Year	−0.07	[0.11]	−0.04	[0.11]	−0.04	[0.11]
Hegemony	−4.94	[5.57]	−8.16**	[4.60]	−8.94**	[4.57]
World Disputes	0.11	[0.17]	0.11	[0.16]	0.11	[0.16]
Targeted Nation						
Major Power	−0.46	[0.39]	−0.46	[0.38]	−0.46	[0.37]
Democracy	0.01	[0.14]	0.02	[0.14]	0.02	[0.14]
U.S. Relations with Targeted Nation						
Alliances	−0.18	[0.15]	−0.18	[0.14]	−0.19*	[0.14]
Trade (billions)	0.01	[0.01]	0.01	[0.01]	0.01	[0.01]
Soviet Involvement	−0.32**	[0.17]	−0.33**	[0.17]	−0.33**	[0.16]
Capability Ratio (log)	−0.07	[0.06]	−0.07	[0.06]	−0.07	[0.06]
Prior, Ongoing Opportunities and Commitments						
Prev. Opportunities	−0.04	[0.06]	−0.04	[0.06]	−0.04	[0.06]
Contemp. Opportunities	−0.00	[0.02]	0.00 ·	[0.02]	0.00	[0.02]
Troops Deployed (log)	−0.03	[0.03]	−0.03	[0.03]	−0.03	[0.03]
Regional Fixed Effects						
North, Central America	0.67**	[0.32]	0.69**	[0.31]	0.69**	[0.31]
South America	0.36	[0.31]	0.38	[0.31]	0.38	[0.31]
Middle East	0.06	[0.25]	0.07	[0.24]	0.07	[0.24]
Asia, Pacific	0.24	[0.24]	0.24	[0.23]	0.24	[0.23]
Western Europe	0.08	[0.38]	0.10	[0.37]	0.09	[0.37]
Eastern Europe	0.54**	[0.34]	0.57**	[0.34]	0.56**	[0.34]
Constant	1.15	[2.23]	1.05	[2.00]	2.22	[1.90]
(N)	1,599,396		1,599,396		1,599,396	

Heckman selection models estimated. The main equation estimates the probability that the United States responds militarily within 30 days to an opportunity between 1945 and 2000, conditional on an opportunity existing. The first stage, which is reported in table B.3 of appendix B, estimates the probability of there being at least one opportunity in a country on a given day, where per capita GDP serves as the identifying variable. Models consist of country-by-day observations. *** = $p < 0.01$; ** = $p < 0.05$; * = $p < 0.10$; one-tailed tests. Huber/White/sandwich clustered standard errors on country-president combinations reported in brackets. Though not reported, models also contain fixed effect terms for each presidential administration. For regional fixed effects, Africa is the reference category. Models that estimate the probability of a military response within 10, 20, 40, 50, and 60 days generate comparable results.

stance, the estimate of rho is always statistically insignificant. This is perhaps the strongest evidence that the generation of opportunities to use force and the decisions presidents make about military deployments are distinct, lending additional credence to the estimates reported in tables 4.1 and 4.2. This fact, in combination with the consistent effects observed for our various measures of congressional support, should assuage any lingering concerns that our results are an artifact of strategic avoidance behavior.

THE TIMING OF MILITARY DEPLOYMENTS

If the previous modeling exercises establish that congressional-presidential politics inform the probability of observing a troop deployment, how might such politics influence the timing of a military action? If a president faces stringent opposition in Congress, will he delay using force in the hopes that alternative policy options will work or that public support for a deployment will rise? Additionally, some may object to our previous requirement that a military response occur within thirty days of an opportunity—after all, might not genuine responses come after longer periods? And why don't we distinguish between those responses that occur one day after an opportunity from those that occur twenty-nine days after? To address these questions and concerns, we introduce a new class of models that explicitly accounts for the timing of military deployments. These event history models, as they are commonly called, were originally created to deal with studies of epidemiology and demography, where concerns often center on how long a person lives, is sick, married, unemployed, or goes through other changes in life status. For our purposes, these models facilitate studies of the time it takes for a president to respond militarily to the opportunities identified in our dataset.

Event history models offer two advantages, which make the results that follow our preferred estimates of Congress's impact on presidential responses to foreign crises. For starters, these models effectively deal with a phenomenon that econometricians refer to as "right-censoring."[52] Just because an individual does not marry or become unemployed during the period when an investigator tracks a population does not mean that she never does so. The trouble is that one cannot differentiate those who remain single or employed for life from those who become married or unemployed just after a study ends. Similarly, in our study we cannot distinguish those opportunities that never received a military response from those that received one at some date after December 31, 2000, when our study terminates, and without this information, the appropriate interpretation of our estimated effects of congressional support on deployment decisions may be unduly restrictive.[53]

In addition, event history models do not establish strict (some would say arbitrary) time windows during which military responses can occur.

Rather than calling an intervention that occurs in twenty, thirty, or forty days of an opportunity a response, we simply identify the most proximate opportunity prior to a use of force. To get a sense of this approach, imagine the chronology of a single country—say, Lebanon. As the time line starts and moves forward, opportunities begin to mount. In our example, as the civil war begins in 1958, more and more opportunities appear, each of which are coded and included in the dataset. Finally, in mid 1958, an opportunity appears and the United States intervenes. In our data, this final opportunity denotes the end of the period of nonintervention—what econometricians refer to as a "spell."[54] These models account for not only the characteristics of this final "triggering" event, but all of the opportunities that preceded it as well.[55]

In our model, the dependent variable counts the number of days between the first observed opportunity and an intervention. Thus, in the case of Lebanon, our dependent variable increases as time elapses from the first opportunity, recorded on May 29, 1945, through July 15, 1958, when U.S. troops were sent into the region. Once a deployment occurs, the counter begins anew with the emergence of another opportunity (in the case of Lebanon, on December 1, 1962) until another intervention occurs (on March 22, 1976).[56] Although some may object that our setup allows responses to events that are too temporally distant, this approach makes the minimal number of assumptions with the data. The alternative would be to organize events in discrete crises and determine responses to those. Yet, this would create more questions than it would answer: are events over long periods always independent? When do new "crises" begin and old ones end? By making a minimal number of assumptions about the data, we can be more confident that our results are not an artifact of ad hoc coding decisions.[55a]

How do we deal with those opportunities that, as of December 31, 2000, do not elicit a response? Herein lies the right-censoring problem we previously discussed. The model still uses the information found in these opportunities, but it recognizes them as being censored. In these cases, the counter simply stops at the end of the time series, but the spell is never coded as "finished," as it would be if an intervention had occurred.

We expect that spells will last longer when presidents face a hostile Congress, as the uncertainties of war and prospect of failure weigh more heavily on the chief executive. In these instances, presidents may wait until more opportunities arise, allowing a crisis to intensify and support within Congress to grow; alternatively, they may directly lobby Congress and attempt to build public support for a mission. Either way, deployments are delayed, spells are lengthened. On the other hand, if the president knows his support in Congress is strong to begin with, he will tend to use force more quickly. With copartisans firmly in control on Capitol

Hill, the president has less reason to fear a legislative backlash should a mission go astray and hence has greater cause to address immediately the perceived exigencies of a foreign crisis.

Other factors obviously influence how long it takes the United States to respond to an opportunity. We therefore include in the statistical models all of the independent variables from the initial analysis in this chapter.[57] Background factors such as the state of the U.S. economy could clearly play into the calculus of whether to respond to a crisis now, or wait until the crisis escalates or until unemployment and inflationary trends shift. Strong economic relationships with potential target states ought to raise the stakes of force, though they also yield other forms of leverage besides force, such as economic sanctions. Similarly, variables such as *Soviet Involvement, Troops Deployed,* and *Capability Ratio* could influence the timing of deployments inasmuch as they alter the military preparations required to use force.

In the dataset, each opportunity constitutes a single observation.[58] A counter that identifies the time elapsed since the first opportunity, resetting with each use of force, serves as the dependent variable. As before, we consider every opportunity to arise when there was not an ongoing major or minor use of force within a targeted nation. The interpretation of the estimated coefficients from event-history models, we note, differs from those of previous models. Here, the estimated coefficients reflect the impact of changes in our independent variables on the "hazard rate," the probability that a spell terminates at a certain moment in time, given that it has not already terminated. A positive coefficient suggests shorter times to intervention, while a negative coefficient suggests delays.

Table 4.4 presents the results. The first thing to notice is that now all three indicators of congressional support powerfully predict use-of-force decisions, in this instance the timing of military responses to opportunities. The estimated effects for *Percent President Party, President Party Power,* and *Unified Government* all suggest that presidents deploy troops abroad sooner when their party holds a larger share of seats within Congress. Moving from one standard deviation below to one standard deviation above the mean of each of the first two variables, and from zero to one on the third, while holding all other continuous variables at their means and discrete variables at their modes, decreases the expected response time by as much as 55 percent.[59] These results, we believe, constitute one of this book's most important findings. Using the most flexible statistical models available and taking advantage of the greatest information about both the opportunities and the major and minor deployments, for the first time we have solid grounds on which to conclude that congressional support for the president increases not only the likelihood of responses to foreign crises but also influences their timing.

TABLE 4.4
Timing of a Military Response, Including Background Controls

	(1)		(2)		(3)	
Congressional Support						
Unified Government	0.63**	[0.31]	—		—	
Percent President Party	—		4.13**	[1.94]	—	
President Party Power	—		—		3.12**	[1.19]
Standard Background Controls						
Unemployment	0.13**	[0.07]	0.12**	[0.06]	0.12**	[0.07]
CPI	−0.02	[0.01]	−0.01	[0.01]	−0.01	[0.01]
Public Approval	−0.01*	[0.01]	−0.01**	[0.01]	−0.01**	[0.01]
Election Year	0.42***	[0.19]	0.51***	[0.19]	0.51***	[0.19]
Hegemony	−6.44	[6.26]	−6.50	[6.52]	−7.74	[6.40]
World Disputes	−0.04*	[0.03]	−0.05**	[0.03]	−0.05**	[0.03]
Targeted Nation						
Major Power	0.25	[0.29]	0.28	[0.29]	0.28	[0.29]
Democracy	−0.50**	[0.24]	−0.50**	[0.23]	−0.49**	[0.23]
U.S. Relations with Targeted Nation						
Alliances	−0.32**	[0.15]	−0.31**	[0.15]	−0.32**	[0.15]
Trade (billions)	−0.12***	[0.04]	−0.12***	[0.04]	−0.12***	[0.04]
Soviet Involvement	−0.31*	[0.22]	−0.30*	[0.22]	−0.31*	[0.22]
Capability Ratio (log)	−0.24**	[0.07]	−0.24**	[0.07]	−0.24**	[0.07]
Prior, Ongoing Opportunities and Commitments						
Prev. Opportunities	0.07***	[0.01]	0.07***	[0.01]	0.07***	[0.01]
Contemp. Opportunities	0.04	[0.11]	0.03	[0.11]	0.03	[0.11]
Troops Deployed (log)	0.04	[0.03]	0.04	[0.03]	0.04	[0.03]
Regional Fixed Effects						
North, Central America	1.67***	[0.30]	1.67***	[0.30]	1.69***	[0.30]
South America	0.16	[0.36]	0.18	[0.36]	0.20	[0.36]
Middle East	1.09***	[0.26]	1.09***	[0.26]	1.10***	[0.26]
Asia, Pacific	0.56**	[0.30]	0.56**	[0.30]	0.57**	[0.30]
Western Europe	0.58	[0.46]	0.58	[0.46]	0.59	[0.46]
Eastern Europe	0.24	[0.36]	0.25	[0.36]	0.25	[0.36]
Constant	−3.08*	[2.18]	−4.75**	[2.27]	−2.44**	[2.27]
(N)	11,101		11,101		11,101	

Event history models that assume a Weibull hazard function estimated. Daily opportunities analyzed for all uses of force and all countries from 1945 to 2000. (For the sake of these analyses, Yugoslavia/ Serbia and Croatia are treated as separate countries.) *** = $p < 0.01$; ** = $p < 0.05$; * = $p < 0.10$; one-tailed tests. Huber/White/sandwich clustered standard errors on country-president combinations reported in brackets. Though not reported, models also contain fixed effect terms for each presidential administration. For regional fixed effects, Africa is the reference category. Cox models, models that include only those countries with substantial numbers of opportunities, and models that include only those countries for which at least one deployment was observed during the time period generate comparable results.

The estimates associated with some of our control variables differ markedly from those previously observed.[60] Strikingly, *Public Approval* is now highly significant and negative, suggesting that higher approval ratings lead to *longer* response times. It is odd that congressional support would hasten a military response, while public support would appear to delay it. The finding, though, is consonant with claims about diversionary war—that is, that heads of states occasionally use military force in order to mute public criticisms about domestic problems.[61] Here, we find that presidents resort to the sword more quickly when their approval ratings decline.[62]

Additionally, we find that *Unemployment, Election Year,* and *World Disputes* all significantly influence the timing of responses. Presidents appear much quicker on the draw when unemployment figures mount and when they, or their successors, are facing an election; presidents tend to stall when other world events compete for their attention. Though *Major Power* continues to register null results, *Democracy* now appears as a powerful predictor in these event history models. Presidents, we find, take considerably longer when responding militarily to opportunities in democracies than to those in nondemocracies. Drawing on the logic of the democratic peace, this result makes sense, as democracies are more likely to resolve their conflicts through peaceful methods.

When estimating the probability of a military deployment, only one of the variables that characterize relations between the United States and a targeted nation was statistically significant. Here, however, all four are. Higher values of *Alliances, Trade, Soviet Involvement,* and *Capability Ratio* all extend the response time of presidents to observed foreign crises. States with more alliances with the United States draw longer response times, perhaps because decisions to use force against an ally prompt added deliberations both within the United States and between the United States and the targeted nation. Presidents also tend to delay military action against nations with whom the United States regularly trades, who are allies to the Soviet Union, and who have relatively weak militaries. Most of these estimates accord with existing literatures arguing that economic interdependence and balance-of-power calculations retard the use of force.[63]

In comparison with our earlier findings, slightly fewer contextual variables now seem to affect presidential decisions involving the use of force. The positive and statistically significant estimate of *Previous Opportunities* suggests that as opportunities pile up within a given country, the United States responds more quickly. We no longer find, however, that either the number of contemporary opportunities occurring in other nations or the numbers of troops stationed in a targeted nation affect the timing of a military deployment. As before, though, we do find that presidents respond significantly faster to crises brewing in the Middle East and North and Central America than in Africa, the reference category among the regional fixed effects.

The International System

All of the models thus far have estimated the impact of congressional support on the probability of a military response to observed foreign crises, conditional on a wide range of background controls. The "international system" hypothesis, however, predicts that the impacts of congressional support will vary for different kinds of crises, involving different types of nations in different regions of the globe. More specifically, it suggests that interbranch dynamics will matter most when opportunities involve nations with which the United States does not have strong political or economic ties. When formal alliances, international treaties, or strong economic relations bind the United States to another country, the dictates of international commitments may ultimately determine whether or not a military deployment materializes—and in these instances, the partisan composition of Congress (as well as other domestic factors) may not figure into presidential decision making as much.

We therefore estimate event history models on subsamples of the data: U.S. allies versus nonallies; Soviet allies versus nonallies; and high versus low trade. The results, shown in table 4.5, are consistent with the international system hypothesis. Partisan effects are concentrated among nations that are not allies with the United States or the Soviet Union, and that maintain relatively low levels of trade with the United States. When crises involve nations with whom the United States regularly trades or who are allies of either the United States or the Soviet Union, the timing of the response is more likely to depend on the terms of the alliances themselves, other alliance partners in an international organization, or other geostrategic and economic considerations. Domestic politics, in these instances, are pushed to the margins of presidential decision making. For nonallied and low-trade states, such factors are absent, allowing domestic politics to play a more dominant role. Thus, it is not only the case that there is an overall difference between response times to crises involving allies and to those involving nonallies, but that the impact of domestic political alignment on response times also depends on U.S. and Soviet relations with the targeted country.

Model Extensions

In chapter 3, we did not find any evidence that the War Powers Resolution materially augmented Congress's influence over the regularity with

TABLE 4.5
Timing of a Military Response for Selected Subsamples of Countries

	Regression Estimates				
	Percent President Party		Constant		(N)
Sub-samples of Countries:					
Allies with United States	−4.39	[4.43]	−3.94	[4.42]	2,920
Non-Allies	7.04***	[2.72]	−7.07***	[2.84]	6,678
Allies with Soviet Union	−4.96	[12.08]	−34.75*	[26.02]	1,305
Non-Allies	3.49**	[2.10]	−3.17	[2.55]	8,293
High Trade with U.S.	3.50	[3.44]	6.31	[4.89]	4,774
Low Trade with U.S.	5.13**	[2.94]	−5.71**	[3.21]	4,824

Event history models that assume a Weibull hazard function estimated. Daily opportunities analyzed for all uses of force and all countries from 1945 to 2000. (For the sake of these analyses, Yugoslavia/Serbia and Croatia are treated as separate countries.) *** = p < 0.01; ** = p < 0.05; * = p < 0.10; one-tailed tests. Huber/White/sandwich clustered standard errors on country-president combinations reported in brackets. "Allies to Soviet Union" includes the Soviet Union. Though not reported, models also contain all background controls included in models in table 4.4. Models that substitute *Unified Government* or *President Party Power* for *Percent President Party* generate comparable results. Additionally, Cox models, models that include only those countries with substantial numbers of opportunities, and models that include only those countries for which at least one deployment was observed during the time period generate comparable results.

which troops are deployed abroad. We now consider the possibility that the resolution might have enhanced Congress's influence over the timing of troop deployments—a distinct possibility, given the dictates of the resolution itself. To do so, we add to the fully specified event-history models an indicator variable for the period following the resolution's enactment and an interaction term between this indicator variable and each measure of congressional support. If the War Powers Resolution convinced presidents to suddenly pay attention to the partisan composition of Congress, then the main effects of congressional support should shrink, while the estimated effects of the interaction term should be large and statistically significant.

Table 4.6 presents the results. The models, plainly, do not perform especially well. In only one of the models is the interaction term statistically significant, and then only barely so. Additionally, though the estimated main effects for the three measures of congressional support remain positive in every model, they are now statistically significant in only one. In two of the models, we do find significant effects associated with the post–War Powers Resolution period. Curiously, though, they suggest that

Table 4.6
Timing of a Military Response, with Period Effects

	(1)		(2)		(3)	
Congressional Support						
Unified Government	0.30	[0.34]	—		—	
Percent President Party	—		2.74	[2.57]	—	
President Party Power	—		—		2.26*	[1.60]
Post-War Powers Resolution	1.15*	[0.75]	−0.21	[1.66]	1.25*	[0.81]
CongressSupport × Post-WPR	0.85*	[0.65]	2.99	[3.52]	1.77	[2.19]
Constant	−3.79*	[2.32]	−4.81**	[2.25]	−3.23*	[2.48]
(N)	11,101		11,101		11,101	

Event history models that assume a Weibull hazard function estimated. Daily opportunities analyzed for all uses of force and all countries from 1945 to 2000. (For the sake of these analyses, Yugoslavia/ Serbia and Croatia are treated as separate countries.) *** = p < 0.01; ** = p < 0.05; * = p < 0.10; one-tailed tests. Huber/White/sandwich clustered standard errors on country-president combinations reported in brackets. Though not reported, models also contain all background controls included in models in table 4.4. Cox models, models that include only those countries with substantial numbers of opportunities, and models that include only those countries for which at least one deployment was observed during the time period generate comparable results.

presidents tend to respond more quickly, not more slowly, to foreign crises following the resolution's enactment. On the whole, then, we conclude that there is not much evidence that the relevance of Congress's partisan composition is confined to either the period following or preceding the enactment of the War Powers Resolution.

We also revisited Gelpi and Feaver's suggestion that veterans within Congress critically affect presidential use-of-force decisions. Table 4.7 presents the results of the same fully specified event-history models, except that now they also account for the percentage of veterans in Congress. The original estimates associated with the partisan composition of Congress appear unaffected by the inclusion of this additional covariate. All three estimates for *Unified Government, Percent President Part,* and *President Party Power* are positive and statistically significant. As we observed in chapter 3, however, these models do not provide any support for Gelpi and Feaver's claims. None of the estimates associated with veterans even approaches standard thresholds of statistical significance. Moreover, other unreported models that substitute veteran-based measures of Congress for partisan-based measures also reveal null effects. We find no evidence that the number of veterans within the House or Senate correlates with the timing of military responses to foreign crises.

TABLE 4.7
Timing of a Military Response, Congressional Parties and Veterans

	(1)		(2)		(3)	
Congressional Support						
Unified Government	0.67**	[0.35]	—		—	
Percent President Party	—		4.23**	[2.05]	—	
President Party Power	—		—		3.26**	[1.27]
Percent Veteran	−1.89	[5.91]	−1.22	[5.61]	−2.39	[5.69]
Constant	−1.88	[4.47]	−4.04	[3.92]	−0.94	[4.31]
(N)	11,101		11,101		11,101	

Event history models that assume a Weibull hazard function estimated. Daily opportunities analyzed for all uses of force and all countries from 1945 to 2000. (For the sake of these analyses, Yugoslavia/Serbia and Croatia are treated as separate countries.) *** = p < 0.01; ** = p < 0.05; * = p < 0.10; one-tailed tests. Huber/White/sandwich clustered standard errors on country-president combinations reported in brackets. Though not reported, models also contain all background controls included in models in table 4.4. Cox models, models that include only those countries with substantial numbers of opportunities, and models that include only those countries for which at least one deployment was observed during the time period generate comparable results.

Finally, we reconsidered possible differences between Republican and Democratic presidents, this time focusing both on the average length of time that elapsed between a use of force and a military deployment, and on the possibility that presidents from one party were more disposed to respond militarily to certain kinds of crises than to others. For the most part, the differences observed were underwhelming. A t-test comparing the mean length of time taken to respond to an opportunity by Democratic and Republican presidents suggests no meaningful difference. A similar t-test comparing the length of time taken to respond to a precipitating opportunity yields an identical result—no substantial differences exist between Republican and Democratic presidents in the timing of their responses.[64] Finally, adding an indicator variable for Republican presidents to our initial model of the timing of deployments yields no differences in our initial estimates. The indicator variable itself, moreover, is not statistically significant.

SUMMARIZING THE EVIDENCE

This chapter addressed three interrelated questions concerning legislative-executive relations and the use of force. First, we asked whether the partisan composition of Congress influenced presidents' decisions to deploy troops, given an opportunity to do so. Second, we examined whether other nations engaged in strategic avoidance behavior. And third, we asked whether partisan politics affected the timing of deployments.

To generate answers, we created a new dataset of "opportunities" to use force abroad. Based on the content of the *New York Times*, this database allowed us to identify the "dogs that didn't bark" and to see how they differed from those that did. When estimating the models that predicted the probability that presidents deployed troops abroad in the aftermath of an observed foreign crisis, we found substantial, albeit not uniform, evidence in support of the "Congress's Composition" hypothesis. We also exposed these models to numerous respecifications and found the results to be quite robust.

By slightly reconfiguring the opportunities dataset, we explored the possibility that strategic avoidance behavior on the part of foreign states yields a selected sample of opportunities. Our findings, for the most part, suggested that it does not. We found that the processes that lead to the production of opportunities and the military responses of presidents appear to be independent of one another. Still, when estimating models of presidential decision making that accounted for strategic avoidance behavior, we again found statistically significant and substantively large effects generated by two of three measures of congressional support.

We also examined the timing of troop deployments. In addition to addressing a substantively new question, event-history models have a number of attractive statistical properties, such as added flexibility and the capacity to deal with censoring issues, that standard models lack. We found, once again, evidence of the importance of partisan politics. The models demonstrate that higher levels of opposition within Congress contribute to longer periods of time between the emergence of an opportunity and the deployment of troops to a targeted country. These findings, too, were quite robust to alternative specifications.

Finally, this chapter presents new evidence in support of the "International System" hypothesis, which underscores the influence of realpolitik considerations on presidential use-of-force decisions. Consistently, we find that presidents take longer to respond militarily to foreign crises that involve allies of either the United States or the Soviet Union and nations with high levels of trade with the United States. Additionally, the influence of domestic political considerations appears to be conditional on these structural variables. Where international alliances and economic considerations predominate, the relevance of domestic politics wanes; but where international obligations and geostrategic considerations abate, the partisan composition of Congress (and the implications this has for the institution's expected behavior should a deployment go awry) weighs more heavily in presidential decision making.

While the data from chapters 3 and 4 lend strong support to our key conjectures concerning partisan politics and the international system, quantitative studies obviously omit important details of particular instances and causal processes. Chapter 5 examines a handful of illustrative case studies to trace some of these dynamics of congressional involvement, presidential anticipation of that involvement, and in two cases, acquiescence on the part of Congress to presidential plans to use force. While the cases are not meant to be definitive tests, they do illustrate some of the underlying processes implied by our quantitative tests; additionally, they illustrate the importance of the media and public opinion to congressional efforts to influence presidential decision making, themes that stand front and center in the book's last section.

CHAPTER 5

Studies in Domestic Politics and the Use of Force

THE LAST TWO CHAPTERS culled large datasets to test variations of three hypotheses about congressional influence over military deployments. This one takes a decidedly different tack. Rather than trace the quarterly frequency with which presidents exercise military force or the changing probabilities that they respond militarily to different crises, and rather than focus exclusively on the hypotheses relating to "Congress's composition," "deployment's size," or "international system," this chapter takes a more expansive view of the domestic politics that informed some of the more important presidential decisions in the modern era about whether to go to war.

We have chosen six major opportunities that arose during the last half-century and have traced each one through the congressional debate and legislative activity that influenced, in varying degrees, the president's ultimate decision about whether to use military force. The case studies include Indochina (1954), Nicaragua (1981–99), Lebanon (1982–84), Panama (1989), Bosnia (1992–94), and Kosovo (1998–99). Collectively, they serve three overarching purposes. First, the case studies illustrate some of the ways in which presidents adjust plans for war to accord with congressional preferences and prerogatives—either by changing when (or if) they send troops abroad, the terms under which they do so, and the scope and duration of the actual deployment. In some of the studies, such as Indochina in the 1950s and Nicaragua in the 1980s, congressional opposition contributed to presidential decisions to withhold troops. In others, such as Bosnia in the 1990s, congressional opposition effectively delayed the initiation of a military campaign. And in others, such as Lebanon in the 1980s and Kosovo in the 1990s, developments abroad effectively muted congressional opposition during the lead-up to a military campaign—though in Lebanon, when the costs of war surfaced, members of Congress steadily voiced their objections and eventually forced Reagan to abandon the fight long before he would have preferred.

Second, the case studies reveal some of the mechanisms—appropriations, legislation, hearings, or public appeals—through which Congress influences presidential decision making. In most of the studies, presidents heeded warnings and doubts that members of Congress expressed through informal channels of communication. And in these instances, presidents either scaled back a military venture or relinquished it altogether, thereby obviating the need for Congress to formulate and then enact restrictive appropriations or legislation. In at least one case study considered below, however, members of Congress confronted an especially recalcitrant president, and it was not until Congress passed a string of resolutions and appropriations calling for the campaign's deescalation that the president finally relented.

Finally, these studies speak to the main assumptions that inform our analysis. They illustrate how presidents anticipate the likelihood of a mission's failure, and of subsequent congressional dissidence, before committing to a military use of force. And they show that when the costs of war materialize, members of the opposition party within Congress are among the first to criticize the president. In virtually every case study considered below, partisan divisions run deep. Though Republican (Democratic) members occasionally criticize Republican (Democratic) presidents, the main fault lines split the two parties. And perhaps most important, the case studies illustrate how the logic of anticipated reaction operates in the real world—that is, how presidents incorporate into today's decisions expectations about how Congress, as well as the American public, the military, and international allies and adversaries alike, will behave tomorrow. The domestic politics of war are profoundly dynamic and interactive. Efforts to isolate Congress's influence from all of the other competing considerations descending on the president will succeed if, and only if, scholars repeatedly ask themselves the following question: How would the president have behaved differently in this moment if he knew that Congress would support (or oppose) him in the next?

We make no pretense that these case studies are indicative of the universe of use-of-force decisions. Having oversampled decisions about major uses of force in countries that are less strategically important, we may have selected cases that overstate Congress's influence. But because we deliberately chose examples that ran counter to our suppositions about the restraining influence of Congress and the importance of interparty divisions over troop deployments, we also may have selected cases that understate the predictive power of our own theory. Though not a hard test of our primary theoretical expectations, these studies do illustrate some of the manifestations of congressional influence, achieved through different courses of action, witnessed in the last half century. And for those readers hungry for some historical facts to hang on either the regression coefficients or error terms found in previous chapters, your appetites are here indulged.

INDOCHINA, 1954

For most Americans, the Vietnam War conjures up images of jungle battlegrounds, domestic protests, Cold War activism, and the social upheavals of the 1960s and 1970s. The war and the protests it sparked, however, need not have played out as they did. Had the Eisenhower administration made a different set of decisions in the early and mid 1950s, the Vietnam War might well have been the Indochina War, and the enemy the United States confronted might not have been able to claim the evictions of two world powers from its domain. Indeed, we focus on an early episode in Vietnam suggesting the eventual deployment of a half-million American troops was not inevitable. Though foreign states and members of his own cabinet pressed for U.S. intervention in 1954 to prevent the fall of Dien Bien Phu, Eisenhower opted to keep his own troops at home. Congress, it turns out, was an important reason why.

It is worth recalling that in the aftermath of World War II, Harry Truman jettisoned Roosevelt's plans to recognize Indochina's independence. To garner the goodwill of his European ally and secure its cooperation in a North Atlantic defense community against the Soviets, Truman openly supported France's continued occupation of Indochina. When the Vietminh battled French Union forces during the late 1940s and early 1950s, Truman lent extensive financial support, running in the hundreds of millions of dollars per year. The 1952 election ushered in a new president from a new party, but it did not signify a serious challenge to these international commitments. Although the Korean War had temporarily interrupted the flow of aid, the war's end prompted Eisenhower to increase U.S. support to the French by fully $785 million.[1]

All of this aid could not secure France's occupation of Indochina. The French had done little to ingratiate themselves with the native population of Indochina, and French forces, rather than indigenous Vietnamese, were left to do the bulk of the fighting against the Vietminh. In 1954, France concentrated its military forces at Dien Bien Phu, which French General Navarre referred to as "a veritable jungle Verdun." There the Vietminh would launch their most intense military assault on the occupying French forces. Although the French outwardly expressed confidence in their chances on the battlefield, their nation's General Paul Ely placed the odds of victory at "about 50-50."[2] Such estimates, not to mention the ferocious battle that would later ensue, forced the Eisenhower administration to reconsider its dealings in the region. How would the United States keep Indochina out of Communist hands? Should the nation aid the French directly at Dien Bien Phu? And if so, should American forces be involved?

Answers to such questions needed to be delivered rather quickly. In January 1954, on the eve of the battle at Dien Bien Phu, the French requested of the United States fifty-four B-26 bombers and four hundred technicians to service the planes. After consulting with his "Special Committee on Indochina," Eisenhower decided to furnish all the planes and two hundred technicians, with the proviso that personnel be stationed at air bases where there was no risk of capture.[3]

Once the public caught wind of the deal, congressional reaction was quick and furious. Senator John C. Stennis (D-MS) "criticized the deal as a dangerous move that might lead to direct intervention." Senator Richard B. Russell (D-GA) "called the mission a 'mistake' likely to lead the United States into piecemeal participation in the war." Senator Walter F. George (D-GA) expected that "only one thing would bring China in, in force. That is if we sent any sizable number of men over there. That would bring on real trouble." And Senator George D. Aiken (R-VT) "complained that the Administration had not advised the Foreign Relations Committee, of which he [was] a member, that the additional air technicians were being sent."[4]

Congressional objections were not altogether surprising. Strong isolationist tendencies remained within the Republican Party,[5] and copartisans within Congress were in short supply. Eisenhower possessed just an eleven-vote majority in the House and, soon into his term, a minority in the Senate, as Senator Taft died and was replaced by a Democrat. "With such a line-up on Capitol Hill," Eisenhower recognized, "I knew from the beginning that noisy, strong-armed tactics would accomplish nothing, even were I so inclined."[6]

With Congress poised to formally rebuke the president, Eisenhower promised to withdraw the technicians by mid summer (June 15), and to replace them, if need be, with civilian contractors. Eisenhower then spent the next two weeks meeting with congressional leaders and issuing statements at press conferences promising to proceed cautiously in Indochina. Perhaps more important, Eisenhower never again took action on Indochina without first consulting with his Republican allies in Congress. Melanie Billings-Yun identifies this backlash as a turning point in the president's thinking about Indochina: "If the legislature raised such fearsome objections to dispatching a couple of hundred mechanics to relative low-risk areas in Indochina, it certainly would not sit passively while the president ordered bombing strikes or otherwise intervened in the war. Eisenhower's instinct was to steer clear of French Indochina. The hackles raised in Congress and the press by the mechanics deal reaffirmed his belief that Vietnam could not be won for the price Americans were willing to pay."[7] Though Congress reacted after the fact to the air technicians deal, it needed to do so only once to convey its views on the matter. Thereafter, no funding cutoffs, investigations, or other legislative threats were needed to keep the president in check.

In the months that followed, Eisenhower continually emphasized the importance of consulting with Congress before making any decision on Indochina. At a March 10 news conference he announced, "There is going to be no involvement of America in war unless it is a result of the constitutional process that is placed upon Congress to declare it. Now, let us have that clear. And that is the answer."[8] At another press conference held less than a month later, the president again paid homage to Congress. When asked whether "as a last resort" he would be willing to exercise military force in Indochina, Eisenhower responded, "Again you are bringing up questions that I have explained in a very definite sense several times this morning. I am not saying what we are prepared to do because there is a Congress, and there are a number of our friends all over this world that are vitally engaged. I know what my own convictions on this matter are; but until the thing has been settled and properly worked out with the people who also bear responsibilities, I cannot afford to be airing them everywhere, because it sort of stultifies negotiation which is often necessary."[9]

At the end of March, Secretary of State John Foster Dulles left for the Geneva Conference, joining representatives from France, China, Russia, and Great Britain to discuss how best to deal with the mounting crisis in Indochina. A *New York Times* editorial then noted, "No Secretary of State in recent memory, not even Dean Acheson in the Truman Administration, undertook a foreign mission with a colder background of congressional nonsupport than will chill John Foster Dulles as he sets off for Geneva."[10] The editorial continued, "It is, therefore, inescapable, in the present atmosphere and in all the circumstances, that the Secretary at Geneva will be under the greatest restraints and sharpest caveats, implied and even at some points explicit, from the practical politicians of his party." While the Geneva Conference proceeded, and as the French position deteriorated at Dien Bien Phu, Congress refused to provide either Dulles or Eisenhower the bargaining leverage needed to assure the international community of the United States' resolve. Dulles had proposed (and in fact drafted) a congressional resolution authorizing the use of force by the navy and air force should the president deem it necessary. Dulles and Secretary of Defense Charles Wilson hoped that the resolution, if passed, would "fill our hand" in negotiations with U.S. allies, and in turn would signal to the world the nation's commitment to the region. Eisenhower, however, did not allow Dulles to even circulate the draft resolution among Republican leaders.

Not until April 3 would Dulles brief congressional leaders on the administration's plans should Dien Bien Phu fall. The meeting, not surprisingly, sparked heated exchange. Dulles's own notes relay the key points of contention: "The Secretary then said that he felt that the president should have congressional backing so that he could use air and sea power in the area if he felt it necessary in the interest of national security. Senator Knowland (R-CA) expressed concurrence but further discussion developed a unanimous reaction of the Members of Congress that there should be no congressional action until the Secretary had obtained commitments of a political and material nature from our allies. The feeling was unanimous that 'we want no more Koreas with the United States furnishing 90 percent of the manpower.'"[11] Congressional leaders then asserted three conditions necessary for their support of U.S. involvement in Indochina: (1) formation of an allied 'coalition'-type force; (2) a French declaration indicating an intent to accelerate independence for the Associated States, which consisted of what would become Laos, Cambodia, North Vietnam, and South Vietnam; and (3) French agreement to continue the Expeditionary Corps in Indochina. Reflecting on this period nearly two decades later, the House Armed Services Committee Report would note, "Thus Congressional opposition put the brake on a possible unilateral U.S. intervention."[12]

After meeting with Secretary Dulles and Chairman of the Joint Chiefs Admiral Arthur Radford, Eisenhower responded to congressional demands with a slightly revised set of conditions under which U.S. military involvement in Indochina would be appropriate. The conditions were "(1) formation of a coalition force with U.S. allies to pursue 'united action'; (2) declaration of French intent to accelerate independence of Associated States; (3) congressional approval of U.S. involvement (which was thought to be dependent upon (1) and (2))."[13] Eisenhower dared not press further, for as he would later admit in his memoirs, "There was nothing in these preconditions or in the congressional viewpoint with which I could disagree."[14]

While facing on Capitol Hill staunch opposition to the use of force, within his own cabinet Eisenhower found support. The president and Army Chief of Staff Matthew Ridgeway were, in fact, the only high-ranking administration officials who consistently appeared hesitant to support unilateral U.S. intervention into Indochina. The Dulles brothers Allen and John, Vice President Nixon, and Harold Stassen (Eisenhower's foreign operations director) all insisted that some military action should be taken if Dien Bien Phu fell, if only to demonstrate to the Chinese that the United States was willing to pay some price to contain the expansion of communism. According to Billings-Yun, Eisenhower often stood as the lone member of the National Security Council (NSC) to take a more measured stance.[15] In an April 6 NSC meeting, Nixon advocated that the president explain to the American people the strategic importance of Indochina, with the hopes that he might garner the public, and eventually the congressional, support needed to launch a U.S. intervention. In response, Eisenhower reiterated the conditions he had developed with Congress, and shortly thereafter Nixon relented. Indeed, during this period congressional opposition proved to be a mainstay of cabinet deliberations on Indochina.

Had Eisenhower thought Congress unimportant, the cabinet might well have pressured the president to capitulate; instead, Eisenhower recognized Congress as an important debating point. His continual reference to the three "conditions" for military action, including strong congressional support, suggests he anticipated, and heeded, the possibility of either a legislative or public backlash in the aftermath of a military deployment. Indeed, were congressional threats not credible, if Eisenhower used Congress as nothing more than a convenient foil, then presumably the cacophony of voices within his administration favoring involvement in that region would have prevailed. Eisenhower's adoption of Congress's conditions would not then have been a showstopper.

A speech Nixon gave in late April 1954 affirmed Eisenhower's belief that unilateral military action was politically impossible. In his remarks, Nixon suggested that in the case of French withdrawal, the United States would need to send ground troops to China. The *New York Times* then proclaimed, "Among the editors who heard the speech, the consensus was that Mr. Nixon was testing the reaction of the public and Congress."[16] The speech set off a firestorm in Congress: "White House Chief of Staff Sherman Adams records that Nixon was 'mortified' by the overwhelmingly negative reaction to his speech in the world press and, especially, in Congress. Even his usual ally, Senator Knowland, joined the opposition. The majority leader articulated a Senate demand that Eisenhower come to Capitol Hill to make a full revelation of his secret plans for invading Indochina."[17]

All the while, the Vietminh continued their assault on Dien Bien Phu. Though the Vietminh suffered considerable casualties between March 13 and late April, France's military legion steadily lost its grip on the region. As a last ditch effort to rally behind the French, the NSC assembled on April 29 to consider its options. At the meeting, Stassen was the clear holdout, continually pushing the president to consider direct intervention to support the French. But Eisenhower ended the discussion by "asking his advisers whether they wanted to bear the burden of starting World War III—and whether they believed the legislature would want to bear it."[18] Nixon followed with a final plea for an air assault to assist the French, which the president rebuffed, stating flatly that he would have to take the issue before Congress and that he lacked assurances, in any case, that the French were even willing to stay in Indochina. After the public controversy over the allotment of technicians to Indochina, Eisenhower recognized, at every step, Congress's proper authority on matters involving war.

Of course, it is possible that Eisenhower never wanted to intervene in Indochina, making congressional opposition nothing more than a convenient excuse for withdrawing U.S. support. This claim, however, seems unlikely. While it is true that on the heels of the Korean War Eisenhower remained skeptical of unilateral U.S. intervention into Indochina, a least three pieces of evidence suggest that Congress wielded independent influence. First, as we previously argued, congressional opposition to the provision of air technicians forced Eisenhower to backtrack quickly from a more supportive stance, while also shaping the president's views about what kinds of aid to the French, if any, would be possible. Second, congressional unease about another military engagement in Southeast Asia tempered the powerful arguments advanced by the more hawkish members of Eisenhower's advisory team. Finally, the steadfastness of Congress eventually persuaded Dulles, Nixon, and to a lesser extent Radford that a unilateral intervention to save the French at Dien Bien Phu simply was untenable.

NICARAGUA, 1981–88

Congressional influence over U.S. foreign policy was on full display in the 1980s on the issue of Nicaragua. Democrats were steadfastly opposed to the president's preferred policy, heavily involved in deliberations concerning the region, and held the administration under continuous scrutiny—through hearings, investigations, and floor debates, all of which received extensive media coverage. Congressional influence over presidential decision making, in this instance, appears profound.

In 1979, rebel forces known by their Spanish acronym FSLN, the Sandinista National Liberation Front, overthrew the Nicaraguan dictatorship of Antonio Somoza Debayle. Though Carter had cut assistance to the Somoza regime because of human rights violations, no one within the administration heralded the rise of the Sandinistas, who maintained close ties to Cuba and the Soviet Union. When Ronald Reagan swept to power in 1980, he made supporting an emerging army of anti-Sandinista forces known as the *contrarevolucionarios,* or the *contras,* a key point of his presidency.

Reagan portrayed the Nicaraguan conflict as only one front of a larger effort to contain Soviet expansion, especially into neighboring El Salvador. According to administration officials, the El Salvador civil war constituted "a textbook case of indirect armed aggression by Communist powers."[19] As Reagan focused renewed attention on Central America, he had reason to believe that his newfound majority in the Senate and a sympathetic ear in the House might usher in significant changes in U.S. foreign policy. House Majority Leader Jim Wright (D-TX) noted that "Central America is probably more vitally important to us than any other part of the world. Our response . . . requires a bipartisan, unified approach."[20]

In the months and years that followed, however, partisan wrangling and accusations of malfeasance would quash any goodwill that characterized Reagan's first weeks in office.

Clashes between the president and Congress soon erupted. In March 1981, Reagan announced a new military aid package for El Salvador, including the deployment of U.S. military trainers. This move alarmed members of Congress, as it invited obvious comparisons to the early stages of the Vietnam War, when Kennedy and Johnson had sent U.S. advisors to train the South Vietnamese Army. Although members of Congress did not limit the amount of funds sent to El Salvador, they did restrict how the funds could be spent.[21] According to State Department official Luigi Einaudi, Congress's involvement at this juncture shaped the path of policy toward the region by shifting power *within* the Reagan administration. Einaudi noted that a debate raged between two options, "go the Argentine route [large-scale military repression of opposition] or bumble along and fight the war and build democracy at the same time. . . . The existence of Congress was crucial. It meant the Argentine solution had to be ruled out."[22]

For Reagan, El Salvador and Nicaragua shared common fates. Administration officials consistently claimed that the Sandinistas were funding and arming Salvadoran leftists, prompting Reagan to support covert operations in Nicaragua to disrupt the flow of cash and arms. This time, however, Congress refused to stand by and watch. In the 1982 intelligence authorization bill, House Intelligence Committee chair Edward Boland (D-MA) authored an amendment prohibiting funds for covert operations to destabilize Nicaragua. The so-called Boland Amendment required that Reagan curtail support of the *contras*. To fill perceived loopholes in the first Boland Amendment, Congress in 1984 approved a second that prohibited any support for military or paramilitary activities by any U.S. agency.[23]

Throughout this period, members took to the floor and the media (both local and national media outlets) to express their opposition to U.S. involvement in Nicaragua, including the funding of the *contras* and the mining of Nicaraguan shipping harbors by the Central Intelligence Agency. Democrats, in particular, argued that many Reagan policies were illegal, under both domestic and international law. Gerry Studds (D-MA) noted that:

> the *contras* have been killing people for 4 years. They have accomplished almost nothing of military significance. Internal political reconciliation seems to be further away than ever. Our policy continues to be divisive rather than a unifying force in that country. But having said that, I think it is a backhanded tribute to our political system that, having adopted a policy that is illegal, ineffective, and wrong, we can proceed to discuss it in public.[24]

The vast majority of members opposed any kind of direct military engagement in Nicaragua. Especially vocal, Michael Barnes (D-MD) proclaimed: "I am also deeply disturbed by the continuation of the war. It seems to me that the military situation continues to have dangers for the United States. I think there is a strong bipartisan consensus, certainly here in the Congress, that the United States should not send combat forces to fight in Nicaragua. I am concerned that step by step the United States is becoming committed to the conflict in a way that may lead to what we all oppose."[25] Senator Jim Leach (R-IA) minced no words when describing the mistrust sown between Congress and the administration: "Anyone who accepts administration sophistry that assistance to groups attempting to overthrow a foreign government does not represent an effort on our part to overthrow that government can also accept the existence of the tooth fairy."[26]

Reagan recognized that Congress, under no circumstances, would permit sending U.S. troops to Nicaragua. After the passage of both Boland amendments, however, he did see fit to challenge Congress's opposition to providing financial assistance to the contras. The president, in fact, promised to return to Congress "again and again" until its members lent support. Throughout 1985, Reagan focused on southern Democrats. And for a while, his efforts paid dividends. House Speaker Thomas P. O'Neill, Jr. (D-MA) noted that "when a president gets to the point that he can pinpoint twenty people and work face to face with them, he's hard to stop."[27] Reagan exploited divisions within the Democratic Party to sway a few votes, tipping the balance of power in his favor. He also benefited from developments within Nicaragua. On the second day of the April 1985 House debate over Nicaragua, its president, Daniel Ortega, made a high-profile visit to Moscow seeking assistance from the Soviet Union. This undercut the Democratic leadership who had downplayed Ortega's links with Cuba and the Soviet Union, making it impossible for some members to hold the line on *contra* aid.[28] On June 12, the House approved $27 million in humanitarian assistance to the *contras*.

On June 25, 1986, the House voted for a larger $100 million aid package, with Senate approval following soon thereafter. As in 1985, however, Congress prohibited U.S. personnel from training the *contras* in Honduras or Costa Rica, ensuring that U.S. military forces would not become directly involved in the conflict. Reagan continued to lobby key members of Congress, with the 1986 midterm elections looming on the horizon: "While Reagan spoke of bipartisanship, his allies on the Republican right were publicly targeting Democrats for defeat in 1986 because they opposed *contra* aid."[29] These efforts, however, ultimately failed, as Democrats actually gained seats in the fall elections.

Despite these small victories involving aid to the *contras*, the president's luck eventually ran out. Right when substantial U.S. aid began to flow to Nicaragua, evidence of an illegal scheme to buy the release of American hostages in the Middle East by selling arms to Iran, and diverting the profits to fund the *contras,* came to light in the U.S. press. The scandal riveted the nation, as millions of Americans watched the likes of Oliver North, Fawn Hall, and John Poindexter testify live on national television, while commentators speculated on how much Reagan knew about the diversion of funds to the *contras.* After all, Congress specifically forbade anyone within the government from providing assistance to the Nicaraguan rebels. Many insisted that if Reagan had done so, Congress could justifiably impeach him. If he had not authorized the operation, critics continued, it shed light on how little control the commander in chief wielded over his own intelligence services.[30] On the heels of these revelations, Congress once again slashed aid, limiting the dispensation to only $20 million for purely humanitarian purposes; again, members repudiated any kind of military assistance to the *contra* rebels.[31]

Reflecting on this history, some political observers have argued that the covert operations funding the *contras* demonstrate Congress's impotence.[32] We draw very different conclusions. Unable to assist the *contras* legally, the administration resorted to selling arms to a country on the State Department terrorist list and diverting the profits to fund the rebels. Reagan (and/or his advisers) anticipated problems in securing assistance for the *contras* and chose to pursue a course of action that would precipitate the largest political scandal in Washington since Watergate. If Congress offered nothing but a rubber stamp approving every presidential request, or if Reagan felt confident that his personal appeals to moderate Democrats would yield the funding he so desperately wanted, the Iran-*Contra* scandal most likely would never have occurred.

Clearly, Congress's power of the purse looms large in this case. Each Boland amendment cut funding for more Nicaraguan aid. Indeed, after the first Boland amendment passed, Reagan had little recourse but to seek private financing for the *contras,* which eventually led to his administration's efforts to convince private arms dealers to serve as conduits for the Iran-*Contra* deal. Moreover, by using Nicaragua as a focal point for rallying public opinion against the president, members of Congress managed to jeopardize much more than Reagan's requests for aid to the *contras.* According to Secretary of State Alexander Haig, many of the president's top advisers feared that turmoil in Central America would sap public support for Reagan's domestic policy agenda. "Some advisers, especially his highest aides, counseled against diluting the impact of his domestic program with a foreign undertaking that would generate tremendous background noise in the press and in Congress."[33]

As Haig's comments imply, public opinion stood at the forefront of debates over Nicaragua during the 1980s. Some in Congress, such as Senator John Glenn (D-OH), clearly felt pressure from constituents to avoid military commitments: "The contacts I have had, and the mail I have been receiving . . . have indicated mostly a very, very great concern about what we're doing in [Central America]."[34] Yet members were not entirely beholden to a fickle public that held strong and independent views about U.S. foreign policy in Central America. Quite the opposite, many members managed to shape public opinion itself. As discussions of military involvement in El Salvador and Nicaragua began early in Reagan's term, members regularly drew connections to Vietnam—a slow, plodding involvement beginning with "advisors" leading to major commitments of U.S. forces without any apparent exit strategy. Representative Henry Gonzalez (D-TX) insisted, "The Congress once again has a chance to use the War Powers Resolution for its intended purpose—and that is to prevent tragedies in Central America as we have failed to prevent in Vietnam and Lebanon."[35] Senate Foreign Relations Committee chair Richard Lugar (R-IN) similarly recognized that while his constituents were concerned with the spread of communism, many were "equating Nicaragua to be . . . another Vietnam."[36] Without broad-based consensus among elites about the efficacy of aiding the *contras,* the public never rallied to Reagan's side. And without public support, the president's policy options were significantly restricted. In Richard Sobel's analysis, "The general sentiment of the public in the post-Vietnam era prevented Reagan from using a possible strategy of direct military intervention. . . . The general public disapproval for involvement in Central America greatly aided opposition legislators in their fight to keep America out of Nicaragua."[37]

The balance of evidence suggests that Reagan, left to his own devices, would have introduced American military forces into the region and probably in significant numbers. The president, after all, did send small troop contingents to El Salvador as "advisors," which first raised the ire of Congress in 1981. In addition, early in Reagan's tenure presidential advisors publicly recognized the possibility of a U.S. military intervention. When Haig was asked in November 1981 whether the administration had ruled out any direct U.S. involvement in Nicaragua, he responded, "No, I would not give you such an assurance."[38] Similarly, on the eve of a 1985 vote on *contra* aid, the *New York Times* printed portions of a classified annex that accompanied the administration's request for aid. Reagan argued that "the direct application of U.S. military force . . . must realistically be recognized as an eventual option, given our stakes in the region, if other policy alternatives fail."[39] According to Cynthia Aronson, "For members of the House leadership, the contents of the classified annex were taken as confirmation that the president was committed to sending U.S. troops to fight in Nicaragua."[40]

In the end, the president had little choice but to accommodate congressional concerns. According to Aronson, "The debate in Congress continued to send political messages to the administration: the existence of controversy appeared to rule out certain options, such as sending U.S. troops to the region."[41] Haig's own assessment of the prerequisites for military action in Nicaragua centered on Congress: "I never envisaged the landing of marines in Central America. This was not necessary; there was no popular consensus to support such an act, and in any case, it was not possible under the War Powers Act without the consent of Congress. Every realistic being knew that such consent would only be given in case of catastrophe."[42]

Reagan did manage to convince some moderate Democrats, especially southern Democrats, to reverse their stand on *contra* aid in 1986. This victory, however, proved short-lived. At every instance, allotments of funds included severe limitations on U.S. involvement. Then, in 1988, Congress promptly cut the funds and launched a massive investigation into Iran-*Contra*, which would mar the president and his party for years to come. The case of Nicaragua during the 1980s, more than most, reveals the extent to which Congress can use appropriations and public appeals, the latter of which are often amplified by extensive media coverage, to limit presidential war powers. Despite his continued efforts to overturn the Sandinista regime, Reagan repeatedly tripped over congressional opposition.[43] Ultimately, he left office largely unable to achieve a key foreign policy goal he had held from the moment he won the presidency.

Lebanon, 1982–84

Interbranch struggles do not distinguish the lead-up to every military deployment. When presidents offer assurances that victory will come at low cost and high speed, and when military plans are then executed with facility, members may not proffer any objections at all. It is when missteps are taken, when engagements protract, and when losses are incurred that presidents have cause for concern. In the aftermath of such eventualities, congressional criticisms typically surface—almost always through public appeals, and occasionally in the form of resolutions and laws that demand the withdrawal of troops or cessation of hostilities. On any given venture, then, presidents face a measure of risk, as even the smallest and seemingly safest of initial military engagements can go awry. When they do, members of Congress—especially members of the opposition party—stand poised to strike. This pattern precisely characterizes the fate of Ronald Reagan's deployments of U.S. troops to Lebanon between 1982 and 1984.

On June 3, 1982, three gunmen, including a Syrian intelligence officer, attempted to assassinate Shlomo Argov, the Israeli ambassador to Great Britain. So doing, they shattered a fragile ceasefire between Israel and the

Palestine Liberation Organization (PLO), which the U.S. ambassador Philip Habib had brokered less then twelve months before. Thereafter, the principal parties traded military assaults. Israeli prime minister Menachem Begin ordered retaliatory air strikes against PLO targets in southern Lebanon; the PLO responded with rocket attacks against towns in northern Israel. Israel then launched Operation Peace for Galilee, an invasion of Lebanon intended to relocate PLO camps and operatives at least twenty-five miles north, out of range of most Israeli towns. After another temporary ceasefire between Syria, Israel, and the PLO collapsed weeks later, Israel began a full-scale assault on Beirut, where at least fourteen thousand PLO troops were stationed. The United States could no longer ignore the political turmoil and the escalating violence it fueled in the region.

At a July 6 press conference, Reagan first admitted the possibility of U.S. armed forces being deployed to Lebanon. From the outset, however, the president emphasized that military commitments would be of limited size and duration. As he put it, the White House had only "agreed in principle to contribute a small contingent of U.S. personnel, subject to certain conditions."[44] In the following weeks, Reagan continually held out the possibility of a peaceful resolution to the crisis and offered further assurances that any military engagements would be short in time and small in size. Meeting with members of Congress in mid July, Reagan insisted that any use of U.S. troops would be "for a very short period."[45]

At an August 20 press conference, President Reagan then announced that "the Government of Lebanon has requested and I have approved the deployment of United States troops to Beirut as part of a multinational force." Again, he assured Congress and the public that in "no case will our troops stay longer than 30 days."[46] Though Reagan had announced that no questions would be taken, one journalist was able to hurriedly ask if U.S. forces would be withdrawn immediately if they were fired upon. Reagan replied unequivocally that they would. That same day, U.S. ambassador Habib negotiated a plan with Israel and the PLO to allow for the peaceful evacuation of PLO fighters from Beirut. U.S. Marines would lead a multinational force consisting of eight hundred U.S. troops, four hundred French, two hundred British, and eight hundred Italian.[47] The mission's stated objective was to aid the evacuation of PLO forces from Beirut and then to promptly withdraw. On August 24, U.S. forces landed in Beirut.

Reagan informed Congress about these affairs in a letter to Speaker of the House Thomas O'Neill (D-MA) and to Senator Strom Thurmond (R-SC). "In accordance with my desire that the Congress be fully informed on this matter," he wrote, "and consistent with the War Powers Resolution, I am hereby providing a report on the deployment and mission of these members of the United States Armed Forces."[48] He then again sought to allay fears of a long, violent conflict, adding that he wanted to "emphasize that there is no intention or expectation that U.S. Armed Forces will become involved in hostilities. . . . Our agreement with the Government of Lebanon expressly rules out any combat responsibilities for the U.S. forces."[49]

Duly informed about the engagements and assured that troops would return home before long, members of Congress raised few objections to these developments. Several Democrats within Congress, such as John Seiberling (OH) and Clement Zablocki (WI), requested that the president abide by the War Powers Resolution. A number of others, including Carl Levin (MI) and Christopher Dodd (CT), cautioned the president about the operation's costs. For the most part, though, members said and did little to complicate either the president's military planning or his negotiations with the various combatants in Lebanon.

With the intervention of U.S., French, British, and Italian troops, PLO forces quickly and safely evacuated Beirut. According to Reagan, Ambassador Habib's efforts had "saved the City of Beirut and thousands of innocent lives" and resolved the crisis in West Beirut.[50] On September 10, U.S. Marines left Beirut—only to return weeks later.

On September 14, Lebanese president-elect Bashir Gemayel, who had the support of the Israeli government, was assassinated, plunging the region back into violence. Israeli forces returned to West Beirut, just as Christian Phalange forces massacred some seven hundred Palestinians.[51] These latter atrocities, in particular, engendered international outrage, so much so, in fact, that Israel withdrew from Beirut a few days later and allowed the Lebanese Army to assume control of the city. Fearing anarchy, the Lebanese government solicited the aid of another multinational force. Responding immediately, President Reagan agreed to send peacekeeping forces back to Beirut. Speaking from the Oval Office on live national television and radio broadcasts, the president reminded the public that in August "our government met its responsibility to help resolve a severe crisis and to relieve the Lebanese people of a crushing burden. We succeeded. Recent events have produced new problems, and we must again assume our responsibility."[52] Then, in yet another attempt to deflect any criticism, Reagan assured the country that "the participation of American forces in Beirut will again be for a limited period. But I've concluded that there is no alternative to their [the Marines'] returning to Lebanon if that country is to have a chance to stand on its own feet."[53]

On September 29, U.S. troops reentered Beirut. Just as he had done a month earlier, President Reagan sent a letter to the Speaker of the House and the president pro tempore of the Senate. "In response to this request of the Government of Lebanon, I have authorized the Armed Forces of the United States to participate in this Multinational Force."[54] As in the August letter, Reagan communicated his "desire that the Congress be fully informed" about all aspects of the military planning. Then, in an another attempt to assuage any lingering worries, Reagan noted that his "agreement with the Government of Lebanon makes clear that they [U.S. Marines] will be needed only for a limited period to meet the urgent requirements posed by the current situation."[55]

Given such assurances, coupled with the previous deployment's rapid success, members of Congress once again raised few objectives. Several did author a letter urging the president to cite section 4(a)(1) of the War Powers Resolution, which would have started the official countdown at the moment when either Congress would have to endorse the president's actions or the president would be required to terminate the venture. Reagan, though, refused to recognize the resolution, which seemed acceptable to most of the public and media. The president, for the most part, had a free hand in handling the Lebanese crisis.

Unfortunately, the second intervention proceeded neither as smoothly nor as quickly as had the first. Whereas the first succeeded in a matter of days, the second dragged on for months. With each passing week and each new catastrophe, Congress expressed more and more outrage, erecting barriers for a president intent on seeing the military's mission through to the end. Objections mounted slowly, with Democrats (and a few Republicans) raising the specter of the War Powers Resolution, insisting that the president either secure a formal authorization or abandon the deployment outright. By the New Year's passing, congressional unease grew palpable.[56]

On March 16, many fears were realized: a rocket-propelled grenade attack wounded five marines and nine Italians on routine patrol. Six months into the deployment, some members of Congress—notably Henry Gonzalez (D-TX)—began to cry foul.[57] The March 16 grenade attack, however, was just a harbinger of worse things to come. On April 18, 1983, a van carrying two thousand pounds of explosives drove into the United States Embassy in Beirut, killing forty-seven and wounding over a hundred more.[58] Reagan called the bombing "a cowardly act" and vowed to "rededicate the efforts of the United States" toward the removal of all foreign forces from Lebanon.[59] "We must do what we know to be right," he said, and reiterated his commitment to Lebanon and the Middle East: "The people of Lebanon must be given the chance to lead a normal life free from violence without the presence of unauthorized foreign forces on their soil."[60]

Members of Congress, meanwhile, grew increasingly anxious. Among congressional Democrats, Gonzalez remained an outspoken critic of the president. On June 16, he introduced a joint resolution (H.J. Res. 298) directing the president to withdraw American troops from Lebanon. "The

President," Gonzalez argued, "is obliged to give the Congress more information than he has concerning Lebanon, but he will not volunteer it. . . . If we are going to be true to our constitutional duties, our responsibility is to ask for that information, understand what is taking place, and then act accordingly."[61] This resolution, plainly intended to undermine the president's foreign policy, never had much chance of passing. But on June 27, the president signed a compromise bill, the Lebanon Emergency Assistance Act (LEAA), which provided $57 million in military aid and $150 million for reconstruction, while also insisting that "the President shall obtain statutory authorization from the Congress with respect to any substantial expansion in the number or role in Lebanon of United States Armed Forces." While offering support for the American mission in Lebanon, the LEAA, for the first time, required the president to consult with Congress before expanding the Lebanese mission.

Conditions around Beirut steadily worsened. On August 28, fighting between Druze and Christian Phalange forces spilled over into a U.S. military compound, leaving two marines dead and fourteen wounded. Responding to the military crisis at hand, the president on September 1 sent two thousand additional troops to be stationed just offshore of Beirut.[62] In addition, the president ordered U.S. troops to not only defend themselves but also other countries in the multinational force as well as the Lebanese Army. Meanwhile, domestically, the administration insisted that the mission's status remained unchanged, and that there was no need to seek a congressional authorization, as the LEAA required. "Under the present circumstances," Secretary of State George Schultz announced, "there isn't any disposition to change our mission."[63]

Increasing numbers of congressional members appeared skeptical of the president's claims, and Democrats launched renewed efforts to start the War Powers clock. Throughout September, members introduced a series of resolutions that, in one way or another, would restrict the president's discretion to continue his mission in Lebanon.[64] Lloyd Bentsen's sentiments were typical: "I will not be a party to the evisceration of the War Powers Act. If the President refuses to invoke the provisions of this act it will be extremely difficult for me to support the continued presence of U.S. forces in an area of combat such as Lebanon. In this instance, I believe the principle is as important as the presence because that principle is the continued role of Congress in decisions regarding war and peace."[65]

Hence, on September 14 Senate Democrats unanimously adopted a resolution calling on the president to report to Congress under section 4(a)(1). Because the marines had entered into a hostile situation, returned fire, suffered casualties, and used force to support other members of the multinational force and the Lebanese army, "Senate Democrats have unanimously further agreed to call upon the president to:

1. Recognize that the operative provisions of Section 4(a)(1) of the War Powers Resolution have been triggered.
2. Transmit to Congress a report pursuant to Section 4(a)(1) of the War Powers Resolution; and
3. Transmit to Congress a specific request for such Congressional authorization as he deems necessary and appropriate, which sets forth with precision the mission of the United States Armed Forces in Lebanon."[66]

Not surprisingly, the president objected to these provisions. By forcing the president to seek congressional approval, the administration claimed, Democrats were sending an "extremely dangerous" message to the Syrians and their backers, the Soviet Union.[67] "Any restrictions," one official remarked, "are certainly read and understood beyond a shadow of a doubt by the Syrians and by the Soviets . . . [and would] enable the Syrians and the Soviets to sit back and simply wait" for American forces to leave.[68]

Recognizing their plight, however, White House officials now appeared willing to compromise with congressional leaders. On September 20, Senator Baker introduced SJ Res 166, which found that the requirements of section 4(a)(1) of the War Powers Resolution became operative on August 29, 1983, and authorized the continued presence of U.S. Marines for another eighteen months. The resolution also limited the functions of peacekeeping roles and required the president to report to Congress no less than once every six months—though later, this requirement was increased to once every three months. After continued debate in the House, Congress finally passed and the president signed the Multinational Force in Lebanon Resolution (MFLR). The resolution was the only law ever to be enacted that formally initiated the War Powers clock, albeit for a considerably longer period than the original resolution had stipulated. The MFLR failed, however, to temper all concerns about the Lebanon mission. In the following weeks, sporadic fighting continued between the marines and Druze forces. On the morning on October 22, a Mercedes-Benz truck piled with explosives drove through the gates of the U.S. Marine Battalion Landing Team headquarters at the Beirut International Airport. The explosion killed 241 servicemen and wounded 70 more.

Congressional Democrats promptly and publicly rebuked the president, and the media paid notice. In the bombing's aftermath, the *New York Times* reported that Senator Alan Cranston (D-CA) declared the situation a "complete mess."[69] Senator Byrd expressed concern that "the role of our marines has not been clearly defined. At present our people are just sitting ducks in a defenseless situation where they don't even know who is attacking them."[70] Senator Riegle (D-MI) insisted that recent events established the fact that American forces remained in imminent danger and ought to be withdrawn within sixty days. According to Senator Samuel Nunn (D-GA), "Our forces in Lebanon now are not a deterrent, they're hostages."[71]

Reagan again affirmed his commitment to staying the course, arguing that "these deeds make so evident the bestial nature of those who would assume power if they could have their way and drive us out of that area; that we must be more determined than ever that they cannot take over that vital and strategic area."[72] Events, though, were plainly slipping out of his control. On November 4, another truck bomb exploded at the Israeli military governor's headquarters, this time killing twenty-nine Israeli soldiers and thirty-two prisoners. In response to renewed attacks on American troops, the USS *Independence* and the *Kennedy* on December 4 launched twenty-eight aircraft to bomb antiaircraft positions in Lebanon. During the assault, an A-6 bomber was shot down and both aviators ejected. One bled to death on the ground after severing his leg, while Syrians held the other captive until Jesse Jackson successfully negotiated his release on January 4, 1984.[73]

Congressional outrage mounted. Speaker of the House Thomas O'Neill said of the administration, "They have to know a message was sent to them that they're running out of time. If the diplomatic process isn't working, we'd better get the hell out of there. There is no way we want to escalate this war."[74] Representatives Les Aspin (D-WI) and Lee Hamilton (D-IN) sent a letter to Reagan accusing him of having "overstated our stake in Lebanon."[75] The *New York Times* reported that "the consensus on Capitol Hill is that if the President can show progress toward a peaceful solution in Lebanon, Congress will stick by its 18-month authorization. But if the situation continues to deteriorate and the violence continues to mount, he could face a new challenge to his authority when Congress returns on January 23."[76] Even Republicans began to express reservations about the continued presence of U.S. troops in Lebanon. Senator Paul Laxalt (R-NV) warned President Reagan, "Republican support is very fragile."[77] House minority leader Robert Michel (R-IL) feared that the deployment could impact the 1984 elections, saying that "members just have to see some movement to justify it with constituents back home. . . . I really think something will have to give."[78]

On February 1, shortly after Congress reconvened, Democrats in the House debated a resolution that would force the immediate withdrawal of American troops from Lebanon. In a final plea, President Reagan conceded that "the situation in Lebanon is difficult, frustrating, and dangerous. But that is no reason to turn our backs on friends and to cut and run. If we do, we'll be sending one signal to terrorists everywhere: They can gain by waging war against innocent people."[79] As debate over the resolution continued, Reagan finally relented. On February 7, the president announced his intention to order marines in Beirut to return to ships off the Lebanese coast; one week later he followed up with a formal letter to Congress. The departure would occur within thirty days, the letter promised, and marines would become part of the regular force in the Mediterranean and thus not subject to the MFLR. By February 26, all the troops had left Beirut, and on March 30, President Reagan sent another letter to Congress pursuant to the War Powers Resolution declaring the termination of military exercises in Lebanon. Despite continued efforts to maintain domestic political support for the engagement, the president ultimately withdrew from the fight, albeit well before any of the mission's primary objectives had been met. More than two decades would pass before Syrians would withdraw from Lebanon. Tensions between the PLO and Israel continued unabated, and as the resolve of the United States faltered, its perceived credibility in the region suffered mightily. As Jide Nzelibe observes, "In the end, President Reagan made it clear that in ordering the withdrawal from Lebanon he was not following his preferred military strategy but one foisted on him by congressional leaders."[80]

The Lebanon deployment illustrates two basic lessons about use-of-force politics. First, Congress is capable of disrupting or dismantling military ventures should it desire to do so. As the situation in Lebanon deteriorated, Congress threatened the administration with more hearings, more reporting requirements, and perhaps most important, more news headlines. What is particularly poignant about this example is that Congress enacted few binding laws (other than triggering an extended War Powers clock) that sought to dismantle the military venture. Though Congress may not always have the political will to deny funding for an ongoing use of force outright, Lebanon suggests the mere threat of doing so can be enough to cause the administration to change its course of action.[80a] Second, by questioning the operation and insisting that the president abide by the War Powers Resolution, members managed to materially affect the ongoing course of the campaign. Most immediately, they forced the president to consult with them more often than he would have liked. By refusing to present a united front, members bolstered Syrian and Israeli recalcitrance and thereby complicated the president's efforts to negotiate a satisfactory settlement to the conflagration. The administration repeatedly complained about the message that congressional opposition would send to its allies and enemies in the region; on at least one occasion, Syria refused to honor an accord brokered by Schultz, holding out for better terms to be negotiated. Just weeks after withdrawing the troops from Beirut, Reagan publicly denounced Congress, whose "second-guessing about whether to keep our men [in Lebanon] severely undermined our policy. It hindered the ability of our diplomats to negotiate, encouraged more intransigence from the Syrians and prolonged the violence."[81]

A clear counterfactual emerges: had more Democratic members held office in 1982, the Lebanon deployment might well have looked very different. If Democrats had maintained control of both chambers of Congress, they might have orchestrated a more effective campaign to bring home the troops, ending the operation far sooner than March 1984. Conversely, if Republicans had ruled both the Senate and House, congressional dissent would have softened, and Reagan might have held firm through the spring and summer of 1984, as he plainly preferred. Interesting parallels exist between the 2003 Iraq War and Lebanon. In both cases, insurgencies began to take a toll on U.S. troops. Yet in Lebanon, the administration faced a Congress whose members had stronger incentives to cast a bright light on its failures. In 2003, by contrast, Republicans retained majorities in both chambers of Congress—not coincidentally, the rising death toll in and around Iraq received comparatively less attention from Congress until 2006, when Democrats regained control of the House and Senate.

PANAMA, 1989

To the extent that Congress influences presidential decisions about the use of force, it almost always performs the function of an institutional brake on military operations. In some instances, members vocally oppose new uses of force at the front end of a venture, as occurred in Indochina. In other instances, as in Lebanon, the initial support that presidents enjoyed waned over time as the costs of military action in money and lives increased. But where influence is detected, it almost always serves as a deterrent, rather than a stimulant, to military action.

Every rule, though, has its share of exceptions. The 1989 Panama invasion shows that Congress every now and again nudges a reluctant president into battle. In September of that year, four separate polling groups asked the American people what they believed was the most important problem facing the country. An overwhelming majority, between 53 and 61 percent across five surveys, identified drugs. Indeed, the proportion of Americans identifying drugs dwarfed the share that any other issue received; runners-up included the economy (topping out at 8 percent), poverty (6 percent), and the deficit (5 percent).[82] One day before the last poll ended, a Panamanian coup presented the Bush administration with a golden opportunity to appear responsive to the public's concern and seize Panamanian strongman and dictator General Manuel Noriega, whom Representative Charles Schumer (D-NY) would later call "the most notorious drug dealer in the world."[83]

If not the most dangerous drug trafficker, General Noriega certainly was among the most familiar. From the time of his indictment by a Miami federal court on February 5, 1988 to October 1, 1989, the *New York Times* referenced Noriega's involvement in the drug trade on almost 150 occasions, including 41 times on the front page. If Willy Horton provided the face of inner-city crime during Bush's presidency, the Panamanian general lent the visage of America's "war" on drugs. So when Bush refused to order U.S. military support for the coup, Schumer was hardly alone in criticizing the president and calling for swift action to serve the dual imperatives of freeing the Panamanian people from the yoke of a ruthless dictator and extinguishing the physical embodiment of a drug trade that riveted the nation.

On October 3, 1989, a group of rebel officers under Major Moises Giroldi seized and detained General Noriega in an attempted coup. The plotters requested that American forces then stationed in the Canal Zone block the main roads into Panama City, offering to surrender Noriega to American forces if U.S. helicopters would airlift the dictator out of the city. The administration's response was slow and confused. United States forces ultimately did block two roads into the capital, but Bush refused to commit any American troops to the coup itself. The president never sent troops into Panama City to apprehend the captive general, nor did he lend American firepower to support the coup's leaders. The window of opportunity to seize Noriega soon closed, as loyal forces freed the general and crushed the insurrection.

While media initially granted the administration cautiously favorable coverage,[84] a maelstrom soon erupted on Capitol Hill. Still smarting from Republican attacks on Michael Dukakis's toughness in the 1988 presidential campaign, congressional Democrats seized the opportunity to return the favor and castigate the Bush administration for its timidity and inaction. Decrying what he deemed to be rampant risk aversion in Washington, Senator Fritz Hollings (D-SC) refuted Bush's claims that caution and restraint constituted the "prudent" response to the Panamanian coup: "Whether in Congress, in the bureaucracy, or in the White House, 'prudence' has become the mask for passivity and paralysis."[85] Mocking another of the president's catch-phrases from the 1988 campaign, Colorado Representative Patricia Schroeder (D) joked, "I, as many other people, applauded his statement that he wanted a kinder and gentler America. But I did not know that that was going to extend to Noriega."[86] West Virginia Democrat Robert Wise went even further, alluding to the administration's decision to block routes into Panama City during the coup: "This is the worst of all worlds, to intervene and not be successful. Being branded the heavy-handed Yankee from the North is bad enough, but being the gringo who cannot even intervene competently is worse."[87]

Raising the hot-button issue of drugs more explicitly, Dick Durbin (D-IL) reminded the House that Noriega was the foremost "drug kingpin of Central America," and that when faced with a golden opportunity to secure his ouster, President Bush "blinked." Chastising the president as a throwback to the Mugwumps of 1884, Durbin derided, "His mug was on the side of attacking drug gangsters, his wump on the side of caution to the point of timidity."[88] In a less caustic, but even more emotionally charged appeal, Butler Derrick (D-SC) castigated a president who "let an opportunity pass to do away with this tin dictator who is allowing the importation of drugs into this country that are killing our youth and going to the very roots of our society."[89]

Even the Senate majority leader, George Mitchell (D-ME), who refrained from criticizing the president for not intervening, expressed incredulity at the extent to which the government was caught unprepared. Noting that the Select Intelligence, Armed Services, and Foreign Relations Committees were all investigating the American response, including conflicting accounts over whether the coup leaders had ever agreed to hand over Noriega to American forces, Mitchell criticized the administration for its inability to capitalize on an outcome that it had itself encouraged: "What is most difficult to understand, in light of the President and the administration's repeated public invitations to elements within the Panama Defense Force to rebel against Noriega, is how the administration could have been so unprepared when what it had been urging finally took place."[90]

Although the Bush administration might have anticipated Democratic opposition, condemnation from several prominent Republican senators must have come as a surprise. North Carolina's Jesse Helms, the ranking member on Foreign Relations, led the charge. Not one to mince words, Helms accused the White House not only of general incompetence in its handling of the crisis, but even of deception: "Mr. President, I believe the U.S. Government had advanced warning that an action was planned against General Noriega, and I also believe, to my sorrow, that no contingency plans had been set in place, other than to do nothing."[91] Helms then submitted an amendment to the National Drug Control Strategy Initiative (S 1711), which would buttress the president's authority to use military force to remove Noriega from power. Justifying the motion, Helms derogatorily noted that there should never be "another occasion where the Keystone Cops run around and bump into each other and say we do not know whether we have the authority or not."[92]

By echoing Helms's forceful criticisms of the administration and again raising the specter of drugs, Senator Alfonse D'Amato (R-NY) kept the heat on the White House. Observing that Noriega had transformed Panama into a haven for drug money-laundering and its border with Colombia into a "superhighway" for narcotics smuggling, D'Amato compared the Panamanians' "thirst for freedom" to that of the Founders and emphasized to his colleagues that the next time a coup arose, "I think we—the United States—have a moral obligation to support them in their quest for freedom." Concluding, D'Amato compared the current president unfavorably with Theodore Roosevelt: "It is about time that the United States begin to adhere to a policy of a great President of the United States, Teddy Roosevelt, when he said 'Speak softly, and carry a big stick.'"[93]

Some senators, including William Cohen (R-ME) and Paul Simon (D-IL), offered tepid support for the president, but their measured expressions of approval were overwhelmed by their colleagues' zealous criticisms. Animadversions from congressional Democrats and Republicans alike attracted substantial and sustained media coverage throughout the two weeks following the aborted coup. Indeed, one of the few representatives to rally behind the president, John Jacobs (R-AZ), cited the torrent of congressional criticism before network television cameras as his primary motivation for speaking out.[94]

When repudiating the president, it is worth noting, members of Congress were not merely relaying public calls for military action. Two surveys in the immediate wake of the aborted coup show that only about one-third of Americans believed Bush should have used U.S. forces stationed in the region to oust Noriega.[95] Nonetheless, the public did desire some kind of action. Sixty percent of Americans believed it was "very important" that Noriega be driven from power, and another 23 percent claimed it was "somewhat important."[96]

The Bush administration quickly assumed a defensive posture. The day after the outpouring of criticism of U.S. inaction on the Senate floor, a senior White House official confided to reporters "this is really our first crisis. We learned a lot. We could have done better." White House chief of staff John Sununu ordered an internal review of the administration's response.[97]

Initially stunned by the onslaught of criticism, the administration tried to blame Congress for the lack of military aid to the Panamanian coup. According to National Security Advisor Brent Scowcroft and Defense Secretary Richard Cheney, the president would have intervened had it not been for Congress's steadfast support for an executive order that banned political assassinations: "The Congress, by its actions and demeanor, certainly leaned us against the kinds of things they're now saying we should have done."[98] This line of argumentation, however, did little to advance the president's case. The Panamanian coup leaders had no intention of killing Noriega, they merely wanted to turn him over to American forces. As such, U.S. involvement in the coup would have done nothing to aide or abet a political assassination. Following Scowcroft on ABC's *This Week*, Senator Boren (D-OK) dismissed such charges, insisting that Congress had provided the president with sufficient funds and grants of authority to pursue American objectives in Panama. When Secretary Cheney again tried to deflect blame, this time in closed testimony before the Senate Intelligence Committee in mid October, even Republican William Cohen, a supporter of Bush's actions, denounced the tactic and inserted into the official record details of previous intelligence orders on Panama that the committee had approved.[99]

Three days later, the president met with senators at the White House in an effort to repair the breach.[100] In a last-ditch effort to propel the administration to the forefront of events then engulfing it, Sununu publicly proclaimed that Noriega's days were numbered. In an interview with CNN, Sununu confidently prognosticated that the odds Noriega would be ousted within the next six months were eight to five.[101]

On December 20, 1989, Bush ordered the invasion of Panama, then the largest U.S. military action since the Vietnam War. American paratroopers and marines bolstered U.S. forces already on the ground in the Canal Zone, and the combined force, supported by American jets patrolling the skies, quickly took control of Panama City. Noriega, however, proved more elusive, slipping through the military's grasp even as a new provisional government was sworn in on a U.S. military base. Complicating matters, Noriega sought asylum at the Vatican Embassy in Panama. Only after weeks of negotiations with the Vatican did Noriega finally surrender to U.S. forces. The military escorted the general to Miami to stand trial, and he is currently serving a forty-year sentence for drug trafficking.

Had Congress not objected, Bush might never have sent the military into Panama. In the fall of 1989, when rebels held Noriega in their grasp, the president refused to commit the necessary troops just to pick him up. Only after Congress railed against the administration's passivity did Bush spring to action. By that time, however, the costs of recapturing Noriega had skyrocketed—to the tune of twenty-three American and four thousand Panamanian lives, and another three hundred Americans wounded.[102]

It is an overstatement to suggest congressional pressure alone drove the Bush administration to intervene into Panama. Nonetheless, this case highlights the potential for Congress to at least stimulate military action. And though we have argued that Congress more commonly acts as a restraint on the presidential use of force, even here we find considerable evidence about the causal processes by which Congress influenced presidential decision making that appears broadly consistent with our general argument. Criticisms raised by Democrats and Republicans alike, and the concerns over electoral fallout they engendered, played an important role in shaping the president's behavior in Panama. Indeed, Congress-driven public debates over the failure to secure Noriega pushed the president toward a harder line in Central America, and certainly contributed to the invasion in December 1989.

BOSNIA, 1992–94

Members of Congress can influence the timing of an operation, determining just how quickly or with how much delay a president deploys troops abroad. Fearing the domestic political fallout of a hasty move to arms, a president may put off risky military ventures, at least until members come around to support him or until foreign crises become so acute that they can no longer be ignored. The debates and consultations that preceded the eventual 1994 military operations in Bosnia illustrate how members of Congress manage to stall deployments by weeks, months, and sometimes years.

With the collapse of communism in eastern Europe in 1989, Yugoslavia's different ethnic groups began to push for independence from the central government in Belgrade, and regional violence quickly escalated. After repeated attempts to hold the country together, key members of the international community (especially Germany and the United States) decided in early April 1992 to recognize the independence of several former Yugoslav states, including Bosnia and Croatia.[103] In response, Serbian nationalists throughout Bosnia and Croatia began land grabs and, before long, the systematic persecution of various ethnic populations.

Having formally recognized the republics, President Bush felt some compunction to address the deteriorating conditions in Bosnia. Later in April, he called for a UN Security Council resolution authorizing the delivery of humanitarian supplies and, if necessary, the use of force. Over the next several months, leading Republicans and Democrats publicly supported military action in Bosnia. In June, Senate Foreign Relations Committee members Claiborne Pell (D-RI), Richard Lugar (R-IN), and Carl Levin (D-MI) all called for action, approving a nonbinding resolution urging UN secretary general Boutros Boutros-Ghali to plan a multinational military deployment to Bosnia. In addition, Senate leaders Bob Dole (R-KS) and George Mitchell (D-ME) strongly supported the use of force to facilitate humanitarian assistance and to pressure Serbs at the negotiating table.

During the summer and fall of 1992, with a Democratic challenger bellowing "It's the economy, stupid!" the Bush administration scrambled furiously to convey its commitment to solving domestic issues. Still, the candidates did not ignore Bosnia, as Clinton called for tougher measures against the Serbs to end atrocities, going so far as to support air strikes and the lifting of a prior arms embargo placed on the Bosnians.[104] In August, the Senate Foreign Relations Committee passed another resolution, this time calling on the president to work with the United Nations to use "all means necessary, including the use of military force" to protect aid shipments to Bosnia. Although Republican senators John McCain (AZ), John Chafee (RI), and John Warner (VA) appeared skeptical of plans to use force in the region, each admitted that a compelling humanitarian case for military action existed.

From the moment he took office, Clinton began to soften his stance on the use of air strikes to stop Serbian aggression, leading Dole to criticize him for having done "far less than he suggested in the campaign."[105] As the spring of 1993 wore on, violence in the Balkans showed no signs of abating. Indeed, Croat and Bosnian forces, which had been loosely allied against the Serbs, began fighting against one another, producing a three-front war and the collapse of the previously brokered Vance-Owen peace process.[106] As evidence of continued Serbian atrocities against Bosnians surfaced, the United Nations authorized the UN Protection Force (UN-PROFOR) to create and guard six "safe areas" for civilians. The inadequacies of this response, however, quickly became apparent, as Serbian forces surrounded five of the safe areas and presented a menacing threat to Bosnian refugees.

At this time, three policy options dominated discussions in the executive and legislative branches: (1) unilaterally terminating the UN arms embargo and arming the Bosnians so that they might fortify the safe areas; (2) conducting limited air strikes to disable Serbian artillery (especially around the safe areas) and pressure the Serbs at the negotiating table; or (3) introducing U.S. ground forces to the region. While the options were clear, consensus proved elusive. On April 23, 1993, Senator Dole suggested that the arms embargo should have been lifted "months ago" and that he would back limited air strikes.[107] Joseph Biden, meanwhile, excoriated the administration for failing to do "a damn thing" to help the Bosnians, while Senate majority leader George Mitchell called for a more aggressive foreign policy in the region.[108] Others, meanwhile, appeared more reluctant to escalate U.S. involvement in Bosnia. John Warner (R-VA) pressed for caution, insisting that air strikes would constitute an act of war "when the first airplane drops the first piece of ordnance."[109] Patrick Leahy (D-VT) warned that bombing might not curb Serbian aggression, obliging the United States to then introduce ground troops. Republican senators John McCain and Hank Brown (CO) raised additional concerns about air strikes, with Brown suggesting, and media outlets reporting, a direct analogy to Vietnam: "The Vietnam experience is a very pertinent analogy because when Americans suffer casualties in Yugoslavia, support for American involvement is going to fade."[110]

During this period, the public appeared just as divided as Congress. Two polls conducted within forty-eight hours of one another during May 1993 revealed considerable ambivalence about the prospect of military action in Bosnia. In a May 6 CBS poll, 52 percent of respondents claimed that the United States had no business intervening in the Balkans and opposed the use of either ground troops or air strikes. By contrast, a May 8

ABC poll found that 65 percent of Americans supported air strikes in response to Serbian aggression.

At the height of this spring debate, the *New York Times* ran an editorial by Anthony Lewis reflecting the mood of most within Congress: "The first premise here is that, in practical terms, President Clinton cannot take military action on his own. Constitutionally and politically, he must have support from Congress and the public."[111] It is worth noting, though, that the partisan divisions over Bosnia did not comport with those that usually dominate interbranch politics. In this instance, Democratic members of Congress, at least those who early on staked out public positions, offered tepid support for a Democratic president, while Republicans tended to stand behind him. The cause of this intraparty conflict, though, is readily identifiable: Clinton did not initiate the debate over the use of force, Bush did; and congressional divisions merely reflected those found at the beginning of the Bosnian crisis, when a Republican occupied the Oval Office.[111a]

Throughout the spring and summer of 1993, Clinton, worried that the Serbs were not bargaining in good faith, held onto the possibility of taking military action. And there is good reason to believe that the president, left to his own devices, might have launched limited air strikes that very year. At an April news conference, he claimed to be giving "serious consideration" to just that option.[112] For two reasons, however, he chose a more cautious route. First, European allies opposed both the lifting of the arms embargo and air strikes. When Secretary of State Warren Christopher briefed the House on the Balkans, he repeatedly noted that European allies were "unwavering" in their opposition to these two policies. Still, even without multilateral support, Clinton could have pushed the issue. A divided Congress, however, convinced him otherwise. According to Thomas Friedman, writing in the *New York Times*, "Mr. Clinton is ready to use air power and arm the Bosnian Muslims, but says he will not commit American ground forces because he is not going to risk his domestic agenda trying to settle a European civil war."[113] Given allied opposition, the possibility of limited air strikes devolving into a ground war, and threats to his domestic political agenda, Clinton opted to forestall military action in Bosnia.

During the fall of 1993, conditions in the Balkans steadily worsened, and peace talks assumed a renewed sense of urgency. All parties recognized that, for any truce to endure, a large military presence in Bosnia would be needed, possibly led by American forces. This anticipation aroused still more debate within and between Capitol Hill and the White House. Although no major figures changed their original positions, even advocates of "doing something" in Bosnia recognized that the president could not secure congressional approval for sending ground forces into the region.

As Dole put it, "It's going to be a tough sell in Congress to send 25,000 Americans. Let's have debate. Let's have Congress decide."[114]

Congressional concerns centered on three main issues. First, some asked, would there be a peace to keep? Absent a preexisting peace, many were wary of placing a large number of troops directly into combat without clear guidelines concerning the circumstances under which the troops would be withdrawn. Second, other members of Congress feared that European allies might not contribute financial or military assistance to the endeavor. And finally, several key members demanded assurances that if the peace collapsed, the West would promptly arm the Bosnians. Most everyone in Congress wanted to avoid a situation wherein U.S. troops fought in vain to impose a peace that none of the warring parties, or any of the European spectators, actively supported.

While the president and Congress debated such matters, dangers continued to gather. During the winter of 1993–94, Serbs repeatedly attacked UN-mandated "safe areas" where Bosnian Muslims had sought refuge. Then, in February 1994, the Serbs launched a major military offensive against the city of Sarajevo. When Serbian forces shelled a crowded marketplace, opinion both in Europe and Congress promptly shifted in support of military action. The North Atlantic Treaty Organization (NATO) established no-fly zones around the "safe areas," and on February 28, U.S. forces operating under NATO auspices shot down two Serbian jets, formally signifying the beginning of the Bosnian war.

Reflecting on this two-year history, a number of observers have ballyhooed over congressional failures to influence presidential decision making. After reviewing statements by key Republican members of the House, for instance, Ryan Hendrickson claims, "In sum, this case illustrates that Congress continued the practice of deference to the president over war powers, despite its earlier ideological commitment to do otherwise."[115] Such conclusions, however, mistake silence for deference, just as they overlook some of the more subtle ways in which congressional influence manifests itself. That members of Congress did not insist that the War Powers clock be initiated, as they had done in Lebanon, or that the president forego any military action whatsoever, as they had done in Indochina, does not mean that the president had his way in Bosnia. In systems of separated powers, where one branch of government continually monitors the doings of another, it can be extremely difficult to identify the origins of influence. For clues, we must look beyond outward repudiations of decisions already cast and the consequent abandonment of military ventures conducted abroad. We must consider how presidential orders differed from presidential preferences—regarding a deployment's size, duration, scope, or timing—and then assess whether Congress contributed to the disjuncture.

In Bosnia, the clearest evidence of congressional influence concerns matters of timing. During the 1992 campaign, Clinton railed against Bush for not having intervened militarily in Bosnia. And during his first year in office, Clinton consistently held out the possibility of launching air strikes against Serbian strongholds in Bosnia and Herzegovina. But with various members of Congress expressing unease about a military deployment, the public wary of anything reminiscent of the Vietnam War, and European allies refusing to take an aggressive stance against the Serbian military, Clinton opted to steer a more prudent course.[116] Rather than pushing for military action that might well have escalated into a ground war, which would have raised the Congress's ire, Clinton instead delayed until the killings in Bosnia reached such proportions that they could no longer be ignored.

Though European allies were certainly a source of the delay, so too was Congress. As the editorial board of the *Christian Science Monitor* noted, "Confusion and cross-purposes about intervening in Bosnia have caused President Clinton to delay approval of military action there. Congress isn't settled. The Europeans are stalling."[117] In a September 1993 news conference with Japan's prime minister, Clinton admitted, "It is clear to everyone that the United States could not fulfill a peacekeeping role in Bosnia unless the Congress supported it. And I will be consulting with all the appropriate congressional leadership in both parties to see what the best manifestation of that is."[118] Even after the air strikes, congressional opposition continued to influence the administration. In the summer of 1995, for example, Clinton asked the UN Security Council to delay a vote on funding UN peacekeepers in Bosnia "to allow time for consultation with Congress."[119] Rather than press on without Congress, Clinton recognized the importance of working with members who, at any moment, might openly balk and withdraw their support.

The political costs to a president of launching a failed military venture are now well known. And here, they are once again on display. At the same time that he voted in favor of a measure to support military operations in Bosnia, Senator Dole openly challenged the president. As Louis Fisher observes, "Senator Dole explained some of his purposes of the bill that passed. One was to shift responsibility from Congress to the President. Dole said that Clinton 'made this decision and he takes responsibility. It was his decision to send troops and his decision alone.' Translation: If anything went wrong it was Clinton's fault, not Congress's."[120] Dole's eventual drift from vocal proponent of a Bosnian intervention to a distant observer of Clinton's war further reveals the fragility of presidential support that resides among members of the opposition party.

It is true that Congress did not raise much of a ruckus during the lead-up to the Bosnian deployment. In part, members did not actively challenge the president because of the previous stances they took on Bosnia. During the spring and summer of 1993, those who most naturally would criticize the newly elected president—namely, Republicans—had just months earlier backed the use of force in Bosnia, when Bush (41) was in office. Republican leader and presidential hopeful Bob Dole stood out in this regard. According to Fisher, "The congressional response depended greatly on what Bob Dole, the Senate majority leader, would do."[121] While Fisher derogates Dole for not doing more to check Clinton's war powers, it was Dole who barely five months before the 1992 election had called on the United States and NATO to send an ultimatum to Milosevic, backing the threat with air strikes if Milosevic did not comply.[122] Although Dole would later criticize aspects of Clinton's Bosnia plans, his preferences concerning the use of force were cast before Bill Clinton had been sworn in as president.

Of course, members of Congress who were newly elected in 1992 and 1994 had a freer hand in criticizing presidential arguments for the use of force. For the most part, however, the president managed to address the concerns that they raised. Clinton provided Congress with considerable information about conditions in and around Bosnia, he set time limits on the duration of various deployments, and he ensured that European allies provided support for military action, largely through NATO. Finally, in the summer of 1995, Congress voted to allow the U.S. military to help arm Bosnians. With each concern met, partisan opponents to the president willingly backed a limited military engagement. By delaying military action, consulting with members of Congress, and then initiating force under NATO's banner, the president managed to avoid an interbranch conflagration—though in doing so, he dealt with the Bosnian crisis in a different manner and pace than he otherwise might have preferred.

Kosovo, 1998–99

Many hoped that the 1995 Dayton Accords, which ended the Bosnian civil war, would bring peace to the Balkans. It did not. On its heels emerged the conflict in the Serbian province of Kosovo, where more than 2 million people lived, 90 percent of whom were ethnic Albanians. Kosovars who had served in Bosnian and Croatian units during the civil war began to flow into the ranks of the Kosovo Liberation Army (KLA), which had theretofore maintained a relatively low profile. As the KLA undertook sporadic attacks against local Serbian police in the spring of 1998, Milosevic began to crack down. Police forces and Serbian Army units shelled areas around the Kosovo capital of Pristina, killing numerous civilians, provoking the KLA to escalate its attacks against Serb forces. With sectarian violence spreading, thousands of civilians streamed into Albania, creating a massive humanitarian crisis.

In response to the offensive maneuvers against civilian areas of Kosovo, the Contact Group—an alliance consisting of the United States, Britain, France, Germany, Italy, and Russia—instituted in May 1998 an arms embargo of Serbia. Simultaneously, President Clinton advocated harsher penalties against the Serbs, including possible military strikes against Milosevic. Secretary of State Madeleine Albright believed that Milosevic would respond only to force, as he had in Bosnia, and that if the strife were to end, the threat of U.S. military intervention must be credible. As she noted in a June news conference in London, "We know from experience that our response must be unequivocal and unambiguous if it is to be effective."[123]

Milosevic, however, pressed onward. In June, Serbian forces launched a sustained military campaign against KLA forces, generating increasing numbers of refugees. In response, NATO threatened an air campaign against Serbian forces to end the offensive, though some NATO allies (France and Germany) remained hesitant to pursue this option without the approval of the United Nations Security Council. Interestingly, the few members of Congress who spoke out at the time supported a hard line against Milosevic—and a number of these members came from the ranks of the opposition party.[124] As Nebraska senator Chuck Hagel (R) noted, "I see a shift on the Republican side on this. The reality is . . . we're probably going to have to put NATO troops in there."[125] Still, the majority of Congress remained silent on the issue. And facing the prospect of an international intervention, Milosevic abandoned the Kosovo offensive later that summer.

Throughout the summer, U.S. ambassador Christopher Hill engaged in shuttle diplomacy between Pristina and Belgrade. Little came of these efforts, and at summer's end, Serbia again attacked the KLA. In response, NATO escalated its threats of air attacks, and on October 6, U.S. negotiator Richard Holbrooke, who crafted the 1995 Dayton Agreement ending the Bosnia war, flew to Belgrade to negotiate directly with Milosevic. On October 12, NATO ordered member states to activate assets for an air campaign (the equivalent of cocking a loaded gun), and NATO approved military action on October 13. As he had responded to previous threats from abroad, Milosevic promptly agreed to withdraw forces from Kosovo, though he would not finally comply until October 27.

During this period, Clinton made a point of informing members of Congress about developments, sending Albright, Cohen, and National Security Advisor Sandy Berger to regular briefing sessions. Democrats, for the most part, tended to quietly side with their president, while Republicans appeared more divided. Senators Gordon Smith (OR), John McCain

(AZ), and Mitch McConnell (KY) all supported air strikes, though they occasionally expressed criticisms of Clinton's planning. Don Nickles (OK) and Richard Lugar (IN), meanwhile, appeared more skeptical;[126] Trent Lott (R-MS) noted that while he favored air strikes, "there's no real plan on how to carry this out."[127] Other Senate Republicans, meanwhile, complained that Clinton had failed to "adequately prepare Congress or the American people for military action."[128]

Although the Holbrooke-authored agreement held firm for a short while, the situation in Serbia would take a drastic turn for the worse. After purging officers of questionable loyalty to Milosevic, including the heads of internal security and his top military commander, Milosovic stood poised to launch his largest assault yet.[129] With Operation Horseshoe, the Serbian military swept through the province and displaced the KLA and ethnically cleansed Kosovo of hundreds of thousands of Albanian civilians.[130] Despite the presence of an unarmed international Kosovo Verification Mission (KVM), Serbian attacks commenced in early 1999, beginning on January 15 with a massacre at the village of Racak.[131]

While violence escalated, both sides to the conflict came to Rambouillet, France, ostensibly to negotiate a ceasefire. Serbia, however, steadfastly refused to accept NATO troops in Kosovo, and NATO resumed its threats of military force. After some delay, Kosovar Albanians signed an interim agreement, although Serbia rejected its terms. With hopes for a peaceful resolution to the conflict dashed, Holbrooke issued one final warning to Belgrade. Operation Horseshoe was by this time in full swing. Literally hundreds of thousands of Albanians were being driven out of Kosovo, terrorized by all manner of atrocities. According to some NATO leaders, "genocide" was at hand.

Around the beginning of the Rambouillet talks, Congress began to reassert itself, debating the wisdom of deploying U.S. troops to the region. Interestingly, some Republicans who had supported Clinton in the early fall now appeared more hesitant. Republican Representative John Kasich (OH), for instance, called Clinton's proposals to place U.S. forces in the Kosovo peacekeeping operation "a terrible decision." Similarly, McCain quipped, "We have no concept of how we want to settle this situation. The American people and the Congress deserve to know that."[132] Meanwhile, a handful of other Republicans, and virtually all Democrats, supported Clinton's efforts to use NATO to pressure Serbia in March, as well as his proposals to contribute U.S. troops to NATO peacekeeping operations. As chairman of the Armed Services Committee John Warner (R-VA) noted, "We have no choice but to commit ground troops, and I'll have to lead that effort to convince the Senate."[133]

When members of Congress debated blocking funds for possible military operations, some noted the body appeared "skeptical" of Clinton's calls for war.[134] Still, on March 11 the House voted by a margin of 219–191 to approve the Clinton plan for U.S. peacekeepers for Kosovo. Twelve days later, after extensive consultations with members of the administration, the Senate too approved military strikes on Kosovo, this time by a vote of 58–41. Neither chamber followed through with their threats to limit funding for the operations. As they typically do, both votes broke along party lines, with just enough Republicans breaking ranks to secure passage. Of note, Speaker Dennis Hastert (R-IL) openly criticized Clinton's foreign policy, but finally voted in support of the measure—perhaps because of the extensive negotiations he held with administration officials over the deployment's terms.

As in the Bosnia case four years prior, a divided Congress reflected, and likely yielded, a divided electorate. Public opinion polls consistently showed Americans split as to proposed actions in Kosovo. A Harris poll on the eve of the NATO bombings (March 23, 1999) found that of those respondents who had heard of the situation in Kosovo, 49 percent favored the use of NATO ground forces while 45 percent opposed. Similarly, 52 percent favored air strikes against Serbian targets, while 42 percent opposed them.[135]

In what would prove to be one of Clinton's longest military operations, on March 24 NATO forces began a sustained bombing campaign of Serbian targets in Kosovo and Serbia proper. In addition, nearly seven thousand U.S. troops joined an overall peacekeeping force of more than fifty thousand. And despite some public protests, members of Congress never opted to restrict funding for the operations, nor did they make any other effort to derail Clinton's military plans.

Several factors help explain why Congress ultimately fell behind the president. First, and perhaps foremost, the importance of conveying national resolve to the international community lingered in the minds of key congressional leaders. Milosevic's continued flouting of NATO deadlines and outright reneging on agreements with the United States and NATO led many members of Congress to perceive him as a bully who would back down only if threatened with force. In this context, as shown in the early spring of 1999, congressional attempts to limit military engagements might only undermine Clinton's efforts to negotiate a peaceful resolution. In particular, during debates over the House resolution approving the deployment of troops, many members of Congress recognized that a vote against the president would effectively ruin any chances of persuading Milosevic to halt his assaults against the Kosovars. In congressional testimony, former Republican Senator Bob Dole put it succinctly: "if there is a 'no' vote tomorrow, there probably won't be an agreement." Dole then proceeded to lay out the ramifications of congressional limits on Clinton's discretion to deploy troops:

I don't know if it would be disastrous, but obviously, [Milosevic] would use it to vindicate his position that there is a feeling that this is a sovereign nation . . . it's none of our concern as a part of NATO. . . . I think even more disastrous would be the Albanian reaction. Why would they sign any agreement if there's not going to be U.S. forces as a part of NATO? Now, I know it's non-binding, but remember, they're in Pristina, they're out in the fields. . . . All they get is the headline, "Congress Says No." That will be the headline, "Congress Says No."[136]

Concerned about the powerful signal that a congressional rebuke would send abroad, enough moderate Republicans decided to back the president to allow the resolution's passage.

Domestic politics also limited Congress's involvement in decisions about how, and when, the president might send troops into the Balkans. At the same time that Milosevic was committing all sorts of atrocities against Kosovars, Washington was embroiled in a heated debate about the president's dalliances with a young White House intern named Monica Lewinsky. Given the single-mindedness with which many Republicans pursued impeachment in the fall and winter of 1998–99, many no doubt lacked interest in attacking Clinton on an issue they felt the public cared less about. Had Republicans within Congress not found such delight in Clinton's parsing of the verb "is" and muddled public apologies, the outcome in Kosovo might well have looked quite different. As a staffer on a congressional foreign affairs committee told the *Washington Post* in October 1998, when discussion of NATO strikes were beginning, "I think we've waited too long on Kosovo. . . . And let's face it. We're in the middle of this other mess [of] a debate about impeachment."[137] Indeed, the most formal attempt to deal with Clinton's threat of air strikes and the deployment of ground forces occurred in early March, *after* the impeachment trial had ended.

The two most important reasons Congress decided to support a military deployment reveal, in turn, two important lessons about use-of-force politics. First, even through nonbinding resolutions that ostensibly have no direct bearing on presidential power, Congress can materially affect the conduct of foreign policy. When members recognized that by limiting Clinton's discretion to exercise force abroad they might embolden Milosevic and incite further Serbian violence, they opted to stand by the president and present a more unified national front. What superficially would appear to be proof of congressional impotence, in this sense, emerged from a recognition of congressional potency. Second, interbranch struggles do not always transpire one issue at a time. Occasionally, debates over the use of force intersect with partisan wrangling over purely domestic considerations. The ability, not to mention willingness, of Congress to take on the president in one domain may depend on expectations about how they are likely to fare in another.

Concluding Remarks

The various domestic political struggles over how best to deal with conflicts arising in Indochina, Lebanon, Nicaragua, Panama, Bosnia, and Kosovo confirm Adam Berinsky's observations that "politics has never stopped at the water's edge. Foreign policy is often as contentious and partisan as domestic policy. Theories of war and politics must account for the effects of the domestic political process."[138] Congress, to varying degrees, appears central in this regard. Amidst every one of these crises, a president confronted members who had reasonably well-defined views about how operations should proceed, if they should proceed, and members who stood poised to lash out should a military venture falter. In almost every instance, the president adjusted course, in one way or another, in order to accommodate some domestic constituency.

Familiar themes run through these case studies. Partisanship, for starters, defines the most salient dimension of presidential-congressional interactions over use-of-force decisions. Within Congress, members almost always divided along party lines, and the first individuals to criticize the president typically came from the ranks of the opposing party. Additionally, when members of Congress opted to intervene directly into a military venture—either by restricting the use of appropriations for specified military purposes, establishing new reporting requirements, or demanding that troops be withdrawn by a specified date—they usually did so after troops had been committed.

During the weeks and months that preceded military action, members of Congress did little more than give public speeches or offer purely symbolic resolutions to a congressional committee or chamber floor. These actions, however, often had immediate policy consequences, either by bolstering (or debilitating) the president's capacity to effectively negotiate with other countries or by fixating the media's (and hence the public's) attention on a set of concerns that the president might just as soon have ignored. In the first instance, congressional appeals signaled to the president Congress's willingness to withstand military losses. They also gave foreign nations, allies and enemies alike, some indication about the nation's resolve to see a military venture through to the end. Repeatedly, members of Congress recognized their roles in presenting a united front and fortifying the credibility of national commitments. In the second instance, the case studies revealed considerable evidence of the political costs of embarking on a long and costly military venture. In 1982, Reagan had every confidence that the second Lebanese intervention would be as short and successful as the first, but when weeks turned to months and then to years, congressional unease steadily mounted, the media insistently reported on members' concerns, public support waned, and Reagan finally withdrew troops well before his original strategic objectives had been met. Note that in nearly every case study in this chapter, presidents and members of Congress were attentive to the public, taking arguments to the media in an effort to court public opinion.

The case studies also illustrate less obvious, and less common, features of use-of-force politics. Occasionally, as in Panama, members of Congress have actively encouraged a wary president to send troops abroad; in such instances, Congress would appear to stimulate rather than restrain military action. Other times, congressional criticisms were more muted than the institution's partisan composition might suggest, either because members were locked into positions they had taken under previous administrations (as in Bosnia) or because they were preoccupied with other domestic and international events (as in Kosovo). Arguments about congressional-presidential relations constitute, at best, central tendencies. They are not hard and fast rules.

One final feature of these case studies deserves special emphasis. Uses of force are not independent of one another. Presidents eschew military force today because of the nation's experiences exercising military force yesterday. Eisenhower shied away from engaging the Indochina insurrection largely because of the shadow that the Korean War cast on his administration. The specter of the Vietnam War loomed large as Reagan, Bush, and Clinton confronted the possibility of sending troops into battle. Reeling from the public and congressional criticisms that accompanied smaller failed interventions—as Clinton plainly was at the end of 1994 when tragedies in Somalia filled American television screens—presidents occasionally expressed reluctance to launch new military ventures abroad. Use-of-force politics do not begin anew every time that the president considers exercising military force. Often, they derive straight from the nation's experiences in past deployments. Though we have little more to say on the topic here, we encourage future research to systematically explore how such dependencies are forged, and the conditions under which they dissolve.

This, then, concludes the second section of the book. It warrants reviewing, if only briefly, just how far we have come. In the book's first section, we recounted some of the tools at Congress's disposal to check presidential war powers, and we then specified the conditions under which they would most likely be utilized. In the second, we extended old datasets, introduced a new one, and then canvassed a half-dozen case studies in order to check whether our expectations about Congress's involvement in use-of-force politics were borne out in the real world. For the most part, we found that they were. Facing numerous partisans within Congress lined up against them, presidents exercised military force with less frequency and were less likely to respond militarily to any specific foreign conflagration abroad. The partisan composition of Congress, however, appeared to matter most when larger military deployments were considered and when the targeted nation was less strategically important to the United States.

Having established the fact of congressional influence on presidential decision making, the book in the third section explores some of the ways in which this influence comes about. Recall that earlier we actually posited two primary mechanisms by which congressional opposition might affect use-of-force decisions—the first emphasizing a president's capacity to credibly convey resolve to the nation's allies and enemies, and the second focusing on the public's willingness to support a planned military venture. We set aside further empirical investigations of the first mechanism for future research. The second, instead, is our central preoccupation. Chapters 6 and 7 demonstrate how congressional debate affects media coverage of a proposed military venture, and how media coverage, in turn, affects the public's willingness to back the president.

PART THREE

One Causal Pathway

CHAPTER 6

Congress and the Media

As THE NATION'S EXPERIENCE in Indochina, Nicaragua, Panama, Bosnia, and Kosovo bears witness, members of Congress at the front end of a prospective military venture usually influence presidential decision making indirectly—raising questions, objections, and concerns that help define the terms of public debate about a prospective operation.[1] One of the surest means of doing so is by staging events that become focal points of media attention, shaping the national conversations that citizens watch on their television screens and read in their morning newspapers. Through hearings, legislative debates, and investigations, members of Congress generally, and the party leadership in particular, can reliably expect to hone journalists', and by extension the public's, assessments of the prospective costs and benefits of military action.

Other scholars have found that the probability that Congress stages such events, and the type of events that it actually holds, critically depends on who fills its chambers.[1a] When the president's party secures strong and cohesive majorities in the House and Senate, a president leading the nation into war is not likely to be subject to especially aggressive hearings, investigations, bills, or resolutions that intentionally limit executive discretion, or to prolonged public debate about legislative actions that criticize his past decisions or constrain his future ones. On the other hand, facing hostile partisan majorities on Capitol Hill, a president is more likely to attract intense congressional scrutiny that is both carefully orchestrated and highly publicized. The partisan divisions that received so much attention in the first two sections of the book crucially determine the number and type of hearings, investigations, and debates about war that Congress conducts.

This chapter takes the analysis another step forward. It demonstrates how the public positions members of Congress take translate into influence over what David Mayhew calls the "public sphere"—that is, the "realm of shared American consciousness in which government officials and others make moves before an attentive stratum of the public, and in which society's preference formation, politics, and policymaking all substantially take place."[2] To do so, this chapter builds on the insights of a group of political communication scholars who have examined the influence of domestic political institutions on national media coverage of planned uses of force. For the most part, contributors to the literature have asserted that national television news broadcasts and newspapers take cues from Congress when establishing the content and scope of foreign policy coverage. Rather than forming independent judgments, journalists turn to other political elites, most frequently senators and representatives, to evaluate White House arguments on behalf of military deployments. At the brink of military action, Congress retains a privileged place in the newsroom, for how its members react to possible uses of force crucially determines whether, and by what degree, critical voices find their way into news stories.

This chapter first summarizes the principal arguments and evidentiary claims on the "indexing hypothesis," which contends that the perspectives expressed by Washington elites effectively determine the tone and content of the news that reaches the public. More than an isolated literature review, this section shows how a group of scholars principally concerned with the prerequisites for a free and independent press have uncovered one of the most important ways in which Congress constrains the president's ability to deploy troops abroad. To test and extend the hypothesis, the chapter then probes a single case study, albeit one of monumental importance during the nation's recent political history: the 2003 Iraq War. By examining a unique database of national and local television news coverage of Iraq during the war's prelude, this chapter presents the first-ever evidence that Congress influences public debates about the use of military force in both national *and* local media outlets, where most Americans turn for news about politics.

INDEXING

How do average citizens evaluate a president's recommendations that American troops be sent into real or potential combat to defuse some foreign conflagration? How can they begin to figure out whether the nation's short- or long-term interests are served by sending the military to Somalia or Haiti or Liberia? With little understanding of the strategic interests involved, and with no firsthand knowledge of the targeted nation or identified crisis, most citizens have an impoverished basis on which to formulate independent opinions.[3] For the most part, everything they know about the planned military initiative, and most every piece of information they can utilize to evaluate the president's actions, comes from the media.

In a classic formulation, Walter Lipmann recognized average citizens' essential ignorance about events occurring outside of their daily lives, and their consequent reliance on the media for guidance:

> Each of us lives and works on a small part of the earth's surface, moves in a small circle, and of these acquaintances knows only a few intimately.

Of any public event that has wide effects we see at best only a phase and an aspect. . . . Inevitably our opinions cover a bigger space, a longer reach of time, a greater number of things, than we can directly observe. They have, therefore, to be pieced together out of what others have reported and what we can imagine.[4]

Unfortunately, when it comes to complex foreign policy issues, media outlets often find themselves in much the same position as average citizens. They too lack basic information about the goings on in the particular region of the world, the likely costs and benefits of a military intervention, the probabilities of success and failure, the details of ongoing diplomatic negotiations between nations, the military's strategic planning, or the merits of alternative—that is, nonmilitary—courses of action. Foreign correspondents and White House contacts may provide some insight into these matters, and by subjecting administration spokespersons to vigorous questioning, journalists may make additional headway. But at the front end of a planned military venture, most media outlets (most of the time) are in an all-too-familiar dilemma: they anticipate the deployment of troops abroad and the exercise of military power, but they are not sure what to say about either. Even if one sees the media's role merely as relaying what others are saying, given time and space constraints, reporters must still make judgments about whose commentary to include.

This book's focus on the domestic politics that precede military deployments retains special significance here. Once a venture is launched, and once successes and failures are revealed, the media have independent means by which to pass judgment on the president. Witnessing early military victories, praise may confidently be bestowed. And at the sight of civilian casualties, friendly fire losses, botched operations, or other mishaps, condemnations may rightly follow. But in the days and weeks that precede a deployment, when every one of the president's arguments rests on hypotheticals and uncertainties, the media have precious few means by which to see into the future—and hence, little basis on which to evaluate the administration's position.

Consider the *New York Times* coverage of the Bush administration during the lead-up to the Iraq War, which this chapter examines in considerable depth. Like virtually every other media outlet in the nation, the *Times* failed to uncover, or at least report, some basic flaws in Bush's case for invading Iraq: namely, that Iraq had neither weapons of mass destruction nor official ties with al-Qaeda and, consequently, that the Saddam Hussein regime probably posed less of a threat to U.S. national security than the Bush administration suggested. Its overblown apologia aside,[5] the *Times*'s oversight was hardly exceptional. According to then executive editor Howell Raines, "It is inevitable that newspaper stories of this kind—

usually based on information from interested parties in government and elsewhere—are incomplete and in some cases reflect the agenda of the sources."[6] Though media outlets might subject the claims of "interested parties in government" to greater scrutiny, key facts often do not surface until after troops are deployed and the political landscape is fundamentally altered.

One particular *Times* story line underscored the media's almost exclusive reliance on official government sources and, in the absence of policy conflict within Washington, its resultant inattention to alternative analyses and perspectives. Relying on highly suspect intelligence reports from the CIA, the Bush administration in September 2002 publicly claimed it possessed "irrefutable evidence" that Iraq was reconstituting its nuclear weapons program. The centerpiece of the administration's claim was Iraq's procurement of sixty-six thousand aluminum tubes, purportedly for use in constructing uranium-enriching centrifuges. But nuclear scientists at the departments of Energy and State, and even some officials within the Central Intelligence Agency, hotly disputed the claim, arguing that the tubes were much better suited for use in conventional small artillery rockets. The first mention of any debate over the tubes' military applicability appeared in the *Times* on September 13, 2002. In the absence of congressional criticism of its position, the administration continued to dominate the news, leading the *Times* to conclude (falsely) that "the CIA had wide support, particularly among the government's top technical experts and nuclear scientists."[7] Marginalized within the administration, and failing to garner much attention on Capitol Hill, opponents of the CIA theory in the Department of Energy sought to influence public discourse by going public with its nonclassified findings with the Institute for Science and International Security. Still, multiple public briefings held by the institute attracted scant media attention, meriting only a back page article in the *Washington Post* and failing to ever appear in the *Times*.

One wonders why such a serious critique of the administration's main casus belli went uncovered. The *Times* itself acknowledged it was "partly because reporters did not realize [the briefings] had been done with the cooperation of top Energy Department experts." Perhaps even more important, though, members of Congress failed to publicly challenge the administration's claims,[8] leading the *Times* to conclude that "while administration officials spoke freely about the agency's theory, the evidence that best challenged this view remained almost entirely off limits for public debate."[9] In this instance, the American public did not receive full information concerning Bush's claims until after the Iraq War was completed and the nation's occupation had begun.

This example reveals an important fact about public debates that precede the use of military force: when evaluating the merits of White House claims, the mainstream print and television media rely heavily on official sources for information, and journalists tend to convey as many criticisms and qualifications of the president's position as top Washington bureaucrats and members of Congress are willing to express publicly. The strategy, from the journalists' perspective, makes the best of a difficult position. Should they step out and offer arguments and evidence that political elites refuse to endorse, and should later events demonstrate their error, journalists (their judgment and reputation in tow) will confront considerable scrutiny. But if they stick mainly to those claims offered by members of Congress, high-ranking bureaucrats, and representatives of the administration—that is, those who direct the nation's foreign policy apparatus— journalists find the cover needed to safeguard their perceived objectivity. For even if the arguments reported are subsequently shown to be wrong, journalists can claim to have only reiterated the official declarations of officials. Given the degree of uncertainty amid rapid advancements toward war, what more could they reasonably be expected to do?

Scholars have long recognized the media's reliance on government officials for information about foreign policy generally, and uses of force in particular.[10] In the last decade, however, they have gone considerably farther, suggesting that the content and scope of media coverage actually mirrors official Washington debate. As W. Lance Bennett argued in his seminal treatment of the subject, "mass media news professionals, from the boardroom to the beat, tend to 'index' the range of voices and viewpoints in both news and editorials according to the range of views expressed in mainstream government debate about a given topic." In addition to using government officials as sources of information about the president's plans, the media key off politicians' words and actions when making a wide variety of editorial decisions about the tone of their coverage, the selection of criticisms that deserve consideration and omission of those that do not, and the ultimate determination of whether to give the president a free pass or force him to address long lists of counterarguments and counterclaims. Though journalists are not mere propagandists working on behalf of the state, they nonetheless take their cues from key elected officials in the federal government. As a result, the parameters of mainstream media debate largely reflect the levels of consensus and conflict that circulate about Washington.

The "indexing hypothesis" highlights the media's dependence on government officials when crafting their foreign policy coverage.[11] Jonathan Mermin identifies its core claims and its implications for the spectrum of debate put before the American public:

The press is independent of the president, but not the government, as it does not offer critical analysis of White House policy decisions unless actors inside the government (most often in Congress) have done so first. This means the media act, for the most part, as a vehicle for government officials to criticize each other, reporting criticism of U.S. policy that has been expressed inside the government, but declining to report critical perspectives expressed outside of Washington.[12]

Those arguments that are aired within the nation's capital are, in turn, articulated on television and in newspapers; those that are not, no matter how valuable the insight or cogent the analysis, rarely find their way into foreign policy coverage. In sum, consensual politics breeds consensual news, just as contentious politics breeds contentious news. Within the media, the president receives as fair a hearing as officials in other branches of government, and in Congress in particular, are willing to grant him.

There are a host of reasons why journalists rely on Washington elites to determine the scope and content of their coverage. Some trace back to the paucity of public information available to evaluate the president's claims, others concern the dictates of maintaining a reputation for objectivity, and still others emanate from an assumed responsibility for following those individuals in government who retain the constitutional authority to formulate and implement foreign policy decisions. Whichever the primary causes of journalists' behavior, substantial empirical research corroborates the basic predictions of the indexing hypothesis. Bennett's original 1990 article demonstrated that *New York Times* coverage of U.S. funding for Nicaraguan contras in the mid 1980s relied overwhelmingly on government officials as sources, while other experts were regularly marginalized. Bennett also found that the scope and content of the newspaper's coverage systematically tracked congressional involvement in, and criticism of, the Reagan administration. When political elites complained, criticism in the newspaper quickly followed; when elites acquiesced, so did the *Times*. Rather than independent assessments of the nation's ongoing involvement in Central America setting the tone of its news coverage and content of its editorials, the *Times* took its cues straight from Congress.

Other analyses found much the same pattern in print and television coverage of the Vietnam War and the 1991 Persian Gulf War.[13] In the first book-length examination of the indexing hypothesis, Jonathan Mermin content-coded coverage by the *New York Times*, *ABC World News Tonight*, and *The MacNeil/Lehrer News Hour* of the 1983 invasion of Grenada, the 1989 deployment to Panama, the 1990 military buildup in the Gulf Region, the U.S. military presence in Somalia in 1993–94, and the 1994 invasion of Haiti. Mermin's analyses reveal startling correlations between the level of Washington political conflict surrounding a presidential use of force and the amount of criticism directed toward the

White House in media outlets. With the single exception of Reagan's bombing of Tripoli in 1986, every crisis received roughly as much media criticism as it did congressional scrutiny.

In the most exhaustive account of Congress and the press conducted to date, Doug Arnold presents evidence that the media closely follow members of Congress.[14] Regional newspapers regularly report on local representatives; news coverage is almost always positive or neutral; stories featuring members of Congress are prominently displayed within the newspapers; and within the news stories themselves, members are usually the primary or secondary subjects. Stories regularly report representatives' views on policy matters, especially when "there is intense conflict between the president and Congress, where presidential prestige is on the line and where the outcome is in doubt"—precisely the conditions that hold during the lead-up to a contentious military venture.[15] If members of Congress decide to take on the president in the weeks and months that precede a military action, they can expect media outlets to relay their views to the broader public faithfully and prominently.

Of course, any discussion of the media and Congress must consider the direction of causation: Is the press taking cues from Congress? Or is Congress taking its cues from the press? Alone, observed correlations between the content of press coverage and public declarations of Congress do not establish who, exactly, is leading whom. Rather than informing media coverage, Congress may simply be parroting perspectives aired on the prior evening's broadcasts. Though political communications scholars often overlook this basic issue, John Zaller and his colleagues have been notably attentive.[16] Drawing from a large body of public opinion research on the ways in which political elites shape and inform mass opinion, Zaller pores over the temporal ordering of the events leading up to military deployments and the stories that appear in the media.[17] Consistently, he finds, the media follow the positions taken by political elites, rather than vice versa. On virtually all domestic policy matters, and many foreign policies, members of Congress carefully monitor public opinion and the media. But in matters involving the use of force, neither the public nor the media are especially informed, and both tend to look to political elites for guidance on how to evaluate the president's position. Dictating conventional wisdom, Zaller concludes, "Elites lead, masses follow, and the press does the bidding of the government."[18]

While the basic thrust of the indexing hypothesis receives virtually unanimous support, scholars disagree over whether indexing merits the status of law or central tendency.[19] At the considerable risk of oversimplification, researchers can roughly be categorized as either strong or weak adherents of the hypothesis. Strong adherents, including Bennett, Mermin, and Zaller, maintain that the boundaries of national media coverage are almost totally defined by Washington debate. Only those arguments that receive some type of presidential or congressional endorsement make their way into the news. Rarely, if ever, does popular dissent or social opposition gain traction in the framing of news stories involving the presidential use of force.

Weak adherents take a more cautious stand. They suggest that Washington debate, while important, does not monopolize media coverage of a planned presidential use of force. Given the demands of twenty-four-hour cable news coverage and the proliferation of think tanks and public experts eager to lend their views, journalists now solicit the perspectives of a widening assortment of political commentators—foreign dignitaries, retired military personnel, area specialists, professors, and political activists. Weak adherents insist that the process of collecting news appears considerably more open, and more independent, than strong adherents of the indexing hypothesis are willing to admit. Though the spectrum of foreign policy coverage may be closely tied to official Washington debate, outsiders nonetheless have opportunities to air their views.

Robert Entman's "cascading activation model" is one of the most recent, and most sophisticated, formulations of weak adherence.[20] Entman fully acknowledges that the media look to political elites when considering how to cover a planned presidential use of force but contends that all political elites do not receive equal consideration. At the top of Entman's theoretical "waterfall" resides the presidential administration—and for good reason, as the president, and those who work directly for him, retains profound informational advantages that allow him to set the terms of subsequent debate. Though the White House establishes the dominant frame, when deciding whether (and how much) to criticize the president's position journalists continue to monitor the reactions of other Washington elites, particularly members of Congress, who occupy the second tier of Entman's waterfall.

Where Entman parts ways with the strong adherents to the indexing hypothesis is in suggesting that other voices (foreign leaders, unelected Washington insiders, and journalists themselves) and other factors (features of the observed crisis and the cultural values that support military action) contribute to the framing of foreign policy coverage. The more expansive scope of the cascading activation model accounts for a variety of phenomena that the indexing hypothesis cannot readily explain, such as instances when administration positions receive favorable exposure in the media even though Congress vehemently objects to the president's plans, and moments when members of the media launch their own critiques of the president. Moreover, the model goes some distance toward explaining when presidents succeed in framing the national debate over a military deployment, when they must contend with diverse viewpoints aired in the national media, and when, ultimately, they fail.

On two matters, however, strong and weak adherents basically agree. First, the president, more than anyone else, sets the terms of the national debate over a planned military venture. The president looms large in the interbranch politics that precede military deployments. For it is his policies, his evidence, and his objectives that stand front and center, and he and his subordinates who set the whole conversation in motion. Second, strong and weak adherents also recognize the importance of Congress. Indeed, more than anyone else, members of Congress determine whether the president's case for military action is given a free pass or is widely contested in the national media. For strong adherents, Beltway reactions carry over, in full, to media reactions; for weak adherents, adjoining branches of the federal government merely set the tone for subsequent reporting. But for all, participants in "official Washington debate" consist almost entirely of people working in the White House and on Capitol Hill, and Congress stands out as the "chief institutional locus of elite opposition" to the president.[21]

Though it has taken root within political communications circles, and hence has stirred anxieties about the independence of our nation's print and television media,[22] the indexing hypothesis also raises concerns about separation of powers, interbranch relations, and the presidential use of force. Specifically, it suggests that Congress exerts considerably more influence over public debates involving the presidential use of force than many had heretofore recognized. As Mermin notes:

> The indexing rule therefore enables a major factor that realists see as extraneous to sound foreign policy—domestic politics—to structure foreign-policy debate in the public sphere. The independent impact of the media on foreign-policy debate is marginal, but the impact of domestic politics turns out to be quite strong. The agenda-setting power journalists decline to exercise does not vanish into air. Instead, it is passed on to politicians.[23]

And it is passed on to members of Congress more than anyone else. Due to indexing, Congress's impact on public debates surrounding the use of force is amplified, as its members can rely on mainstream media to convey their objections to the public at large.[24] The media typically devote extensive coverage to Congress's legislative initiatives, hearings, floor debates, and public pronouncements on planned presidential uses of force. These actions, in turn, fundamentally shape the case for sending troops abroad that is ultimately put before the American people. When members pass resolutions backing the president, when they express solidarity with him on Sunday morning talk shows and evening news, when they stand before their colleagues and pronounce the vital interests being served by sending American troops abroad, the media tend to fall right in line behind the chief executive. When, instead, member after member insists that the presidential use of force violates basic constitutional principles, party leaders raise hard questions about the fate awaiting the nation's soldiers, or key committee chairs demand an exit strategy before a mission has even been launched, criticisms abound in the media. By extension, as the next chapter demonstrates, these criticisms are reflected in the minds of average voters struggling to understand their president's foreign policy.

It is worth emphasizing that Congress is not just one of many voices attempting to sway public opinion in favor of, or against, a planned military venture. If the indexing hypothesis is correct, Congress stands out as the single most important institution to check the kinds of arguments that the president can effectively make to the American public. As the media disregard many who would challenge the exercise of military power, it is often Congress alone that determines whether the president can proceed to the military action at hand. Even as the president continues to set the agenda and dominate the debate, possibilities for popular dissent critically ride with Congress.

The indexing hypothesis research, of course, is hardly the first body of work to suggest that Congress affects the tone and content of media coverage of foreign policies formulated within the executive branch and, by extension, public perceptions of the president. An entire subfield within American politics is devoted to studying the ways in which political elites frame public discourse and assign meaning to each other's actions, and some of the empirical studies in this tradition have examined the presidential use of force. Richard Brody, for example, argues that the probability that presidential approval ratings jump in the aftermath of a national crisis critically depend on congressional reactions.[25] By Brody's account:

> [Members of Congress] provide opinion leadership for the public. When they rally to the president or run for cover, the public will be given the implied or explicit message "appearances to the contrary notwithstanding, the president is doing his job well." Given this message, it is not surprising that, in the aggregate, the public rallies behind the president. When opinion leadership does not rally or run for cover, the media must and do report this fact. The public now receives countervailing elite evaluations of presidential performance and, in the aggregate, appears to look to the events themselves for information with which to update its judgment of how well the president is handling his job.[26]

Adam Berinsky echoes these sentiments, arguing:

> When political elites disagree as to the wisdom of intervention, the public divides as well. But when—for whatever reason—elites come to a

common interpretation of a political reality, the public gives them great latitude to wage war. Thus it is not the direct influence of events themselves that matter. Instead, it is the conflict among political elites concerning the salience and meaning of those events that determines if the public will rally to war.[27]

Rather than patriotic fervor automatically welling up in the hearts of every American every time the president sends troops abroad, public approval ratings vary according to the public reactions of party leaders and committee chairs within Congress. Absent any vocal criticism by the opposition party, citizens who are predisposed for ideological or partisan reasons to oppose their president may be swept up by the tide of events and images dominating the news. But when political opponents launch their attacks on the administration and its policies, like-minded citizens react to familiar partisan or ideological cues and withdraw their support for the president and his policies. Elite dissension, as it were, breeds confrontational media coverage, which, in turn, polarizes public opinion. Only when congressional elites stand beside the president does this causal chain produce anything resembling rally effects.[28]

All of these tendencies must be understood in probabilistic terms. That Congress objects does not automatically imply that the media will saturate the airwaves with critical coverage, nor that members of Congress will mobilize the public against a planned military action. Congress is fighting an uphill battle when it challenges the president on matters involving military force. Adherents of the indexing hypothesis, both weak and strong, recognize the structural and information advantages that the president enjoys in matters involving military policy.

Still, if the indexing hypothesis is correct, Congress plays a key role in shaping public debate. Congressional opposition may be a necessary, but perhaps not a sufficient, condition for widespread criticism of the president's position to take hold in the mainstream media. If the president often appears to enjoy a free ride in the press, this is only because members of Congress have chosen to either support him in the early stages of a military campaign or to step aside and await its early returns. But when party leaders in Congress rise up in defiance, the politics that precede the use of force may become notably contentious, and the longer-term political costs of a failed military venture rise in equal proportion.

Herein lies the key reason why the indexing hypothesis plausibly, if only partially, explains our empirical findings showing that presidents are less inclined to use military force when large and unified congressional majorities oppose them. The indexing hypothesis suggests that the scope and content of media criticism of presidents ought to covary with the scope and content of congressional dissent. We have already seen that members of the opposition party are much more likely to vote against an authorization to use force, and to vote for restrictions on the president's discretion to oversee an ongoing military venture. If members' involvement in public arguments about the efficacy of a planned use of force mirrors their voting behavior—and we shall soon show that it does—then we should expect congressional dissent to ring most loudly when the opposition party holds a preponderance of congressional seats. And when it does, media portrayals of a planned use of force ought to turn more and more negative.[29] If the indexing hypothesis is correct, partisan politics have important implications for the foreign policy news that average citizens read and watch.

LOCAL NEWS

To date, every empirical test of the indexing hypothesis has focused on national print and television news.[30] Scholars usually justify this exclusive focus on national news by pointing to one of two conflicting arguments. Some claim that local media follow national media, especially in foreign policy, and hence empirical tests of local news are redundant. For instance, Jonathan Mermin and Doris Graber contend that elite media—by which they mean network news and the *New York Times*—remain the most important sources of information for the middle of the political spectrum, particularly in foreign affairs.[31] If Mermin and Graber are correct, then all of the evidence in national news supporting the indexing hypothesis should carry over to local news. Other scholars who support excluding local news from empirical tests of the indexing hypothesis argue that local news outlets are influenced by local factors. According to Bennett, "The [indexing] hypothesis is an attempt to explain the behavior of 'leading' press organizations (i.e., the prestige national newspapers, wire services, television networks, and the 'big three' news magazines) that set professional press standards and influence the daily news agenda. It stands to reason that small-audience news outlets in the sway of ideological missions or local tastes would deviate from this norm."[32] While national media may index coverage of international policies to official Washington debate, Bennett suggests, local news outlets probably do not. On the whole, then, the existing scholarship is divided as to whether local media parrot or are independent of national media sources.

Whether local media index foreign policy coverage to Congress is not merely an academic question. Americans depend on local television broadcasts more than any other outlet for their domestic and foreign policy news. As political communication scholars Frank Gilliam and Shanto Iyengar note, "Local news is America's principal window on the world."[33] According to a 2004 survey conducted by the Pew Research Center for the People and the Press, 59 percent of Americans regularly watch local television news, as compared to 38 percent who watch cable news, 34 percent nightly network news, 22 percent network television magazines, and 22 percent morning news; as for other sources, 42 percent read newspapers, 25 percent read magazines, 40 percent listen to the radio, and 29 percent go online for their news.[34] Local news also remains a primary source of information for America's most educated citizens. Among college graduates, 54 percent of Americans regularly watch local television news, as compared to 38 percent who watch cable news, 35 percent who watch nightly network news, 43 percent network television magazines, and 21 percent morning news. According to the poll, 56 percent read newspapers, 33 percent read magazines, 51 percent listen to the radio, and 29 percent go online for their news.

The news that indexing hypothesis scholars have examined is not the news that the modal citizen actually views. When evaluating the merits of a planned military venture in Bosnia, Somalia, or Iraq, most Americans do not read the *New York Times* or watch *PBS*. At the end of their workdays, they turn to local news. But if local news does not privilege the opinions and arguments of congressional representatives, as the national media appear to do, then the institution's influence may be less than scholars assume. To date, no one has constructed a database of local news coverage of military policy. Indeed, to our knowledge, no one has constructed so much as a purely descriptive case study of local news and the use of force. To initiate this line of inquiry, we present findings on Congress's influence over local media coverage during the lead-up to the 2003 Iraq invasion.

Debating Iraq in 2002

During the summer and fall of 2002, the nation was fixated on the prospect of war against Iraq. Roughly 90 percent of Americans claimed to be closely following the situation—an extraordinary figure given the public's general apathy toward foreign policy matters. With a military victory against the Taliban regime in Afghanistan just completed, and the specter of September 11 looming over the national conscience, the Bush administration sought to expand its "war on terror" by confronting an old nemesis, Saddam Hussein.

In the nation's push toward war, President Bush stood out in front. Both domestically and abroad, almost everyone responded to an agenda that he set, a schedule he advanced, and a set of arguments he formulated. At the core of Bush's argument for war was a conviction that past measures taken to deal with Hussein—inspections, no-fly zones, economic sanctions, limited military strikes—had proven futile. Since the 1991 Gulf War, Hussein had repeatedly violated United Nations resolutions, had assembled an arsenal of weapons (including anthrax, mustard gas, sarin nerve gas, VX nerve gas, and ballistic missiles) that threatened the stability of the Middle East, and had strengthened his ties with al-Qaeda and other terrorist organizations. As Bush noted in a national address given in Cincinnati, Ohio, on October 7, "Saddam Hussein is harboring terrorists and the instruments of terror, the instruments of mass death and destruction."[35] And the nation, Bush insisted, could no longer stand by and watch. Only the credible threat of military action, the argument ran, could force Hussein to immediately reveal and destroy all of his weapons programs and stockpiles, and then to terminate his relationships with terrorist organizations.

Bush spent months trying to rally Congress, the American public, and the United Nations behind a military invasion that would serve the dual purposes of toppling the Hussein regime and advancing democracy in the region. As he told the General Assembly on September 12, 366 days after the terrorist attacks, "We must choose between a world of fear and a world of progress. We cannot stand by and do nothing while dangers gather. We must stand up for our security and for the permanent rights and the hopes of mankind. By heritage and by choice, the United States of America will make that stand."[36] From the administration's vantage point, the evidence was overwhelming, and the need for action clear. With or without UN support, Bush insisted, the United States would hold Hussein accountable for his past misdeeds and the present threat he posed to his own citizens and the world at large.

From the halls of Congress, a wide range of reactions to Bush's initiative emerged. Almost uniformly, Republicans came out in support, endorsing the president's prerogative to define both the nature of the problem and the course of corrective action. In a speech on the Senate floor, John Ensign (R-NV) made the argument for action and the urgency of rallying behind the president most forcefully:

"There is a time for all things," the Rev. Peter Muhlenberg told his congregation on the eve of the Revolutionary War, "a time to preach and a time to pray. But those times have passed away. There is a time to fight, and that time has now come." We have listened and we have prayed. Now we must fight. For the best honor we can bestow on those who have died for our nation, and those who will die for our nation, is victory. Victory over terrorism.[37]

Mitch McConnell (R-KY) concurred:

The fact is that President Bush is giving the United Nations and the international community a final chance to disarm Saddam Hussein through diplomatic means. But under no illusions of Saddam Hussein's violent and irrational character, the President has made clear that if reason fails, force will prevail. I am reminded of President Franklin Roosevelt['s] insights into Nazi Germany and Adolph Hitler: "No man can tame a tiger into a kitten by stroking it. There can be no appeasement with ruthlessness. There can be no reasoning with an incendiary bomb."[38]

The Democrats, meanwhile, appeared more divided on the issue. Some, such as Joseph Liebermann (D-CT) and Evan Bayh (D-IN) in the Senate and Richard Gephardt (D-MO) in the House, were willing to grant Bush broad latitude to decide whether and when to invade Iraq. For the most part, these Democrats only requested that before going t o war the president issue a formal determination that diplomatic alternatives had been exhausted and, once military action commenced, that he regularly consult with Congress. Other Democrats appeared willing to endorse military action, but preferred stronger limits on its scope and the establishment of clear commitments that the president would first exhaust all diplomatic solutions to the Iraq crisis. In the Senate, Foreign Relations Committee chairman Joseph Biden (D-DE) and Armed Services Committee chairman Carl Levin (D-MI) both pushed for an authorization that would restrict military efforts to uncover and disarm Iraq's weapons programs, that would force Bush to secure a UN Security Council resolution backing military action, and that would require the president to issue a formal determination before actually going to war. Finally, other members expressed outright opposition to any military venture whatsoever. Jim McDermott (D-WA) and David Bonior (D-MI) within the House and Paul Wellstone (D-MN) and Robert Byrd (D-WV) within the Senate raised numerous concerns, ranging from lack of evidence that Iraq posed an imminent threat to the United States' national security to Congress's supposed abrogation of its constitutional warmaking responsibilities.

By all accounts, Byrd was the most loquacious of Democrats, and the most willing to take on a popular president during the lead-up to war. With a long sense of history, he is worth quoting at some length:

The Polycraticus of John of Salisbury, completed in 1159, says that Nero, the sixth in line from Julius, having heard the Senate had condemned him to death, begged that someone would give him courage to die by dying with him as an example. When he perceived the horseman drawing near, he upbraided his own cowardice by saying: "I die shamefully." So saying, he drove the steel into his own throat and thus, says John of Salisbury, came to an end the whole House of the Caesars. Mr. President, here in this pernicious resolution on which the Senate will vote soon, we find the dagger that is being held at the throat of the Senate of the United States.[39]

Ever the stalwart defender of Congress's rightful place in debates over the use of force, Byrd continued:

> Mr. President, with reference to this Commander in Chief business that we hear about—oh, the Commander in Chief, they say. I listen to my friends across the aisle talking about the Commander in Chief. We must do this for the Commander in Chief; we must stand shoulder to shoulder with the Commander in Chief. The Commander in Chief. Of what is he Commander in Chief? The army, the navy, and the militia of the several States. But who provides the army and the navy? Who provides for the calling out of the militia of the several States? Congress. So much for the term "Commander in Chief." Charles I used that term in 1639—Commander in Chief. You know what happened to Charles I of England? The swordsman cut off the head of Charles I on January 30, 1649. So much for Commander in Chief. Parliament and the King of England fought a war. Can you imagine that? Can you imagine Congress fighting a war with the President of the United States? They did that in England. Yes, Parliament and the King fought a war. Who lost? The King. Who was it? King Charles I. A high court convened on January 1, I believe it was, 1649, and in 30 days they cut Charles I's head off—severed it from his body. So much for Charles I. That was the Commander in Chief. Yes. Hail to the chief.[40]

And so, while the president barnstormed the country highlighting the dangers of the Iraqi regime, the United Nations attempted to conduct weapons inspections, and the U.S. marshaled its forces to attack Iraq, arguments about the merits of military action dominated the national news. During late September and October 2002, all of Congress entered the fray, formally debating an authorization to use force against Iraq. On September 26, senators Tom Daschle (D-SD) and Trent Lott (R-MS) introduced a resolution based on the original White House proposal authorizing the use of force in Iraq. A few days later, Joseph Lieberman (D-CT) introduced to the Senate a slightly modified version, just as Speaker of the House Dennis Hastert (R-IL) and 136 cosponsors introduced to the House HJ Res. 114. On October 10, the House voted 296 to 133 in favor of the "Authorization for Use of Military Force Against Iraq Resolution of 2002," which granted the president authority to "use the Armed Forces of the United States as he determines to be necessary and appropriate in order to (1) defend the national security of the United States against the continuing threat posed by Iraq; and (2) enforce all relevant United Na-

tions Security Council resolutions regarding Iraq." By a margin of 77 to
23, the Senate followed suit the next day. In a Rose Garden ceremony, the
president signed the authorization into law,[41] securing his right to deploy
troops as he saw fit.

LOCAL AND NATIONAL NEWS STORIES ON IRAQ

The indexing hypothesis suggests at least two ways in which Congress
may affect media coverage. On the one hand, if journalists do not retain
any independent view of the president's position but instead merely
mimic official Washington debate, then we should expect to see as much
coverage as there is talk around Capitol Hill. On any given day, the president should receive as much positive coverage as there were positive arguments made about Congress during the previous news cycle, and the
total volume of coverage should match the intensity of debate around
Washington. On the other hand, if journalists rely on political elites when
updating their own views of a pending use of force, then a slightly different expectation emerges. While the volume of coverage may coincide with
congressional debate, news content should become noticeably more positive once Congress grants the president the power to exercise military
force.

Of course, the indexing hypothesis may be altogether wrong, and the
content and volume of news coverage may not track congressional activity in any discernible way. It is also possible that Bennett's intuition is correct, and that national television and print media index their coverage to
official Washington debate, while local television outlets pay little if any
attention to goings on about Congress. To explore these varied possibilities, we examine national and local news stories on Iraq broadcast between September 17 and October 31, a period when congressional involvement in and opinion about the impending Iraq War varied markedly.
The data consist of all news stories that aired on local affiliates of the
major networks (Fox, CBS, NBC, and ABC) in the nation's fifty largest
media markets,[42] where 66 percent of the American population resides.
By sampling the highest-rated early- and late-evening local and national
news broadcasts, we have one of the most comprehensive and systematic
collections of local television news ever gathered, and certainly the most
detailed inventory of local news coverage of a planned use of force.[43] In
addition, for purposes of comparison, we independently collected every
news story on Iraq published during the same period in the *New York
Times*.

Because electronic search engines were available, the collection of *Times*
stories on Iraq proved fairly straightforward. The assembly of local and

national television news broadcasts on Iraq, however, was a more challenging task. More than 10,000 news broadcasts and 5,500 hours of news programming from 122 local stations and 4 national affiliates initially required viewing. We and our team of coders at Harvard University and the University of Wisconsin watched all of these broadcasts and then clipped those stories that centrally concerned Iraq. In total, we identified 2,389 local television news stories, 162 national television stories, and 290 *Times* stories. Having identified the relevant news, we then content-coded each story, collecting information on the kinds of people who were either quoted or given air time, the kinds of arguments (positive and negative) they made on the use of force against Iraq, and the general slant of the story as a whole. In the analyses that follow, we focus on the 1,471 local stories, 117 national stories, and 206 *Times* stories that presented arguments for and against the use of force. The rest reported on events occurring domestically or abroad, but did not engage in any substantive way the ongoing debate about whether Congress or the public ought to rally around the president and support a military intervention in Iraq.

While this survey of news coverage of a planned use of force is unprecedented, it nonetheless presents unique challenges of its own. It is not clear, for instance, that there exists a single critical test of the indexing hypothesis. These data concern but one debate over one use of force, something about which we will have more to say later in this chapter. None of the analyses to follow establishes, definitively, the power of Congress to check those arguments and policies that the president puts before the American public. Collectively, however, the preponderance of the evidence suggests that the institution contributed to and in some instances shaped the volume and content of news coverage of Iraq. When understood within the broader array of empirical investigations on prior uses of force, we have solid grounds for concluding that Congress plays a vitally important role in shaping the news, and thereby the domestic politics, that surrounds the use of force.

MEDIA APPEARANCES

We start with the simple observation that news stories involving Iraq regularly feature members of Congress.[44] Table 6.1 shows the distribution of people who appear in news stories in our dataset.[45] As one might expect, more than anyone else journalists turned to the president and personnel within his administration—members of the State and Defense departments, intelligence officials, White House staff, and presidential advisors—for commentary on the mounting crisis in Iraq. At least one member of the president's administration (including the president himself) appeared in 52 percent of local television news stories, in 44 percent of national tel-

TABLE 6.1
Who Appears in Stories on Iraq

	Appearances in Stories	Number of Stories
All Media Outlets		
Administration	49.6%	1,794
Congress	21.0%	1,794
Other Politicians	3.8%	1,794
Other	26.0%	1,794
Local TV News		
Administration	52.3%	1,471
Congress	21.2%	1,471
Other Politicians	3.7%	1,471
Other	23.1%	1,471
National TV News		
Administration	43.6%	117
Congress	20.5%	117
Other Politicians	5.1%	117
Other	35.9%	117
New York Times		
Administration	33.5%	206
Congress	19.9%	206
Other Politicians	4.3%	206
Other	33.5%	206

Sample restricted to stories that present arguments for and against use of force in Iraq.

evision news stories, and in 34 percent of stories in the *New York Times.* Such findings are hardly surprising. As presidents retain the most information about unfolding foreign crises, and as presidents ultimately are the ones to decide whether the nation will deliver a military response, presidents secure the most space and airtime in the news.

Of course, Congress too has critical information about and constitutional authority over foreign policy making. And journalists clear considerable space for them. In this instance, members of Congress presented arguments on the mounting Iraq crisis in a remarkably high percentage of stories. On average, they appeared in roughly one in five stories overall, slightly more often in local television news and slightly less in the *Times.* The media granted members of Congress almost as much exposure as they did to all of the people placed in the "other" category combined: foreign heads of state, members of Saddam Hussein's regime, scholars from Washington think tanks, professors, United Nations and NATO representatives,

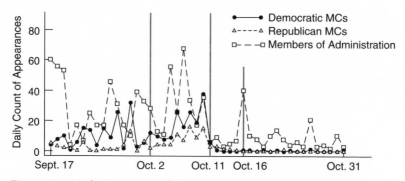

Figure 6.1. Media Exposure of Washington Politicians. October 2, congressional debate begins; October 11, Congress passes authorization; October 16, president signs authorization.

retired generals, and dignitaries. Other domestic politicians (mayors, governors, members of state legislatures) figured in a small fraction of the news stories.

Figure 6.1 further disaggregates the data, this time tracking the daily number of media appearances by Democratic members of Congress, Republican members of Congress, and personnel within the president's administration. Three features of this figure are worth noting. First, throughout the time period, members of the administration appeared in more news stories than either Democratic or Republican members of Congress, though not always the two combined. The gaps appear largest between September 17 and 20, when the Bush administration went before the United Nations to advocate for additional resolutions demanding that Iraq's weapons regime be dismantled, and on October 16, when Bush signed the authorization. But throughout, the president's administration effectively kept pace with congressional appearances in the news. Second, media appearances by all political actors intensified rather noticeably while Congress debated the use-of-force authorization. Whereas members of Congress appeared in the media, on average, 12.6 times per day before October 2, they appeared in 16.2 stories per day on average between the 2 and 16. Third, after the president signed the authorization into law, Republican and Democratic members of Congress completely disappeared from stories involving Iraq, affording the president considerable freedom to speak directly to the American citizenry. The moment Congress withdrew from the airwaves, a "one-way flow of information" took hold.[46]

ARGUING ABOUT IRAQ

Few observers would find it surprising that when reporting on Iraq, journalists turned to political actors from within the executive and legislative branches with such regularity. But the indexing hypothesis takes the case one step forward, suggesting that media coverage of Iraq actually tracks official Washington debate. To test this proposition, we need to pay special attention to the arguments for and against the use of force that members of Congress advanced, and then check whether different media outlets constructed stories that matched the content and volume of these arguments.

To do so, we coded all 708 speeches on Iraq that appeared in the *Congressional Record* between September 16 and October 31 for the kinds of claims made about an impending Iraq War. We then did the same for all local television, national television, and *New York Times* stories in our sample. In each instance, we checked whether the speech or story presented a number of specific arguments for or against the use of force—arguments involving issues ranging from the purported assembly of weapons of mass destruction to the ability of the United Nations to contain a rising Iraq threat.[47]

The findings tend to confirm the indexing hypothesis. When members of Congress spoke on the House or Senate floors, they presented, on average, a total of 3.8 different arguments; 3.1 supported the use of force (roughly 80 percent), and 0.7 opposed it. Similarly, within the various media outlets, stories on Iraq presented a total of 2.4 arguments; 1.7 supported the use of force (roughly 70 percent), and 0.7 opposed it. Among the media outlets, the *Times* printed a slightly higher proportion of arguments against the use of force, and local television news presented a slightly lower proportion. Overall, however, the balance of arguments in Congress and in the media appeared in general concordance with one another.

Table 6.2 identifies the regularity with which specific arguments appeared in congressional speeches and news stories on Iraq. Among arguments for the use of force, there was considerable overlap between congressional and media discussions. While speeches tended to cite more arguments, the rank ordering of arguments appearing in congressional speeches and news stories match one another rather closely. In every source, claims that Iraq was developing weapons of mass destruction, that it defied the United Nations and/or the world, and that it must be disarmed ranked among the most commonly identified reasons for using force. Meanwhile, concerns that the United Nations was incapable of meeting the task and that Iraq posed a threat to its own people were the least commonly identified reasons for using force. To be sure, a few discrepancies arose: congressional speeches contained more references to the threat that Iraq posed to American lives and the region than did the media, and fewer references to whether Bush had made a convincing case for going to war. On the whole, though, the distributions of arguments for using force against Iraq were roughly comparable in all four samples.

Congressional speeches and the media also tended to offer a similar sampling of arguments against the use of force. The most commonly cited

TABLE 6.2
Arguments on Iraq Made in Congress and the Media

		Forum		
	Congress	Local T.V. News	National TV News	NY Times
Percent of arguments for use of force that note:				
Iraq developing WMD	63.6	32.2	38.5	48.5
Iraq defied United Nations, world	47.2	23.9	25.6	33.5
Iraq must be disarmed	41.8	28.5	21.4	21.8
Iraq threat to American lives	35.6	13.7	6.8	10.2
Iraq violates human rights	32.1	5.1	5.1	16.5
Iraq threat to region	29.4	3.5	2.5	8.2
Iraq linked to terrorist groups	23.9	10.3	11.1	16.0
Iraq threat, no specific subject	16.9	15.8	17.9	9.2
Iraq threat to own people	9.6	3.6	2.6	8.3
Bush made convincing case	9.2	19.9	14.5	5.3
United Nations inadequate	5.1	2.5	1.7	2.4
Percent of arguments against use of force that note:				
War against Iraq would be costly	25.0	5.2	6.0	7.8
Bush has not made case for war	16.7	30.9	31.6	28.2
Iraq not threat to American lives	11.7	1.4	0.1	1.9
No Iraq links to terrorism	5.8	1.8	6.8	7.3
Iraq not a threat to its people	3.7	0.0	0.0	0.0
Iraq has disarmed	2.3	0.2	0.0	1.0
Iraq not threat, no specific subject	1.6	1.1	0.0	3.4
No evidence of WMD	1.6	8.2	7.7	7.8
Iraq not defied United Nations, world	0.6	0.3	0.8	2.9
Iraq not a threat to region	0.1	0.1	0.1	0.0
Iraq does not violate human rights	0.0	0.0	0.0	0.0
(N)	708 speeches	1,471 stories	117 stories	206 stories

Figures refer to the percentage of times that an argument for or against the use of force appeared in a speech made in Congress or in a story that aired in local television news, national television news, or in the *New York Times*. In order, arguments in support of the use of force included: Iraq has or is developing weapons of mass destruction; Iraq has defied the United Nations and/or the world; Iraq must be disarmed; Iraq is a threat to American lives; Iraq violates the human rights of its citizens; Iraq is a threat to the region; Iraq has links to terrorist groups; Iraq is a threat, no specific threat mentioned; Iraq is a threat to its own people; the Bush Administration has made a convincing case to attack Iraq; the United Nations is inadequate to address the threat posed by Iraq. Arguments in opposition to the use of force included: a military venture is likely to involve many casualties and high financial costs; the Bush Administration has not made a convincing case to attack Iraq; Iraq is not a threat to American lives; Iraq has no links to terrorist groups; Iraq is not a threat to its own people; Iraq has disarmed; Iraq is not a threat, no specific threat mentioned; Iraq has no or is not developing weapons of mass destruction; Iraq has not defied the United Nations, world; Iraq is not a threat to the region; and Iraq does not violate human rights of its citizens.

reasons for opposing military action centered on the costs of war, concerns that Bush had not made a case for war, and the fact that links between Iraq and terrorism were not well established. Similarly, the four samples rarely contained arguments that Iraq did not violate human rights, that it was not a threat to the region, and that it had not defied the United Nations. Again, some discrepancies arose. Members of Congress were less likely than the three media sources to claim that Bush had failed to make the case for war or that there was no evidence of weapons of mass destruction. In addition, members were more likely to raise concerns about the financial and human costs of military action and to assert that Iraq did not pose a threat to American lives. Overall, though, members of Congress and the media tended to agree on the most and least important reasons for opposing military action.[48]

As one would expect, the balance of arguments attributed to congressional Republicans and Democrats differed markedly from one another. In their speeches on the House and Senate floor, congressional Republicans presented, on average, 4.1 different arguments for the use of force and just 0.1 arguments against. By contrast, congressional Democrats in their speeches presented 2.4 arguments for and 1.1 arguments against the use of force. In television and print news stories, arguments advanced by members of the two parties differed just as greatly. When they appeared in the media, congressional Republicans presented 1.6 arguments for the use of force and 0.2 arguments against, and congressional Democrats presented 0.7 arguments for and 1.1 arguments against.[49]

Interestingly, there also was a strong temporal dynamic to the arguments advanced by Republicans and Democrats. The balance of arguments for and against the use of force advanced by congressional Republicans and Democrats varied rather markedly before (September 17–October 1), during (October 2–16), and after (October 17–31) the formal authorization debate. Before the debate, the support of congressional Republicans for military action appeared somewhat tepid. When delivering speeches in Congress, these individuals offered, on average, 2.6 arguments for the use of force and 0.4 arguments against. The moment Congress began to debate the authorization vote, however, congressional Republicans fell in line behind their president, offering an average of 4.2 arguments in favor of the use of force, and only 0.1 against it. After the president signed the authorization, congressional Republicans were not to be heard from. Only three congressional speeches in the final weeks of October featured a GOP legislator, as compared to 281 speeches during the formal authorization debate and 19 speeches in the two weeks that preceded it.

Congressional Democrats, meanwhile, marched to an altogether different drummer. Before the debate, congressional Democrats gave speeches that regularly argued against the use of force, and only occasionally did they present evidentiary claims or prognostications in support. During this period, Democrats presented 0.6 arguments for the use of force and 1.9 against before the authorization debate. Once the House and Senate took up debate, congressional Democrats changed their tune rather markedly, offering 2.7 arguments for the use of force and just 1.0 argument against.[50] Following the debate, they too withdrew from public sight, giving only 7 speeches during the last two weeks of October—as compared to 353 speeches during the first two weeks and 53 speeches in the final weeks of September.[51]

Panel A of figure 6.2 plots the daily output of congressional arguments for and against the use of force against Iraq.[52] During the period preceding the formal authorization debate, members advanced a modest number of arguments both for and against military action. During this period, Congress presented on average 5 arguments per day for the use of the force and 7 against. As the figure makes apparent, however, the levels of argumentation took off once the formal authorization debate began. Moreover, the balance of arguments turned markedly more supportive for the president. Between October 2 and October 16, an average of 130 arguments were presented per day in support of military action and 23 arguments against—as the graph plainly shows, this level of activity peaks between October 8 and October 10, when an average of 759 arguments per day were presented. Thereafter, however, members of Congress fell silent. Between October 17 and October 31, a grand total of 10 arguments were presented within Congress, a daily average of less than 1.

Knowing the patterns of activity and representation of Democrats and Republicans within Congress, and knowing the arguments that members of both parties advanced, the indexing hypothesis generates rather clear predictions about the overall volume and tone of media coverage. With regard to volume, moderate levels of argumentation should precede the authorization; while Congress formally debated the use of force against Iraq, arguments should escalate within the media; and then, after the president signed the authorization, precious few arguments either for or against the use of force should appear in the media. With regard to tone, we would expect that arguments against the use of force should constitute a larger proportion of total arguments in the weeks leading up to the authorization debate; throughout the period under consideration, arguments on behalf of using force should outnumber arguments against.

The production of local news (presented in panel B) follows a similar trajectory. In September, when debate within Congress was beginning to simmer, a moderate flow of stories on Iraq are observed. Between October 2 and October 11, when Congress debated the merits of granting the president the authority to use military force against Iraq in order to ensure compliance to various UN resolutions, both the local and national

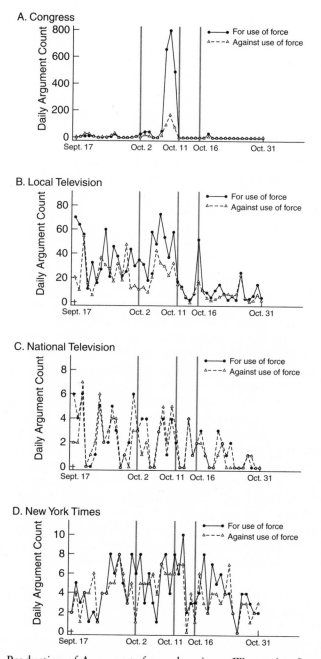

Figure 6.2. Production of Arguments for and against a War against Iraq. Counts represent number of arguments in *Congressional Record* (panel A) or news stories (all other panels) for and against the use of force. October 2, congressional debate begins; October 11, Congress passes authorization; October 16, president signs authorization.

series peaked. Then, having authorized the use of force, congressional activity and media coverage dropped off markedly—at least until October 16, when the president signed the bill into law. Thereafter, members of Congress were not to be heard from, and the media slipped into a quiet slumber. Between October 17 and October 31, members of Congress made a few last speeches on the floor before going into recess, while the media's coverage of the issue completely bottomed out. The correlation between *Congressional Record* speeches on Iraq and media activity is 0.59.

Local television news coverage, in this instance, matches our expectations almost perfectly. A steady supply of arguments flowed through local media outlets during the lead-up to the authorization debate, and once the formal debate began, local television news devoted a rising share of time to the topic of Iraq. But as soon as Congress passed and the president signed the authorization, local news turned to other kinds of stories. The balance of stories for and against the use of force also appears consistent with the indexing hypothesis. For much of the period leading up to the authorization debate, arguments for and against the use of force appeared in roughly equal measure. Once the authorization debate began, however, the former consistently outpaced the latter, and in the final weeks of October, when the volume of news production dropped off, the tone of stories continued to favor the president's position.

It was hardly a foregone conclusion that local media coverage of Iraq would appear so closely aligned to congressional activity. Congress, after all, was but one institution involved in a much larger debate about the efficacy of using force in the Middle East. During this period, Bush continuously lobbied on behalf of military action; Saddam Hussein's regime was actively defending itself before the world community; foreign policy experts were writing various reports about the purported threat that Iraq did or did not present to the country's security interests; European nations, especially France, Germany, and Russia, were publicly announcing their reservations about abandoning diplomatic solutions to the Iraq problem; the United Nations was preparing to debate resolutions designed to reintroduce weapons inspections; and large public protests (both domestic and international) were common. To be sure, from the evidence presented, it does not appear that Congress introduced the topic. Well before Congress launched its official debate, the media was devoting considerable airtime and column space to issues involving the use of force against Iraq. It is noteworthy, though, that the volume of media coverage intensified when Congress formally considered the authorization. Perhaps most remarkably, though, media coverage died down precisely when Congress withdrew from the debate, even as the president continued to face considerable domestic and international opposition. Moreover, important logistical questions remained unanswered: How long would a military intervention last? What was the exit plan? Which countries would join in support? How much would the intervention cost? Did the benefits of military action outweigh the risks? Members of Congress may have signed off in order to campaign for an upcoming midterm election, but by any reasonable standard, the Iraq issue remained alive and charged. Judging from the media coverage during the final weeks of October, however, viewers just would not know it.

While still broadly consistent with the indexing hypothesis, national television news did not so closely mimic the ebb and flow of official Washington debate. Take a look at panel C of figure 6.2. From mid September through October, the total volume of coverage did steadily decline, but the October 2 and October 16 transitions were not as abrupt as the indexing hypothesis would suggest. Furthermore, there is no evidence that the number of arguments presented in national news during the authorization debate surpassed the number presented before.[53] And on any given day, the national news presented a roughly equal number of arguments for and against the use of force. While these patterns may adhere to norms of balance and objectivity, they do not reflect the pattern of arguments coming out of Congress and the executive branch.

There is very little evidence, meanwhile, that the *New York Times* indexed its coverage of Iraq to official Washington debate (see panel D of figure 6.2). Coverage of Iraq remained relatively steady throughout the period—even during the last two weeks of October, when national and local television news affiliates devoted considerably less time to the impending use of force against Iraq. And on any given day, a roughly equal number of arguments for and against the use of force appeared within the newspaper's pages. Collectively, the pattern of coverage observed in figure 6.2—the relatively low frequencies with which members of Congress and the executive branch appeared in its stories shown in table 6.1, along with the higher percentages of "other politicians" and "others" voicing their opinions—suggest that the *Times,* more than national and local television news, engaged the issue on terms that were not set by leading members of either the legislative or executive branches. There is a certain irony in the fact that the *Times,* and the *Times* alone, devoted so much space in subsequent years to lamenting its failure to expose errors in Bush's case for using force against Iraq.[54]

So far, three findings deserve special consideration. First, consistent with the empirical findings in chapters 3, 4, and 5, partisanship continues to matter. When debating the use of force against Iraq, politics clearly did not stop at the water's edge; indeed, party identification proves to be a powerful predictor of who was saying what, when. Second, the indexing hypothesis finds support, not only because Congress is the major nonadministration source of arguments concerning Iraq, but also because the volume of media coverage devoted to Iraq systematically tracks the volume of congressional activity on the topic. Remarkably, the moment that legislative discussions over the use of force settled, and the instant government conflict was resolved, local television news immediately moved on to other issues. Third, and finally, evidence of indexing is stronger in local television news (which political communication scholars have mostly overlooked) and weaker in national print and television news (which prior scholars have studied in considerable depth). If the trends observed here apply generally—a topic we revisit at the end of the chapter—then previous empirical studies of the indexing hypothesis may actually understate the extent to which Congress affects popular deliberations about the potential use of force.

CONTENT OF INDIVIDUAL STORIES

Up until now, we have scrutinized the representation of Washington politicians in news stories involving Iraq and basic trends in reporting on the use of force. And we have found considerable, albeit not uniform, evidence that public debates over the use of force track Congress's involvement in the issue. The clearest evidence of Congress's impact on public deliberations concerns the minimal space and airtime devoted to the issue of Iraq once Congress resolved to authorize the use of force. It is possible, though, that the media devoted fewer stories to the topic without ever changing the content or tone of any individual one. Media clamoring over the use of force, as such, may have quieted down during the weeks after congressional debate, but within each story, journalists may have presented just as many arguments for and against the use of force and subjected Bush's claims to just as much scrutiny as before.

To investigate such possibilities, this section estimates some simple regression models that assess whether congressional activity covaries with the number and types of arguments presented in individual stories on the use of force. The number of arguments within each story is posited as a function of the period during which it was issued (*Pre-Authorization, Authorization,* or *Post-Authorization*) and its media source (*Local Television News, National Television News,* or *New York Times*).[55] The model results are presented in table 6.3.[55a] (Descriptive statistics are provided in table C.1 of appendix C).[56]

When considering the total number of arguments that are presented in a story (see column 1), the estimated effects are perfectly consistent with the indexing hypothesis. Relative to the pre-authorization period, the number of arguments presented in news stories spiked while Congress formally debated the use of force, just as it plummeted after the president signed the authorization.[57] During the authorization period, arguments per story increased by roughly one-third of a standard deviation; there-

TABLE 6.3
Volume of Arguments on Iraq Presented in News Stories

	All arguments presented		Arguments for use of force		Arguments against use of force	
	(1)		(2)		(3)	
Congressional Activity						
Authorization	0.68***	(0.09)	0.72***	(0.08)	−0.04	(0.04)
Post-Authorization	−0.45***	(0.09)	−0.31***	(0.08)	−0.14***	(0.05)
Source						
Local TV News	−0.61***	(0.17)	−0.29*	(0.15)	−0.32***	(0.07)
National TV News	−0.51**	(0.22)	−0.39**	(0.19)	−0.11	(0.10)
Constant	2.70***	(0.17)	1.72***	(0.15)	0.98***	(0.08)
(N)	1,794		1,794		1,794	
R^2	.07		.07		.02	

Least squares regressions estimated. *** = $p < 0.01$; two-tailed test; ** = $p < 0.05$; * = $p < 0.10$. Robust standard errors reported in parentheses. Dependent variable in column 1 is the total number of arguments presented in story; in 2, total number of arguments for use of force; in 3, total number of arguments against use of force. Sample restricted to stories that present arguments for and against use of force in Iraq. *Pre-Authorization* and *New York Times* are the reference categories for the two sets of variables.

after, they declined by roughly one-quarter of a standard deviation. Both the local and national television news registered negative and statistically significant results, suggesting that the *Times* conveyed more arguments per story than its television news counterparts.

When isolating arguments for and against the use of force (columns 2 and 3), results again are largely consistent with the indexing hypothesis. There are, however, a few differences between the models that are worth noting. First, while arguments for the use of force peaked during the authorization period, congressional debate registered null effects for arguments against the use of force. The total volume of arguments for the use of force increased within news stories while Congress debated the use of force; the number of arguments against the use of force within each story appeared unaffected by the initiation of debate over the authorization. Interestingly, while media source effects remain significant and negative in column 2, the coefficient for national news is insignificant in column 3, indicating that the *Times* and national television news presented an equivalent number of arguments against the use of force per story.[58]

The evidence presented thus far suggests that both the volume and content of local news coverage of Iraq tracked congressional debate on the topic. Obviously, though, many forces other than Congress contribute to news production. Recall Bennett's speculation that local news does not index official Washington debate, but rather caters its coverage to "ideological missions or local tastes." To account for such factors, we focus on local news and estimate a statistical model that posits the number of arguments within a story as a function of the period during which it aired, the network affiliate that aired it, the day of the week that it appeared on television, and a host of market demographics.[59] Table 6.4 presents the results.

The findings are consistent with those observed for local news in tables 6.2 and 6.3. During the authorization period, stories presented significantly more arguments overall, and arguments for the use of force in particular; thereafter, they presented significantly fewer. Throughout the period under consideration, stories presented a roughly equivalent number of arguments against the use of force. Temporal variability in the content of each story, as such, appears to be a function of the number of arguments on behalf of using force against Iraq, rather than the number of arguments against.

The additional controls that the models include, for the most part, have little bearing on local news coverage of Iraq. In columns 1 and 2, virtually all of the market controls generate insignificant effects. Interestingly, though, local news in richer and more Democratic media markets presented a higher number of arguments against the use of force within each story. In all three models, Fox affiliates presented significantly more arguments concerning the use of force, as did ABC in columns 1 and 2, than did CBS, the reference category. There is also some evidence of weekly news cycle effects. On Sundays, news stories presented significantly more arguments for using force, and significantly fewer against, than during the week, the reference category; similar patterns are observed on Saturdays, though the effects are only significant in column 3.

Thus far, each of these models predicts the total number of arguments— for and against the use of force—that different media sources present within each story. And again, we can attribute a fair amount of variation across stories to changes in congressional involvement in the debate. But does congressional involvement in the debate have any bearing on different media outlets' willingness to present a higher or lower proportion of arguments for or against the use of force? On balance, that is, do news stories become more positive or negative toward Bush during each of the periods under consideration? To investigate the matter, we revisit our three previous regression models, this time substituting as the dependent variable the proportion of arguments that support the use of force.[60] We present the results in table 6.5.

Column 1 shows that local news stories, for the most part, report a higher proportion of arguments that support Bush's position than did stories in either national television news or the *Times*. The models also

TABLE 6.4
Volume of Arguments on Iraq Presented in News Stories, with Background Controls

	All arguments presented		Arguments for use of force		Arguments against use of force	
	(1)		(2)		(3)	
Congressional Activity						
Authorization	0.70***	(0.09)	0.75***	(0.08)	−0.06	(0.04)
Post-Authorization	−0.46***	(0.09)	−0.39**	(0.09)	−0.08	(0.06)
Affiliate						
Fox	0.49***	(0.12)	0.32***	(0.12)	0.17***	(0.07)
NBC	−0.06	(0.10)	−0.04	(0.10)	−0.02	(0.05)
ABC	0.22**	(0.11)	0.20**	(0.10)	0.02	(0.05)
Weekly News Cycles						
Saturday	−0.10	(0.11)	0.04	(0.11)	−0.14**	(0.06)
Sunday	0.78***	(0.17)	0.95***	(0.16)	−0.16***	(0.06)
Market Controls						
Pct Democratic	0.99*	(0.57)	0.25	(0.52)	0.74**	(0.30)
Pct Minority	−0.28	(0.51)	−0.31	(0.47)	0.03	(0.25)
Pct Born US	−0.62	(0.80)	−0.97	(0.76)	0.35	(0.41)
Pct College Graduate	−0.99	(2.66)	−1.23	(2.40)	0.24	(1.43)
Population (in millions)	−0.12	(0.17)	−0.10	(0.16)	−0.01	(0.09)
South	0.01	(0.09)	0.03	(0.09)	−0.02	(0.05)
Per Capita Income (in ten thousands)	0.17	(0.19)	−0.05	(0.18)	0.21**	(0.09)
Constant	1.80	(1.21)	2.30**	(1.15)	−0.51	(0.62)
(N)	1,471		1,471		1,471	
R^2	.12		.14		.04	

Least squares regressions estimated. *** = $p < 0.01$, two-tailed test; ** = $p < 0.05$; * = $p < 0.10$. Robust standard errors reported in parentheses. Dependent variable in model 1 is the total number of arguments presented in story; in 2, total number of arguments for use of force; in 3, total number of arguments against use of force. Sample restricted to stories that present arguments for and against use of force in Iraq. Pre-Authorization, CBS, and Weekday are the reference categories for the first three sets of variables.

present strong evidence of temporal effects—though as column 2 and 3 make clear, effects vary markedly across the three media sources. The estimates in column 2 suggest that before the authorization vote, local news stories were significantly more positive toward the use of force than were *New York Times* stories. Once Congress began to formally debate the authorization, local news stories turned even more positive. But in the

TABLE 6.5
The Balance of Arguments for and against a War against Iraq

	All Stories		All Stories		Local Stories	
	(1)		(2)		(3)	
Congressional Activity						
Authorization	0.08***	(0.02)	—		0.08***	(0.02)
Post-Authorization	−0.03	(0.03)	—		−0.08***	(0.04)
Source						
Local TV News	0.07**	(0.03)	—		—	
National TV News	−0.02	(0.05)	—		—	
Congress/Source Interactions						
Local (Pre-A)	—		0.10*	(0.05)	—	
Local (A)	—		0.18***	(0.05)	—	
Local (Post-A)	—		0.03	(0.06)	—	
National (Pre-A)	—		0.03	(0.07)	—	
National (A)	—		0.02	(0.08)	—	
National (Post-A)	—		0.12	(0.11)	—	
New York Times (A)	—		0.08	(0.06)	—	
New York Times (Post-A)	—		0.06	(0.07)	—	
Affiliate						
Fox	—		—		0.04	(0.03)
NBC	—		—		0.02	(0.03)
ABC	—		—		0.00	(0.03)
Weekly News Cycles						
Saturday	—		—		−0.04	(0.03)
Sunday	—		—		−0.08***	(0.03)
Market Controls						
Pct Democratic	—		—		0.28*	(0.15)
Pct Minority	—		—		0.06	(0.13)
Pct Born US	—		—		0.29	(0.21)
Pct College Graduate	—		—		0.10	(0.67)
Population (in millions)	—		—		0.02	(0.05)
South	—		—		−0.00	(0.03)
Per Capita Income (in ten thousands)	—		—		0.07	(0.05)
Constant	0.59***	(0.03)	0.55***	(0.05)	−0.25	(0.32)
(N)	1,794		1,794		1,471	
R^2	.02		.02		.04	

The dependent variable is the proportion of total arguments that support the use of force within each story. Least squares estimated. *** = $p < 0.01$, two-tailed test; ** = $p < 0.05$; * = $p < 0.10$. Robust standard errors reported in parentheses. Columns 1 and 2 consider stories from all media outlets; column 3 focuses only on local stories. All samples restricted to stories that present arguments for and against use of force in Iraq. Pre-authorization, *New York Times* (Pre-A), CBS, and Weekday are the reference categories for the first five sets of variables.

weeks that followed, when the total volume of coverage plummeted, local news stories appeared no more positive toward the use of force than were *Times* stories before the authorization vote. On national television news, meanwhile, stories predictably turned more positive as Congress rallied behind the president, though the effects are not statistically significant. And once again, the *New York Times* coverage of Iraq appeared unrelated to Congress's involvement in the issue.

Members' campaigning strategies for the midterm elections, we suspect, account for the observed differences across media sources. During the weeks immediately following the authorization vote, members of Congress constituted a disproportionate share of the guests on local news stories involving Iraq—even though they almost never appeared in the *New York Times* or national news. Moreover, those members who appeared in local news stories tended to be Democrats interested in explaining their votes against the use of force; meanwhile, Republicans and Democrats who voted for the authorization rarely if ever appeared in local news stories on Iraq. As a consequence, local news stories, on average, turned more critical toward Bush after he won the authorization vote, while national television news turned positive, and the *New York Times* remained altogether unaffected.

It is intriguing that local news stories were especially critical of Bush after Congress enacted the authorization—an outcome that is difficult to reconcile with the indexing hypothesis. For two reasons, however, we should not make too much of this finding. First, all of the evidence suggests that when Congress began formally debating the use of force, Republicans uniformly fell behind their commander in chief and Democratic opposition assumed a more evenhanded stance; concomitantly, local news stories presented more and more arguments for using force against Iraq. Second, the finding is based on a tiny number of observations, as local news on Iraq virtually disappeared during the last few weeks of October. Though an average of 5.8 local news stories on Iraq were aired daily in each media market during the authorization period, just 1.8 aired, on average, during the last two weeks of October. So local news stories may have turned negative toward the end of October; at the time, however, there were very few stories in circulation.

SUMMARIZING THE EVIDENCE

When introducing the data for this chapter, we noted that the indexing hypothesis generates two predictions about how congressional debate over the use of force might affect media coverage. First, journalists could have engaged the topic as much (or as little) as Congress did on any given day, and the scope and content of its coverage could have reflected the range of voices then heard within the executive and legislative branches. Alternatively, once Congress signed off on the use of force, journalists might have offered a steady stream of stories that supported the president's argument, no matter what individual members of Congress said or did during the proceeding weeks. Which outcome was observed, we speculated, very much depended upon the underlying processes of news making. If journalists were merely holding up a mirror to official Washington debate, then the former possibility seemed likely. But if they were updating their own beliefs about the efficacy of a planned military venture based on what members of Congress had to say, then the latter scenario seemed more plausible.

The preponderance of the evidence suggests that journalists merely reflected views expressed within Washington. The total volume of coverage tended to track the levels of congressional activity on Iraq, peaking during the authorization period and rapidly declining thereafter. And the number of arguments for and against the use of force that were presented within each story followed similar trajectories. There is little evidence that the congressional authorization convinced journalists about the merits of using force against Iraq or that they adjusted the slant of their coverage to reflect this new consensus. The larger effects, instead, suggest that journalists became convinced that the issue was resolved—even though, as a factual matter, it plainly was not—and that they should now turn their attention to other policy matters, just as most members of Congress were doing.

Local television news, national television news, and the *New York Times* incorporated congressional debate into their coverage of Iraq in different ways and to different degrees. Members of Congress regularly appeared in local television news. And the volume of local news on Iraq, as well as the number of total arguments presented within each story, almost perfectly mirrored Congress's involvement in the issue. Curiously, though, after the president signed the authorization, the tone of local news turned negative—a fact that directly challenged the supposition that journalists might rely on Congress as an institution to inform their own judgments about a planned military action. National media outlets, meanwhile, looked somewhat different. The *New York Times* regularly reported the opinions of experts outside of Congress and the presidential administration, while the volume of its coverage appeared relatively constant during this period. Nonetheless, within each newspaper article, the number of arguments presented on Iraq did run in concert with activity levels within Congress. National television news, for its part, also featured the views of nongovernmental officials. The congressional authorization debate hardly interrupted the steady decline of time devoted to the issue of Iraq, while the number of arguments presented within each broadcast failed to reveal much temporal variability.

Evidence of indexing, as such, appears contingent on the media source consulted—with members of Congress enjoying the greatest influence over local news. To be sure, though, the findings presented in this chapter concern just one case, and as such, they hardly constitute an exhaustive study of the indexing hypothesis in particular, much less of all the factors that contribute to media coverage of foreign policy more generally. One wonders, for instance, whether a congressional vote against the use of force might inflame criticisms against the president within national and local media outlets; whether congressional votes on uses of force against lesser-known nations and regimes generate comparable effects; and whether heated congressional debate that occurs outside the context of a formal authorization vote materially influences the volume or content of local media coverage. This chapter leaves important questions unanswered, and we, quite consciously, leave to another day the work required to answer these.

Still, the 2002 debates over what turned out to be the 2003 Iraq War constitute a difficult test for the indexing hypothesis. This, after all, was not an instance of the president recommending military action in some distant region of the world about which average citizens knew little or nothing. During the period under consideration, all kinds of political actors, foreign nations, and organizations were actively engaged in the debate, and media outlets, as such, were hardly wanting for expert opinion. In 2002, unlike 1982 (much less 1962), there were numerous media sources—the internet and cable television most prominently—engaged in the debate, further challenging the federal government's capacity to dictate the terms or scope of discussion over the use of force. And many of the journalists covering the debate had experience with the previous Iraq War, which further muted those factors (low information, lack of onsite observers, among other things) that encourage news outlets to index their coverage to official Washington debate. Given such a large number of potential news sources, such high levels of public awareness, and so many media forums, it seems unlikely that opposition voices within Congress would materially influence television or print news. That they do, especially in local news, is quite remarkable.

Three other distinguishing facts about these debates are worth noting. First, debate over an Iraq War came on the heels of September 11 and a largely successful, and popular, military campaign in Afghanistan. The president enjoyed remarkably high approval ratings, and the public, by and large, appeared willing to follow his lead. Second, by the president's own account, this was a preemptive strike. There was no discrete and discernible event that precipitated the military strike, one that political elites could carefully study and interpret. Journalists did have information about the region and experience from which to draw. But the justification for this military strike was based largely on new intelligence that the president had and Congress did not. Both of these factors suggest that indexing is likely, but that the president, more than Congress, dictates the flow of information from Washington to mass publics.

Third, and finally, this was a massive military intervention with a long prelude. Not all uses of force are so large or receive so much media and public attention. Often, presidents launch targeted initiatives without consulting with Congress, and the media do not learn about military operations until troops are placed in the field. And almost always, uses of force are smaller in scope and shorter in duration than what turned out to be the 2003 Iraq War and subsequent occupation. The fact that these uses of force are not subject to such media coverage, and that Congress does not have much of an opportunity to motivate and shape public debate, may help elucidate why congressional effects in chapter 3 were isolated to major uses of force.

Whether or not the September and October 2002 debates over Iraq present a hard case for indexing generally, and congressional influence over news coverage in particular, they still concern but one prospective military operation. As such, the findings presented in this chapter should not be considered in isolation, but rather juxtaposed with all of the prior empirical investigations of the indexing hypothesis. In a number of regards, the data examined here are unique: they include local television news stories, they link a formal authorization vote within Congress to changes in the volume and content of media coverage, and they distinguish the balance of arguments advanced by congressional Democrats and Republicans. But when reflecting on the wider body of evidence that scholars have amassed on the indexing hypothesis, there is an even stronger basis for stipulating that Congress, perhaps more than any other domestic or international political institution, serves as a check on the arguments that presidents articulate in the media. We still do not know whether the precise trends in local television coverage generalize to other events or other times. But we can conclude with some certainty that Congress contributes to media coverage of those debates that precede the use of force.

If David Mayhew is correct that much of politics consists of jockeying over positions and making "moves" designed to shape public discussions about a range of policy issues, then the evidence presented in this chapter would seem to bode well for members of Congress.[61] By influencing the volume and content of media coverage of a planned use of force, members of Congress intercede in the president's ongoing struggles to direct the news coverage—and all of the deliberations, expectations, and assessments of the nation's resolve that flow from it—of a prospective military venture. When members object, it would seem, their voices carry well beyond the halls of Congress.

In the next chapter we suggest that congressional influence extends further still. For by shaping media coverage, members of Congress both directly and indirectly affect the willingness of average citizens to support a presidential use of force. Using a variety of observational and experimental datasets, chapter 7 demonstrates that congressional influence over the media results in influence over public opinion, which can, in turn, influence presidential decision making. And by prompting public unease about the downsides of an impending military venture, we shall suggest, members of Congress find the means by which to retard, and occasionally even reverse, the president's plans for war.

CHAPTER 7

The Media and Public Opinion

LINKAGES BETWEEN CONGRESS and the media appear strong. A large literature on the indexing hypothesis demonstrates that Congress, more than any other political institution, determines whether critical perspectives about a planned use of force are aired to the public. Interestingly, scholars working within this literature restrict their empirical investigations to national print and television news, yet the previous chapter presents evidence that congressional influence registers most clearly in local media coverage. While the executive and legislative branches debated the merits of launching military strikes against Iraq, local media outlets followed suit, presenting as many arguments for and against the use of force as appeared in official Washington debate. Congressional opinions over the planned use of force, it would seem, not only spill over into local news broadcasts—they actually dictate the intensity of voices put before the American public.

Typically, scholars working on the indexing hypothesis suspend their analysis once stories are crafted and published, leaving readers to wonder whether the forces that Congress sets in motion have any discernible impact on the thinking of average citizens. This chapter addresses this issue. Revisiting the debates over the Iraq War in 2002 and introducing new experimental findings, it presents evidence that local television news influenced people's support for Bush's Middle East policy, and that congressional support for and opposition to the president also affect the probability that individuals will back a new proposal for military action. By shaping the content of news stories on military operations, Congress influences public support for the president and thereby gains an important foothold in White House deliberations over whether, and when, to send troops abroad.

SCHOLARSHIP ON NEWS AND PUBLIC OPINION

Enormous literatures within political science examine how average citizens understand television news and whether the mass media inform their views about politics and public policy.[1] Although we cannot possibly summarize this work here, we draw three useful lessons about citizens' involvement in politics, as well as the probability that new information presented to them about a prospective use of force will influence the views they hold. Stripped of the caveats and qualifications that rightly preoccupy scholars of political behavior, these lessons provide a backdrop for the empirical tests presented later in this chapter and establish a basis for believing that Congress's influence over the media translates, in turn, into influence over public opinion.

The first lesson is perhaps the most basic: most citizens' views on policy matters are unorganized, unstable, and ill-informed. People's political views on one issue often have little relationship to their views on other, ostensibly related issues. The views they express in the context of surveys often change from month to month and year to year, and the opinions they formulate about a particular issue often rest on fragmentary, and sometimes fallible, information. The result, Philip Converse claimed some forty years ago, is that citizens are best understood as having "non-attitudes."[2] And in many ways, the field of political behavior since Converse's seminal article can be understood as an ongoing effort to understand how, and whether, poorly informed and inattentive people navigate a complicated and evolving political universe, using as guides their partisan affiliation,[3] retrospective voting,[4] stereotypes,[5] or other heuristics.[6] To be sure, disagreements linger about whether people succeed or fail in this endeavor, and what implications this has for the health of our democratic institutions. And much about the cognitive processes that people use to understand politics remains poorly understood. Still, the facts that motivate these higher-order debates, for the most part, remain uncontested—namely, average citizens know very little about politics, and they know even less about specific policies that do not have a direct bearing on their own lives or on those around them.[7]

If this is true of matters involving domestic politics, it is doubly true of international affairs. Average citizens' views about events occurring in far-off lands tend to be less organized, less stable, and less informed.[8] Individuals may have firm opinions on such charged and polarizing issues as the death penalty, abortion, and gun control—and many track a single policy that affects their lives immediately, such as dairy or ethanol subsidies. But foreign policy is generally different, as people tend to know less (and, often, care less) about the doings of their government abroad. To be sure, international affairs often do attract widespread attention, such as during the post-9/11 period, the 1991 Gulf War, and even the beginnings of the Bosnia crisis in the early 1990s. Additionally, the prospect of war surely catches the public's attention. On the whole, though, most citizens, most of the time, come to foreign policy discussions with fewer well-defined and independently formulated prior beliefs than they do to domestic policy debates; and the opinions that citizens formulate in foreign policy discussions are not usually moored to the strongest of ideological principles.[9]

The second lesson is a rather obvious extension of the first. With little information about politics, especially international politics, and without a strong ideological edifice to direct their political choices, people are susceptible to persuasion and, some would say, manipulation. By restructuring policy options, by priming essential values, or by framing options strategically, polling organizations can elicit from respondents what would appear to be wildly divergent views about the same substantive issue. The answers given on either telephone surveys or voting ballots depend critically on the options presented and the language used to describe them. How this manipulation happens and to whom remain subjects of continued and vibrant research.[10] Many voters hold at least a handful of policy views from which they are not easily dissuaded, and not all appeals and manipulations by either survey outfits or political elites induce equivalent responses from all citizens. But precisely because most people are ill-informed about policy issues generally, and foreign policy issues in particular, few hold steadfast to preexisting views, discounting every countervailing argument that is presented to them. Whether by changing the wording of a survey question or a ballot initiative, it is possible to elicit from some citizens a considerably wide range of policy choices.

This leads us to the third lesson: because most citizens pay little attention to politics, and because they are susceptible to persuasion, the news they watch has the potential to influence their views.[11] As Shanto Iyengar and Donald Kinder argue, "Television news is in fact an educator virtually without peer . . . it shapes the American public's conception of political life in pervasive ways . . . television news is news that matters."[12] To be sure, objective news, tempered and balanced, may not sway average citizens' views about politics and policy options.[13] For news to persuade, it may need to present a disproportionate number of arguments either for or against a public policy.[14] But when news leans forcefully in one direction, it may succeed in arousing viewers' attention and convincing them of the merits of one policy option or another.

All of these lessons, of course, are only central tendencies. Survey respondents exhibit varying amounts of prior knowledge about political issues, foreign and domestic. Some respondents are more susceptible to persuasion than others, and some learn about certain policy options from direct experience and independent investigation rather than from print or television news. These lessons, nonetheless, serve as useful guides when trying to understand the public debates that often precede the use of military force abroad. During such periods, virtually all the information available to average citizens on foreign policy comes through the media. Most do not have any direct insight into the conditions in Sudan or Liberia or Haiti—nor do they know anyone who does. What Americans know about these countries, how they understand the problems these countries face, and whether they relate these problems to notions of national interest or personal welfare critically depend on the news that they watch. If ever news matters, it ought to matter during the lead-up to a military venture conducted abroad.

Though these three lessons on political behavior suggest that television news should affect average respondents' thinking about prospective military interventions, the practical realities of conducting quantitative research on the topic are daunting. A variety of modeling and measurement problems complicate the endeavor. Two stand out. The first involves matters of causal inference. Do the people who construct the news for local media outlets come from the same pool of individuals as respondents to national surveys? And if so, how do we know that one group is informing the other? Perhaps, instead, newscasters tailor the arguments they present in their stories to suit the opinions, and political leanings, of their audience. In this case, the views of average respondents percolate upward, informing the arguments that elites make in the news. This claim does run contrary to much of the public opinion literature, which posits elites as senders and mass publics as receivers of information; conventional wisdom, after all, dictates that "public opinion seem(s) to follow, not lead, the agenda set by the press."[15] Nonetheless, efforts to identify media influence over public opinion must account for the possibility that newscasters select and present news to please their audience. And depending on how one understands the issue, this possibility requires statistical solutions to the problems of either omitted variable bias or endogeneity.

The second challenge is more pedestrian, but no less vexing—namely, how to adequately identify and summarize the news to which respondents are exposed. The less we know about the viewing habits of respondents, the more difficult it is to establish a link between what appears in media outlets and what individual people think about a range of political subjects.[16] With the increasing volume and differentiation of media outlets, the problem is only compounded. The *New York Times* presents a very different kind of news than the Fox News Network, which, in turn, differs markedly from many Fox local affiliates. Respondent X may import his views on Candidate Y or referendum Z directly from what he reads in a newspaper or what he sees on television—but unless we, as social scientists, observe what he has watched or read, it is difficult to trace the origins of his choices. As a consequence, tests of news and public opinion that rely on observational (as opposed to experimental) data will have a difficult time finding significant effects. All too often, we are left with strong reasons for believing that news matters, but few findings that demonstrate the fact.

SUPPORT FOR THE IRAQ WAR, SURVEY DATA

The Pew Research Center for the People and the Press is an independent organization that regularly conducts national surveys that track attitudes toward the press and a variety of salient public issues. Fortuitously, on October 10, 2002, and then again on October 30, the Pew Research Center released national surveys that asked a broad array of questions regarding the impending war in Iraq.[17] The surveys asked about people's political views, their attention to the ongoing debate over Iraq, and most critically, their views on the efficacy of military action. One question, asked in both surveys, gets to the heart of the matter: "Would you favor or oppose taking military action in Iraq to end Saddam Hussein's rule?" Assuredly, there were other competing reasons for using military force against Iraq that did not concern the toppling of Hussein's regime, but this question does a better job than any other in the two surveys of gauging respondents' general views on the efficacy of a military intervention against Iraq. As such, it serves as the basis for most of the empirical investigations presented in this chapter.

The Pew surveys coincide almost perfectly with our data on television and print news coverage on Iraq, providing a unique opportunity to assess the relationships between people's views on the use of force and the content of local news. Unfortunately, we do not know the exact source of news that each respondent turns to for information about foreign affairs, and hence our measures of news coverage are unavoidably crude. We do not know, for instance, who routinely read the *New York Times*, who watched NBC national television news, who watched Fox local news, and who perused some combination of the three. All we know is that a respondent resided within one of the fifty largest media markets; as a consequence, the only source of identifiable variance concerns the content of local news that aired across them.[18] This fact, if anything, should bias our tests toward finding no effects. Because some respondents relied on other news sources to inform their views about Iraq, and because those respondents who did turn to local news may have watched only one affiliate, the tests presented below are likely to understate the true relationship between news coverage and public opinion.

Abiding John Zaller's insight that "what matters for the formation of mass opinion is the relative balance and overall amount of media attention to contending political positions,"[19] we summarize the news in each media market by measuring the proportion of total arguments presented in the local news that opposed the use of force against Iraq. As table D.1 of appendix D indicates, the measures reveal a fair amount of variation across media markets, with negative arguments constituting somewhere between 0 and 50 percent of all arguments during this period, with a mean of 25 percent and standard deviation of roughly 10.[20] The media coverage breaks in expected ways: the five media markets to air the lowest percentage of negative arguments include Phoenix, Kansas City, Raleigh, San Antonio, and Charlotte; the five media markets with the highest proportions of negative arguments include Seattle, Philadelphia, Harrisburg, Chicago, and Miami.

Obviously, people's views about any given policy depend on much more than the local news that airs on their television screens each night. Fortunately, we can account for many of these factors. The Pew surveys contain demographic indicators about each respondent—gender, education, race/ethnicity, religion, among other things. In addition, we can identify the kinds of neighborhoods that respondents inhabit. Drawing from the 2000 Census and electoral returns, we have a large body of information about the socioeconomic standing and partisan composition of communities within each media market. These data, as we argue below, help address a variety of potential statistical problems that make it difficult to discern the true relationship between the news people watch and the opinions that they hold.

FINDINGS

To begin, we assess the basic relationship between respondents' willingness to support military action against Iraq and the local news coverage on the subject. Imagine for a moment that the views people hold on foreign policy matters perfectly reflect the news that airs on television—that is, that respondents lack any ideological predispositions or personal traits that potentially mitigate the media's influence on their support for war. Were this imagined world to approximate the real world, then individual views on Iraq should depend solely on the arguments that air on local television news. We therefore estimate a simple logistic regression that posits support for the use of force as a function of *News*, a variable that measures the proportion of arguments against the Iraq War on local television news that were aired on the four local news affiliates during the prior three weeks.[21] Column 1 of table 7.1 presents the results.[21a]

From the perspective of those congressional members intent on checking presidential power—members who, as chapter 6 demonstrates, exert considerable influence over the content and volume of local news coverage over the use of force—the preliminary findings are rather encouraging. When local news airs a higher proportion of arguments against the use of military force in Iraq, the public appears significantly less likely to support war. Moving from the sample minimum value (0.00) to the maximum value (0.48) on *News* correlates with a twenty-point decline in the probability that a respondent backs the use of force against Iraq, as support drops from 64 to 44 percent. For every ten-percentage-point increase

TABLE 7.1
Impact of Local News Coverage on Public Support for a War against Iraq

	Early October 2002 Survey			Late October 2002 Survey		
	(1)	(2)	(3)	(4)	(5)	(6)
Proportion of arguments in local news against use of force (in tens)	-1.73*** [0.61]	-1.45** [0.68]	-1.34** [0.66]	-1.94*** [0.62]	-2.03*** [0.69]	-1.43** [0.61]
Respondent's political orientation						
Conservative Republican	—	1.35*** [0.26]	1.35*** [0.27]	—	1.10*** [0.26]	1.04*** [0.27]
Moderate Republican	—	1.26** [0.33]	1.24*** [0.33]	—	1.15*** [0.21]	1.11*** [0.21]
Moderate Democrat	—	0.17 [0.16]	0.17 [0.16]	—	-0.15 [0.24]	-0.16 [0.23]
Liberal Democrat	—	-1.16*** [0.26]	-1.17*** [0.27]	—	-0.81*** [0.28]	-0.84*** [0.27]
Respondent's race/ethnicity						
White (non-Hispanic)	—	0.41 [0.29]	0.39 [0.29]	—	0.80*** [0.24]	0.81*** [0.25]
African American (non-Hispanic)	—	-0.64* [0.34]	-0.74** [0.34]	—	-0.90*** [0.33]	-0.95*** [0.31]
Hispanic	—	0.29 [0.32]	0.30 [0.33]	—	0.55* [0.32]	0.52 [0.32]

	(1)		(2)		(3)		(4)		(5)		(6)	
Other Respondent Characteristics												
Education	—		−0.26***	[0.09]	−0.23***	[0.09]	—		−0.14**	[0.06]	−0.10	[0.06]
Age (in tens)	—		−0.25***	[0.05]	−0.25***	[0.05]	—		−0.18***	[0.04]	−0.18***	[0.04]
Male	—		0.53***	[0.17]	0.53***	[0.16]	—		0.30**	[0.14]	0.31**	[0.14]
Parent	—		0.29	[0.18]	0.29	[0.18]	—		0.36***	[0.13]	0.36***	[0.13]
Community Characteristics												
Pct Vote Democratic in 2000	—		—		0.24	[0.79]	—		—		−0.99*	[0.61]
Pct Minority	—		—		0.37	[0.79]	—		—		0.84	[0.67]
Pct Born in United States	—		—		0.59	[0.93]	—		—		0.34	[0.91]
Pct College Graduate	—		—		−2.10	[1.98]	—		—		−3.95**	[1.62]
Population (in millions)	—		—		−0.25	[0.41]	—		—		0.28	[0.34]
South	—		—		0.05	[0.20]	—		—		0.19	[0.15]
Per Cap. Income (in ten thousands)	—		—		0.23	[0.33]	—		—		0.49	[0.33]
Constant	0.83***	[0.17]	1.86***	[0.45]	1.09	[1.07]	0.62***	[0.16]	0.79**	[0.42]	0.35	[1.03]
(N)	941		920		920		1091		1026		1026	
Pseudo-R^2	.01		.14		.15		.01		.14		.15	

Logistic regressions estimated. *** = $p < 0.01$, two-tailed test; ** = $p < 0.05$; * = $p < 0.10$. Robust standard errors that adjust for clustering on media markets are reported in brackets. The dependent variable is coded 1 if the respondent claimed to favor "taking military action in Iraq to end Saddam Hussein's rule," and zero if they opposed or had no opinion. For political orientation, "independent/other party" is the reference category; "other" is the reference category for race/ethnicity.

in the proportion of arguments against the use of force aired in a media market's local news, average support for the use of force drops by roughly four points.

The simplest possible model supports our intuition that news coverage on Iraq ought to matter. Reality, of course, is considerably more complex, with a swarm of factors contributing to people's beliefs about the efficacy of war. To account for some, specifically respondents' background characteristics, we reestimate the previous regression model, this time adding controls for partisan leanings, education, age, gender, and parental status.[22] Column 2 presents these results. Though the magnitude of the estimated impact of *News* attenuates somewhat, the coefficient remains quite large and statistically significant. The content of local news that aired in respondents' media markets continues to exert a strong impact on public support for the use of force against Iraq.

Not surprisingly, respondents' individual characteristics also inform their views about a prospective Iraq War. Significant and negative impacts are associated with African-Americans, education, and age, while men appear positively predisposed to support the military action. Some of the largest effects concern party identification. As one would expect, Republicans were significantly more likely to support the use of force, and Democrats to oppose. But divisions appear only within one party. The estimated coefficients for conservative and moderate Republicans are indistinguishable from one another, while significant and negative effects are observed only for liberal Democrats. This breakdown mirrors partisan divisions observed among political elites during this period. Just as Democratic members of Congress during the authorization debate presented arguments both for and against the use of force, while Republican members uniformly supported the president (see chapter 6), so do Democratic respondents appear split and Republican respondents united.

To recover an unbiased estimate of the impact of *News*, we may need to do more than just add controls for each respondent's partisan identification and socioeconomic profile. Recall that all of the leverage for estimating the effect of local television news comes from variance in local television news coverage across media markets. There is reason to believe, however, that the respondents answering the Pew survey and the journalists constructing local news come from common pools. Respondents and journalists may be moving in sync without the actions of one having any bearing on the decisions of another. Both respondents and journalists in Madison, Wisconsin, and Cambridge, Massachusetts, are likely to be liberal; respondents and journalists in Dallas, Texas, and Phoenix, Arizona, are likely to be conservative. In all cities, public opinion predictably follows news coverage, though not necessarily because of media influence. The observed effects, instead, may simply conflate each region's general

liberalism or conservatism. Unless we account for the relevant characteristics of the communities that respondents inhabit, our estimates may suffer from omitted variable bias.

To address this problem, we collected an assortment of county data
from the 2000 Census and 2000 presidential election returns,[23] including
the percentage of people who voted for Al Gore (the Democratic candidate) in the 2000 presidential election; the percentages of respondents
who are minority, who were born within the United States, and who graduated from college; the population of the media market; an indicator for
respondents who live in the South; and the per-capita income. We add
each of these control variables to the previous regression model and reestimate the parameters.[24] Column 3 presents the results.[25]

Many of the county characteristics have the expected signs, but none
are statistically significant. More important, at least for our purposes, the
estimated effect of *News* remains unaltered. While the magnitude of the
coefficient in column 3 is roughly 20 percent smaller than that observed
in column 1, it remains both statistically and substantively significant.
Where local news is most positive, the model estimates the probability
that the modal respondent will support military action at almost 70 percent; where local news is most negative, estimated levels of support drop
below 50 percent. The balance of arguments for and against the use of
force in Iraq that appeared in local television news bore heavily on the
public's willingness to support military action, extending even further the
reach of congressional influence revealed in chapter 6.

Taken as a whole, these results are rather impressive, especially given
that we lack a strong exposure measure for each individual respondent.
The observed effects of local news on public opinion are both substantively and statistically significant. They appear robust to a variety of
model specifications and modeling strategies. If members of Congress
hope to rally public support for or against the presidential use of force,
influencing the content and volume of local news would appear an effective strategy.

REPLICATION

Three weeks after releasing its early October survey, Pew issued a second
national survey that contained, verbatim, the same measure of public
opinion on the use of force against Iraq. In the late October survey, we
have roughly 100 more respondents in the top fifty media markets, and
these respondents come from slightly more counties. Otherwise, as table
D.1 in appendix D shows, the profile of respondents in the early and late
October surveys looks much the same.[26]

For the late October survey and an updated summary measure of news
coverage, columns 4 through 6 of table 7.1 present the estimates from our

three regression models. In almost every instance, the findings replicate those observed in the first three columns. In every model, the coefficients for *News* appear large and statistically significant; their magnitudes, if anything, slightly exceed those observed in the earlier survey. Moving from the minimum to the maximum values for *News* corresponds with a drop in the probability that a respondent will support a war in Iraq from 62 percent to 49 percent. Moving from one standard deviation below the mean of *News* to one standard deviation above translates into a seven-percentage-point decline in the probability that a respondent will do so.

The regression results for the individual and county control variables reveal additional similarities to the early October survey. Conservative and moderate Republicans remain equally likely to support the use of force, while moderate and liberal Democrats part ways. African Americans, more-educated people, and older individuals are less likely to support the use of force, while men are more likely to do so. Again, most of the county-level controls appear unrelated to individuals' support for military action against Iraq. A few variables appear statistically significant in the late October survey that were not so in the earlier survey. The effects associated with whites and parents now are positive and significant, while those associated with percent Democrat and percent college graduate are significant and negative. On the whole, however, the major points of cleavage and the estimated effects for the primary variable of interest remain much as they were earlier in the month.[27]

EXTENSIONS

We now turn to a key factor that might mitigate the effect of *News* on *Support*: each individual's party affiliation. We know that Republicans, both conservative and moderate, were overwhelmingly likely to support the use of force and that Democrats appeared more divided on the issue. It is possible that Republicans expressed support without much reflection—all they needed to know, after all, was that the nation faced a military crisis abroad, and that their president (himself a Republican) supported action. Democrats, meanwhile, were torn between the kinds of national allegiances that spawn rally effects during times of war and political allegiances that encourage suspicion of (Republican) White House claims. Democrats, therefore, may have thought longer and harder about the probable costs and benefits of military action. Other survey data also show that Democrats are more likely to watch television generally, and local television news in particular.[28] If true, then Democrats may have received more exposure to the arguments that *News* measures. We have, then, a variety of reasons to expect that local news will have little bearing on Republicans' views, while arguments presented against the use of force may

TABLE 7.2

Impact of Local News Coverage on Republicans', Democrats', and Independents' Support for a War against Iraq

	No Controls		Individual Controls		Individual and Media Market Controls	
	(1)		(2)		(3)	
Early October Survey						
Republicans	−0.03	[1.34]	−0.01	[1.33]	−0.20	[1.34]
Democrats	−2.78***	[1.01]	−2.99**	[1.27]	−2.16*	[1.28]
Independents	−1.22	[1.60]	−1.74	[1.77]	−2.61	[1.75]
Late October Survey						
Republicans	−0.29	[0.89]	−1.43	[1.06]	−1.99	[1.21]
Democrats	−3.18**	[1.62]	−2.58	[1.77]	−0.96	[1.59]
Independents	−2.07**	[0.98]	−2.39***	[0.82]	−1.96**	[0.89]

Separate logistic regressions estimated for each population with same controls as in table 7.1. *** = $p < 0.01$, two-tailed test; ** = $p < 0.05$; * = $p < 0.10$. Robust standard errors that adjust for clustering on media markets are reported in brackets. The dependent variable is coded 1 if the respondent claimed to favor "taking military action in Iraq to end Saddam Hussein's rule," and zero if they oppose or have no opinion. The early (late) October survey contained 297 (355) Republicans, 310 (343) Democrats, and 264 (344) independents.

check any impulse that Democrats feel to rally behind their president during the lead-up to military conflict.

The results, for the most part, appear consistent with these claims. Table 7.2 shows that in none of the models in either of the surveys does *News* have a significant impact on *Support* for Republicans; indeed, in four of six models, the estimated coefficients hover right around zero. For Democrats, the estimates are always large, and in four of six, they are statistically significant. Similar patterns hold for Independents, for whom estimates are always negative and appear statistically significant in all three models included in the second survey. According to the survey data, Republicans, Democrats, and Independents were equally attentive to the debate over Iraq. The three groups, however, were not equally impressed by arguments and evidence that challenged their ideological priors. *News,* it seems, mattered most to individuals outside of the Republican Party.[29]

Thus far, the preponderance of evidence suggests that local television news had an appreciable impact on peoples' views of an impending war in Iraq. The tests employed thus far, however, considered only one measure of public support for the war and pooled all respondents, raising concerns about the scope of the findings. To address such concerns, we present models that use alternative measures of public support. Specifically, we ask the following question: does the influence of local television news reach beyond respondents' conclusions about the efficacy of war to inform their evaluations of the probable consequences of military action?

The late October survey contains additional questions that provide opportunities to further test the effect of *News* on respondents' support for war. Specifically, the survey asks whether respondents, when "thinking about a possible war with Iraq," worry "a great deal," "a fair amount," or "not much" about eventualities ranging from high U.S. casualties to the escalation of armed conflict throughout the Middle East. Presumably, when local news airs a higher proportion of arguments against the use of force, viewers (or, more exactly, potential viewers) ought to exhibit greater concern for the risks of war. It is possible, though, that respondents worry about each of these outcomes and still support military action. To the extent that each respondent's support depends on her assessment of likely consequences of action or inaction, however, we should expect that *News* will yield effects, if perhaps smaller and more sporadic, on these additional items.

TABLE 7.3
Impact of Local News Coverage on Public Concerns about a War against Iraq

	No Controls		Individual Controls		Individual and Media Market Controls	
	(1)		(2)		(3)	
Possible outcomes of war:						
High U.S. casualties	−0.44	[0.33]	−0.17	[0.33]	0.03	[0.35]
Iraq use biological weapons	−0.35	[0.46]	−0.38	[0.40]	−0.47	[0.34]
High Iraqi civilian casualties	−0.40	[0.37]	−0.42	[0.44]	−0.57	[0.42]
Increase terrorism	0.17	[0.33]	0.50	[0.37]	0.70*	[0.38]
Destabilize Iraq and region	0.37	[0.43]	0.48	[0.50]	0.46	[0.54]
Lead to all-out war in Middle East	0.60	[0.45]	0.81	[0.50]	0.80*	[0.43]

Ordered probits estimated. * = $p < 0.10$, two-tailed test. Robust standard errors that adjust for clustering on media markets are reported in brackets. For each item in the late October survey, respondents were asked the following: "Thinking about a possible war with Iraq, how worried are you that [INSERT ITEM]—a great deal, a fair amount, or not much?" In reverse order, response categories were coded 1, 2, and 3. Items include: "U.S. forces might sustain a lot of casualties:" "Iraq might use biological or chemical weapons against U.S. troops;" "many Iraqi civilians might be killed;" "this might increase the chances of a terrorist attack within the U.S.;" "it will take a long time to make Iraq a stable and peaceful country after the war;" and "it might lead to an all-out war in the Middle East."

To test this possibility, we estimated a series of regressions that model the extent to which respondents worry about six possible outcomes of war: high U.S. casualties, the use of biological weapons, high Iraqi civilian casualties, increased terrorism, the destabilization of the Middle East, and the escalation of conflict to all-out war.[30] To conserve space, table 7.3 presents the results for just the *News* variable, though the models include the same explanatory variables as in our previous regression models. Though statistically smaller, the results are consistent with those observed in tables 7.2 and 7.3. On four of the six items, null effects are observed. On two, however, large, positive, and statistically significant effects emerge. As the proportion of arguments against the use of force increases in local news coverage, respondents within corresponding media markets are more likely to express concerns about the possibility that military action against Iraq will lead to increased terrorism within the United States and all-out war in the Middle East. There is some evidence, then, that local news influences not only respondents' willingness to back military action but also the particular concerns they have about proceeding to war.

SUPPORT FOR WAR, EXPERIMENTAL DATA

The findings presented until now largely confirm our expectations. Proceedings within Congress appear to influence the tone and volume of local television news coverage and, in turn, local television news influences public opinion. One problem with potentially important statistical implications, however, remains: endogeneity. If local news outlets design their coverage to suit the independently formulated political views of their audience, then the causal arrow would seem to point from public opinion to news, rather than the other way around. If this is true, then the estimates presented in tables 7.1–7.3 are potentially biased.

Conventional wisdom about the relationships between political elites and the mass public suggests that concerns about endogeneity, especially in matters involving foreign affairs, are inflated.[31] Recall that we are examining the effect of news on public opinion over foreign policies—where average respondents have the least amount of information and depend most on the media for what information they do have. In addition, these models examine how yesterday's news affects today's public opinion. Hence, for news to be endogenous, at least one of two following conditions must hold: (a) public opinion on the use of force must be stable over time, or (b) journalists must have the capacity to forecast future public opinion, and then they must cater to it when writing contemporary news. Given the lessons from the public opinion literature that were outlined at the beginning of this chapter, neither condition is likely, and therefore concerns about endogeneity may be overwrought.

But what if the existing public opinion literature overstates the public's reliance on television news for information about foreign policy options? What if, instead, public opinion, at some level, informs the content of news coverage? Statistical solutions to these kinds of problems usually involve the estimation of systems of equations, whereby public opinion is posited as a function of news coverage and other background controls, and then news coverage is posited as a function of some exogenous variable and controls. Unfortunately, it is not clear what this exogenous variable—commonly referred to as an instrument—would look like in this context. And without a variable that does a reasonable job of predicting local news coverage but is unrelated to public opinion—the two criteria for an effective instrument—the system of equations cannot be identified.

To help ameliorate this problem, analysts may choose to abandon the world of observational data and consider experimental research, where they can randomly expose respondents to different kinds of information about a planned use of force and thereby formulate claims about causal inferences with considerably more ease. It is no coincidence that some of the best research on news and public opinion relies almost exclusively on experimental data.[32] Of course, experimental data have problems of their own, most of which concern the extent to which findings observed in a survey or lab hold up in real-world settings. Yet, if experimental findings appear consistent with observational findings, we may proceed with somewhat more confidence that the estimated effect of news on public opinion is not an artifact of any specific dataset or any particular modeling strategy.

In the fall of 2004, within the context of a large, national postelection public opinion survey,[33] we conducted a very simple experiment. In a telephone survey, one-third of the sample was told the following: "According to the president, Eritrea (a small country on the east coast of Africa) is harboring terrorists. The president is prepared to use military force against this country." Another third received exactly the same information, except that this time they were also told, "Members of Congress, however, have cast doubts on the president's claims; and a majority in Congress opposes military action." For the final third, we exchanged the previous sentence for the following: "Members of Congress have reiterated the president's claims; and a majority in Congress supports plans for military action." Based on the information presented, we then asked all respondents whether they believed that Eritrea, in fact, was harboring terrorists and whether they supported military action to resolve the problem. Because respondents were randomly assigned to one of the three conditions, differences observed across the three groups can be reliably attributed to statements about congressional opposition to or support for the president's claims and not to other factors that contribute to their opinions about foreign policy.[34]

For several reasons, we chose to name a specific country, and Eritrea in particular, as a potential target of military action. Most important, we did not want respondents to presume that we were talking about Iraq. We chose Eritrea because very few Americans have heard of the country, mitigating the possibility that prior knowledge of or allegiances to its people or government would condition people's responses to the experiment. Still, for those who have heard of Eritrea, and for those who were attuned to that nation's recent history, terrorism within its borders would appear a distinct possibility. Though Eritrea and Ethiopia ended a two-and-a-half-year border war in 1998, agreeing to UN peacekeeping in 2000, relations between the two states have remained extremely tense and a border dispute continues to simmer. In addition, Eritrea sits only miles across the Red Sea from Yemen, on whose government the United States has exerted immense pressure to shut down suspected al-Qaeda cells operating within its borders.

If the public looks to the president, and the president alone, when formulating its views about foreign policy, then reported levels of confidence and support should not vary across the three conditions. That the president says there is a problem, and that he identifies a course of action, should be all that matters. In this particular instance, it is reasonable to suspect that congressional support or opposition may not influence public assessments of presidential claims. In every condition, the president's position is presented first, with congressional opposition or support conveyed as an addendum. Given their abiding concerns about terrorism and national security, respondents on the right of the political spectrum may be quick to endorse any sign of trouble abroad, and any action designed to address it. Given their belief that the president sold the nation a false bill of goods in Iraq, respondents on the left may oppose the president no matter what Congress does or does not say. Meanwhile, everyone in between may simply refuse to support or oppose the president given the minimal amount of information provided.

On the other hand, respondents' answers may vary across the different experimental conditions. Rather than take the president at his word, or reject the president's claims outright, many respondents may look to a separate branch of government to corroborate his claims. Without any alternative source of information about this particular crisis, the public may well incorporate congressional support or opposition into their evaluations of White House claims. To the extent that they do, and to the extent that subtle manipulations in the information presented to respondents affect public support for presidential claims, we will have uncovered additional evidence of Congress's continuing relevance to the domestic politics over the use of military force.

Table D.1 of Appendix D presents summary statistics for all the survey items used in the analyses to follow, and table 7.4 presents the experiment's main results. When asked whether they believed that Eritrea was harboring terrorists and whether they supported the use of military force, many respondents hedged their bets. Over 55 percent of respondents claimed that they neither agreed nor disagreed that the country was harboring terrorists, and more than one-third claimed they neither supported nor opposed the use of force. On the basis of the paltry information provided, however, the remaining respondents still saw fit to offer an opinion. Congressional silence, opposition, and support appeared to systematically affect the opinions voiced. When the president alone presents the claims (see column 1), 24 percent of respondents agreed that Eritrea was harboring terrorists; when respondents are told about congressional skepticism (column 2), that number drops to just under 20 percent; and when Congress confirms the president's claims (column 3), the number jumps to 30 percent. Congress, as such, effects as much as a 10-percentage-point change in support for the president's claims and policies. If the president's first task in mobilizing the country for war is to convince the citizenry about the existence of a foreign crisis, then Congress would appear to play a vital role.

When examining public support for the use of force, comparable findings are observed. When the president alone presents his case for military force, 27 percent of the public supports him; when Congress second-guesses his prescribed course of action, only 22 percent of the public falls behind the president; and when Congress openly supports the president, support jumps to 32 percent—once more, yielding a 10-percentage-point swing in public opinion.[35] Again, because respondents were randomly assigned to one of the three conditions, differences observed can be attributed to alterations in the wording of the vignettes. The mere mention of congressional support or opposition, it would seem, has a marked impact on public opinion regarding the use of force.

Because so many respondents remained undecided on both questions, it is worth comparing the percentages of respondents who believed the president and supported the use of force to those who remained more skeptical and opposed military action. When the president alone presented his claims, more people agreed that Eritrea was harboring terrorists and that military action was needed than disagreed with the president and opposed plans to use force. When Congress questioned the president's claims, however, the public quickly turned against the president. More respondents

Table 7.4
Experimental Manipulations of Congressional Position Taking

	Only President's Claims Presented[1]		President's Claims, Congress Opposes[2]		President's Claims, Congress Supports[3]	
	(1)		*(2)*		*(3)*	
Is country harboring terrorists?						
Completely agree (4)	10.0%		6.7%		11.9%	
Somewhat agree (3)	14.3		13.2		18.0	
Neither agree nor disagree (2)	58.2		56.7		55.0	
Somewhat disagree (1)	9.4		9.9		8.8	
Completely disagree (0)	8.2		13.5		6.2	
Total	100.0%	[918]	100.0%	[926]	100.0%	[927]
Average agreement (0–4 scale)	2.09		1.90		2.21	
Support use of force?						
Completely support (4)	11.6%		7.2%		12.5%	
Somewhat support (3)	15.3		15.5		19.0	
Neither support nor oppose (2)	38.0		36.8		37.4	
Somewhat oppose (1)	17.1		18.2		15.2	
Completely oppose (0)	18.0		22.4		15.9	
Total	100.0%	[924]	100.0%	[931]	100.0%	[932]
Average support (0-4 scale)	1.86		1.67		1.97	

Number of observations reported in brackets. Column (1) reports answers for respondents who only heard about president's claims; (2) reports answers for respondents who heard about president's claims and congressional opposition; and (3) who heard about president's claims and congressional support. Possible agreement (support) scores range from 0 to 4, where 0 indicates complete disagreement (opposition) and 4 indicates complete agreement (support). Post stratification-weights used.

[1] Respondents were told: "According to the president, Eritrea (a small country on the east coast of Africa) is harboring terrorists. The president is prepared to use military force against this country."

[2] Respondents were told: "According to the president, Eritrea (a small country on the east coast of Africa) is harboring terrorists. The president is prepared to use military force against this country. Members of Congress, however, have cast doubts on the president's claims; and a majority in Congress opposes military action."

[3] Respondents were told: "According to the president, Eritrea (a small country on the east coast of Africa) is harboring terrorists. The president is prepared to use military force against this country. Members of Congress have reiterated the president's claims; and a majority in Congress supports plans for military action."

disagreed than agreed with the president's claims, and almost twice as many respondents opposed as supported the use of force. Here, public wariness over the expansion of military deployments beyond the Middle East and skepticism about Bush's undocumented claims about a new foreign crisis appear on full display. When Congress reiterates and reinforces presidential claims, twice as many respondents claimed to believe the president as did not, and a roughly equal number of respondents supported and opposed the use of military force. To persuade at least those respondents willing to stake out a position when presented with minimal information about a perceived foreign crisis, it would appear critical that the president secure congressional support or, at least, mute its dissent.

One feature of these findings deserves special emphasis. The losses in public belief and support associated with congressional opposition exceed the gains associated with congressional backing. To see this, look at the average scale scores for agreement and support.[36] Moving from columns 1 to 2, agreement and support scores drop 0.2 point, but when moving from columns 1 to 3, the scores only jump 0.1 points.[37] While engaging Congress, soliciting the opinions of its membership, and rallying their support can yield valuable gains for the president, these also are risky ventures. Should Congress raise doubts about the efficacy of a planned military venture, the president stands to lose almost twice as much ground as he would have gained had Congress instead lent its confidence and support. Put most bluntly, congressional opposition hurts more than congressional support helps. When uncertain about what Congress will do or say, the president might rightly minimize members' involvement in discussions and debates that precede military strikes abroad.

In addition to the national sample of respondents, we also looked separately at various subpopulations. The findings for Democrats, Republicans, and Independents are especially noteworthy.[38] As one would expect, Republicans were more likely to believe and support the president than were either Democrats or Independents. Interestingly, though, the differences observed across the three experimental conditions are comparable for respondents from all three groups. Congressional support tends to increase positive assessments of the president's position by 0.06 to 0.10 points, and congressional opposition depresses public assessments by 0.11 to 0.34 points. We do not find any evidence that only Democrats, or Republicans, or Independents incorporate the views of Congress when formulating their own opinions about the use of force. To the contrary, in one way or another, Congress affects the opinions of every group considered.

In addition to their partisan affiliations, some respondents may draw on broader foreign policy principles and the nation's recent experiences exercising force abroad when weighing presidential and congressional claims about terrorism in Eritrea. The survey, fortunately, allows us to explore this possibility. Just before the experimental question, the survey posed a series of questions about the relative value of diplomacy and military solutions to foreign policy items,[39] the value of working through international institutions such as the United Nations and World Trade Organization as opposed to "going it alone,"[40] and finally the success or failure of the Iraq War.[41] For the most part, the findings for these various subpopulations follow the same patterns as those previously observed. Whether or not one preferred diplomatic over military solutions to perceived foreign policy crises, or whether one thought that the Iraq War was or was not worth the cost, congressional support for and opposition to the president systematically figured into respondents' thinking about prospective military actions. And as before, the decline in public opinion associated with congressional opposition almost always exceeded the gain in public opinion associated with congressional support.[42]

If the Pew surveys from October 2002 are any indication, a variety of personal background characteristics correlate with foreign policy views, independent of the arguments and information that are presented to respondents. In both of those surveys, Republicans, males, parents, and whites supported the use of force against Iraq, while liberal Democrats, African Americans, more-educated people, and older respondents came out in opposition. Many of the people in those surveys, however, probably had already formulated views about Iraq before being interviewed. The issue dominated the news at the time, and respondents had ample opportunities to sort through their political allegiances and offer a considered view on the matter. It is possible, therefore, that when survey respondents are presented for the first time with a new foreign crisis, like the one imagined in Eritrea, a very different set of relationships emerges.

Table 7.5 shows how, within a regression framework, levels of public belief and support varied across the three experimental conditions. As columns 1 and 3 report, congressional support and opposition both have statistically significant and substantively important impacts on the levels of belief in the president's claim and support for the use of force.[43] Because respondents were randomly assigned to the three experimental conditions, the inclusion of additional background controls should not impact these estimated coefficients—if anything, they should improve the efficiency of estimates and therefore reduce the standard errors. This is exactly what we find. The coefficients reported in columns 2 and 4 are virtually equivalent to those in columns 1 and 3, while the standard errors are slightly smaller. When members of Congress cast doubt on the claim that Eritrea is harboring terrorists, and when members oppose the use of force to resolve the problem, average respondents are significantly less likely to either believe the president or endorse his recommended course of action.

TABLE 7.5
Public Belief in and Support for the President, Including Background Controls

	Believe President's Claims		Support Use of Force	
	(1)	(2)	(3)	(4)
Experimental Condition				
Congress Opposes	-0.22*** [0.05]	-0.24*** [0.05]	-0.12*** [0.05]	-0.15*** [0.05]
Congress Supports	0.15*** [0.05]	0.14*** [0.05]	0.13*** [0.05]	0.12*** [0.05]
Party ID				
Democrats	—	-0.35*** [0.05]	—	-0.34*** [0.05]
Republicans	—	0.73*** [0.05]	—	0.84*** [0.05]
Ethnicity/Race				
White (non-Hispanic)	—	0.05 [0.12]	—	0.14 [0.12]
African American (non-Hisp.)	—	0.00 [0.13]	—	0.10 [0.13]
Hispanic	—	0.03 [0.14]	—	0.12 [0.13]
Other Characteristics				
Education	—	-0.06*** [0.02]	—	-0.12*** [0.02]
Age (in tens)	—	-0.02 [0.01]	—	-0.03** [0.01]
Male	—	0.11*** [0.04]	—	0.15*** [0.04]
Parent	—	0.04 [0.05]	—	0.06 [0.05]
(N)	2,771	2,771	2,787	2,787
Pseudo-R²	.01	.07	.00	.08

Ordered probits estimated. *** = p < 0.01, two-tailed test; ** = p < 0.05; * = p < 0.10. Robust standard errors reported in brackets. Cut points not reported. The experimental condition where Congress is silent, "independents/other," and "other race/ethnicity" are the reference categories for the first three sets of variables.

Interestingly, the political and social cleavages that defined public opinion on Iraq reappear when respondents are asked about a tiny, obscure country in Africa. Democrats, for the most part, are more skeptical of the president and more likely to oppose the use of force, while Republicans tend to believe the president and support his plans for military action. Though respondents from different ethnic backgrounds and parents and nonparents are equally likely to believe the president and support the use of force, important differences are observed on the remaining background variables. Men, once again, are much more likely to believe and support the president; the old are less likely than the young and the more-educated less likely than the less educated to back the president. While the impact of age is significant only in column 4, all of the estimated coefficients retain the same sign whether the dependent variable concerns levels of belief about the existence of state-sponsored terrorism in Eritrea or levels of support for the use of force to resolve the problem.

The experiment, admittedly, leaves important questions unanswered. One wonders whether Democrats would be any more (and Republicans would be any less) likely to believe the president and support the use of force were a Democrat residing in the White House, rather than a Republican; whether Congress's mediating influence over public opinion is stronger or weaker during periods of unified or divided government; whether larger or smaller effects would be observed were the president contemplating military action in a larger, more prosperous country in some region of the world other than Africa; and whether it matters much that the source of political support for or opposition to the president is a member of Congress, rather than, say, a UN representative or a foreign government or a prominent interest group. By introducing other manipulations to the experimental design, one could get a handle on such issues. While a number of scholars are pursuing such lines of inquiry,[44] for now, we underscore a more basic point that is consistent with all of the evidence presented in this chapter, both observational and experimental: either by shaping the contents of local television news or by speaking directly to average citizens, members of Congress exert considerable influence over public support for military action. In the battle over public opinion during the lead-up to a planned military venture abroad, the president may reign supreme, but if he hopes to rally the public behind an especially risky and potentially long-term deployment, he ought not forget about Congress.

SUMMARIZING THE EVIDENCE

That Congress influences media coverage over military deployments appears well established. The primary contributions of chapter 6 were to extend to local television news prior scholars' work on the relationship between political elites and the media, and to probe the various ways in which members of Congress influence the volume and content of a particularly salient public debate over the use of force. The contributions of this chapter, meanwhile, may be more far-reaching. Here, we offer evidence that congressional influence over local television news extends to influence over public support for a planned military venture. Either by shaping news coverage (as the observational data show) or by speaking directly to the American public (as the experimental data show), members of Congress can mobilize public opinion either behind or in opposition to the president. In doing so, they contribute in important ways to the politics that precede military deployments abroad.

The data in this chapter present an especially difficult test of the proposition that congressional influence over the media translates into influence over public opinion. First, lacking information about the newspapers survey respondents read or the television news they watched, we must rely on the fact that local television news coverage on Iraq varied across media markets. Given the noise in such a measure of local news coverage, strong biases against finding significant effects are built into the statistical models. Moreover, the observational data draw together information collected from five independent sources: two national public opinion surveys, a survey of local television news coverage, U.S. Census data, and the 2000 election returns. Given the practical difficulties of merging so many different kinds of data, one might well expect that the models would generate few results of interest. It is rather astonishing, therefore, that the models consistently demonstrate that people's support for the Iraq war systematically covaries with the tone of local news coverage on the topic.

Just as the media data in chapter 6 revealed the differences between the arguments advanced by elected Republicans and Democrats, the observational data presented in this chapter demonstrate the importance of partisanship for mass publics. Republicans, predictably, were significantly more likely to support military action than Democrats. Though conservative and moderate Republicans were indistinguishable from one another, moderate and liberal Democrats parted ways. Moderate Democrats were as likely as Independents to support military action against Iraq, while liberal Democrats were significantly less likely to do so. The late-October survey also suggests that television news had a greater impact on the views about war of some respondents than on the views of others. Though Democrats appeared especially sensitive to the content of local television news within their media markets, the effects for Republicans were more muted.

Beyond addressing some nagging statistical complications, the experimental data yield new insights of their own. Congressional support for and opposition to the president again appear to matter greatly, affecting both the probability that individuals believe the president and the probability that they back the recommended use of military action. Interestingly, though, some of the descriptive statistics suggest that opposition hurts the president more than support helps him. Though supporters and detractors of military action are equally represented when the Congress backs the president, detractors outnumber supporters two-to-one when Congress casts doubt on the president's claims. The observed differences across the experimental conditions, moreover, apply to a wide range of populations, defined both by their partisan affiliations and their prior beliefs about different foreign policy principles.

One should not push the evidence too far, however. Amidst the findings presented in chapters 6 and 7 are indications of the limits of congressional influence over the media and public opinion. During September and October 2002, while much of the content and volume of local television news on Iraq tracked congressional involvement in the issue, national television news and the *New York Times* were less attentive. Some of the arguments that dominated congressional debate—such as reservations about the war being costly and Saddam Hussein not representing a genuine threat to American lives—received very little play in any of the media outlets. There is hardly any evidence that Congress introduced the issue of war against Iraq to journalists of either television or print news. Throughout the period, moreover, all news sources gave a disproportionate amount of time and space to claims advanced by the White House.

Similarly, findings from the observational and experimental datasets presented in this chapter attest to the limitations of congressional influence over public opinion. Though local news had a significant effect on public support for the war in both the early and late October surveys, Congress was but one among several contributors to this news, and baseline levels of support appeared unchanged, even though Congress had authorized the use of force in the middle of the month. In addition, the experimental data show that congressional support or opposition to the president alters levels of public support by just 10 percentage points. In all experimental conditions, the modal response category remains undecided. Members of Congress matter, to be sure, but just like all other domestic political actors during the weeks and months that precede a military deployment abroad, they struggle for influence over a decision that ultimately rests with the president.

How do the findings in chapters 6 and 7 help explain the influence of Congress over presidential decision making documented in the second section of this book? Stripped of all its embellishments, the argument is straightforward. During the lead-up to a military venture, members typically affect presidential decision making by engaging in a larger public argument about the efficacy of the planned venture. Actual behaviors, when observable, consist of public speeches on the floors of the House and Senate and media appearances where members stake out positions either in favor of or in opposition to the proposed military action.

What members of Congress say publicly during these periods can serve as an important signal to presidents about what members will do when, and if, a military operation goes awry. If members uniformly and steadfastly express support for a military operation, the president may rightly infer that they will continue backing him when the costs of military actions materialize. On the other hand, if congressional support appears more tepid, and if members grumble about the potential risks involved, then presidents have reason to proceed more cautiously. The president may interpret these speeches as fair warning that if scandals emerge or atrocities occur or objectives wane during the course of a military campaign, members of Congress will pile on additional criticisms, moving to enact legislation that further restricts his ability to see the campaign to a successful resolution. As Truman learned in Korea, Johnson learned in Vietnam, and Clinton learned in Somalia, military operations do not always go according to plan, and Congress has the power to turn a difficult situation into a seemingly impossible one. From the beginning, presidents have considerable reason to forecast how Congress will respond when, and if, things go poorly. The public declarations members offer during the lead-up to a military venture constitute an important indicator of the sentiments that are likely to be aired once troops are in the field.[45]

As we have seen, however, the speeches that members make during the prelude to a military operation also have more immediate consequences. When members of Congress raise concerns about a use of force and cast doubt on the president's ability to protect and promote American interests abroad, media coverage turns sharply negative. Although the literature on the indexing hypothesis presents considerable evidence of congressional influence over national television and print media outlets, the findings from the Iraq War data suggest that local television news, where most respondents obtain their news about domestic and foreign policy, is especially responsive to congressional influence. Influence over the media extends, in turn, to influence over the public. We have seen that when television and print media begin to cast doubts on the efficacy of a planned military operation, public support for the president promptly erodes.

These findings extend to a related and well-established body of research suggesting that the rally-around-the-flag effect is at least partially conditional on the level of bipartisan congressional support for the use of force. Research by Richard Brody, Bruce Russett, John Oneal, John Zaller, and others shows that bipartisan support for a military conflict leads to larger and more robust increases in public support for the president.[46] When the public sees that political elites (including members of Congress) oppose the president, they are less likely to stand behind an actual deployment. The observational and experimental data presented in this chapter help explain why. As members of Congress rise to voice concerns over a deployment, their reluctance hits the airwaves, minimizing public support for a use of force, both before and after troops are actually sent abroad.

Obviously, the data presented in the last two chapters concern one use of force, which pits one Congress and one president against each other. The larger argument being advanced here suggests a clear counterfactual: had more Democrats held congressional seats in 2002, a higher proportion of arguments against the use of force would have emerged from Capitol Hill; media coverage of the Iraq War, in turn, would have been distinctly more critical; and as the public relies on the media for information about foreign policy, public support for the use of force would have been lower. The corresponding scenario also seems likely. Had Republicans retained more seats in Congress, the Washington debate over the Iraq War would have been even more perfunctory, media coverage would have been more positive, and the public would have been even more supportive than it was. Because congressional opposition to a presidential use of force almost always comes from the opposition party, the partisan profile of Congress has huge implications for the levels of disagreement raised within Washington, the media, and the public to a use of force. It is little wonder that levels of partisan opposition to the president consistently register statistically significant and substantively large impacts on the presidential use of force.

COMPLETING ONE CAUSAL ARGUMENT

Congress, we have shown, wields considerable influence over media coverage of a planned use of force, and influence over the media, we have seen, translates into additional influence over public opinion. But does influence over public opinion, in turn, have any bearing on presidential decision making? Fortunately, much of the evidence needed to complete this causal argument has already been assembled and analyzed. As we discussed in chapter 1, plenty of other scholars have documented the fact of public influence over presidential war planning.[47] Rather than once again summarize highlights from this literature, here we merely identify some of the more important reasons presidents consult public opinion before initiating military action. To begin, along with Congress, the public figures prominently in international diplomacy. If congressional dissent alone can undermine a president's capacity to credibly convey resolve to a foreign enemy, congressional dissent buoyed by popular unrest only exacerbates matters. In the fall of 2002, when public support for war languished below 40 percent, Fergal Keane predicted that Saddam Hussein "will calculate that public opinion in the U.S. and Britain will either forestall an attack, or revolt when the military and civilian cost becomes too high. Saddam may well be willing to allow a war to start in the belief that it will collapse from political pressures well before U.S. armor ever reaches the gates of Baghdad. Thus, he has little incentive to cave in now to what are likely to be very tough demands on weapons inspections."[48] Sensing a politically vulnerable president, an adversary—in this case an Iraqi dictator—has cause to fight longer and harder, to rebuke demands made by the United States and its allies, and to hold out for even greater concessions. For appearances alone, the president therefore has strong incentives to shore up public support for a military venture and to proceed more cautiously when none is forthcoming.

Second, the president monitors public opinion in matters involving war for the simple reason that once the public is motivated and informed, it can have a profound impact on the likelihood that Congress will meddle in an ongoing military venture. Up until now, we have focused on congressional influence over public opinion during the weeks that precede a military deployment. Once informed, however, the public becomes a player in its own right, as citizens introduce important feedback effects that may reinforce members' intentions to criticize or praise the president's military planning. Popular wars are not likely to invite widespread congressional involvement, even when operations do not go according to plan. When the public turns against the president, however, members of Congress have considerable cause to issue laws, resolutions, or appropriations that effectively restrict the president's discretion to continue onward. During the course of unpopular military ventures—prominent past examples including those conducted in Korea, Vietnam, and Lebanon—the public may demand that Congress call back troops, cut funding for certain operations, or hold hearings on perceived war crimes or abuses of power. And eager to please their constituents, members of Congress may follow suit.

Finally, but perhaps most obviously, it is to the public that the president must appeal at the next election. In this sense, public opinion about military operations matters specifically because public opinion matters generally. Every four years, either an incumbent president or his party's chosen successor must stand before the electorate and ask that the public once again entrust in him the vast arsenal of executive powers. Having prudently exercised military powers in the past, the president stands a decent chance of securing reelection. Having launched ill-considered and unpopular military ventures abroad, on the other hand, the president's reelection prospects, as well as those for his party, may dim. For next to a bad economy, a bad war is perhaps the surest way of losing the seat of power.

It is little wonder, then, that Bush remained preoccupied with the state of public opinion during the lead-up to the Iraq War. Throughout the fall of 2002 and winter of 2003, Bush launched a concerted public relations campaign designed explicitly to rally public support for the war.[49] According to the *New York Times,* Bush executed "a meticulously planned strategy to persuade the public, the Congress and the allies of the need to confront the threat from Saddam Hussein."[50] Bush and members of his administration—notably Secretary of State Colin Powell, Secretary of Defense Donald Rumsfeld, and Deputy Secretary of Defense Paul Wolfowitz—gave more than fifty major speeches on Iraq between November 2002 and March 2003, in places ranging from Dearborn, Michigan, to New York City to the District of Columbia.[51] Concurrently, White House personnel regularly made appearances on the local news of key media markets. The president strategically released classified documents containing evidence of a purportedly active Iraqi weapons program, documents that later became the centerpiece of Powell's February 2003 United Nations presentation and call for new resolutions demanding that Hussein immediately disclose and dismantle all of his regime's biological, chemical, and nuclear weapons systems. This media blitz appears to have worked. While public support for a war against Iraq measured in the mid 50s at the end of August 2002, it peaked at 71 percent in mid March of 2003, just three days before the actual war began.[52]

Outwardly, the president claimed not to care much about public opinion. In press conferences and speeches, he regularly insisted that he intended to lead the country and protect its vital interests and not to slavishly cater to the latest poll results. At a March 2003 press conference that came on the heels of worldwide protests against the impending war, Bush defended his position of effectively ignoring public dissent. "I appreciate societies in which people can express their opinion. My most important job is to protect the security of the American people. That's precisely what I'll do . . . I don't run my administration based upon polls and focus groups." Most political observers, however, saw through this charade. Carroll Doherty of the Pew Research Center commented, "Although the White House likes to say they don't read polls, public opinion is having a powerful effect in many ways."[53] The *New York Times* observed just a month earlier, when Bush had made similar comments following another rash of antiwar protests, "What President Bush doubtless meant was that confronting Iraq is necessary, whether or not that makes him popular in Paris or Peoria. But he, too, is well aware of public opinion."[54]

Having secured in October 2002 congressional authorization to exercise military force against the Iraqi regime, the president did not immediately launch a full-scale invasion. By all accounts, he would have preferred doing so long before March 2003.[55] Nonetheless, he waited. And he did so for a reason. Bush recognized the importance of securing public support before launching a large-scale military venture, one with potentially great costs and considerable sacrifices. He, like many of his predecessors on the eve of war, actively engaged in public debates about the use of force because these debates mattered. For him, a contest with public support as its prize was well worth entering.[56]

Still, we need not be Pollyannaish about the state of American democracy. For Congress to effectively check presidential power via this particular causal pathway, every interlocking relationship must hold firm. There are reasons to expect that one or another will occasionally break. Preoccupied with Michael Jackson's trial or college basketball finals or a natural disaster in the Indian Ocean, the media may not cover ongoing congressional debates about the efficacy of using military force against Iraq. Even when they do, large portions of the American public may be too distracted with their own affairs to take much notice. Perhaps most important, when the need for military action is especially urgent, the president may take the nation to war regardless of any particular constituency's verdict on the matter. That Congress can affect the media, which can affect public opinion, which can affect presidential decision making, does not mean that each necessarily will. When one link in the chain snaps, Congress's influence over presidential decision making is unavoidably diminished.

In addition, long and involved periods of debate do not precede every use of force. Sometimes, presidents launch military ventures without ever giving members of Congress, the media, or the public much of an opportunity to weigh in on the matter. They are forced to learn about a foreign crisis as the nation responds to it, formulating their opinions while troops are in the field. This is especially true of minor uses of force, which may explain why the partisan composition of Congress does not have a discernible impact on the frequency with which presidents launch them.[57] Even when larger operations are at hand, either the exigencies of the foreign crisis or the president's own strategizing may shorten the period of reflection and debate, placing Congress and those that it would influence in a defensive posture, struggling to keep pace with a chief executive who exercises his unilateral powers with all the energy and dispatch that Alexander Hamilton lauded some 225 years ago.

That Congress does not always influence presidential decision making on matters involving war, however, does not mean that it never does. While acknowledging the strategic advantages that unilateral powers impart to the president, we also recognize Congress's vital contributions to the interbranch politics that precede war. During the lead-up to a planned military venture, a period infused with uncertainty, politics typically center on public arguments about the likelihood of success, the prospects of failure, and the larger public good being served. And during these periods, especially when the nation mobilizes for large military engagements, the voices of Congress occasionally ring loudly. So doing, they set in motion political forces that materially affect the public's willingness to stand by the president and, as the literature on credible commitments attests, that either bolster or undermine the president's efforts to convince allies to join in a cause and adversaries to abandon a fight. When members of Congress vocally object to a planned military venture, presidents have reasons to listen.

CHAPTER 8

Conclusion

IN THE MODERN ERA presidents have consistently bestridden U.S. deliberations about when, and whether, to exercise military force abroad. This power eclipses that of their nineteenth-century predecessors and is of a magnitude that they could only dream of exercising over domestic policy. Let there be no mistake about it: presidential power reaches its apex when the nation stands on a war footing. "'When the blast of war blows in our ears,'" Clinton Rossiter reminds us, "the President's power to command the forces swells out of all proportion to his other powers."[1]

During the lead-up to a military venture, however, presidential power is far from absolute. Just because modern presidents exercise influence that would astound the Founders or that would delight the fancies of some of their more aspiring nineteenth-century kin does not mean that modern presidents can do as they please. Domestic political institutions, though weakened, can readily punish an overzealous or reckless chief executive. And the president who ignores these institutions does so at considerable peril.

It is of some consequence, then, that we find so much evidence that the partisan composition of Congress factors into presidential decision making about the nation's response to assorted foreign crises. Estimating a wide range of statistical models, we find that those presidents who face large and cohesive congressional majorities from the opposite party exercise military force less regularly than do those whose party has secured a larger number of seats within Congress. Additionally, other statistical models reveal that partisan opposition to the president reliably depresses the likelihood of a military response to specific crises occurring abroad and significantly extends the amount of time that transpires between the precipitating event and the eventual deployment. Modern presidents consistently heed the distinctly political threat posed by large, cohesive, and opposing congressional majorities—a threat that is all too often latent, but that when mobilized, materially affects the president's efforts to rally public support for an ongoing deployment and to communicate the nation's foreign policy commitments to both allies and adversaries abroad.

Congressional influence, though, is not omnipresent. When a relatively small number of congressional opponents stand in the way, presidents usually can proceed as they choose. Unless they hold a sizable share of congressional seats, members cannot hope to dissuade a president intent on exercising military force abroad. Additionally, the partisan composition of Congress appears to have less bearing on the regularity with which presidents deploy smaller contingents of U.S. troops abroad, nor does it seem to influence whether presidents respond militarily to crises occurring in foreign nations with which either the United States or the Soviet Union has long standing alliances. To the great consternation of constitutional scholars, members of Congress do not feel much of a duty to thwart any and all challenges to the foreign policy powers and responsibilities laid out in Article I. Rather, congressional checks on presidential war powers materialize under well-specified conditions, having to do with the institution's partisan composition, the size of a proposed deployment, and the strength of international obligations.

Why should presidents ever heed domestic political opposition to a planned military deployment? This book identifies two core reasons. The first, which we borrow from existing formal literatures within political science, concerns the president's ability to credibly convey resolve to foreign states. When members of Congress vocally oppose a use of force, they undermine the president's ability to convince foreign states that he will see a fight through to the end.[2] Sensing hesitation on the part of the United States, allies may be reluctant to contribute to a military campaign, and adversaries are likely to fight harder and longer when conflict erupts—thereby raising the costs of the military campaign, decreasing the president's ability to negotiate a satisfactory resolution, and increasing the probability that American lives are lost along the way. Facing a limited band of allies willing to participate in a military venture and an enemy emboldened by domestic critics, presidents may choose to curtail, and even abandon, those military operations that do not involve vital strategic interests.

Beyond sketching out some basic theoretical expectations, this book does not empirically document the ways in which congressional opposition undermines the president's position in an international contest of wills.[3] Instead, it focuses on the media and public opinion, which constitute a second (though obviously related) mechanism by which congressional opposition to a planned use of force can influence presidential decision making. When members dissent, they can set in motion political forces that raise the domestic political stakes involved, altering both the content of news stories and the public's willingness to support the president. Congressional speeches, we have seen, shape media coverage of prospective uses of force, which in turn impacts public opinion about the war. And as we observed in chapters 1 and 7, there are ample reasons for presidents to cultivate public support for prospective military engagements abroad. All sorts of trouble, political and otherwise, await the president who loses public support for an ongoing military venture.

SCHOLARSHIP

This book does not presume to cover all aspects of the domestic politics of war. Instead, it considers how one branch of government, Congress, restricts the capacity of another, the executive, during the lead-up to a military venture. It says very little about the actions of other domestic political institutions—such as the courts or the bureaucracy—on presidential decision making. Though it occasionally ventures across that vital temporal marker when troops are actually committed to the field, it does not in any systematic way examine Congress's influence over the numerous decisions that presidents must make during the ongoing course of a military venture—whether to escalate or deescalate, to stay the course or withdraw, to negotiate a peaceful resolution or fight onward. And quite consciously, this book sets aside normative considerations about what Congress ought to do, whether by reference to its constitutional obligations, its involvement in the writing of domestic policy, or expectations about how a system of separated powers should operate in practice. The fact that we are able to document congressional checks on presidential war powers may not, and we believe should not, allay critics' concerns that Congress is not presently doing an adequate job of restricting presidential power in matters involving war.

We conclude this book, nonetheless, with some reservation. For even within the province of study for which we assume responsibility, vital questions remain underexamined. On this book's analytic dimension—its characterizations of Congress, the presidency, the international arena, the media, and public opinion—more can, and must, be said. This section briefly identifies a handful of issues that are particularly ripe for continued study, with the hope that future scholars will pick up where this book leaves off.

We began chapter 2 with the recognition that Congress is not a unitary actor, but rather a collective decision-making body consisting of 535 voting members distributed across two chambers, forty standing committees, and numerous other joint and subcommittees. Hence, when trying to assess the probability that Congress will check presidential power, one must scrutinize the behavior of the institution's individual members. We then argued that the single most revealing characteristic of members during the lead-up to war is their partisan identification. Because of their common conceptions about when military action is appropriate, their shared electoral fortunes, and their ability to effectively communicate with one another, Republican members of Congress are much more likely to back Republican presidents during the lead-up to war. Similarly, Democratic members of Congress are more likely to raise questions about the efficacy of Republican presidential uses of force, and to object vehemently when, and if, a venture should go awry. Knowing the partisan composition of Congress, we demonstrated, provides considerable leverage in predicting the propensity of presidents to exercise military force abroad.

That partisanship is the first distinguishing characteristic of members' behavior, however, does not mean that it is appropriately understood as the last. Much more can be said about the internal organization of Congress—about its committee system, party leadership, and its interchamber dynamics. Though a member's partisan identification may say much about her stance vis-à-vis the president, it says relatively little about her entire capacity to set the legislative agenda; attract media attention; shape the content, tone, and length of congressional hearings; and thereby check the president's war powers. Where there are more partisan opponents within Congress, we have shown, presidential discretion to exercise military force abroad reliably weakens. But the ability of individual members, situated within different places in Congress, to check presidential power probably varies widely. When voicing objections about a prospective use of force, committee chairs, party leaders, and senators may wield more influence than sitting members, rank and file, and representatives, respectively. Future scholars would do well to scrutinize such possibilities and to further elucidate how turnover within specific committees, party leadership positions, and chambers, rather than in Congress as a whole, bears on the president's capacity to wage war abroad.[4]

If Congress is not a unitary actor, then neither is the executive. Though he sits alone atop his governing institution and retains considerable powers to ensure the compliance of those below him, when preparing for war the president still must coordinate with all sorts of advisors within the Executive Office of the presidency; navigate tensions that often arise between the State and Defense departments; allay the concerns of current and past generals who, increasingly, have demonstrated a predilection for showing up on television news; and manage the production of often conflicting intelligence reports that weigh on the president's case for war and the probable benefits of alternative courses of action. How the president does this and what troubles he encounters along the way deserve greater consideration than this book gives. Fortunately, at present there are massive literatures on both the evolving organization of the Executive Office of the presidency and the decision-making processes that occur within it.[5] By distilling from these literatures lessons that concern presidential decisions involving military deployments, and by relating them to the kinds of separation of powers issues that have preoccupied this volume, further insights will be gained into how presidents take us to war.

This book also yields at least three potential avenues for future research in international relations. For starters, one might examine the extent to which findings about the United States transport to other states. Though the prospects for the use of force in any country can elicit debates among policymakers, different democracies may confront these types of foreign policy challenges in different ways. Do parliamentary democracies, with executives who answer more directly to a legislature, demonstrate similar dynamics similar to those witnessed here? What kinds of recourse might be lacking in presidential systems but available to opposition members in parliamentary ones? How do politics in coalitional governments differ? Or do the same underlying processes work across democratic systems? Extending the scope of study to include other democratic and non-democratic systems could generate important empirical and theoretical insights. Of course, as a global superpower, the United States stands out as a good place to launch this line of inquiry. Obviously, though, other countries (notably the permanent five members of the UN Security Council) have responded to many crises around the world. Gathering data on relevant opportunities in a cross-national effort would yield valuable evidence about intervention choices across different types of governmental types and domestic institutions.

Second, our theoretical development and empirical tests consider only the use of military force (albeit differentiated by scope) as a possible U.S. response to observed foreign crises. Clearly, though, executives have a number of policy levers to pull in response to international crises, and few of these are mutually exclusive. Having assembled a dataset of all opportunities to use force, a richer response model could be estimated where outcomes are not limited to force/no force, but encompass a broader array of policy options. For example, a large literature exists on economic sanctions, which constitute an escalation beyond hostile diplomacy but short of military force.[6] This literature suffers from a similar problem as the use-of-force literature—it tends to ignore instances when sanctions *could* have been used but were not. Our opportunities dataset, or a revised one that accounts for a broader array of triggering events, might address this issue. Similarly, foreign policy responses such as diplomatic demarches, expulsions of diplomatic personnel, and military threats could be modeled as a part of a foreign policy choice model where various opportunities, as we have defined them, could elicit any number of conflictual or cooperative responses.

Finally, in our attempt to bridge levels of analysis, we have shown empirically that the relevance of some forces at the domestic level varies according to other systemic or interstate factors. We hope this is a step toward integrating various levels of analyses in international relations, rather than considering domestic and international forces as necessarily, and irreconcilably, opposing. We suggest that other questions in the realm of foreign policy could be approached in such a manner. We suspect that similar international conditions may influence the presence or dynamics of other processes such as rally effects during crises or, more broadly, public support for the president in foreign policy. Scholars should be mindful of such possibilities, given that systemic factors may condition the constraints of domestic institutions or political leaders.

Perhaps the most straightforward subject of continued empirical study may concern Congress's influence over the media and public opinion. In chapters 6 and 7, we presented the first evidence ever collected of Congress's ability to shape local television news during the lead-up to war, and we traced the various implications this has for the public's willingness to endorse military action. The evidence, however, came from just one military deployment and centered on the height of congressional involvement at the time—specifically, during the authorization debates. We do not know whether individual members effectively gained entrée to the local or national media outlets in the period between the 2002 midterm elections and the outbreak of war; whether Congress exerted comparable influence over the local or national media during the lead-up to other military deployments; or whether Congress's influence over local television news extended to alternative news sources, such as the cable news, the blogosphere, or online news agencies. And with regards to public opinion, our empirical studies invite refinements: with surveys that identify the specific news outlets that individuals watch, for instance, analysts should be able to reduce much of the noise that infects models of public opinion and the media; and with experiments that allow for multiple messengers to comment on a president's preferred policy, analysts may be able to distinguish the particular influence that members of Congress wield over public discussions involving war from more general framing effects that have consumed so much of the existing public opinion literature.[7]

Looking Back on Wars against Iraq, Afghanistan, and Terror

We began research on this book in the fall of 2002, when fighting in Afghanistan was in full swing, and public debates about an impending war in Iraq were just getting underway.[8] At the time, academic treatments of congressional checks on presidential powers appeared exactly that—academic. The president, it seemed, remained entirely unconstrained in the realm of military policy. By exercising his unilateral powers, George W. Bush could accomplish almost any foreign policy objective, and members of Congress had little choice but to tag along.

Using national security directives, executive orders, proclamations, and a wide assortment of other measures, Bush exercised extraordinary control over military actions waged against foreign regimes and the terrorists that they purportedly harbored. In the immediate aftermath of September 11, Bush unilaterally created a series of agencies—the Office of Homeland Security, the Office of Global Communications, and the Commission on the Intelligence Capabilities of the United States Regarding Weapons of Mass Destruction—to collect and disseminate new intelligence while co-ordinating the activities of existing bureaus. He issued a national security directive lifting a ban (which Ford originally instituted via executive order 11905) on the CIA's ability to "engage in, or conspire to engage in, polit-ical assassination"—in this instance, the target being Osama bin Laden and his lieutenants within al-Qaeda. He signed executive orders that froze all financial assets in U.S. banks that could be linked to bin Laden and his terrorist networks. Perhaps most controversially, Bush unilaterally estab-lished special military tribunals to try noncitizens suspected of plotting terrorist acts, committing terrorism, or harboring known terrorists. And through national security directives, the president developed a massive international infrastructure to detain and interrogate (and, some charge, torture) foreign combatants.

The most visible of Bush's unilateral actions, of course, consisted of military strikes in Afghanistan and Iraq. Having secured congressional authorizations to respond to the mounting crises as he saw fit,[9] in the fall of 2001 Bush directed the air force to begin a bombing campaign against Taliban strongholds, while special forces conducted stealth missions on the ground. In the spring of 2003, he launched a massive air and ground war against Iraq, plunging the United States into the most protracted military conflict since the Vietnam War. During the subsequent occupa-tion, most policies related to intelligence gathering, the rebuilding of infrastructure, the training of Iraqi troops, and the governing transition came not through laws, but through unilateral actions of one sort or an-other. Within a year Bush's orders resulted in the collapse of the Taliban and Baathist regimes, the flight of tens of thousands of refugees into Pak-istan, Iran, and Turkey, the destruction of Afghanistan's and Iraq's social and economic infrastructures, and the introduction of new democratically elected governments.

Over time, most observers appeared awestruck by the president's in-domitable power. Bush's willingness to bypass Congress in pursuit of a sweeping set of foreign policy objectives revealed considerable aplomb, audacity even. *The Economist* recognized that "most presidents like to try and expand their powers. But in repeatedly invoking his constitutional authority as commander-in-chief in the 'war on terror' to bypass both domestic laws and international treaties, George Bush has taken the art to new heights."[10] David Moberg lamented "the threat of an imperial presidency, which has reached its highest level under Bush."[11] Stephen Graubard noted that "the perils of exaggerated executive power were never more conspicuous than in the first years of the twenty-first century when the king, courtiers, and warriors domiciled in Washington, D.C." (2004, 32). And other scholars spoke more eloquently still about the various constitutional, legal, and moral implications of the current administration's brash exercise of presidential power.[12]

Evidence of congressional checks on this president, meanwhile, appeared in short supply. During the first six years of Bush's administration, Bush's foreign policy agenda did not suffer grand defeats at the hand of congressionally enacted statutes or judicial rulings. Though an epic interbranch showdown may yet erupt, during Bush's first term, conflicts proved rather muted—even though the president, quite explicitly, sought to exalt his own power and to denigrate Congress's, insisting on more than a few occasions that members should not, and constitutionally cannot, meddle in his campaigns against terrorism at home and abroad. Among critics, the president's defiant stance generated a growing consensus, articulated in a *New York Times* editorial, that "the system of checks and balances is a safety net that doesn't feel particularly sturdy at present."[13]

Three factors, in our judgment, help explain why friction between Congress and the presidency has not yielded the kinds of sparks that might allay scholars' lingering worries about the health of our system of separated powers. First, and perhaps most obviously, is September 11. Having been attacked stateside, and with the horrific images of the Twin Towers collapsing fresh in the public's mind, the nation automatically looked to its president to formulate a response. Congress and the courts, it seemed, could not move quickly enough to get out of the president's way. And so it is during the aftermath of genuine catastrophes. The bridle that Congress might otherwise place on the president temporarily slackens; and for a period, the chief executive enjoys considerable freedom to do as he will.

The second boon to presidential power during Bush's first term and the early part of his second—and the one most pertinent to the analyses included in this book—concerns the partisan composition of Congress. Republicans retained control of both chambers of Congress; with this control, they managed to limit legislative hearings about the Iraq War, squelch initiatives to establish fixed timetables for the return of troops, and temper legislative efforts to amend or overturn various aspects of the president's military and diplomatic agenda. Imagine how the hearing on the Abu Ghraib scandals might have differed had Democrats retained control of either chamber; or the momentum that Representative John Murtha's 2005 recommendation that troops return home might have gained if his party set the legislative agenda in the House; or how Senator Russ Feingold's push to censure the president might have fared if his party controlled the Senate. During the first six years of his presidency, Bush benefited mightily from the disciplined control that his party wielded in Congress.

Third, and finally, there is much that members of Congress can do short of enacting laws that formally amend or overturn especially objectionable executive actions. As we have argued throughout this book, when trying to assess congressional checks on presidential power, it is a mistake to fixate exclusively on legislative challenges; for in doing so, one overlooks the more subtle, yet tangible, ways through which members of Congress can affect the president's strategic calculus. As the Iraq War dragged on, casualties mounted, an insurgency grew, and the president's approval ratings languished in the low 30s and high 20s, members of Congress increasingly lodged public complaints against this president. After the 2004 election, the Democrats objected most consistently to the president's war in Iraq. Increasingly, though, moderate Republicans also chimed in, trying to distance themselves from a president who, due to this war, increasingly looked more like a liability than an asset. In the words of one *Washington Post* columnist, "grumbling in some GOP quarters seemed likely to persist, fueled in part by Republican concern over Bush's declining approval ratings. Those ratings, at 33 percent in a recent AP-Ipsos poll, the lowest of his presidency, have emboldened Republicans to speak out when they don't agree with the president, something that didn't happen during Bush's first term. Congressional Republicans have been battered by a string of White House woes."[14]

There is, moreover, considerable evidence that congressional complaints have dampened the president's ability to conduct military operations in Afghanistan and Iraq as he would have liked. In the wake of congressional opposition during his two terms, Bush had to make a variety of substantive concessions—recall his backtracking on whether to allow Condoleeza Rice and Donald Rumsfeld to testify before Congress; on the creation of a Department of Homeland Security; on domestic surveillance initiatives; and on the creation of the 9/11 commission. In every one of these instances, Bush took bold stances in support of his favored foreign policy position only to backtrack later when critics assembled and objected in unison. And in the one showdown where the president patently refused to budge—the Dubai Port deal, during the winter of 2005—Bush watched as his entire policy ran aground.

Bush's travails are hardly unique. In 1950, when he retained large democratic majorities in the House and Senate, Truman launched the Korean War and nary a whisper of dissent emanated from around Washington; in 1965, when he retained even larger majorities in both chambers, Johnson justified retaliatory attacks against the North Vietnamese without facing any congressional opposition; and in 1982, when he retained control over the Senate, Reagan sent a large contingent of troops into Lebanon without any organized opposition in the federal government crying foul. But as each of these deployments became protracted, mishaps and atrocities were publicized, and the prospects of success dimmed, objections from within Congress grew increasingly strident—and presidents were forced to prematurely abandon either the venture itself (Reagan) or their political careers (Truman and Johnson).

Again, imagine how these deployments might have differed had these presidents faced strong, large, and unified partisan opponents within Congress throughout their tenures. Though, in each instance, the president might well have sent in the troops anyway, the timing of the deployments, their size, and their duration might have differed. With partisan opponents poised to hold long investigative hearings, publicly denounce every misstep, and possibly legislate restrictions on the conduct of the wars, would Truman have pursued the communists past the thirty-eighth parallel? Would Johnson have moved so quickly to respond militarily against the purported attacks on U.S. vessels in the Gulf of Tonkin? Would Reagan have kept troops in Lebanon for months, rather than weeks, after the bombing of the marine barracks? Perhaps. We, of course, can only imagine how events might have transpired in these alternate realities. The quantitative findings and case studies laid out in this book, however, suggest that the presidents might have behaved differently than they did, implying that our system of checks and balances, though perhaps not especially sturdy, at least shows signs of life.

And so our system continues to function, especially recently. June 2006 started like many months in Iraq—continued sectarian violence and lingering worries about the stability of the country's new government. Two events, however, would make the month quite notable. On June 9, American military forces killed Abu Musab al-Zarqawi, the self-proclaimed leader of al-Qaeda in Iraq. With a long-awaited victory in the "war on terror," Bush appeared cautiously optimistic about the prospects of a political settlement taking hold. And shortly after al-Zarqawi's death, the president paid Iraq a surprise visit. Developments at home, however, would quickly turn America's attention away from these encouraging developments abroad. On June 16, the House closed a long day of acrimonious debate by approving a resolution rejecting any deadline for American troop withdrawals from Iraq.[15] A few days later, the Senate began a similar debate over a pair of Democratic proposals to begin troop withdrawals. Both measures failed after several days of rancorous debate.[16]

Two features of these debates especially concern the themes of this book. First, despite a dizzying set of events on the ground in Iraq, the American media turned their focus to Congress the moment that formal debate began. Gone were reports about the fallout from the death of Zarqawi, the "intelligence bonanza" discovered by the Iraqi government, and the continued violence in Iraq, including the death of several American troops. Instead, local television, newspapers, and opinion pages zeroed in on congressional debate, structuring their coverage around the arguments and evidence advanced by members of Congress. Second, party allegiances continued to dictate members' behavior. In the House, Republicans rallied behind their president with 90 percent voting against troop pullouts, while 75 percent of Democrats voted for some cut in troops. Similarly in the Senate, the nonbinding resolution calling for troop reductions without a set timetable failed with all but one Republican voting against, and all but six Democrats voting in favor. If Iraq tells us anything about the domestic politics of war, it is that partisan wrangling does not abet at water's edge. Even after troops have been committed to the field, it plays a prominent role in debates over the use of force.

Looking Forward to Iran

The recent resumption of legislative activities should assuage some concerns that the events surrounding September 11 and the wars that succeeded them permanently crippled Congress's capacity to check presidential powers. It is worth recalling, though, that such events fall outside of this book's primary domain. From the outset, we have announced our intention to examine the interbranch politics that precede military action, to scrutinize the strategizing of presidents when the nation stands on a war footing, and to discern the extent to which Congress figures into their thinking. During those periods when dangers gather abroad, we have suggested, presidents struggle mightily to forecast the likelihood of military success and to discern Congress's likely reaction in the event of failure. The latter possibility has given us cause to intermittently document what actually happens when military ventures do go awry. The book's focus, however, lies on the domestic politics that precede war, not in the politics that ensue during its execution. Contemporary deliberations about how best to handle Iran's nuclear program, therefore, fit more naturally within this book. This section, then, briefly reflects on the implications of our findings for military action being taken against Iran in the near future.

First, some background. Since 1979, the United States has not maintained any sort of diplomatic relations with Iran. After the Islamic revolution unseated a long-time ally of the United States, Shah Reza Pahlavi, and American hostages were held for 444 days in Tehran, bilateral relations were put on permanent hold. Despite Iran's pivotal position in the Middle East, despite a potential mutually beneficial economic relationship, despite a thirty-year military and political alliance, relations between the two countries have remained hostile for more than a quarter century.

In 2005, U.S.-Iranian relations suffered further setbacks when President Mahmoud Ahmadinejad ascended to power. Ahmadinejad, who replaced the more moderate Mohammed Khatami, invited all sorts of controversy on issues ranging from the holocaust (which he denies the existence of) to American foreign policy in the Middle East (which he labels imperialist). His rhetorical outbursts were all the more irksome, given that they were made against the backdrop of Iran's admission that it was attempting to enrich nuclear material that could be used for constructing nuclear weapons.

Of course, the history of the Iranian nuclear crisis predates Ahmadinejad. In the fall of 2002, as the United States debated whether to wage war against Saddam Hussein in Iraq, Iranian exiles began reporting that it was not Saddam's nuclear program that should worry the United States, but rather Iran's. Although Iran was a member of the 1968 Non-Proliferation Treaty (NPT), exiles, Israeli intelligence, and some American intelligence officials suggested that Iran had secretly built facilities to process uranium that could be used in nuclear weapons. Iranian leaders denied the charge, insisting that even if work on nuclear material was occurring, it was merely for the purposes of generating electricity.

The crisis accelerated rapidly in December 2002, when U.S. satellite reconnaissance photos revealed evidence of Iranian efforts to develop nuclear technology, including the enrichment of nuclear material. Immediately, the Bush administration accused Iran of attempting to build nuclear weapons. Iran initially responded by reaffirming its claim that the work was for civilian purposes and by allowing the International Atomic Energy Agency (IAEA) to inspect the facilities. In February 2003, Iranian President Khatami announced formally that Iran wished to develop nuclear power facilities and soon thereafter, the IAEA began its inspections.

During the summer of 2003, the IAEA announced that it had discovered trace elements of enriched uranium. Then, under pressure from several European Union (EU) states, Iran agreed to an IAEA protocol allowing spot inspections of its nuclear facilities. By the winter of 2003, the IAEA chief Mohammed ElBaradei claimed to see no evidence that Iran was pursuing weapons. But by early 2004, new IAEA evidence and reports from Pakistan indicated that Iran had attempted to create a bomb.[17] In response, the Bush administration assumed a hard-line stance against Iran, calling for sanctions and immediate punishment by the international community. The IAEA also demanded that Iran halt its nuclear activity. Buoyed by these objections, EU states brokered a deal to halt the enrichment of uranium; and in November 2004, the IAEA placed seals on several of Iran's nuclear facilities.

Iranian elections then intervened. In August 2005, Ahmadinejad entered office and within days, he announced that Iran would resume nuclear enrichment activities. By early 2006, Iran had launched full-scale uranium enrichment, removing IAEA seals from all facilities. Thus far, no foreign state or international organization, including the IAEA, the UN Security Council, and Russia, has convinced Iran to abandon the project. Though the United States, France, and Great Britain continue to support efforts to halt Iran's nuclear activities, including economic sanctions, both Russia and China have threatened to veto any sanctions until diplomacy has run its course. As of this writing, Iran has ruled out compromise and rebuffed efforts by both Security Council members and EU members to broker a settlement.

Though Bush has refused to forsake the possibility of military force, thus far he has relied on "aggressive diplomacy" to deal with Iran. With the Iraq war dragging, the president's standing with allies and the American public languishing, and Iranian bellicosity in full bloom, the administration has steadfastly pursued multilateral negotiations and UN Security Council action. Some observers have noted the distinct difference between the more direct and militarily aggressive stand on Iraq and the diplomatic overtures on Iran. As one senior fellow at the Council on Foreign Relations observed, "The Bush administration in the second term has been much more mindful of the need to engage in diplomacy. . . . After the difficulties of Iraq, we see it on Hamas, we see it on Iran, and we've seen a reemphasis on the need for European strength and unity."[18] Of course, more than domestic politics have induced this shift. The expected losses incurred in an Iran war constitute one (if not the single most important) explanation for the administration's reliance on diplomacy. Moreover, Iran possesses numerous military options that Iraq lacked, raising the expected costs of military action. But Congress too has played an important role. Beginning in the fall of 2005 and the spring of 2006, when the administration refused to rule out using force and as negotiations between Iran and the international community intensified, many members of Congress appeared in the media. If the administration was looking for open support for a preemptive war with Iran (which they claimed they were not), they found little on Capitol Hill. Instead, members offered pleas for caution and diplomacy.

As expected, most objections to the use of military force arose from the opposition's ranks. Senator Christopher Dodd (D-CT) opined that "I don't think we've been muscular enough, if you will, on the diplomatic front. I don't disagree that we ought to leave the military option on the table, but I don't think we've been working hard enough on the diplomacy side of this."[19] In response to a *New Yorker* article that claimed Bush was planning for the possibility of a nuclear-led preemptive strike, Senator Diane Feinstein (D-CA) denounced the administration: "I don't know why we would even talk about using tactical nuclear weapons when we haven't directly spoken with the Iranians. It doesn't make sense."[20] Other Democrats, including Evan Bayh (D-IN) and Bill Nelson (D-FL), echoed these calls.

This time around, Republicans did not automatically fall in line behind their president. Senate Armed Services Committee Chair John Warner (R-VA) called for direct negotiations between Washington and Tehran, with other Republicans joining the ranks. Richard Lugar (R-IN), chair of the Senate Foreign Relations Committee, John McCain (R-AZ), and Nebraska Republican Chuck Hagel noted in a *Financial Times* editorial, "Allies of the US will support tough action against Iran only if they are confident America is serious about achieving a negotiated, diplomatic solution. The continued unwillingness of the U.S. to engage Iran will make other states hesitate to support, and possibly oppose, these tougher measures."[21]

In May 2006, the administration denounced as simple propaganda the first communication directed from Iran to the United States since the 1979 revolution. The *Los Angeles Times,* however, noted a different possibility—that the letter from the Iranian president "may add mounting pressure on Bush from U.S. allies and some Congress members to engage in direct talks with Tehran before resorting to sanctions or military action."[22] And there is some evidence that the letter had its intended effect. Thereafter, members of Congress called on the president to launch direct negotiations with Tehran, contra the administration's preferred strategy of negotiating through European and Russian mediators.

In the spring of 2006, the nomination hearings for General Michael Hayden provided members of Congress with further opportunities to publicly criticize the administration's failed intelligence in Iraq and to examine their implications for how best to handle Iran.[23] Senator Pat Roberts (R-KS) complained about the paucity of reliable information on Iran's nuclear weapons program: "We don't know, and the people providing the answers don't know."[24] Having learned its lesson in Iraq, members in Congress appeared in no mood to hear about the "slam dunk" case on Iran. Hence, they pressed General Hayden on the CIA's efforts to collect intelligence on Iran. Senator Feinstein led the charge, asking Hayden, "Given the problems with estimates of Iraqi weapons of mass destruction, how can the American public be confident of the accuracy of estimates regarding Iranian plans and programs?"[25] Such concerns clearly established a basis for questioning future attempts by the administration to quash the Iranian threat. Ironically, even Secretary of Defense Donald Rumsfeld drew a link between failed Iraq intelligence and the politics of pressuring Iran. *Newsday* noted that "even Rumsfeld said last week that the Iraq intel fumbles give him pause about Iran."[26]

Cognizant of their own influence, reminiscent of Kosovo in 1999, some members of Congress nonetheless expressed concern about the importance of signaling resolve in a crisis. Members ranging from Dodd to McCain, while criticizing the Bush administration, made a point of ending their remarks with calls to "leave force on the table." McCain consistently noted that "force should not be ruled out." Yet, these same members insisted that military action would be justifiable in only a limited set of circumstances. McCain claimed that "everybody knows we're not going to have two wars [at once]." These comments were relayed by the *Financial Times*, which noted that they "illustrate the opposition within the president's own party to any effort to use the military to tackle the problem."[27]

During this period, members of Congress did more than just issue public appeals on Iran. Occasionally, the legislative machinery whirred to life. A 2006 concurrent resolution introduced by House Democrats expressed "the sense of Congress that the President should not initiate military action against Iran with respect to its nuclear program without first obtaining authorization from Congress." The bill had thirty-two cosponsors, all Democrats; in the spring, it was referred to the House Committee on International Relations. Signs of bipartisanship emerged in late April 2006 when the House passed a bill, 397 to 21, authorizing financial backing of prodemocracy groups inside Iran.[28] When Congress attempted to independently gather and analyze information, however, partisan divisions returned with a vengeance. Also in April, the House defeated a measure that would have required the Bush administration to report every ninety days on the status of Iran. Although the purported justification for a "no" vote was that a report could be requested at any time, the vote was split along party lines—Republicans supporting their commander in chief, Democrats pushing for stricter reporting requirements.[29]

Congress's public appeals and legislative maneuvering seem to have influenced the public's thinking about a possible war in Iran. An April 2006 poll by the *Los Angeles Times* found that 48 percent would support taking military action against Iran, while 40 percent stood opposed.[30] Barely four months prior, public opinion was noticeably more favorable: 57 percent of Americans then supported military action against Iran. This nearly ten-percentage-point drop in support could be traced to a host of factors, ranging from continued American struggles in Iraq to the president's declining popularity; yet as our own findings in chapter 7 suggest, tepid congressional support for military action also may have stirred public doubts about the wisdom of military action in Iran. Should Congress continue to criticize the administration, public support for military action against Iran may fall further still.

Congress's involvement in public debates about Iran illustrates several lessons that by now should be all too familiar. Initially, partisanship remains the single best predictor of members' positions on matters involving military action. It is the case that Republicans occasionally aired grievances about the Bush administration and the possibility of military strikes. Doing so, moreover, these Republicans attracted considerable media attention, not least because their actions signaled potential rifts within the party, which could tip the balance of power on this issue to the Democrats who steadfastly and uniformly opposed the president. Were Lugar, McCain, and Hagel the only three senators to raise questions about the use of force against Iran, they would hardly warrant such widespread attention. Because they joined a solid minority of Democrats voicing similar concerns, however, their voices resonated throughout Washington and beyond.

Additionally, debates about military deployments do not occur one at a time. In this instance, the shadow of Iraq cast a long shadow on Iran. As casualties continued to mount in Iraq, as Afghanistan experienced an upsurge in violence, and as the president's popularity continued to fall, Congress appeared increasingly reticent to cede full authority over Iran to the president. Unlike the immediate aftermath of September 11, now Congress appears insistent on greater public scrutiny of presidential decision making regarding future military ventures into the Middle East.

Finally, just because Congress has not insisted that the president abide by the War Powers Resolution, or that it has not passed new legislation detailing when military force can be used against Iran, does not indicate that its members are wholly excluded from deliberations about this evolving crisis. As we have seen, members of Congress took advantage of a variety of venues to influence the course of public debate—on cable talk shows, floor debates, the confirmation hearings of presidential appointees, and local television outlets. So doing, they managed to shape the tone and direction of elite discourse on Iran, the public's willingness to support a military operation there, and Iranian views about the likelihood that the United States and its allies would follow through on their threats.

What does the future hold? Much, of course, depends on what is learned about the state of Iran's nuclear program, for the current intelligence remains, if not speculative, at least uncertain. Whether Iran decides to cooperate with an inspections regimen, too, will influence the president's calculus of the costs and benefits of military action. Developments within the international arena—whether Iran continues to openly threaten Israel; whether Russia and China insist that all diplomatic options be thoroughly exhausted before even considering sanctions or the use of force; whether the UN Security Council takes any serious action against Iran—too will surely dictate the range of options available to the president.

And still another factor will critically affect the direction of U.S. foreign policy in the Middle East—namely, the 2006 congressional elections.

THE 2006 MIDTERM ELECTIONS, AND BEYOND

For the first three and a half years of the Iraq War, Bush insisted that American troops would remain in the Middle East as long as it took for the sectarian violence to subside, the Iraqi security forces to assume responsibility for citizens' welfare, and the newly installed Iraqi national government to function effectively. Throughout, Bush reaffirmed his stalwart commitment to winning the war on terror and his refusal to cow to a rising insurgency within Iraq. To convey this resolve, the president and members of his administration reiterated the same catchphrase again and again: the United States must "stay the course." But in October 2006, Bush publicly retired the phrase, claiming that it did not adequately reflect his commitment to "adjust[ing] to the enemy on the battlefield."[31] Quite suddenly, the administration appeared willing to set "benchmarks" and "milestones" for progress in the Middle East, respond flexibly to events on the ground, and, if only implicitly, admit U.S. intentions to eventually withdraw from Iraq.

In its lead editorial the day after Bush's announcement, the *New York Times* reflected on the cause of his apparent change in course:

> The generals who told President Bush before the war that Donald Rumsfeld's shock-and-awe fantasy would not work were not enough to persuade him to change his strategy in Iraq. The rise of the insurgency did not do the trick. Nor did month after month of mounting military and civilian casualties on all sides, the emergence of a near civil war, the collapse of reconstruction efforts or the seeming inability of either Iraqi or American forces to secure contested parts of Iraq, including Baghdad, for any significant period. So what finally, after all this time, caused Mr. Bush to very publicly consult with his generals to consider a change in tactics in Iraq? The president, who says he never reads political polls, is worried that his party could lose some of its iron grip on power in the Congressional elections next month.[32]

The *Times* then proceeded to excoriate the president for allowing domestic politics, rather than dispassionate assessment of the war itself, to influence his decision-making.

It is not at all clear, though, that Bush was mistaken to anticipate (and then heed) the prospect of a Democratic Congress. By almost all accounts the Democrats planned to launch hearings and investigations into the various mishaps, scandals, and tactical errors that plagued the military campaign. Given a majority of seats, Democrats in Congress would fixate on no-bid contracts, intelligence failures, decisions to ignore the military's advice about increasing troop levels, and other perceived abuses and blunders—all with the aim of honing media (and by extension public) attention on Bush's failures to execute the war, and thereby setting the stage for further Democratic gains in Congress and the White House in 2008.

On this, almost everyone agreed. According to reports during the final weeks of the midterm election campaigns, with control of Congress Democrats would launch "made-for-television hearings [that] would focus on faulty intelligence used to justify the invasion of Iraq, strategic and tactical missteps once there and the sending of troops into combat with insufficient armor."[33] Said Norman Ornstein of the American Enterprise Institute, "Two things will change: there will be lots of investigations, on Iraq, torture, intelligence failures, and so on; and there will be more congressional pushback on the unprecedented expansion of executive power."[34] Or, as *Washington Post* columnist Jeff Birnbaum noted, "If Democrats take control of the House, the Senate, or both, expect oversight and investigative hearings—and not very friendly ones from Bush's standpoint—to pop up on issues ranging from Darfur to North Korea."[35]

Democrats themselves made no secret of their plans. Asked what a change in party control of Congress would yield, Ike Skelton (D-MO) responded:

> Oversight. I'll repeat it: oversight, oversight, oversight! Congress has done a poor job of overseeing the conduct of the war, the corruption in the reconstruction program in Iraq, the recruiting problems, particularly in the Army. They have rubber-stamped the Pentagon. What we need today is a Truman Commission."[36]

Carl Levin (D-MI) insisted that a Democratic takeover would constitute a "referendum" on changing course in Iraq.[37] According to Democratic strategist Victor Kamber, "First and foremost will be tough questioning on the Iraq War. . . . We need open, honest hearings to understand what our military is saying, what we really know and didn't know, when we knew it and why we're there."[38]

Prolonged hearings, observers anticipated at the time, would pose a variety of challenges for the Bush administration. For starters, hearings probably would displace other features on the administration's legislative agenda, such as proposed immigration, social security, entitlement, and tax reforms. Depending on the public's reactions, a Democratic majority might also follow up the hearings with legislation designed to further restrict the president's discretion to wage war abroad. As one observer noted:

> Oversight is not just a matter of playing political piñata with administration witnesses. Such hearings can convert unfocused anxieties into irresistible momentum for budget cuts, budget increases, or reform legislation. Bipartisan revolts have already speeded up new armor for troops in Iraq; reduced the executive branch's discretion to spend money

through leasing, "other transaction authorities," or "multiyear procurement"; and increased the size of the Army over the Pentagon's objections. Those votes indicate that Republican defectors are ready to
move if the Democrats hit the right pressure points.[39]

A sudden shift in the tone and volume of media coverage on the Iraq
War, many expected, would also follow Democratic-initiated hearings
within Congress. Sounding much like the communications scholars discussed in chapter 6, *National Journal* columnist William Powers noted:

> Journalists like to think they are reporting just the facts, straight and
> unaffected by circumstance. The story is the story is the story. In fact,
> news is a highly atmospheric product: the way a story is presented,
> framed, and played (up or down) depends heavily on matters beyond
> the facts themselves. In Washington, the balance of power between the
> parties on one hand and between the administration and the media on
> the other is a hidden but immensely important factor in determining
> how the news reads and sounds.

What impact, then, would a transfer of power within Congress have on
the media's coverage of the Iraq War? Powers continued, "A November
defeat for the Republicans will change everything. If Bush suffers a major
political setback, the media will feel freed up to tear into this war as they
have never done before."[40] And as we discovered in chapter 7, the kinds
of news reported on television and in newspapers has immediate implications for public opinion.

The downstream consequences of congressional hearings and investigations could be more far reaching still. Indeed, they might well stoke
doubts among European allies and Middle Eastern adversaries about the
willingness of U.S. citizens to see the current struggle through to its end.
During the campaign, in fact, Republican strategists attempted to exploit
these very doubts for electoral gain. Republican candidates regularly
warned voters that a Democratic victory would send the "wrong message" to the nation's Middle Eastern allies and adversaries.[41] Bush declared at one campaign rally, "The Democrat approach in Iraq comes
down to this: The terrorists win and America loses."[42] According to
Danielle Pletka from the American Enterprise Institute, "If the Osama bin
Ladens, Mahmoud Ahmadinejads, and Kim Jong Ils of this world already
believe Washington is weak and divided, they will only be encouraged by
a Chairman Murtha, who believes America is 'more dangerous to world
peace than Iran or North Korea,' an empowered Senator Kerry, who
longs for an end to the focus on terror, and a Speaker Pelosi, who believes
an immediate withdrawal from Iraq is the wisest course."[43]

As we now know, Republican entreaties did not have their intended effect. On November 7, the Democrats swept to power in both the House and Senate. And as we write these concluding paragraphs, Bush is announcing the resignation of Donald Rumsfeld—a secretary of defense who the president had defended against any number of previous attacks, whose resignation he had twice rejected, and who stood to be a lightning rod in subsequent congressional hearings. Having previously insisted that Congress had hardly a say over decisions involving war, the president appears downright eager to work alongside Democratic Party leaders in order to adjust course in Iraq. In his postelection press conference, Bush announced:

> I look forward to working with [the Democrats]. And I truly believe that Congresswoman Pelosi and Harry Reid care just about as much. They care about the security of this country, like I do. . . . We have different views on how to do that, but their spirit is such that they want to protect America. That's what I believe.

Still, ever aware of the international consequences of domestic political strife, the president also saw fit to speak directly to the insurgents within Iraq. "Amid this time of change, I have a message for those on the front lines. To our enemies: Do not be joyful. Do not confuse the workings of our democracy with a lack of will. Our nation is committed to bringing you to justice."[44]

While reciprocating gestures of bipartisanship in the immediate aftermath of the elections, Democrats also reaffirmed their intentions to launch hearing and investigations on Iraq. Said the *Los Angeles Times,* "Representative Ike Skelton knows what he will do in one of his first acts as chairman of the Armed Services Committee in the Democratic-led House: resurrect the subcommittee on oversight and investigations."[45] Representative John Murtha, one of the outspoken Democratic critics of the war (and in line to chair the Appropriations subcommittee on military spending) promised hearings on Iraq: "In the long run, in order to solve the problem, we have to have hearings. We have to establish who was accountable for all the mistakes that have been made."[46] Such investigations, and the media attention to follow, would have implications that extend well beyond the nation's dealings with Iraq. In the words of one observer: "The Democratic takeover of Congress will raise the profile of lawmakers who have repeatedly urged the Bush administration to talk to key adversaries such as Iran, North Korea, and Syria, increasing pressure on the White House to stop placing restrictions or conditions on such discussions."[47]

At the start of the 110th Congress, neither Nancy Pelosi (D-CA) nor Harry Reid (D-NV), the new Speaker of the House and Senate Majority

Leader, will dictate U.S. foreign policy in the Middle East. Nor will Bush feel obliged to withdraw immediately from Iraq or to forsake a military solution to other challenges posed by Iran, North Korea, or any other nation. The president's views continue to loom largest in public debates over war. But if the findings presented in this book serve as any guide, the president, now stripped of his partisan majorities in Congress, will be less likely to resort to war during the last two years of his tenure than he was in the first six. Before the 2006 midterm elections, Robert Byrd (D-WV) made a habit of railing against a Congress that had been "ominously, dreadfully silent."[48] With the elections now over, Congress is silent no more. And this president, like so many presidents before him, finds himself at the center on an inter-branch struggle—charged by partisan politics—to direct U.S. military policy abroad.

Tables Relating to Chapter 3

Table A.1
Descriptive Statistics for Chapter 3 Analyses

	Mean	Standard Deviation	Minimum	Maximum
Dependent Variables				
All Force	1.71	1.49	0	7
Minor Force	1.08	1.18	0	5
Major Force	0.63	0.86	0	5
MIDs	0.95	1.05	0	5
Independent Variables				
Unified Government	0.39	0.49	0	1
Percent President Party	0.50	0.09	0.35	0.68
President Party Power	−0.00	0.14	−0.24	0.27
CPI	4.22	3.57	−2.7	18.9
Unemployment	5.51	1.64	1.1	10.7
Public Approval	55.19	13.21	23.0	87.0
Election Year	0.19	0.39	0	1
Ongoing War	0.24	0.43	0	1
Cold War	0.80	0.40	0	1
Hegemony	0.33	0.06	0.26	0.52
World Disputes (non-U.S.)	5.54	3.08	0	17
Percent Veteran	0.61	0.11	0.38	0.74

N = 224 for each variable

TABLE A.2
Frequency of All Uses of Force, Including Background Controls

	(1)		(2)		(3)	
Unified	0.28	[0.31]	—		—	
Percent President Party	—		0.68	[2.12]	—	
President Party Power	—		—		0.85	[1.25]
Unemployment	0.23***	[0.04]	0.24***	[0.05]	0.23***	[0.04]
CPI	0.06**	[0.03]	0.05**	[0.02]	0.05**	[0.02]
Public Approval	−0.00	[0.01]	−0.00	[0.01]	−0.00	[0.01]
Election Year	0.14**	[0.09]	0.14*	[0.09]	0.16**	[0.08]
Ongoing War	−0.57***	[0.20]	−0.52***	[0.20]	−0.54***	[0.19]
Cold War	0.47***	[0.06]	0.49***	[0.05]	0.47***	[0.06]
Hegemony	−0.38	[2.11]	−0.52	[2.16]	−0.14	[1.13]
World Disputes	−0.01	[0.02]	0.01	[0.02]	0.01	[0.02]
Constant	−1.39**	[0.62]	−1.85	[1.28]	−1.29**	[0.55]
(N)	224		224		224	

Negative binomial regressions estimated. Quarterly number of uses of force analyzed from 1945 to 2000. For all table entries: *** = $p < 0.01$, one-tailed test; ** = $p < 0.05$; * = $p < 0.10$. Huber/White/sandwich standard errors clustered on presidential administrations reported in brackets. Though not reported, models also contain fixed effect terms for each presidential administration.

Text and Tables Relating to Chapter 4

THE OPPORTUNITIES DATABASE

WHILE MANY INTERNATIONAL relations scholars have examined presidential uses of force, only one other, James Meernik, actually built a database that permits explorations of why presidents seize on some opportunities to commit U.S. troops abroad, but not others.[1] Surveying a wide range of sources (*Facts on File, Keesing's Contemporary Archives, New York Times, Royal United Services Institute,* and *Bracey's Defense Yearbook*), Meernik identified threats posed by state and nonstate actors to the security, economic, or political interests of the United States, each of which constituted an opportunity to exercise military force abroad. Meernik found 458 such opportunities from 1948 to 1988, of which 245 elicited a U.S. military response.[2] These opportunities occurred in every region around the globe, most frequently in the Middle East and Central America. Every president faced at least 20 opportunities to exercise military force, but Reagan and Eisenhower faced the most, topping out at 104 and 82, respectively.

With these data, Meernik estimated a series of regressions that posit presidential responses to each individual opportunity as a function of a variety of domestic and international indicators. Meernik found that levels of U.S. military aid, the prior use of military force, anti-American violence, and Soviet involvement consistently yield significant impacts on the probability that the president exercises military force, while presidential popularity, election years, and a weighted misery index do not. On the basis of these findings, he concluded that arguments about domestic political forces are "overstated."[3] The realists would seem to have it right: when presidents (and other heads of state) contemplate military action, all of the action occurs between states rather than within them.

There are a variety of reasons, however, to question Meernik's conclusion that domestic politics explicitly, and domestic political institutions by implication, are trivial influences over presidential decision making. To begin, Meernik excludes from his analyses any measures of congressional opposition to the president. Never does he estimate regressions that include the kinds of covariates first presented in chapter 3, and additional concerns arise about those covariates he does include. If, for instance, the provision of military aid and prior decisions to exercise military force themselves are functions of domestic politics, then his conclusions about the negligible influence of Congress is unwarranted. The largest problems, however, do not concern issues of model specification, but rather the actual construction of the opportunities database. Three stand out, each of which underscores a basic challenge associated with building an events-based database on the use of military force.

The first concerns the definition of an "event," which, in this instance, identifies an opportunity to use military force. This would appear a rather trivial matter. But on reflection, this turns out to be an extraordinarily nettlesome issue. Consider the following: is a civil war a singular event, or might there be multiple events (such as a coup, a massacre, a clash with troops) embedded within larger events (such as an interstate war, an ongoing border dispute, a disagreement about neutral territories such as airspaces and waterways), each of which might be called an opportunity? How many "events" occurred during the first or second Intifadas, the Indian/Pakistani dispute over Kashmir, or during the ongoing skirmishes between North and South Korea? These are difficult questions, to be sure— and ones to which Meernik is sensitive. To "avoid over-counting," Meernik proposes to include only "specific and extraordinary circumstances during ongoing crises."[4] We are less convinced than he, however, that this addresses the underlying problem. Indeed, it raises new issues, as it requires coders to discern the most "extraordinary" developments of an ongoing crisis. The basic issues about the defining, and limiting, features of an "event" remain unresolved, and we are left with few hard and fast rules that let us know whether we are working with one, two, or more events at any given time.

The second problem concerns the criteria used to identify qualifying events. In addition to developing classes of events that might evoke some kind of military response, Meernik attempts to intuit "presidential perceptions" in order to further winnow the field of potential uses of military force. To be counted as an opportunity, the president must "perceive" a danger, conflict, or loss as a problem, and subsequently must have "considered" the use of force. This data collection strategy poses two problems. First, as analysts, we simply cannot see the world through the president's eyes. We cannot, with complete confidence, identify those foreign crises that each president perceived as potentially warranting military action, a limitation Meernik readily admits.[5] Beyond the hazards of divining the president's thoughts at any given moment, this data collection strategy also introduces systematic biases into our sample selection, as the mere consideration of using military force is itself endogenous—in other words, evidence of threat perception and the consideration of military options are as much cause as consequence of the actual decisions that presidents eventually make. Benjamin Fordham, for instance, notes that presidents are more likely to "perceive" threats when the domestic economy is flagging, and not when the economy is strong.[6] If Fordham is right, then Meernik's sample likely biases against finding economic effects, for by design it excludes instances when the president did not perceive a crisis, and such instances occur disproportionately during times of economic prosperity.

There is every reason to believe that presidents issue public declarations about foreign conflagrations strategically, paying close attention to the domestic and international political environments they face. When relying on such declarations to build a dataset that permits tests of the influence of domestic political factors, one risks introducing systematic biases against finding evidence of influence. As such, it will not do to rely on presidents to identify the larger universe of opportunities. We are better served relying on third-party observers to do so.[7]

In part because of the role of perception in Meernik's coding criteria, and also because of a somewhat imprecise list of precipitating events, there arises a final concern about replicability. Using Meernik's coding criteria, the analyst has considerable latitude in deciding whether a particular event qualifies as an opportunity. For example, one criterion instructs the coder to include all events "perceived as having led, or likely to lead to advances by ideologically committed opponents of the U.S. (i.e., communists or 'extreme leftists' broadly defined) be they states, regimes, or regime contenders." Such vague language sets the stage for coding volatility from one researcher to another. For example, during the period from 1995 to 1997, the New York Times cross-referenced four coups, one each in Nigeria, Burundi, Cambodia, and Sierra Leone. Meernik includes Sierra Leone and Cambodia in his dataset, but he excludes Nigeria and Burundi. Elsewhere in his dataset, similar ambiguities hold for riots and other forms of domestic violence. Meernik deems that some uprisings presented the United States with the opportunity to intervene, such as Egypt (1981) and South Korea (1979), while others allegedly did not, such as Macedonia (1995) and Israel (1995). Judging from the events themselves, though, it is difficult to justify this particular case selection.

A NEW DATASET

To examine whether Congress exerts any influence over the probability that presidents respond militarily to specific developments abroad, we have attempted to construct an entirely new opportunities dataset. Presidents' perceptions play no part in the data collection effort, and we do not require any evidence that the president intended to exercise, or even contemplated exercising, military action. Rather than counting events that occur around the globe, we identify media reports of these events. The resulting database consists of media stories on selected types of international crises that received prominent domestic coverage.

To begin, it may be useful to identify data points that lie outside the boundaries of our analysis.[8] There are plenty of instances when the president acts on intelligence that his administration has gathered but that is not available to the public. Lacking access to these flows of information, we do not include them in the data. This rather pragmatic concern motivates the first limiting condition—that a crisis receives domestic media coverage, specifically coverage on the front page of the *New York Times*.

The second limiting condition concerns the nature of the crisis itself. We recognize that the president may also deploy the military in an effort to stem negative political or economic trends, or to ward off anticipated future problems. This dataset, however, is restricted to those instances when discrete events occur around the world. It is not enough for concerns about authoritarianism or communism to reach a tipping point—something needs to happen along the way, an event we can readily identify as a crisis unto itself.

We also provide no account of those instances when presidents send troops abroad as part of routine training missions, as symbolic displays of military might to would-be competitors, or as confirmation of national allegiances to allies. This database is designed to identify when presidents deploy troops abroad to address a well-defined crisis or a series of crises.

The United States occasionally sends a fleet of ships to a foreign nation's shores as an act of solidarity with a newly elected regime. Some of the minor uses of force described in chapter 3 were precisely these kinds of missions. As a proportion of all occurrences, elections so rarely prompt a military intervention that they cannot be reasonably identified as a systematic "opportunity" to exercise military force. This leads us to our final eligibility criterion, that the crises stand a nontrivial chance of eliciting military action. There are plenty of foreign events that constitute crises, but for which military strikes do not provide solutions—such as the collapse of a foreign nation's economy, a contested election, a natural disaster, or famine. Though these plainly are crises, and though they often receive extensive domestic media coverage, they nonetheless are excluded from the database.

Within these constraints, we identify a wide variety of opportunities to exercise force abroad. The database inventories the following kinds of crises: attacks on United States embassies and consulates; instances when United States ambassadors, consuls, or military personnel are killed; hijackings that include human casualties; stateside attacks perpetrated by foreign groups; civil wars; interstate armed clashes; coups (or attempts thereof); assassinations (or attempts thereof) of heads of state; declarations by states of emergency or martial law; any downing of an aircraft by a foreign military; hostile claims to international waters; attacks on United Nations personnel; crimes against humanity on a mass scale; military violations of United Nations territorial mandates; nuclear proliferation; and violations of agreements to dismantle weapons of mass destruction. We make no claim that these classes of events constitute every opportunity that the United States has to exercise force abroad. Indeed, we know that this is not the case, as presidents occasionally use the military to intervene in the international drug trade or to deal with immigration flows or to provide disaster relief to tsunami victims. We were not convinced, however, that a sufficient share of stories written about drug usage or immigration or natural disasters constituted a genuine opportunity to use force. All of those crises that we have deemed opportunities, by contrast, stood a reasonable chance of eliciting a military response from the United States.

Of course, many issues arise when trying to figure out whether a story fits into any of our crisis categories. At what point does the repression of a domestic constituency become a "crime against humanity?" When are internal conflicts civil wars, and not just domestic unrest? How do we know that international agreements were, in fact, violated? And does it matter? How, for instance, should we handle those cases where one state accuses another of violating a territorial mandate but the other pleads innocent? Below, we detail solutions to these and the many other vexing challenges that unavoidably arise when building a database such as this. With the working criteria we have developed, trained undergraduate and graduate students can easily discern whether a reported event qualifies as an opportunity to use force abroad. In 91 percent of cases, our coders sorted articles the same way, yielding a Cohen's kappa, which is a standard intercoder reliability rating, of 0.81.[9]

The building blocks of the database consist of front-page *New York Times* news stories about foreign crises rather than, as in Meernik's database, the precipitating events themselves.[10] The upsides of this decision are explained in chapter 4. The one downside, however, is the workload involved. It is not enough to catch a declaration of martial law in Albania, a military clash between the Turkish government and Kurdish rebels, or a border dispute between Ecuador and Peru. Instead, we must capture every single article on these events. To accomplish as much, we proceeded in two steps. First, we used Proquest's electronic search engine to identify those stories that involve subject matter that meet our definition of an opportunity. When constructing our library of search terms, considerable efforts were made to ensure that we did not exclude any relevant articles.[11] Such precautions, though, came at a cost, as we were left with literally tens of thousands of stories that required additional sorting. With a team of graduate and undergraduate students, we read every one of these stories to determine whether they qualified as reports of opportunities to use force. Every qualifying story was read by at least two coders, one of which was a senior member of the research team. The research team as a whole regularly convened to discuss difficult cases, and it reached consensus as a group about whether these cases constituted opportunities that required coding.

Having identified reports of different countries' involvement in relevant crises, we then were left with the monumental task of coding each for a range of contextual factors that might contribute to the president's decision to use military force. In each instance, we identified the time-frame when events occurred—that is, whether the event occurred in the last twenty-four hours, the last week, month, or year.[12] We coded each report for the type of opportunity discussed (attacks on U.S. embassies and consulates, instances when U.S. ambassadors, consuls, or military personnel are killed, etc.). In addition, we identified whether the story was a direct report on a crisis, an investigation into an alleged crisis, or a response by either the United Nations or a foreign government to an ongoing crisis. And finally, we collected a variety of kinds of contextual information, such as whether the United States already had military commitments in the region; whether the Soviet Union or a NATO ally was involved; the number of people killed; and whether the president, a member of his administration, or Congress offered any public reactions to the events.

Before defining exactly what we mean by an "opportunity" to use force, two complications to our data collection strategy are worth mentioning. First, the size of the front page of the New York Times shrunk markedly during the postwar period. Indeed, between 1945 and 2000, the number of articles appearing on the front page of the Times dropped by almost 50 percent. It is possible, then, that opportunities to use force are overrepresented in the early period of the time series, and underrepresented in the latter period. We see little reason, however, to expect that this possibility biases our main estimates of interest—namely, the effect of Congress's partisan composition on the probability that presidents respond militarily to observed foreign crisis. Just the same, in the main statistical models in chapter 4 we controlled for the annual average number of articles on the front page of the Times, both as linear and quadratic terms. Never were either of these covariates statistically significant, nor do our main estimates of interest change appreciably.

Second, the probability that the Times reports on a foreign crisis may depend on the editors' expectations about the likelihood of a U.S. military intervention. Knowing that the president will not use military force, the Times may opt not to cover a minor skirmish in Africa; alternatively, it may relegate the story to the newspaper's back pages. But when military action appears imminent, the *Times* may ramp up its coverage. On this matter, two observations are worth noting. First, it is not at all clear how any other data collection strategy could guard against this possibility. Surveys of other newspapers, historical accounts, and even embassy communications all confront this same problem. And second, to the extent that this fact introduces any bias into our statistical models, it ought to point against the predictions of our theory. If the *Times* systematically underreports foreign crises to which the U.S. military is not likely to respond, and if the probability of observing a military response depends on the partisan composition of Congress, then our opportunities data effectively censor those instances when hostile congressional majorities dissuade the president from exercising force abroad. If true, then the effects reported in chapter 4 may actually underestimate Congress's true influence over presidential use-of-force decisions.

SPECIFIC CODING CRITERIA

Below, we provide working definitions of classes of events and illustrative examples of cases that do and do not qualify as opportunities.

VIOLENT ACTS PERPETRATED AGAINST THE UNITED STATES
    OR ITS REPRESENTATIVES

Attacks on U.S. Embassies or Consulates

We exclude U.S. foreign missions and cultural centers as often too small and insignificant to represent official U.S. interests abroad. Consulates are included because of their representation of U.S. commercial interests and the official status of the consul. Examples of included events: a bomb explodes in the southeastern Turkish city of Adana, July 30, 1977; rocket-propelled grenade is fired at U.S. embassy in Moscow, September 14, 1995. Examples of excluded events: ransacking of U.S. Mission in Laos, May 13, 1975; Pakistanis storm American cultural center in Islamabad, February 13, 1989.

U.S. Ambassadors, Consuls, or Military Personnel Killed

We exclude CIA personnel because of the different nature of covert operations. We exclude kidnapping, injuries, and other mishaps short of death as too small to serve as focusing events that might trigger a U.S. response. We exclude killings of U.S. civilians abroad as such events are quite frequent and the details often in dispute. Examples of included events: three Iranian terrorists slay two USAF officers in Iran, May 21, 1975; North Korean soldiers attack American soldiers in Panmunjom, June 30, 1975;

U.S. soldier is killed in Haiti, January 13, 1995; U.S. soldier is killed by a landmine in Bosnia, February 4, 1996; bombing of U.S. military housing complex in Saudi Arabia, June 27, 1996. Examples of excluded events: three American Rockwell employees abroad are killed by terrorists, August 28, 1976; U.S. seaman is wounded in Philippines, December 11, 1976; gunmen slay CIA station chief in Athens, December 23, 1995.

Stateside Attacks Perpetrated by Foreign Groups

Examples of included events: hijacking of TWA 727 and planting of bomb in New York City's Grand Central Terminal by Fighters for a Free Croatia, September 11, 1976. Examples of excluded events: bombing of U.S. Senate offices in protest over U.S. presence in Lebanon and invasion of Grenada, November 8, 1983; Oklahoma City bombing, April 19, 1995.

THREATS TO REGIME STABILITY

Civil Wars

An article is coded as a civil war even if it only mentions an ongoing conflict in a region without specifically discussing any new engagements between rebel and government troops. The *New York Times* is in such cases drawing attention to an ongoing conflict in the world to which the United States could respond. Civil strife and street violence are not sufficient—only clashes between armed rebels and government soldiers or security forces are included. A note regarding the Palestinian-Israeli conflict: clashes taking place within Israel must involve Palestinian National Authority insurgents or rebels attacking Israeli military targets. The article must explicitly link the Palestinian insurgents or rebels involved in the clash to the Palestinian National Authority (PNA). Attacks perpetrated by Hamas or other such groups or by individuals only thought to be aligned with the PNA are considered terrorist acts, not a civil war constituting an opportunity. Examples of included events: civil war in Angola, August 18, 1996; civil war in Afghanistan, Taliban seizes Kabul, September 29, 1996; civil war erupts in Zaire as Rwandan Army aides Kabila and Zaire rebels, November 3, 1996. Examples of excluded events: Italian police, reinforced with army troops, clash with armed communist miners, July 17, 1948; Palestinian suicide bombing kills four in a Tel Aviv café, March 21, 1997.

Interstate Armed Clashes

This category includes instances when guerrilla groups cross a border from a host country and clash with the target government's soldiers or security forces. When a third party joins an existing conflict, clashes between its troops and the existing parties also constitute an opportunity. The category excludes domestic acts of terror such as suicide bombings. Even when the terrorist groups are sponsored by foreign states, if the clash only involves government troops and terrorists, it is excluded. Instances when guerrillas cross boundaries and attack only civilian targets are excluded as are clashes between guerrillas and police. A note regarding the Palestinian-Israeli conflict: all cross-border clashes between organized groups and Israeli military targets constitute an opportunity to use force. However, to reiterate, clashes taking place within Israel must involve Palestinian National Authority insurgents or rebels attacking Israeli military targets. Examples of included events: Algerian-backed guerrillas kill twenty-five Moroccan soldiers, May 5, 1976; Cuban soldiers are killed in Angola by pro-Western forces, December 14, 1977; Peru-Ecuador border clash, March 2, 1995; border clashes in Kashmir, August 27, 1997. Examples of excluded events: random acts of violence perpetrated across South Korean countryside by communists believed to be supported by North Korea, May 10, 1948; terrorist clash with Egyptian police after slaughter of tourists at Luxor, November 18, 1997.

Coups and Attempted Coups

To qualify, the article must explicitly recognize observed behaviors as part of an effort to overthrow a sitting regime. Reports of widespread dissent, therefore, do not qualify. Examples of included events: aborted coup in Nigeria, February 16, 1976; coup in Burundi, August 4, 1996; Cambodian coup, July 9, 1997. Examples of excluded events: sectarian riots and clashes in Egypt, June 22, 1981; prodemocracy demonstrators in Tiananmen Square prompt a military crackdown, May 22, 1989.

Assassinations or Attempted Assassinations of Heads of State

Examples of included events: attempted assassination of Macedonian president, October 4, 1995; Rabin assassinated, November 5, 1995. Examples of excluded events: stabbing of British Royal Governor of Sarawak, December 5, 1949; assassination of Benigno Aquino, former senator and rival to Filipino President Ferdinand Marcos, August 23, 1983.

State of Emergency or Martial Law Declared

Examples of included events: China places Tibetan capital under martial law, March 8, 1989; national state of emergency in Albania, March 3, 1997. Examples of excluded events: British impose strict curfew on Palestine,

November 2, 1948; twenty-four-hour curfew declared in some parts of El Salvador, November 15, 1989.

Any Downing of Aircraft, Civilian or Military, by Military Forces

This category also includes attacks on unidentified/foreign aircraft over a country's territorial airspace, such as KAL 007. Examples of included events: South Korea opens fire on U.S. cargo plane that strayed into its airspace, October 14, 1976; Southern Yemen shoots down Iranian fighter, November 25, 1976. Examples of excluded events: RAF plane accidentally collides with Swedish passenger jet in heavy fog shrouding an English airport, July 5, 1948; terrorist bombing of Pan Am 103 over Lockerbie, Scotland, December 22, 1988.

VIOLATIONS OF INTERNATIONAL LAW

Hostile Claims to International Waters

This category includes all officially announced claims to international waters, and all clashes on the high seas involving two or more navies. Clashes over fishing rights that involve fishing vessels and one country's navy are not sufficient. Examples of included events: after numerous fishing disputes, British frigates ram two Icelandic patrol boats, May 22, 1976; Libya claims Gulf of Sidra as its own territorial waters, March 27, 1986. Examples of excluded events: Cambodian gunboat clashes with Thai fishing boats in Thai waters, June 12, 1975; Argentine Navy fires on and hits Soviet and Bulgarian trawlers in its territorial waters, October 1, 1977.

Attacks on UN Personnel

This category identifies attacks on United Nations personnel only. We exclude attacks on personnel from other domestic relief agencies. Examples of included events: two UN observers come under fire from Albanian mortars while monitoring the Greek border during civil war, March 22, 1948; Bosnian Serbs use UN soldiers as human shields, May 27, 1995. Examples of excluded events: three American nuns and a lay mission worker are killed in El Salvador, presumably by security forces, December 6, 1980; six International Red Cross workers are killed in Chechnya, December 18, 1996.

Evidence or Reports of Crimes against Humanity Committed on Mass Scale

This category is meant to capture only reports or accusations of mass scale atrocities, such as genocide or ethnic cleansing. While often sparking international outrage, allegations of more minor or smaller scale human rights abuses do not meet our standard of an opportunity to use force. Examples of included events: U.S. spy photos show apparent mass graves near the fallen safe area at Srebrenica, August 10, 1995; reports of ethnic cleansing in Yugoslavia, October 11, 1995. Examples of excluded events: Guatemalan army massacres more than sixty people in village "trouble spot," September 15, 1982; Yugoslavs and Croats levy conflicting charges of war crimes against civilians, but nothing verified on a mass scale, December 19, 1991.

Military Violations of UN Territorial Mandates

Examples of included events: Bosnian Serbs attack UN safe havens of Goradze and Srebrenica, July 23, 1995; Iraqi troops cross Northern Exclusion zone and seize Kurdish city, September 1, 1996. Example of excluded events: Iraqi aircraft violate the southern no-fly zone, which is not specifically authorized by UN resolutions but patrolled by U.S. and British aircraft, December 28, 1992.

Violation of Neutral Territory

An article is coded as a violation of neutral territory if a state restricts access to or sends troops into a UN-mandated neutral territory, a neutral territory created by a Four Powers agreement, or a neutral territory created through other forms of international agreement. Examples of included events: Soviet troops restrict access into West Berlin, April 6, 1965; North Korean troops enter the DMZ, April 8, 1996. Examples of excluded events: U.S. accuses Yugoslavia of "Bolshevization" of their zone of Trieste, but no troop border violations alleged, March 27, 1948; German police from western sector clash with eastern communists trying to occupy Mercedes Palast, no military forces involved, February 6, 1950.

PROLIFERATION OF WEAPONS OF MASS DESTRUCTION

This category captures reports or evidence of the testing, development, or acquisition of nuclear, chemical, or biological weapons by a state that did not previously possess such weapons. Examples of included events: Cuban Missile Crisis, October 23, 1962; Libyans accused of building a chemical weapons manufacturing facility, January 1, 1989. Example of excluded events: suspected sale of MIGs to Nicaragua, November 8, 1984.

TABLE B.1
Opportunities to Use Military Force, 1945–2000

Israel	1402	Ethiopia	65	Azerbaijan	12
France	1081	Germany	65	Bangladesh	11
Egypt	871	Philippines	62	Slovenia	11
Soviet Union	697	Guatemala	59	Zambia	11
Lebanon	694	Haiti	56	Mexico	10
Syria	662	Tanzania	54	Armenia	9
United Kingdom	637	Malaysia	52	Guinea	9
Algeria	495	Bolivia	50	East Timor	8
Iraq	431	Kenya	50	Georgia	7
Republic of Vietnam	412	Zimbabwe	50	Grenada	7
El Salvador	339	Costa Rica	49	Sweden	7
China	320	Somalia	49	Brunei	6
India	282	Sudan	49	Cameroon	6
Nicaragua	267	Thailand	46	Trinidad and Tobago	5
Laos	266	Oman	45	Botswana	4
Bosnia	264	Panama	43	Gabon	4
Democratic Republic		Chad	42	Ireland	4
of the Congo	253	Belgium	40	Togo	4
Jordan	253	Turkey	40	Uruguay	4
Cuba	228	Venezuela	40	Benin	3
Iran	225	Uganda	39	Central African	
Vietnam	216	Saudi Arabia	38	Republic	3
Afghanistan	197	Peru	37	Guinea-Bissau	3
Pakistan	193	Kuwait	36	Mali	3
Argentina	189	Spain	36	Australia	2
Indonesia	175	Myanmar	35	Bhutan	2
Angola	135	Sri Lanka	34	Canada	2
Cambodia	134	Italy	33	Congo	2
Yugoslavia/Serbia	132	Colombia	31	Fiji	2
Greece	131	Chile	29	Jamaica	2
Poland	130	Mozambique	29	Latvia	2
Tunisia	122	Romania	29	Lesotho	2
Hungary	111	Albania	27	Singapore	2
South Korea	105	Rwanda	27	Austria	1
South Africa	101	Dominican Republic	25	Bahrain	1
Morocco	94	Brazil	22	Barbados	1
Taiwan	90	Japan	22	Comoros	1
Yemen	90	Ghana	21	Denmark	1
Nigeria	88	Ecuador	20	Madagascar	1
Libya	87	Burundi	17	Maldives	1
Croatia	83	Namibia	17	Malta	1
Cyprus	81	Lithuania	15	Mauritania	1
Netherlands	77	Paraguay	15	Niger	1
North Korea	76	Guyana	14	Seychelles	1
Honduras	75	Sierra Leone	13	The Bahamas	1
Portugal	70	Bulgaria	14	Suriname	1
Czechoslovakia	67	Liberia	14	Swaziland	1

Nations not listed did not contribute any opportunities to the database.

TABLE B.2
Descriptive Statistics for Chapter 4 Analyses

	Mean	Standard Deviation	Minimum	Maximum
Dependent Variable				
Military Response	0.10	0.30	0	1
Independent Variables				
Unified Government	0.32	0.47	0	1
Percent President Party	0.49	0.09	0.35	0.68
President Party Power	−0.00	0.14	−0.24	0.27
Unemployment	5.82	1.83	2.4	11.4
CPI	62.17	41.41	21.9	173.7
Public Approval	55.57	13.54	23.0	89.0
Election Year	0.19	0.40	0	1
Hegemony	0.20	0.04	0.14	0.32
World Disputes	6.80	2.95	0	17
Alliances	0.40	0.68	0	3
Major Power	0.19	0.39	0	1
Democracy	0.26	0.44	0	1
Trade (in billions)	1.51	4.90	0	139.58
Soviet Involvement	0.21	0.41	0	1
Capability Ratio (log)	3.75	1.66	0.03	9.31
Prev. Opportunities	11.83	15.12	0	111
Contemp. Opportunities	0.36	1.16	0	10
Troops Deployed (log)	−1.71	2.81	−6.91	5.79
North/Central America	0.09	0.28	0	1
South America	0.03	0.17	0	1
Middle East	0.37	0.48	0	1
Asia/Pacific	0.19	0.39	0	1
Western Europe	0.15	0.35	0	1
Eastern Europe	0.09	0.29	0	1

Values based on the 13,327 observations included in the logistic regressions estimated in tables 4.1–4.2.

TABLE B.3
Results from the First Stage of Models Presented in Table 4.3

	(1)		(2)		(3)	
Congressional Support						
Unified Government	−0.06**	[0.04]	—		—	
Percent President Party	—		−0.14	[0.17]	—	
President Party Power	—		—		−0.09	[0.11]
Instrument						
Per Capita GDP	−0.03***	[0.01]	−0.03***	[0.01]	−0.03***	[0.01]
Background Controls						
Hegemony	−0.11	[0.36]	−0.30	[0.35]	−0.29	[0.35]
World Disputes	0.22***	[0.03]	0.22***	[0.03]	0.22***	[0.03]
Major Power	0.54***	[0.07]	0.54***	[0.07]	0.54***	[0.07]
Democracy	−0.11**	[0.05]	−0.10**	[0.05]	−0.11**	[0.05]
Prev. Opportunities	0.18***	[0.01]	0.18***	[0.01]	0.18***	[0.01]
Troops Deployed (log)	0.01	[0.01]	0.01	[0.01]	0.01	[0.01]
North, Central America	0.25***	[0.10]	0.25***	[0.10]	0.25***	[0.10]
South America	0.01	[0.08]	0.01	[0.08]	0.01	[0.08]
Middle East	0.44***	[0.08]	0.44***	[0.08]	0.44***	[0.08]
Asia, Pacific	0.18**	[0.08]	0.17**	[0.08]	0.17**	[0.08]
Western Europe	0.09	[0.10]	0.08	[0.10]	0.08	[0.10]
Eastern Europe	0.09	[0.09]	0.09	[0.09]	0.09	[0.09]
Constant	−2.88***	[0.08]	−2.80***	[0.11]	−2.88***	[0.08]
Rho	−0.37	[0.41]	−0.40	[0.37]	−0.40	[0.37]
(N)	1,599,396		1,599,396		1,599,396	

First stage of Heckman selection models presented. The first stage, which is reported here, estimates the probability of there being at least one opportunity in a country on a given day, where per capita GDP serves as the identifying variable. The main equation, which is reported in Table 4.3, estimates the probability that the United States responds militarily to an opportunity within 30 days, conditional on an opportunity existing. Models consist of day-by-country observations. *** = $p < 0.01$, one-tailed test; ** = $p < .05$; * = $p < 0.10$; one-tailed tests. Huber/White/sandwich standard errors clustered on country-president combinations reported in brackets. Though not reported, models also contain fixed effect terms for each presidential administration. For regional fixed effects, Africa is the reference category. Models that estimate the probability of a military response within 10, 20, 40, 50, and 60 days generate comparable results.

Table Relating to Chapter 6

TABLE C.1
Descriptive Statistics for Chapter 6 Analyses

	Mean	Std. Dev.	Min.	Max.	(N)
Dependent Variables					
Number of all arguments	2.37	1.70	1	14	1,794 stories
Num. args for use of force	1.69	1.56	0	11	1,794 stories
Num. args against use of force	0.68	0.79	0	5	1,794 stories
Proportion args for use of force	0.32	0.18	0	0.83	1,794 stories
All Story Characteristics					
Local TV news	0.82	0.38	0	1	1,794 stories
National TV news	0.07	0.25	0	1	1,794 stories
New York Times	0.11	0.32	0	1	1,794 stories
Authorization period	0.39	0.49	0	1	1,794 stories
Post-authorization period	0.15	0.35	0	1	1,794 stories
Local TV Story Characteristics					
Fox	0.19	0.40	0	1	1,471 stories
NBC	0.25	0.44	0	1	1,471 stories
ABC	0.28	0.45	0	1	1,471 stories
Saturday	0.13	0.34	0	1	1,471 stories
Sunday	0.12	0.33	0	1	1,471 stories
Media Market Characteristics					
Pct Democratic	0.48	0.09	0.26	0.67	50 media markets
Pct Minority	0.28	0.11	0.09	0.52	50 media markets
Pct Born US	0.88	0.08	0.64	0.97	50 media markets
Pct College Graduate	0.14	0.02	0.10	0.18	50 media markets
Population (millions)	0.38	0.35	0.15	2.02	50 media markets
South	0.44	0.50	0	1	50 media markets
Per Capita Inc. (ten thousands)	2.21	0.30	1.74	3.16	50 media markets

Table Relating to Chapter 7

TABLE D.1
Descriptive Statistics for Chapter 7 Analyses

	Mean	Std. Dev.	Min.	Max.	(N)
Early October Survey					
Support Use of Force	0.61	0.49	0	1	941 respondents
Conservative Republican	0.17	0.37	0	1	941 respondents
Moderate Republican	0.11	0.31	0	1	941 respondents
Moderate Democrat	0.24	0.43	0	1	941 respondents
Liberal Democrat	0.09	0.29	0	1	941 respondents
White (non-Hispanic)	0.71	0.45	0	1	941 respondents
Af. American (non-Hispanic)	0.12	0.32	0	1	941 respondents
Other Religious	0.11	0.32	0	1	941 respondents
Education	2.68	1.01	1	4	932 respondents
Age (tens)	4.50	1.76	1.8	9.7	928 respondents
Male	0.48	0.50	0	1	941 respondents
Parent	0.34	0.47	0	1	941 respondents
Pct Democratic	0.46	0.12	0.14	0.86	376 counties
Pct Minority	0.18	0.15	0.01	0.73	376 counties
Pct Born US	0.92	0.08	0.52	0.99	376 counties
Pct College Graduate	0.23	0.10	0.07	0.60	376 counties
Population (millions)	0.04	0.07	0.00	0.95	376 counties
South	0.41	0.49	0	1	376 counties
Per Capita Inc. (ten thousands)	2.18	0.54	0.87	4.50	376 counties
Proportion News Against War	0.25	0.11	0	0.47	50 markets

	Mean	Std. Dev.	Min.	Max.	(N)
Late October Survey					
Support Use of Force	0.53	0.50	0	1	1091 respondents
Conservative Republican	0.19	0.39	0	1	1042 respondents
Moderate Republican	0.13	0.34	0	1	1042 respondents
Moderate Democrat	0.25	0.43	0	1	1042 respondents
Liberal Democrat	0.10	0.30	0	1	1042 respondents
White (non-Hispanic)	0.70	0.46	0	1	1091 respondents
Af. American (non-Hispanic)	0.12	0.33	0	1	1091 respondents
Hispanic	0.12	0.32	0	1	1091 respondents
Education	2.64	1.03	1	4	1088 respondents
Age (tens)	4.48	1.72	1.8	8.9	1074 respondents
Male	0.48	0.50	0	1	1091 respondents
Parent	0.38	0.48	0	1	1087 respondents
Pct Democratic	0.45	0.12	0.14	0.86	393 counties
Pct Minority	0.19	0.16	0.01	0.87	393 counties
Pct Born US	0.92	0.08	0.52	0.99	393 counties
Pct College Graduate	0.23	0.10	0.07	0.55	393 counties
Population (millions)	0.04	0.07	0.00	0.95	393 counties
South	0.41	0.49	0	1	393 counties
Per Capita Inc. (ten thousands)	2.16	0.53	0.77	4.50	393 counties
Proportion News Against War	0.25	0.09	0	0.39	50 markets
Experimental Findings					
Believe President's Claims	2.06	1.00	0	4	2771 respondents
Support Use of Force	1.83	1.21	0	4	2787 respondents
Democrats	0.38	0.49	0	1	2837 respondents
Republicans	0.31	0.46	0	1	2837 respondents
Independents	0.29	0.45	0	1	2837 respondents
White (non-Hispanic)	0.73	0.45	0	1	2837 respondents
Af. American (non-Hispanic)	0.12	0.32	0	1	2837 respondents
Hispanic	0.11	0.31	0	1	2837 respondents
Education	2.60	1.02	1	4	2837 respondents
Age (in tens)	4.54	1.65	1.8	9.5	2837 respondents
Male	0.48	0.50	0	1	2837 respondents
Parent	0.31	0.46	0	1	2837 respondents

Post-stratification weights used for survey data.

Notes

PREFACE

1. (Corwin 1948, p. 208).
2. (Howland 1928, p. 110).
3. (Buzzanco 1996, p. 21).
4. During the nineteenth and early twentieth centuries, however, the federal courts actively engaged separation of powers issues on matters involving war. For a useful summary, see (Fisher 2005).
5. (Keynes 1982, p. 7).
6. *Mottola v. Nixon*, 464 F. 2d 178 (1972); *Holtzman v. Schlesinger*, 484 F. 2d 1307 (1973).
7. *Rumsfeld v. Padilla*, 124 S. Ct. 2711 (2004); *Hamdi v. Rumsfeld*, 124 S. Ct. 2633 (2004).
8. This assertion of American jurisdiction is one way the court claims it differs from the *Eisentrager* precedent, which ruled that "aliens detained outside the sovereign territory of the United States [may not] invoke a petition for a writ of habeas corpus." *Johnson v. Eisentrager*, 70 S. Ct. 936 (1950).
9. *Hamdan v. Rumsfeld*, November 8, 2004, Civil Action No. 04-1519.
10. See, for example, Press Secretary Tony Snow's Press Briefing on June 29, 2006, available at: www.whitehouse.gov/news/releases/2006/06/20060629-6-html.
11. (Ornstein and Mann 2006a, p. 68). See also (Ornstein and Mann 2006b).
12. Senate majority leader Frist disclosed his intention to introduce new legislation authorizing tribunals after the July 4 recess. Judiciary Committee members Lindsay Graham (R-SC) and John Kyl (R-AZ) seconded Frist, announcing: "We intend to pursue legislation in the Senate granting the executive branch the authority to ensure that terrorists can be tried by competent military commissions. Working together, Congress and the administration can draft a fair, suitable, and constitutionally permissible tribunal statute." Charlie Savage, "Justices Deal Bush Setback on Tribunals; High Court Says Guantanamo Action Illegal," *Boston Globe*, A1. See also: CNN.com. 2006. "Bush Says He'll Work with Congress on Tribunal Plan." http://www.cnn.com/2006/POLITICS/06/29/hamdan.reax/index .html.
13. Bush, George W. "Remarks on Signing the Military Commissions Act of 2006." *Public Papers of the President.* October 17, 2006. http://www.presidency .ucsb.edu/ws/index.php?pid=24200&st=military+commissions+act&st1=.
14. Charles Babington and Jonathan Weisman, "Senate Approves Detainee Bill Backed by Bush: Constitutional Challenges Predicted," *The Washington Post,*

September 29, 2006. http://www.washingtonpost.com/wp-dyn/content/article/2006/09/28/AR2006092800824.html.

15. Quoted in David Sanger, "Iraq Makes U.N. Seem 'Foolish,' Bush Asserts," *New York Times,* October 28, 2002, p. 15.

16. Quoted in David Rennie, "U.S. Prepares to Do without UN," *Daily Telegraph,* October 28, 2002, p. 20.

17. Quoted in "Showdown with Iraq," *USA Today,* January 22, 2003, p. 4A.

18. For research on congressional checks on presidential power during the ongoing course of a military venture, see (Kriner 2006).

19. (Russett 1990, p. 130).

20. So too does congressional involvement in use-of-force politics change once the president has committed troops to action. How Congress responds to presidential claims surely differs when a military deployment is contemplated versus when it is executed. On the one hand, as reports come back from the field about a venture's successes and failures, members of Congress can criticize the president more effectively. As field reports and firsthand observations displace military forecasting models, members are better able to participate in conversations about the war effort. On the other hand, as already noted, individual members who opposed the deployment may experience strong constituency pressures to fund, and even publicly support, a military venture that is up and running. As John Kerry learned in 2004, it is difficult to justify a vote against the provision of aid to troops already in the field, no matter how misguided or poorly planned their mission may be.

21. (Blechman and Kaplan 1978).

CHAPTER 1

1. (Schlesinger 1973, p. ix)
2. Quoted in (Eagleton 1974, p. 11).
3. (Katzmann 1990, p. 35).
4. (Ely 1993, p. 49).
5. (Irons 2005, p. 7).
6. (Fisher 2000, p. 65).
7. (Weissman 1995, p. 17).
8. (Ely 1993, p. ix).
9. (Katyal 2006, pp. 2316, 2318).
10. (Gowa 1999, p. 42). See also (Hinckley 1994).
12. (Fisher 2002, p. 673).
11. (Ornstein and Mann 2006a, p. 68). See also (Ornstein and Mann 2006b).
13. Though legal scholars squabble over some of the most straightforward of constitutional passages, almost universally they agree on one matter: the Framers originally intended for Congress and not the president to decide whether the nation would enter into wars, both small and large (Ely 1993; Adler and George 1998; Berger 1974; Fisher 2004; Irons 2005). As Louis Fisher notes, "Questions about framers' intent invariably cause scholars to scatter and divide. Not so with the war power. There is remarkable agreement among experts on the war power that the framers broke with available monarchical precedents and vested in Con-

gress the sole power to initiate hostilities against other nations" (2000, p. 13). This being the case, one must recognize that Congress abdicates its constitutional responsibilities when it allows the president to exercise military force abroad without first securing a declaration of war or, minimally, a formal authorization. (In *Bas v. Tingy* [1800] the Supreme Court ruled that Congress could authorize the limited use of force without a formal declaration of war.)

That the Framers gave Congress primary authority over matters involving war and that they did not intend for presidents to exercise any powers outside of those delineated in Article II suggest that the modern practice of presidential power hardly matches the principles laid out at the constitutional convention some 230 years ago. During an era when presidents launch hundreds of military ventures abroad without ever securing Congress's formal consent, there exists a "gross disjuncture between law and practice" (Adler 1996, p. 39). Although the courts have been reticent to correct this course of events, it certainly is fair to conclude that the Constitution's division of foreign policy powers between the executive and legislative branches has not fared especially well during the past half century.

14. (Howell 2005; Howell 2003). For a sampling of the research literature on unilateral powers, see (Mayer 2001; Cooper 2002; Mayer 1999; Mayer and Price 2002; Moe and Howell 1999a; Moe and Howell 1999b; Krause and Cohen 1997; Krause and Cohen 2000; Deering and Maltzman 1999; Howell and Lewis 2002; Pious 1991; Marshall and Pacelle 2005).

15. (Lindsay 1995, p. 98).

16. Bob Franken, "House Mulls over Several Amendments on Haiti," CNN News, October 6, 1994.

17. Yet, when members of Congress do act legislatively to influence the conduct of an ongoing military action, they do so to considerable effect. Kriner (2006) shows that roll call votes on binding legislative initiatives to set a timetable for troop withdrawal, cut off funding for an ongoing deployment, or otherwise curtail a military operation, even when they fail to secure final passage on the floor, raise the political costs to the president of staying the course and significantly decrease the expected duration of an overseas commitment.

18. As quoted in (Doherty 1990).

19. For more on this point, see (Canes-Wrone, Howell, and Lewis forthcoming).

20. (Dahl 1950, p. 63).

21. (Peterson 1994, p. 271). Or as Edward Corwin notes: "The verdict of history, in short, is that the power to determine the substantive content of American foreign policy is a divided power, with the lion's share falling usually to the President, though by no means always" (Corwin 1948, p. 208).

22. Lindsay continues, "[The appropriations power] stands as Congress's foremost instrument for shaping military policy" (1999, p. 179). Richard Grimmet reiterates these claims: "In cases of significant differences with the President over foreign policy, especially deployments of U.S. military forces abroad, Congress has generally found the use of its Constitutionally-based 'power of the purse' to be the most effective ways to compel a President to take actions regarding use of U.S. military force overseas that he otherwise might not agree to" (Grimmet 2001, p. 1). Because defense department appropriations must be passed every year, members of Congress must revisit at regular intervals the formal debates about how

funds should be used when the military is protecting or advancing the nation's interests. By cutting funds or attaching various restrictions to their use, members may convince the president to either terminate or curtail a particular military venture.

23. In particular, Roosevelt feared that Congress would refuse to support the Second New Deal. And his concerns were not without justification. On the same day that they denied lifting the arms embargo in the summer of 1939, members of Congress denied emergency monetary powers under the president's Second New Deal proposal.

24. Turner Catledge, "Doubt Suddenly Arises on Arms Embargo Fate," *New York Times*, September 24, 1939, p. 75.

25. Quoted in (Kennedy 1999, p. 434).

26. Frank L. Kluckhohns, "Neutrality Move May Be Limited to Arming Ships," *New York Times*, October 6, 1941, p. 1.

27. "Taft Asserts Foreign Policy Puts Our Survival 'in Doubt,'" *New York Times*, January 27, 1952, p. 1.

28. Felix Belair, "Republican Chiefs Charge Ineptness in Foreign Affairs," *New York Times*, February 12, 1963, p. 1.

29. James Reston, "Foes Put Kennedy on the Defensive," *New York Times*, April 1, 1963, p. 1.

30. "President Meets Congress Chiefs on Foreign Policy," *New York Times*, February 19, 1963, p. 1.

31. H.R. 19911, P.L. 91-652.

32. H.R. 9055, P.L. 93-50. See also H.J.Res. 636, P.L. 93-52.

33. S. 3394, P.L. 93-559.

34. (Kissinger 1979, p. 513). Additionally, a White House "Vietnam White Paper" on the January 1973 peace accords bristled with frustration about the "incessant attacks from the United States Congress. . . . No president has been under more constant and unremitting harassment by men who should drop to their knees each night to thank the Almighty that they do not have to make the same decisions that Richard Nixon did" (Berman 2001, p. 238).

35. P.L. 94-212.

36. P.L. 94-329. See also P.L. 94-330.

37. Clifton Daniel, "Angolan Aid Ban Signed by Ford," *New York Times*, February 11, 1976, p. 1.

38. P.L. 98-473.

39. P.L. 98-119.

40. Of course, Congress is not powerless to overcome these informational disadvantages. Through reporting requirements, for instance, Congress has managed to wrest from the executive branch information about the conduct of a military venture and White House plans for its continued execution. Every time that Congress has authorized the use of force, it has required the president to issue regular reports about the ongoing conduct of the military campaign and to consult with members about courses of future action. Between 1973 and 2004, the president submitted 114 reports under the War Powers Resolution, though only one (regarding the 1975 Mayaguez incident under Ford) actually cited the relevant section of the law (Grimmet 2004). During this period, presidents informed Congress about all sorts of imminent and recent military activities around the globe: in Chad,

Lebanon, and Grenada in 1983; the Philippines and Panama in 1989; Macedonia, Haiti, Bosnia, Somalia, and Iraq in 1993; Albania, Congo, Gabon, Sierra Leone, Bosnia, and Cambodia in 1997; and in Bosnia, East Timor, Sierra Leone, Kosovo, Bosnia, and Yemen in 2000. To be sure, the fact that presidents report these activities to Congress does not mean that those reports factor into congressional decision making or views on the matter—the mere action is never, in itself, evidence of influence. Nonetheless, the reports afford members some opportunity to review the military actions taking place around the world.

41. See S.J. Res 45, February 4, 1993.

42. Some allowances were made for the protection of U.S. citizens and diplomats. P.L. 103-139.

43. P.L. 103-335.

44. (Barnett 2003; Melvern 2004; Power 2002).

45. Another supplemental appropriations bill added $50 million to aid Rwanda. See P.L. 103-306. Quotes found in *Congressional Quarterly Almanac*, 1994, p. 493.

46. P.L. 103-335 [H.R. 4650].

47. H.R. 1569, April 28, 1999.

48. See, for example, H.J.Res 44, which would have declared a state of war between Yugoslavia and the United States, but which was defeated 2–427 on April 28. Later that same day, the House defeated another bill, S.Con.Res. 21, which supported the use of force in Kosovo. On May 4, 1999, the Senate tabled another resolution, S.J.Res. 20, which would have authorized military operations in Kosovo.

49. See Andrew Taylor, "GOP Seizes Kosovo Supplemental as Defense Spending Vehicle," *CQ Weekly*, April 24, 1999, pp. 955–56. Still, Republicans within Congress did spearhead a lengthy court challenge to Clinton's actions. *Campbell v. Clinton*, 52 F. Supp. 2d 34 (D.D.C. 1999).

50. Quoted in *Congressional Quarterly Almanac*, 1999, pp. 2–157.

51. (Ferejohn and Rosenbluth 2005, p. 32). Emphasis added.

52. (Mayhew 1974, p. 107).

53. Within the American politics literature, this observation borders on conventional wisdom. A host of scholars have persuasively demonstrated that perfunctory confirmation hearings and regular budgetary outlays do not constitute prima facie evidence of congressional failure to oversee the bureaucracy (McCubbins, Noll, and Weingast 1989; McCubbins and Schwartz 1984); that infrequent efforts to overturn executive orders does not establish, once and for all, that presidents can exercise their unilateral powers however they choose (Howell 2003); or that consistent abidance by court rulings does not demonstrate that legislative constraints on judicial decision-making are entirely vacuous (Epstein and Knight 1997). To properly measure power, and infer influence, scholars must do considerably more than just inventory the number of times that Congress takes positive steps to undo the actions of administrative agencies, presidents, or courts.

54. Jim Hoagland, "The Unimperial Presidency," *Washington Post*, April 7, 1994, p. A27.

55. (Ely 1993, p. 4). As Edward Corwin noted decades ago, in foreign policy the president "is usually in a position to *propose*," while members of Congress "are often in a technical position to at least *dispose*" (Corwin 1948, p. 208).

56. Other scholars have demonstrated that these actions too have a tangible effect on presidential war making. According to (Kriner 2006), congressional sanction for a military intervention, even if granted by only a single chamber, tends to extend the duration of large-scale military actions.

57. The War of 1812 is another such example, when the War Hawks in Congress pushed hard for national expansion and a forthright rebuttal of the British practices of pressing U.S. citizens into Royal Navy service and blockading European ports. President James Madison, initially reluctant to enter into war, eventually acquiesced to congressional demands. In chapter 5, we present one contemporary case study where Congress stood out in front and advocated on behalf of a smaller military action: the 1989 Panama invasion. Of course, there also are instances when individual members of Congress, or groups of members, advocated on behalf of military action before the president was willing to commit troops. As previously discussed, some Republicans in Congress called for continued naval aggression after the Cuban Missile Crisis; also recall, during Clinton's tenure, Robert Dole on Bosnia and the black caucus on Haiti. Still, we know of no laws or resolutions that Congress passed during the modern era that demanded military action in the face of presidential opposition.

58. For a useful summary of these factors and events, see (Gelb 1979, pp. 96–177).

59. (Churchill 1996 [1930], p. 232).

60. (Thucydides 1972, pp. 81–82). Special thanks to Bruce Russett for this quotation.

61. Michael Barone, "Presidents at War," *U.S. News and World Report*, January 30, 2006, p. 51.

62. For more on the electoral consequences of battlefield losses, see (Cotton 1986).

63. Frank Baumgartner and Bryan Jones have identified fully 253 formal congressional hearings between 1946 and 2000 on "direct war related issues," including treatment of prisoners of war; the commitment of troops to different regions of the world; bombing campaigns in Vietnam and Cambodia; the provision of military supplies; ground-level operations in Kosovo, Somalia, Bosnia, Grenada, Panama, and Iraq; Nicaraguan incursions into Honduras; and attacks on military personnel stationed in the Middle East. (The data are available online at http://www.policyagendas.org/datasets/index.html. Hearings on "direct war related issues" were coded under sub-topic 1619.) One hundred fifty of these hearings were held in the House, 100 were held in the Senate, and 3 were held jointly. In total, Congress devoted almost two full years (699 days) to these hearings, which were hardly the province of a single committee or select handful of congresspersons. Fourteen different House committees, 10 Senate committees, and 2 Joint Committees held hearings at one point or another on war-related issues. Many of these hearings focused on the various costs of war, financial, human, and diplomatic. During the Korean, Vietnam, and Persian Gulf wars, Congress held hearings to investigate claims that defense department appropriations were misspent. Congress held a series of hearings that scrutinized the atrocities of war, raising the stakes for all parties involved. Over the past fifty years, hearings have focused on the massacres at Katyn Forest and Malmeddy (World War II) and Mai Lai (Vietnam

War); the bombing of Marine barracks in Lebanon and Beirut; alleged war crimes and the treatment of POWs during World War II, the Korean War, the Vietnam War; and the health problems experience by veterans who served in the Persian Gulf War. Through these hearings, Congress erected forums for publicizing the president's (and his advisors') missteps, misdeeds, and miscalculations. The costs of war were put in stark relief before the American public, and the political fall-out was often considerable.

64. The reverse is also true. When Congress does authorize the use of force, the president may find cover from subsequent criticisms if things go poorly. By way of example, contrast the treatment members of Congress gave presidents Truman and Bush (43) during the Korean and Iraq Wars. In the former case, as we have already noted, Congress came down hard on the president when conditions on the ground worsened. As Gary Hess notes, "A resolution of congressional support would not have precluded eventual criticism, but it would have put some constraints on that opposition. As the war became more controversial, Truman could have always pointed to Congress's endorsement, while critics in Congress (assuming they had voted for the war resolution) would always have to explain why they no longer supported Truman's policy" (Hess 2001, p. 38). By securing a congressional authorization before starting the Iraq War, Bush earned such protections, at least while Republicans maintained control of Congress. The news from Iraq during 2004 could hardly have been more disturbing, as beheadings of foreign nationals, car bombings, and widespread unrest were regular occurrences. Criticisms from Congress, though, were strangely muted. Though Democratic presidential candidate John Kerry struggled mightily to advertise the president's failings—ranging from the administration's scorn of international allies to its lack of planning for the occupation—he stumbled almost every time he was forced to explain why he had voted for the original authorization.

65. U.S. Congress, House Committee on Armed Services, United States-Vietnam Relations, 19, 12 vols. Washington: U.S. Government Printing Office, 1971, vol. 1, part 2, p. B-5.

66. Anthony Leviero, "Eisenhower Limits U.S. Participation in Indo-China War," New York Times, February 11, 1954, p. 1.

67. U.S. Congress, House Committee on Armed Services, United States-Vietnam Relations, 19, 12 vols. Washington: U.S. Government Printing Office, 1971, vol. 1, part 2, p. B23-4.

68. (Billings-Yun 1988, p. 27).

69. Steven Roberts, "Congress and White House at Odds Over Growing Presence in Gulf," New York Times, May 21, 1987, p. A19.

70. Tom Lantos, "Keep U.S. Flags off Kuwaiti Tankers," New York Times, May 31, 1987, p. E29.

71. As quoted in (Hendrickson 2002, p. 53).

72. As quoted in ibid., p. 88.

73. These do not exhaust the tolls of domestic political dissent on presidential power. Under certain conditions, for instance, overcoming congressional opposition to a planned use of force may have deleterious effects on other aspects of the president's policy agenda. The longer it takes to satisfy concerns about a proposed military venture, and then the longer it takes actually to achieve a mission's stated

objectives, the more likely it is that important features of a president's policy agenda will be tabled for another term. When media discussions over the use of force intensify, the president must expend additional resources to build and sustain arguments for action—resources that might otherwise be spent on other domestic or foreign policy initiatives. Debates over the use of force, after all, do not occur in a vacuum. They proceed contemporaneously with arguments over tax policy and gay marriage and social security reform. By directing journalists' attention to the costs of war, members of Congress may derail, or at least delay, White House efforts to build the consensus and momentum required to advance other initiatives that they can only secure through legislation.

74. (Schultz 1998, p. 840).

75. (Ibid.; Smith 1998; Fearon 1994; Smith and Guisinger 2002).

76. *Public Papers of the President*, 2002, p. 1669.

77. Ibid., p. 1740.

78. Of course, signaling resolve is an ongoing challenge. When the costs of war surface, members of Congress, especially those from within the opposition party, may complain loudly. When they do, the president may have a more difficult time reassuring his allies and convincing his enemies that he will see a military campaign to the end. The results can be devastating. Emboldened by the international and domestic media criticism, insurgents within Iraq launched a concerted campaign of beheadings, car bombings, and suicide missions to further weaken allied commitments to the region. As Bush noted in a December 2004 news conference, "No question about it, the bombers are having an effect. You know, these people are targeting innocent Iraqis. They're trying to shake the will of the Iraqi people, and frankly, trying to shake the will of the American people. And car bombs that destroy young children or car bombs that indiscriminately bomb in religious sites are effective propaganda tools." Full text of press conference available at: http://www.whitehouse.gov/news/releases/2004/12/20041220-3.html (website accessed January 4, 2005).

79. As quoted in News Wire Services, "Bush: No Timetable for Pulling Out Troops," *The Buffalo News*, June 25, 2005, p. A1.

80. (Brody 1991, 1994; Brody and Shapiro 1989).

81. In addition, consumed by deliberations over the use of force, the public is unlikely to mobilize behind the enactment of new and unrelated legislation. Forced to address the public's preoccupation with the prospect of war, presidents may have to temporarily abandon other elements of their policy agenda.

82. "Excerpts from Address of Weinberger," *New York Times*, November 29, 1984, P. A5.

83. Ibid.

84. Writing in the 1940s, 1950s, and 1960s, a number of scholars examined the foreign policy views of average citizens (Rosenau 1961; Almond 1950; Rosenau 1967; Lippmann 1992; Markel 1949). Consistent with other public opinion research at the time, these scholars took a rather dim view of the American public and its capacity to formulate stable opinions about complex foreign policies. For the most part, though, these scholars did not examine what impact, if any, public opinion had on the views of political elites. Recent examinations of the topic, for the most part, provide a stronger basis for optimism. In addition to those scholars

described below, see (Foyle 1999; Wittkopf 1990; Rosenau 1961; Powlick 1995; Bartels 1991; Hartley and Russett 1992; Hinckley 1988, 1992; Kull and Destler 1999). The Center for International and Security Studies at the University of Maryland has released a series of reports on public attitudes toward interventions in Somalia, Bosnia, Haiti, and Iraq (see http://www.cissm.umd.edu/). The Center on Policy Attitudes and the Program on International Policy Attitudes, also at the University of Maryland, has assembled rich datasets on public opinion about a variety of international affairs (see http://www.americans-world.org/). And for an examination of the influence of public opinion on use-of-force decisions in European nations, see (Everts and Isernia 2001).

85. (Holsti 1996).

86. Ibid., pp. 59–60

87. Holsti argues that the general public is consistently less likely to support military action than are "opinion leaders." See ibid., table 4.4, pp. 118–19.

88. (Aldrich et al 2006, p. 496).

89. (Sobel 2001). See also (Sobel and Shiraev 2003; Sobel 1993, 1989).

90. (Sobel 2001, p. x).

91. (Baum 2003, 2004a, 2004b).

92. (Baum 2004b, p. 188).

93. Ibid, p. 193. This is consistent with John Zaller's concept of "anticipated future opinions" (1994b, p. 251).

94. (Jacobs and Page 2005).

95. Ibid., p. 118.

CHAPTER 2

1. For more on this point, see (Shepsle 1992).

2. (Weingast and Marshall 1988; Krehbiel 1992).

3. (Krehbiel 1998; Binder 1999, 2003; Howell et al. 2000; Mayhew 1991; Bond and Fleisher 1990, 2000).

4. Information asymmetries assuredly decline over the course of a military campaign, as interest groups, the media, and members of Congress collect and disseminate relevant information. But when military force is initiated, the period this book seeks to explain, the information available to presidents from the Central Intelligence Agency, the National Security Council, the Department of Defense, and the State Department is unparalleled.

5. Both quotes in Carroll J. Doherty, "Two GOP Leaders Personify Party's Rift Over Kosovo," *CQ Weekly,* April 10, 1999, p. 836.

6. The seminal treatment of this subject is (Crawford and Sobel 1982). For some extensions and modifications, see (Canes-Wrone 2005; Gilligan and Krehbiel 1990; Lupia and McCubbins 1994).

7. (Krehbiel 1992, p. 81).

8. (Wittkopf and Dehaven 1987; Baker and Oneal 2001).

9. (Campbell and Sumners 1990).

10. On September 14, 2001, the House and Senate authorized the use of force

for those responsible for the September 11 attacks by 98–0 and 420–1, respectively. In this paragraph, we only discuss authorization votes that were considered by both chambers of Congress before troops were deployed.

11. PL 102-1, January 12, 1991.

12. H.J. Res 77, January 12, 1991.

13. S.J. Res. 2, January 12, 1991.

14. H.Con.Res. 42, March 11, 1999.

15. S.Con.Res. 21, March 23, 1999. The House would later defeat the Senate resolution, on April 28, 1999, after strikes against the Federal Republic of Yugoslavia had begun.

16. P.L. 107-243, H.J. Res. 114, October 11, 2002.

17. (Hendrickson 2002, pp. 21–42). More generally, Kriner (2006) finds that partisanship was by far the most powerful predictor of all votes to curtail an ongoing use of force in the 1980s and 1990s. Congressional Republicans (particularly compared to Democrats) were highly unlikely to vote to constrain presidential discretion under Reagan, but were three times more likely than Democrats to vote to curtail an ongoing military action when Clinton inhabited the Oval Office.

18. S.J. Res. 45, May 25, 1993. The Senate passed the resolution by voice vote on February 4.

19. For a list of congressional roll call votes on U.S. uses of force, see (Brown 2003).

20. See, for example, (McCormick and Wittkopf 1990).

21. See (Fowler and Law 2005).

22. (Peterson 1990; Rudalevige 2002; Howell et al. 2000).

23. (Edwards 2003, p. 10).

24. The classic treatment of member's reelection incentives is (Mayhew 1974). For extended discussions of the legislative process's various obstacles and challenges, see (Epstein and O'Halloran 1999; Cox and McCubbins 1993; Krehbiel 1998; Moe 1999).

25. (Auerswald and Cowhey 1997, p. 523).

26. While realists and neorealists often emphasize the importance of military factors in structural theories, other structural theories such as world systems theory emphasizes economic factors such as trade and finance.

27. For examples of structural theories, see (Waltz 1979; Wallerstein 1974; James 2002). We use "structural" and "systemic" interchangeably following Fearon (1998), although some scholars make distinctions between these two types of theories.

28. (Waltz 1979, p. 122).

29. (Waltz 1967, p. 16).

30. (Waltz 1979; Wagner 1986).

31. See (Rosecrance 1966; Kaplan 1957; Morgenthau 1967; Deuth and Singer 1964).

32. Indeed, among political scientists, a rigorous debate emerged as to whether the new system was still bipolar, multipolar, or unipolar. See (Krauthammer 1991; Huntington 1999; Haas 1999).

33. (Organski and Kugler 1980; Levy 1985; Kugler and Lemke 1996). Some early scholars conceptualize balance of power as a truly systemic variable where an

overall balance of forces may inhibit conflict. More recent literature treats balance of power dyadically–the comparison of two states' relative capabilities. Our own usage is consistent with the latter. While true structural theorists would not consider a unit attribute such as capabilities a structural characteristic, it would certainly be considered by classical realists as a constraint.

34. A classic statement of this reasoning comes from (Gullick 1955). See also (Waltz 1979, pp. 164–67).

35. See (Morrow 1994; Fearon 1995).

36. (Russett and Oneal 2001, pp. 60–61).

37. On conflict and alliances, see (Siverson and Sullivan 1984; Levy 1981; King 1998, pp. 224–29; Smith 1995). For a general review of how alliances are related to conflict, see (Vasquez 1987). On the question of alliances and extended immediate deterrence, see (Huth 1988, 1999; Huth and Russett 1984).

38. (Leeds 2003, p. 437).

39. See (Russett and Oneal 2001; Mansfield and Pollins 2001; Gartzke, Li, and Boehmer 2001; Pevehouse 2004). For a challenge to this view, see (Barbieri 2002).

40. We note that this argument highlights the importance of political pressure from economic agents—states as entities trade very little. One could argue that pressures to avoid conflict may manifest themselves through Congress. Most work on the domestic politics of trade policy, however, argues that presidents, because they serve no particular geographic constituency, generally favor open trade (see Goldstein 1996). We point this out not to say that presidents will always avoid conflict if trade is at stake, but rather to emphasize that it need not be the case that presidents rely on Congress as a conduit for trade policy preferences. Presidents favor open trade since (in theory) it maximizes the welfare of a population as a whole versus particular constituent groups.

41. Chief adherents to this view are (Gartzke, Li, and Boehmer 2001; Morrow 2003).

42. Although this claim has historically been linked to Hobson and Lenin, more modern variants appear in dependency theory and those critical of globalization.

43. (Fearon 1998, p. 298).

44. (Howell 2003, 2005a, 2005b; Moe and Howell 1999a, 1999b).

45. Ibid.

46. With regards to the use of force, interinstitutional dynamics shift somewhat, as a clear asymmetry defines the relationship between Congress and the president. While members of Congress can punish the president for deploying troops abroad, as discussed in the previous chapter they cannot readily impel military action in the face of presidential resistance. As such, in this realm—unlike policymaking generally, where Congress has the option of legislating when the president refuses to issue a unilateral directive—Congress's impact manifests itself principally as a constraint on presidential power.

CHAPTER 3

1. This chapter builds on (Howell and Pevehouse 2005).

2. (Blechman and Kaplan 1978).

3. See ibid., pp. 1–20, for a description of the kinds of deployments included in the analysis. It is worth noting, however, that subsequent scholars abandoned many of the restrictions Blechman and Kaplan placed on their data. Rather than require that deployments serve some kind of political purpose, scholars merely have catalogued movements of military forces to regions of the world where troops were not already stationed.

4. (Ostrom and Job 1986).

5. Ibid., p. 545.

6. (James and Oneal 1991).

7. (Fordham 1998b).

8. (Stoll 1984).

9. (Waltz 1979).

10. (Meernik 1994; Meernik and Waterman 1996; Meernik 2000).

11. (Meernik 1994, p. 136).

12. (Gowa 1998).

13. (Moore and Lanoue 2003).

14. For important exceptions, see (Meernik 1994, 2000). Meernik argues that quantitative studies of U.S. use of force suffer from selection bias. There are myriad domestic and international contexts in which the United States does *not* respond. By only examining actual uses of force, Meernik argues, scholars have assembled an incomplete view of the dynamics of presidential decision making. This concern establishes the primary motivation for the statistical tests included in chapter 4.

15. Mitchell and Moore (2002) and Fordham (2002) have raised important issues of data comparability (scholars use different years in analyzing their hypotheses) and temporal dynamics (uses of force may be clustered together in time) that may compromise other scholars' findings.

16. For the vast majority of scholars contributing to this enterprise, the data to be analyzed consist of extensions and slight modifications of the original Blechman and Kaplan time series.

17. Although in this chapter we use a similar approach to maintain comparability, in chapter 4 we revisit these questions with new, and richer, data.

18. For a partial exception, see (Morgan and Campbell 1991; Morgan and Bickers 1992). Morgan and Campbell (1991) examine cross-nationally "legislative constraints" on executive war powers. Unfortunately, executives are coded as being constrained only when "legislatures have the ability to overturn [them]." Morgan and Campbell do not provide the data required to assess the varying capacities of individual legislatures to constrain their executives over time. Morgan and Bickers (1992) examine the influence of partisanship and public opinion on decisions to use force in the context of diversionary war.

19. (Gowa 1999, 1998; Fordham 2002; Clark 2000).

20. (DeRouen 1995).

21. (Meernik 1993). Clark (2000) introduces two versions of divided government (instances in which both chambers are held by parties opposite the president, and instances in which either or both chambers are) and also considers the percent of votes in Congress that support positions taken by the president. So doing, Clark differentiates himself from these other scholars by finding large congressional

effects on the frequency with which presidents deploy troops abroad and the duration of these military ventures.

22. (Meernik 1994, pp. 122–23). Meernik (1995) examines the conditions under which members invoke the War Powers Resolution and other measures designed to constrain the presidential use of force. These actions, Meernik argues, place "political restraints on the executive branch" (p. 380) and "may ultimately make it more difficult for presidents to exercise national leadership" (p. 387). But Meernik also insists that Congress "never succeeds in handicapping the president's power to deploy the armed services abroad" and that "such attempts will either not meet with success or will not be pursued to their logical conclusion" for "although the temptation to use the power at its disposal is there, the will to carry though on the threat is not" (p. 380). Meernik characterizes Congress as a highly risk-averse institution that periodically "register[s] loud complaints with the executive branch," but that seeks cover at the first signs of trouble, and that rarely accomplishes anything of consequence in its efforts to constrain the president.

23. (Gowa 1998, p. 307).

24. For an innovative test of diversionary war, see (Richards et al. 1993).

25. For critiques, see (Meernik 2000; Meernik and Waterman 1996; Levy 1989; Blainey 1988).

26. There are, of course, numerous variants on this theme. Morgan and Campbell (1991), for instance, have argued that diversionary war effects crucially depend on citizens' partisan identification.

27. According to a Gallup/CNN poll ending September 10, 2001, 51 percent of the American public approved of Bush's job performance; according to another poll that concluded on September 15, that number jumped to 86 percent. Polls conducted by the Associated Press and by the Pew Research Center revealed comparable changes in the president's job approval ratings. For all of Bush's ratings, see http://www.pollingreport.com/BushJob.htm. (Website accessed July 22, 2005).

28. (Mueller 1973; MacKuen 1983; Ostrom and Simon 1985; Wittkopf and Dehaven 1987; Lian and Oneal 1993).

29. For important exceptions, see (Brody 1991; Brody and Shapiro 1989).

30. (Morgan and Bickers 1992, p. 26).

31. (Stoll 1987).

32. (Hinckley 1994, p. 80).

33. (Peake 2001, p. 60).

34. (Fordham 1998a; Fordham and Sarver 2001; Zelikow 1987). To identify uses of force post-1995, we replicated the procedures described in Fordham 1998a. We also made several adjustments to the original Blechman/Kaplan time series and amendments made to it by subsequent scholars. Specifically, we removed two classes of events: those uses of force which were prescheduled (e.g., Operation Team Spirit) and those carried out by troops already deployed to a crisis area (e.g., attacking Iraqi antimissile batteries after being fired on in the no-fly zone). None of the findings presented below change significantly when the original 1945–95 datasets are analyzed.

35. See, for example, (Fordham 1998a, 1998b). The severity of the use of force is determined by information available at the *outset* of the crisis. Thus, while neither Congress nor the president know the eventual severity or duration of a conflict,

they do have information regarding the size and nuclear capability of the troop deployment, which distinguishes major from minor incidents. Largely for measurement reasons, the quantitative use-of-force literature excludes the Korean and Vietnam wars from the time series. (Given their magnitude and duration, it is virtually impossible to dissemble these wars into their constituent parts). We note, however, that the series does include many of the smaller, discretionary deployments that preceded these full-scale wars; additionally, the statistical models that follow include a control variable for ongoing war.

36. This definition of major versus minor force is standard in the use-of-force literature (DeRouen 1995, 2000; Fordham 1998a, 1998b; Mitchell and Moore 2002). Changing the definition of major uses of force to include only level 1 and 2 deployments on the Blechman/Kaplan severity scale yields positive coefficients for all versions of our independent variable of interest, but these estimates vary in their statistical significance. This result is not surprising given the large number of quarters during which no level 1 or 2 deployments occur.

37. Yearly data are used in the graphs simply for purposes of visual coherence. All analyses use quarterly data.

38. Versions of all key explanatory variables that focus exclusively on the Senate, which arguably plays a disproportionate role in defining Congress's foreign policy positions, generate comparable results.

39. (Brady, Cooper, and Hurley 1979).

40. The LPPC score for either chamber in any given term is calculated as follows: Chamber LPPC = [(majority party size in percent) × (cohesion of majority party)] − [(minority party size in percent) × (cohesion of minority party)]. *Congressional Quarterly's* party unity scores are utilized.

40a. For purposes of comparability with the other measures of congressional support, we also divide the adjusted LPPC scores by 100.

41. (Fordham 1998a; James and Oneal 1991; Fordham 2002).

42. (Ostrom and Job 1986).

43. In the handful of quarters missing approval data, we fill the data by using a linear interpolation. We also interpolated by using the last known poll. The results are consistent regardless of the method used.

44. (Gaubatz 1991).

45. Fordham's election variable differs from ours. While we isolate the three quarters leading up to the national election, Fordham (1998a) isolates all four quarters in an election year, as well as the first quarter of the following year when an incumbent is reelected.

46. (Mansfield 1994).

47. (Small and Singer 1990).

48. (Meernik 1994).

49. For a description of the MID 3.0 data, see (Ghosn and Palmer 2003).

50. F-tests regularly reject the null that the presidential fixed effects are jointly insignificant.

51. Specifically, we estimate the following event count model: Force = f(CongressSupport, PRESIDENT). If our expectations about the relevance of Congress hold, the estimated regression coefficient for CongressSupport should be positive. As previously indicated, we estimate multiple models that interchange the various measures of *Force* and *CongressSupport*. Autocorrelation function plots reveal

negligible temporal dynamics. Three of the first four autocorrelations of the major and minor time series are statistically significant, but the largest value of rho observed is only 0.19. Estimates obtained from general estimation equations models that correct for an AR(1) process yield virtually identical results to traditional event count models (Zorn 2001). (The ACF plots and results from GEE models are available from the authors on request.) For the sake of simplicity, we report estimates from negative binomial regressions with robust standard errors that account for clustering on each president. We use negative binomial models since Poisson models assume that events within an observation period are independent (King 1998: 50–51). In this case, the presence of military action may spur further military action in close proximity. Negative binomial models are not limited by this independence assumption.

52. Although theory suggests that the size of the president's party affects the discretion of the president to use force abroad, it is largely silent with regard to the functional form of the relationship. On reflection, however, there is good reason to expect that the impact of *Percent President Party* and *President Party Power* could be nonlinear. Incremental changes at the tails of the distribution may not have an appreciable impact on the frequency with which presidents exercise force abroad. Shifts around the center of the distribution, meanwhile, may induce large changes in the use of presidential force. To test for the possibility of nonlinear effects, we also took the logistic transformations of *Percent President Party* and *President Party Power* and reestimated the fixed effects models. Again, we found that changes in the partisan composition of both houses of Congress do not have any appreciable impact on the frequency with which presidents deploy minor uses of force, or uses of force overall. Once again, however, significant and positive impacts were observed for major uses of force, with changes in predicted counts nearly identical to the nontransformed results previously discussed. The greater the size and unity of the president's party, relative to that of the opposition party, the more often presidents initiate larger military deployments abroad.

53. Specifically, we estimate the following model, which incorporates many of the alternative hypotheses in this literature: Force = f(CongressSupport, Unemployment, CPI, Approval, Election, War, ColdWar, Hegemony, WorldDispute, PRESIDENT). Again, we expect that the coefficient for *CongressSupport* will be positive; and again, we estimate separate models for each version of *Force* and *CongressSupport*.

54. Models for all uses of force are presented in table A.2 of appendix A.

55. Models that pool major and minor uses of force never generate statistically significant impacts for congressional support for the president.

56. These models are also consistent with (Fordham 1998a).

57. (Gowa 1998; Meernik 1994).

58. This is consistent with the findings of both Meernik and Fordham.

59. When estimating models that also include a variable that measures the quarterly number of "opportunities" to use force abroad, we consistently observe significant and positive effects on the frequency with which troops are deployed. In chapter 4, we introduce and analyze the "opportunities dataset."

60. (Edwards 1986; Wildavsky 1989).

61. (Blechman 1990, p. 10).

62. There is reason to question this standard view. For a powerful challenge to

the conventional depiction of Congress during the Cold War, see Robert Johnson's recent book, *Congress and the Cold War* (2006). This book marshals substantial evidence that through hearings, appropriations, and public appeals, Congress managed to redirect foreign policy in important ways during an era that is supposed to have been defined by consensus and congressional abdication.

63. Because the resolution passed at the end of the 1973 calendar year, we begin our coding in 1974. These estimates, however, are not sensitive to this choice of year.

64. If the War Powers Resolution reestablished Congress's rightful place in deliberations over the use of force, then congressional effects may be concentrated in the post-1974 period. One mitigating factor, however, is worth noting. By establishing strict reporting requirements, the resolution may have reduced the informational asymmetries between the executive and legislative branches. As we note in part 1 of this book, copartisans within Congress are especially likely to support the president because, in part, they can better trust his assessment of a military intervention's efficacy. If the resolution achieved its intended objectives (a subject of considerable controversy; see [Fisher 2000, 2004]), then information may replace trust, and the importance of partisanship may decline.

65. These findings are consistent with (Kriner 2006), which also reports significant impacts associated with the partisan composition of Congress on the duration of deployments pre– and post–War Powers Resolution.

66. (Jones, Bremer, and Singer 1996).

67. (Fordham and Sarver 2001).

68. (Pevehouse 2004).

69. (Gowa 1999, p. 42). Taking the use-of-force time series back to 1870 would appear to be a strength of Gowa's analysis. Unfortunately, her statistical models do little to account for the marked changes in presidential power, presidential-congressional relations, and the nation's standing in the international order pre- and post-FDR, even though she recognizes the marked increase in the number of MIDs observed in the modern era (1998, p. 318). Moreover, as Fordham has pointed out, Gowa fails to account for temporal dynamics in her dependent variable that, uncorrected, generate potentially spurious results (Fordham 2002).

70. (Clark 2000, p. 376).

71. When examining the same period that Gowa considers (1945–92), we replicate her null finding on *Unified Government*. Effects for *Percent President Party* and *President Party Power*, however, remain positive and statistically significant.

72. (Feaver and Gelpi 2005). Gelpi and Feaver also claim that veterans are more likely to support a major deployment than a minor one, given that a decision to use force has been made.

73. (Gelpi and Feaver 2002, p. 792). Even as just a face validity check, Gelpi and Feaver do not report results that indicate that veteran members of Congress are less likely to vote against authorizations to use force abroad. If recent trends are any indication, they are not. In 2002, 69 percent of veteran members of the House supported the Iraq Authorization, as compared to 72 percent of nonveterans—a difference that is neither substantively nor statistically significant. (Results for the Senate are virtually identical, though veterans there were slightly more

likely to have voted in favor of the authorization.) Partisan divisions, by contrast, ran deep. Fully 98 percent of House Republicans, versus just 39 percent of House Democrats, voted in favor of the authorization.

74. We examine the period between 1945 and 2000, while Gelpi and Feaver consider the period between 1816 and 1992. It is worth noting that rather than estimate the frequency with which presidents deploy troops abroad, Gelpi and Feaver estimate the probability that the United States enters into conflict with other "politically relevant" nation states. When estimating such models for the postwar period, the focus of this book, Gelpi and Feaver's main findings disappear entirely, while those for partisan measures of Congress appear stronger. For others who also find a weak link between the percentage of veterans in Congress and policy outcomes, see (Bianco 2005).

75. When examining only male members of Congress, as Gelpi and Feaver do, the effects appear significant for the "major" time series. We see no theoretical reason, however, for restricting the sample to only one gender.

76. (Gowa 1998, p. 308). Fordham (1998a, 1998b) and Clark (2003) argue that Democratic and Republican presidents respond differently to unemployment and inflation when contemplating military action. They do not, however, argue that the baseline proclivity to exercise force differs systematically across the two parties.

77. Angus Campbell and his colleagues (1964, pp. 107–8), for instance, found that Republican politicians had a stronger reputation among the general public for "getting tough" with the Soviets and China.

78. When substituting an indicator for Republican presidents for all of the presidential fixed effects, the Republican indicator variable is positive and highly statistically significant, while the main effects for the various measures of congressional support remain positive and statistically significant.

79. A related question concerns the relative sensitivity of Democratic and Republican presidents to varying domestic institutional constraints: does Congress figure more or less prominently in the calculations of Republican and Democratic presidents who are considering the use of military force? This question is more nuanced than the first, as it concerns the salience of congressional support to Republican and Democratic presidents who are contemplating military action. Moreover, it suggests the possibility that presidential preferences (as defined by their partisanship) may interact with institutional constraints (as measured by the partisan composition of Congress) in ways that heretofore have been overlooked. To examine this possibility, we added to the fully specified models interaction terms between each measure of congressional support and an indicator variable for Republican presidents. We find little consistent support that Democratic presidents are any more or less sensitive to the partisan composition of Congress than are Republican presidents. Though the interaction terms are occasionally significant, the estimates are quite sensitive to the particular measure of congressional support for the president and the particular use of time series considered. Lacking strong theory that supports the expectation that the impact of congressional support on troop deployments should vary systematically according to the president's partisanship, we are hesitant to place much weight on these findings.

80. (Meernik 1994, 2000).

CHAPTER 4

1. "As such," James Meernik points out, "it is not possible to evaluate adequately the significance of decision-making inputs since there is no set of cases where force may have plausibly been employed, but was not, to use as a basis for comparison" (1994, p. 122). For further discussion on the limitations of event count data in international relations research, see (King and Lowe 2003).

2. Using the *New York Times* for content coding, whether the subject of analysis be laws, court cases, executive orders, or foreign crises, is standard practice among political scientists. For one description of this data source's advantages, in this instance measuring issue salience, see (Epstein and Segal 2000).

3. To be included in the database, a story had to discuss events that occurred within the previous six months. With some regularity, the *Times* published stories on the anniversary of past crises (such as the attack on Pearl Harbor or massacres in Central America) or stories that traced the historical evolution of a longstanding regional crisis (such as in Algeria or Korea). Though they may have discussed events that fit one of the criteria laid out in appendix B, such stories could not readily be considered new opportunities to exercise force abroad. Hence, they were excluded from the database.

4. When building the use-of-force data, Blechman and Kaplan applied the same principle: through 1976, when their original dataset ends, never are there overlapping dates in military deployments to target nations. In the 1980s and 1990s, however, we do find some instances of simultaneous deployments—namely, when no-fly zones are established and military systems are placed abroad. As these uses of force can transpire for years on end, we were wary of eliminating from the database every subsequent report of an opportunity to use force against the targeted nations. We therefore estimate statistical models that include and exclude qualifying media reports that occurred contemporaneously with no-fly zones and the placement of new military systems. In both, the main results appear consistent.

5. We exclude outright all opportunities that concern the Korean, Vietnam, or first Gulf Wars. Additionally, we exclude opportunities that concern actions by a country where, and at a time when, it was the target of an ongoing major or minor use of force. Hence, we omit from the database reports about assassination attempts on a head of state or local citizens firing on U.S. troops when they occur during the ongoing course of a military venture within the same country. To be sure, such events certainly are important, as they give cause to escalate or deescalate standing deployments. Because we have fixed our analytic focus on the politics that precede military deployments, however, we omit them.

6. Note, that to be included in the dataset, a nation's involvement in the crisis must be direct. Hence, only two observations result from a report about the provisions of financial or military aid by country X to country Y that is warring with country Z—namely, countries Y and Z.

7. In the statistical models that we estimate in chapter 4, we account for the fact that observations in this database cannot be considered independent.

8. The one exception to this rule concerns direct, stateside attacks against the United States. In these instances, targets need not be foreign states.

9. Event types are not mutually exclusive. It is possible, therefore, for an opportunity to be classified as both a coup and an assassination attempt. Seventy-nine percent of cases were classified into just one category, 19 percent into two, and 2 percent into three or more.

10. We code the number of Americans killed as missing in cases where the *Times* does not mention the deaths of Americans. This results in a high number of missing observations (40 percent of the opportunities sample). Recoding these missing observations as zero changes the 4 percent U.S. death rate to nearly 2.5 percent.

11. Figure 4.1 identifies the number of opportunities that different countries contributed to the database, but may not reflect the actual location of the opportunities themselves. France and Britain, for instance, are among the top ten countries, not because numerous conflicts erupted within their borders, but instead because they were parties to ongoing conflicts in Africa and South America. We code region based on the actor involved rather than the target location since in our statistical models, we emphasize the characteristics of each potential target state involved.

12. The United States is completely white because, by design, we exclude all domestic parties who might elicit a military deployment.

13. After the Gulf of Tonkin (August 1964), we cease to code events in Vietnam since we define them as elements of a full-blown war.

14. To identify political-military allies of the United States and also the Soviet Union, we rely upon the Correlates of War alliance data, which includes defense pacts, nonaggression treaties, and ententes (Gibler and Sarkees 2004). While some might argue that military action against an ally is never a possibility and these should be excluded as opportunities, we leave this as an empirical question and choose to model this possibility.

15. The Correlates of War Project defines major powers as states with large military capabilities and power resources (Singer and Small 1994). During our period of observations, the Project identifies Great Britain, the United States, France, China, and Russia/Soviet Union as major powers.

16. To identify democracies, we draw from (Jaggers and Gurr 1995), which places countries on a scale ranging from −10 to +10, whereby larger (smaller) values correspond to more democratic (autocratic) governing systems. The scale is constructed by measuring a regime's institutional characteristics, including openness of executive recruiting and the electoral system. As is common in the international relations literature (see, for example, Mansfield and Snyder 2002), we identify democracies as countries with values of greater than 6. To bring the time series up through the present, we rely on (Marshall 2005).

17. See (Graber 2001).

18. Trade data are taken from (Gleditsch 2002) and are expressed in billions of U.S. dollars. The trade data have certain limitations, which are worth keeping in mind. The IMF data from which the data are taken confound zero or minimal trade with missing data on trade. Although Gleditsch and others have gone to great pains to rectify this situation, there are still a high number of zeros in the dyadic trade data. Still, even if these data were completely accurate, their real values would likely be near zero.

19. This latter figure refers to average levels of trade between the United States

and all other nations. Average trade for all nation-by-nation dyads worldwide is $161 million.

20. For a description of these data, see (Singer and Small 1994).

21. A number of international relations scholars have suggested as much, though the empirical support for the claim tends to be rather circumscribed, applying only to certain countries at specified times. See, for example, (Fordham 2005; Clark 2003; Leeds and Davis 1997; Smith 1996; Miller 1999).

22. (Fordham 2005).

23. Inflation rates here are represented by the consumer price index (CPI). Data are taken from the Bureau of Labor Statistics: www.bls.gov.

24. It is possible, of course, that the prospect of U.S. involvement might actually increase the probability of an opportunity arising. Anticipating the protection of the United States, for instance, some states might act more aggressively toward rival states. If true, then those opportunities observed during periods of high inflation or unemployment might arise from the strategic behavior of foreign actors. Later in this chapter, we introduce some multivariate models that allow for the further exploration of this and other possible explanations for the occurrence of opportunities.

25. Unemployment rates are calculated for persons 16 years or older. Data are taken from the Bureau of Labor Statistics: www.bls.gov.

26. Event-count models that posit the quarterly number of opportunities as a function of all of the covariates included in the main models of chapter 3 generate estimates for *Unified Government* that are consistently significant, while those for the other two measures of congressional support are not. In addition, public approval ratings, unemployment rates, and inflationary trends uniformly generate null effects.

27. We use the use-of-force data from chapter 3 to determine when troops were deployed. We use both minor and major deployments in this chapter—a decision we discuss below. Also, 9 percent may seem to be a large number of deployments, but recall that a single deployment could yield several responses since any story concerning a crisis is coded as being responded to so long as it is within the one month window.

28. It is worth recognizing that presidents have ample alternative options to military action. In response to a foreign crisis, they instead might demand a UN resolution, impose economic sanctions, give public speeches, or simply do nothing at all. Nothing in the statistical models that follow distinguishes between these options. Future research, however, might use the opportunities database to model the fuller range of U.S. military and diplomatic responses to foreign crises.

29. Here too, we estimated models that included the logistic transformations of *Percent President Party* and *President Party Power*. In most instances, the results are consistent with those reported below.

30. We identify the most recent Gallup poll to precede each opportunity.

31. We identify the average unemployment and inflation rates during the month that preceded an opportunity.

32. In some of the models estimated, especially those using subsamples of all opportunities, more than one of the presidential fixed effects are omitted to facilitate convergence.

33. We consider the Soviets involved if the *Times* mentions their involvement in the story in question.

34. See (Gibler and Sarkees 2004). We include all types of alliances (mutual defense pacts, ententes, etc.) in this sum.

35. On the democratic peace, see (Chang 1997; Russett and Oneal 2001).

36. We code democracies according to the Polity dataset (Jaggers and Gurr 1995). Democracies are counted as any state receiving a 7 or above on the –10 to +10 democracy scale. For current iterations of the data, see (Marshall 2005).

37. For the period of observation, China, Great Britain, France, the Soviet Union/Russia, and the United States are considered the major powers (Singer and Small 1994).

38. The variable is the same as previously defined. For a review of the liberal arguments concerning trade and conflict, see (Mansfield and Pollins 2001).

39. Specifically, we estimate the following logistic regression: Force = f(CongressSupport, PRESIDENT). If our expectations about the relevance of Congress hold, the estimated regression coefficient for each version of CongressSupport should be positive.

40. In the main models presented below, we estimate whether the United States responded militarily to observed foreign crises with either a major or a minor use of force, as originally defined by Blechman and Kaplan. We also estimated models that focused exclusively on major deployments. For the most part, the main results hold. In the few instances when differences arise, however, we mention them in footnotes below.

41. Here we estimate the following logistic regression: Force = f(CongressSupport, Unemployment, CPI, Approval, Election, Hegemony, WorldDispute, Alliances, MajorPower, Democracy, Trade, SovietInvolvement, CapabilityRatio, PrevOpps, ContemOpps, TroopsDeploy, REGION, PRESIDENT). As in chapter 3, we estimate separate models for each version of CongressSupport. If our expectations about the relevance of Congress hold, the estimated coefficient for CongressSupport should be positive. When adding to the model either fixed effects for the different types of opportunities or an indicator variable for whether an article mentions U.S. casualties, almost all estimates for the new variables are insignificant and those for the main variables of interest remain unaltered.

42. When estimating these models, we lose just over 2,000 observations due to missing data among the covariates. Data on international trade, GDP, and troop deployments is notoriously spotty (see, for example, Gleditsch 2002). When estimating models that intermittently exclude these variables, and hence add cases to the sample, we consistently observe comparable effects to those presented in table 4.2.

42a. For reasons explained in Appendix B, we are reluctant to make strong causal claims about this finding. The heightened coverage that precedes a military venture may reflect the *New York Times'* anticipation of a deployment rather than the newspaper's independent assessment of the importance of the crisis to U.S. interests abroad.

43. Given that the use of force is relatively rare in our data, we reestimated the models of table 4.1 using King and Zeng's (2001) Rare Events Logit procedure. The results are nearly identical to those previously reported.

44. Both *Percent President Party* and *President Party Power* are positive and statistically significant for both models of majors only and minors only. *Unified* is not statistically significant for either group.

45. Models that only include presidential fixed effects as controls and that focus exclusively on major deployments never yield statistically significant results for the three measures of Congress's partisan composition.

46. These two-stage selection models were pioneered by Heckman (1979). We use a version of his original model known as Heckman's probit, which allows for both stages to be discrete variables.

47. If multiple opportunities for the same country exist on the same day, the information from each report is collapsed into one entry in this new dataset. We therefore change the coding slightly of *Contemporaneous Opportunities* to include n-1 additional opportunities, where n is the number of opportunities for that country that day.

48. Data are taken from (Gleditsch 2002).

49. Instruments, as they are commonly called, must predict when opportunities exist, but also be unrelated to when military force is used. Empirically, *Per-CapGDP* satisfies both conditions. The variable regularly generates significant effects in the first stage of the model; and in separate analyses, it appears unrelated to U.S. deployment decisions. Nonetheless, we also estimated models using as instruments a nation's total GDP, as well as indicator variables that distinguish states that were former colonial holdings and that indicate whether a state has gone through a transition to or from democracy within the past five years. Such variables have been used to predict civil violence, unrest, and military disputes (for example, see Fearon and Laitin 2003). Though weaker instruments, these models produce estimates for our primary measures of the partisan composition of Congress that are consistent with those reported below.

50. The actual model to be estimated is: [EQ. 1]: Opportunity = f(Congress-Support, WorldDispute, Hegemony, PerCapGDP, Democracy, MajorPower, TroopDeploy, PrevOpps, REGION). [EQ. 2]: Force = f(CongressSupport, Unemployment, CPI, Approval, Election, Hegemony, WorldDispute, Alliances, MajorPower, Democracy, Trade, SovietInvolvement, CapabilityRatio, PrevOpps, ContemOpps, TroopsDeploy, REGION, PRESIDENT). Models that include all of the covariates from equation 2 in equation 1 had trouble converging.

51. Estimates from the first stage, which predicts the number of opportunities to arise in a country on a given day, are presented in table B.3 of Appendix B.

52. Right censoring was an important impetus to the creation of event history models (Box-Steffensmeier and Jones 2004). The models can also cope with left censoring (not knowing when a person entered a study or sample), yet we assume that a country enters our sample on the date the first opportunity after January 1, 1945.

53. The data analyzed in earlier models did identify military responses in early 2001 to opportunities that arose in late 2000.

54. Just as individuals may experience multiple spells of being married and/or employed, so too do states experience multiple spells when opportunities arise that might elicit a U.S. military intervention. The event-history models accommodate the existence of multiple spells.

55. Of course, by constructing our data and statistical analyses in this fashion, we are making important assumptions about state responses to foreign crises. Most important, we assume that the temporally most proximate event to a military venture acts as a trigger, either because a developing foreign crisis surpasses some unobserved tipping point or because the opportunity itself was sufficiently grave to warrant a U.S. military response. One can imagine instances, however, when the president decides to intervene, yet for logistical reasons a period of time passes (allowing more opportunities to arise) until troops enter the field, and on these occasions, the opportunities that immediately preceded a deployment may not have contributed to the president's decision. Unfortunately, efforts to model this alternative process are fraught with problems of their own. For starters, it is impossible to know which among the many opportunities that preceded a deployment convinced the president to use force. Moreover, if one instead opts to tag collections of opportunities, one reintroduces the same problems that we confronted in the logit models—specifically, there are no theoretically informed fixed time bounds for distinguishing opportunities that received a military response. Given these problems, plus the empirical fact that periods between presidential decisions to use force and initiations of conflict tend to be quite short, we opt to identify the temporally most proximate opportunity as the triggering event.

55a. For further discussion on this point, see appendix B.

56. It is true that a series of opportunities in the distant past may be unrelated to the current use of force, but often different types of events cumulate to create an impetus for intervention. For example, although Clinton's intervention in Haiti was in response to the deposing of Jean-Bertrand Aristide, past events such as coups and civil unrest contributed to the discussions surrounding the potential intervention. Additionally, we note that event-history models often are estimated using unbalanced data, as done here. (Rather than every month or year, information about the state of the world is only modeled when opportunities arise). There is one potential downside of structuring the data as we have done: namely, we do not model the length of time between the final opportunity and the actual deployment. Fortunately, these periods are typically quite small, the median interlude lasting just four days.

57. The hazard model to be estimated is specified as follows: Time to Intervention = f(CongressSupport, Unemployment, CPI, Approval, Election, Hegemony, WorldDispute, Alliances, MajorPower, Democracy, Trade, SovietInvolvement, CapabilityRatio, PrevOpps, ContemOpps, TroopsDeploy, REGION, PRESIDENT). We initially specify the functional form of the hazard model as a Weibull distribution based on a plot of the underlying hazard model of the raw data.

58. We collapse multiple opportunities observed for the same country on the same day. Hence, the number of observations in these models in somewhat lower than those for the previous logistic regressions.

59. For *Unified Government,* the effect is 55 percent; for *Percent Party President,* it is 35 percent; and for *President Party Power,* it is 20 percent. Response times have a mean of approximately 700 days, and a median of 500 days.

60. When estimating the logit models on the subsample of states used here, very little changes. The one exception is *Trade,* which is negative and significant for countries with greater than 250 opportunities, and insignificant for the larger

sample. Hence, all other differences between the logit and event history models can be attributed to modeling assumptions and not the selection of states to analyze.

61. For a review of this argument, see (Levy and Vakili 1992).

62. In chapters 6 and 7, we examine the interplay between Congress, the president, the media, and public opinion more explicitly.

63. (Russett and Oneal 2001; Mansfield and Pevehouse 2005).

64. In the first test, p = 0.93. This test only computes the mean number of days since the first opportunity in cases where force is deployed. In the second test, p = 0.89.

CHAPTER 5

1. (Billings-Yun 1988, p. 22).

2. See The Pentagon Paper, Gravel ed., vol. 1, document 26, Memorandum from Arthur Radford for the Joint Chiefs of Staff for the President's Special Committee on Indochina, "Discussions with General Paul Ely," 29 March 1954, http://www.mtholyoke.edu/acad/intrel/pentagon/doc26.htm. Site accessed January 2, 2006.

3. (Duiker 1994, pp. 150–53.).

4. All quotes in Anthony Leviero, "Eisenhower Limits U.S. Participation in Indo-China War," *New York Times*, February 11, 1954, p. 1.

5. Indeed, when Ohio Senator Robert Taft battled Eisenhower for the Republican nomination in the 1952 election, he ran on a strong isolationist platform.

6. (Eisenhower 1963, p. 192).

7. (Billings-Yun 1988, p. 27).

8. James Beston, "Eisenhower Bars War Involvement without Congress," *New York Times*, March 11, 1954, p. 1.

9. Eisenhower, *Public Papers of the President*, March 17, 1954, p. 389.

10. William S. White, "China Issue is a Headache for the G.O.P., Too," *New York Times*, March 28, 1954, p. E3.

11. Dulles's conference with congressional leaders, April 3, 1954. United States Department of State. 1982. *Foreign Relations of the United States, 1952–54,* vol. 13 (Indochina). Washington: U.S. Government Printing Office, p. 1224.

12. U.S. Congress, House Committee on Armed Services. 1971. United States-Vietnam Relations, 1945–67: A Study Prepared by the Department of Defense. Washington: U.S. Government Printing Office, vol. 1, part 2, section B, p. B23–24.

13. U.S. Congress, House Committee on Armed Services. 1971. United States-Vietnam Relations, 1945–67: A Study Prepared by the Department of Defense. Washington: U.S. Government Printing Office, vol 1, part 2, section B, p. B-12.

14. (Eisenhower 1963, p. 347).

15. (Billings-Yun 1988, pp. 149-53).

16. Morris, John D. "Nixon is Revealed as Author of Stir over Indochina," *New York Times*, April 18, 1954, p. 1.

17. (Billings-Yun 1988, p. 133).

18. Ibid., p. 152.

19. (Aronson 1993, p. 56).

20. Ibid., p. 57.

21. Ibid., p. 67. See also (Sobel 2001, p. 102).

22. (Aronson 1993, p. 72).

23. According to this second amendment, "During fiscal year 1985, no funds available to the Central Intelligence Agency, the Department of Defense, or any other agency or entity of the United States involved in intelligence activities may be obligated or expended for the purpose or which would have the effect of supporting, directly or indirectly, military or paramilitary operations in Nicaragua by any nation, group, organization, movement, or individual." 98 Stat. 1935, sec. 8066(a) (1984). Still unsatisfied, in 1986 Congress passed additional legislation that barred U.S. military personnel from operating in Nicaragua. See 100 Stat. 3341-307, sec. 216(a) (1986). Nor were these legislative maneuvers isolated incidents. As Barbara Hinckley notes, between 1982 and 1988 issues regarding Nicaragua constituted almost half of Congress's foreign policy agenda (1994, p. 154).

24. Gerry Studds, "Review of the President's Report on Assistance to Nicaragua's Opposition," House of Representatives, Committee on Foreign Affairs, Subcommittee on Western Hemisphere Affairs, December 5, 1985, p. 27.

25. Michael D. Barnes, "Review of the President's Report on Assistance to Nicaragua's Opposition," House of Representatives, Committee on Foreign Affairs, Subcommittee on Western Hemisphere Affairs, December 5, 1985, p. 1.

26. Jim Leach, *Congressional Record,* July 27, 1983, vol. 129, pt. 14, p. 21201.

27. Edward Walsh, "Reagan Allies in Contra Vote Were Compromise, Fatigue," *Washington Post,* June 27, 1986, p. A1.

28. (Aronson 1993, pp. 198–200).

29. (LeoGrande 1993, p. 41).

30. For a detailed account of Iran-Contra from the special prosecutor, see (Walsh 1998). See also (Draper 1991).

31. Andrew Taylor and Lenore Webb, "Chronology of Hill-Reagan Tug-of-War over U.S. Involvement with the Contras," *Congressional Quarterly Weekly Reporter* 46: 1988, pp. 806–7.

32. See (Hinckley 1994, pp. 160–61).

33. (Haig 1984, p. 127).

34. (Aronson 1993, p. 66). See also (Sobel 2001, pp. 136–37).

35. Gonzalez, *Congressional Record,* January 24, 1985, vol. 131, pt. 1, p. 892.

36. As quoted in (Sobel 2001, p. 133).

37. Ibid., pp. 138–39.

38. John M. Goshko, "Haig Won't Rule Out Anti-Nicaragua Action," *Washington Post,* November 13, 1981, p. A1.

39. Hedrick Smith, "A Larger Force of Latin Rebels Sought by U.S.," *New York Times,* April 17, 1985, p. A1.

40. (Aronson 1993, p. 195).

41. Ibid., p. 83.

42. (Haig 1984, p. 124).

43. (Aronson 1993, p. 275).

44. Reagan, *Public Papers of the President,* p. 899.

45. (Smyrl 1988, p. 102).

46. Reagan, *Public Papers of the President,* pp. 1062–63.

47. (Hall 1991, p. 137).

48. Reagan, *Public Papers of the President,* p. 1078.

49. Ibid., pp. 1078–79.

50. Ibid., p. 1103.

51. (Hall 1991, p. 138).

52. Reagan, *Public Papers of the President,* p. 1188.

53. Ibid., p. 1188.

54. Ibid., p.1238.

55. Ibid., p. 1238.

56. Drew Middleton, "Marines' Tour in Lebanon: Stateside Jitters Mount," *The New York Times,* February 4, 1983, p. A3.

57. *Congressional Record,* vol. 129, part 5, pp. 608–83.

58. (Hall 1991, p. 140).

59. Bernard Gwertzman, "Reagan Calls Bombing Cowardly," *New York Times,* April 19, 1983, p. A1.

60. Ibid., A1.

61. *Congressional Record,* vol. 129, part 12, 16083.

62. William E. Farrell, "U.S. Positioning 2,000 Marines Off Beirut Coast," *New York Times,* September 2, 1983, p. A1.

63. Bernard Gwertzman, "Western Nations Refuse to Widen Role in Lebanon," *New York Times,* September 11, 1983, p. A1.

64. See, for example, SJ Res 159 and HJ Res 348.

65. *Congressional Record,* vol. 128, part 17, 24042.

66. SJ Res 163. *Congressional Record,* vol. 128, part 17, 24055.

67. Steven Weisman, "White House Warns a War Powers Fight Hurts U.S. Interests," *New York Times,* September 17, 1983, p. A1.

68. Ibid.

69. Steven V. Roberts, "Beirut Gives Congress Some Second Thoughts," *New York Times,* December 18, 1983, p. E2.

70. Steven V. Roberts, "Legislators Say Reagan Must Reassess U.S. Role," *New York Times,* October 23, 1983, p. A8.

71. Ibid.

72. Ronald Reagan, "Reagan's Remarks on Attacks," *New York Times,* October 24, 1983, p. A8.

73. (Hall 1991, p. 145).

74. David Rogers, "Congress Warns Reagan to Show Progress on Lebanon or Face Crumbling Support," *Wall Street Journal,* December 14, 1983, p. A2.

75. Lou Cannon, "President Ties Troops' Recall to a 'Collapse,'" *Washington Post,* December 15, 1983, p. A1.

76. Steven V. Roberts, "Beirut Gives Congress Some Second Thoughts," *New York Times,* December 18, 1983, p. E2.

77. David Rogers, "Congress Warns Reagan to Show Progress on Lebanon or Face Crumbling Support," *Wall Street Journal,* December 14, 1983, p. A2.

78. Ibid.

79. "What President Reagan Has Said about the Marines' Role in Lebanon," *New York Times,* February 9, 1984, p. A12.

80. (Jide 2005, p. 37).

80a. For more on this point, see (Kriner 2006).

81. "Excerpts from President Reagan's Speech on Foreign Policy and Congress." *New York Times,* April 7, 1984, p. 6. See also Steven Weisman, "President vs. Congress: Reagan's Speech Brings New Confrontation that Further Embroils His Foreign Policy," *New York Times,* April 17, 1984, p. 1; Bernard Gwertzman, "President Assails Congress over Use of Forces Abroad; Sees Harm in Reluctance," *New York Times,* April 7, 1984, p. 1; Francis Climes, "Reagan Attacks Congress's Role on Many Fronts," *New York Times,* April 4, 1984, p. 1.

82. ABC News/Washington Post poll, September 28 to October 3, 1989; AP poll, September 14 to September 24, 1989; CBS/*New York Times* poll, September 17 to September 20, 1989; Gallup poll, September 7 to September 10, 1989; CBS/*New York Times* poll, September 6 to September 8, 1989.

83. Charles Schumer, *Congressional Record,* October 5, 1989, H6734.

84. "Sensible Restraint on Panama," *New York Times,* October 5, 1989, p. A30; "The Coup that Failed," *Washington Post,* October 5, 1989, p. A30; "Proper Restraint on Panama," *Boston Globe,* October 5, 1989, p. A22.

85. Ernest Hollings, *Congressional Record,* October 16, 1989, S13491.

86. Patricia Schroeder, *Congressional Record,* October 5, 1989, H6734.

87. Robert Wise, *Congressional Record,* October 10, 1989, H6835.

88. Richard Durbin, *Congressional Record,* October 12, 1989, H6987.

89. Butler Derrick, *Congressional Record,* October 5, 1989, H6734.

90. George Mitchell, *Congressional Record,* October 11, 1989, S13020.

91. Jesse Helms, *Congressional Record,* October 5, 1989, S12657.

92. Ibid.

93. Alfonse D'Amato, *Congressional Record,* October 7, 1989, S 12990.

94. John Jacobs Rhodes III, *Congressional Record,* October 12, 1989, H6989.

95. Time/CNN poll, October 9 to October 10, 1989; USA Today poll, October 4, 1989.

96. Gallup poll, October 5 to October 6, 1989.

97. Bernard Weinraub, "White House to Study Handling of Panama Crisis," *New York Times,* October 6, 1989, p. A11.

98. Stephen Engelberg, "Bush Aide and Senator Clash Over Failed Coup in Panama," *New York Times,* October 9, 1989, p. A1.

99. Ibid., A1. For Cohen's general support of the administration's reaction to the coup, see William Cohen, "Noriega: Not Worth American Killing," *Washington Post,* October 17, 1989, p. A27.

100. Michael Gordon, "Bush and Senators Meet on the Coup that Failed," *New York Times,* October 12, 1989, p. A12.

101. Stephen Engelberg, "Bush Aide and Senator Clash Over Failed Coup in Panama," *New York Times,* October 9, 1989, p. A1.

102. Larry Rohter, "Panama and U.S. Strive to Settle on Death Total," *New York Times,* April 1, 1990, p. A12.

103. Bosnia had declared its independence in late February 1992. There was significant fighting before international recognition, but the recognition served to bolster the Serbian nationalists' cause—giving them a rallying point to promote the idea of recovering a "Greater Serbia."

104. (Clinton 2004, p. 510–11). See also (Hendrickson 2002, pp. 72–73).

105. Carroll J. Doherty, "Clinton on Diplomatic Tightrope with New Policy on Bosnia," *Congressional Quarterly Weekly Report* 51 (7), February 13, 1993, p. 322.

106. Trying to end the bloodshed in Bosnia, former U.S. Secretary of State Cyrus Vance and Lord David Owen recommended the division of Bosnia into multiple ethnic enclaves. The plan attracted widespread European support, but American officials, including Clinton, remained skeptical that the plan offered a permanent, workable solution.

107. Elaine Sciolino, "In Congress, Urgent Calls for Action against the Serbs," *New York Times,* April 20, 1993, p. A9. Clifford Krauss,"Many in Congress, Citing Vietnam, Oppose Attacks," *New York Times,* April 28, 1993, p. A10.

108. Carroll J. Doherty, "Democrats Become More Vocal in Urging U.S. to Take Action," *Congressional Quarterly Weekly Report* 51 (17), April 24, 1993, p. 1031.

109. Ibid., p. 1032.

110. Clifford Krauss, "Many in Congress, Citing Vietnam, Oppose Attacks."

111. Anthony Lewis, "The Moment of Truth," *New York Times,* May 7, 1993, p. A31.

111a. As discussed in chapter 2, though, standard party divisions would promptly return when members of Congress would later vote on resolutions concerning the Bosnian war.

112. Gwen Ifill, "Conflict in Balkans; Clinton Considers Bosnia Air Strikes; Sees Allied Accords," *New York Times,* April 23, 1993, p. 1. Or as the president explained to CNN's Larry King, "We have always committed to use our air power to protect your [our?] troops and any other troops. We have not wanted to get the United States involved in the conflict there unless there was a settlement. I have always [said] that we would send appropriate military personnel to be part of United Nations enforcement of the settlement." *Public Papers of the President,* July 20, 1993, p. 1144.

113. Thomas Friedman, "Conflict in the Balkans," *New York Times,* May 7, 1993, p. A10. See also Martin Walker, "The Debate in the U.S.: Clinton Hesitates as a Nation Divided Shies away from War," *The Guardian,* April 29, 1993, p. 13.

114. Stephen Engelberg, "Senator Nunn Sets Tough Conditions to Send U.S. Troops to Bosnia," *New York Times,* September 27, 1993, p. A7.

115. (Hendrickson 1998, p. 257). See also (Fisher 2004, pp. 189–91); and Charles Krauthammer, "Bosnia: The Aborted Debate," *Washington Post,* December 1, 1995, p. A27.

116. For an example of Clinton's consultations with congressional leaders, see Steve Greenhouse, "Washington at Work," *New York Times,* December 25, 1994, p. 12.

117. *Christian Science Monitor,* May 13, 1993, p. 20.

118. *Public Papers of the President,* September 27, 1993, p. 1620–21.

119. Michael Dobbs, "French President Chirac asks Congress to Fund More Peacekeepers in Bosnia," *Washington Post,* June 15, 1995, p. A34. See also Barbara Crossette, "Washington Seeks Delay on Expanding U.N. Force in Bosnia," *New York Times,* June 14, 1995, p. A15.

120. (Fisher 2004, p. 191).

121. Ibid., pp. 189–90.

122. Juan Walte, "NATO Ultimatum," *USA Today,* June 23, 1992, p. 4A. See

also, Johanna Neuman and Bill Nichols, "Clinton Shrugs off Criticism, Remains Firm on Yugoslavia," *USA Today,* July 29, 1992, p. 4A.

123. Robin Wright, "Serbs Put on Notice; Allies Set Deadline for Kosovo Cease-Fire," *Chicago Sun Times,* June 15, 1998, p. 17.

124. David Marcus, "US may push for troops in Kosovo," *Boston Globe,* June 8, 1998, p. A1.

125. Steven Erlanger, "First Bosnia, Now Kosovo," *New York Times,* June 10, 1998, p. A14.

126. Eric Schmitt, "Republicans Criticize Clinton on Kosovo," *New York Times,* October 3, 1998, p. A3.

127. Dana Priest, "Lott Questions Timing on Kosovo," *Washington Post,* October 5, 1998, p. A14.

128. R. Jeffrey Smith, "Kosovo Talks Produce Little Progress," *Washington Post,* October 6, 1998, p. A1.

129. By some accounts, this offensive was actually designed in October, just after Serbia had implemented the Holbrooke agreement. See: R. Jeffrey Smith and William Drozdiak, "Serbs' offensive was meticulously planned," *Washington Post,* April 11, 1999, p. A1.

130. Craig R. Whitney, "Allies Expecting 'Many More Weeks' of Air Campaign," *New York Times,* April 11, 1999.

131. See Barton Gellman, "The Path to Crisis," *Washington Post,* April 18, 1999, p. A1.

132. Stephen Barr, "Clinton's Balkan Deployment Policy Draws GOP Fire," *Washington Post,* February 15, 1999, p. A26.

133. Elizabeth Becker, "US Aides Pushing Plan to Use GI's in a Kosovo Force," *New York Times,* January 30, 1999, p. A1.

134. Ann Scales, "For Clinton, Prospect of 1st Deaths in Combat," *Boston Globe,* March 23, 1999, p. A1.

135. HarrisInteractive, "Kosovo: Public Split Right Down the Middle on Bombing Serbs and Use of U.S. and NATO Troops," http://www.harrisinteractive.com/harris_poll/index.asp?PID=59. Site accessed May 21, 2005. The poll found that among all respondents (informed and uninformed), the split on both questions was 46 percent in favor, 44 percent opposed.

136. Bob Dole, *Hearing of the House International Relations Committee: Kosovo and the Possible Deployment of US Troops,* Federal News Service, March 10, 1999. Henry Kissinger and Jeane Kirkpatrick, relying on much the same logic to argue for the resolution, also testified at the committee hearings.

137. David L. Marcus, "US Offers Planes for NATO Strikes," *Washington Post,* October 7, 1998, p. A2.

138. (Berinsky 2005, p. 5)

CHAPTER 6

1. Among the case studies presented in chapter 5, Lebanon is omitted from this list. For recall, during the lead-up to Reagan's deployment to Lebanon, Congress

remained conspicuously silent. It was not until missteps were taken and casualties were suffered that members of Congress took to the airwaves.

1a. (Fowler forthcoming; Fowler and Law 2005).

2. (Mayhew 2000, p. xi).

3. As discussed in chapter 1, a substantial body of research demonstrates that average citizens know considerably less about foreign policy than domestic policy. See, for example, (Baum 2004a; Graber 1984; Sobel 1989).

4. (Lippmann 1992, p. 59).

5. See NY Times Editorial, "The Times and Iraq," May 26, 2004, p. 10; or Daniel Okrent, "Weapons of Mass Destruction? Or Mass Distraction?" May 30, 2004, p. 2.

6. See http://poynter.org/forum/?id=misc#raines: URL accessed June 14, 2004.

7. Judith Miller and Michael Gordon, "White House Lists Iraq Steps to Build Banned Weapons," New York Times, September 13, 2002, p. 13. The aluminum tubes story broke with no mention of the debate within the intelligence community in Michael Gordon and Judith Miller, "U.S. Says Hussein Intensifies Quest For A-Bomb Parts," New York Times, September 8, 2002, p. 1.

8. To justify their silence, congressional Democrats have since cited fears of leaking classified information and a senior CIA official admitted cautioning members in closed session not to breach confidentiality lest the Iraqis seize on the alternative theory as an excuse to justify the tubes' purchase and conceal their true aims.

9. David Barstow, William J. Broad, and Jeff Gerth, "How the White House Embraced Disputed Arms Intelligence," New York Times, October 3, 2004, p. 1.

10. See, for example, (Sigal 1973; Tuchman 1978).

11. There are, of course, many other research traditions within political communications that make this same point. Scholars who have studied informational subsidies (Gandy 1982), public diplomacy (Manheim 1994; Davison 1974), and news routines (Hallin 1992; Dennis and Ismach 1981; Gans 1979) also argue that journalists regularly turn to political elites for guidance on foreign policy coverage. Other scholars, who take a considerably more impoverished view of the media, suggest that political elites strategically employ journalists to advance their own policy agendas, yielding a body of coverage that does more to suit the interests of those in power than to advance truth in reporting (Herman and Chomsky 1988). For two reasons, though, we highlight the indexing hypothesis in this chapter. First, more than anyone else, scholars who have worked on the indexing hypothesis have focused singularly on the domestic politics surrounding use-of-force decisions. And second, the indexing hypothesis provides the clearest analytic framework for thinking about how Congress, in particular, checks the arguments made by White House officials of behalf on exercising military force abroad.

12. (Mermin 1999, p. 7).

13. (Hallin 1986).

14. (Arnold 2004).

15. Ibid., p. 122

16. (Zaller 1994a, 1994b; Zaller and Chiu 1996).

17. For more recent examples of this research, see (Jacobs and Shapiro 2000). Of course, the causal arrow need not point in one direction. For examples of

studies that demonstrate manners in which public opinion shapes foreign policy decision making, see (Foyle 1999; Page and Shapiro 1992).

18. (Zaller 1994b, p. 250). In the next chapter, which focuses on Congress's mediated influence on public opinion, we revisit these issues.

19. For exceptions, see (Livingston and Eachus 1996), who argue that the indexing hypothesis is time bound, an artifact of cold-war consensus; but see (Livingston and Bennett 2003). Others find that the views of foreign sources and journalists themselves often find airtime in media coverage of the military deployments (Althaus 2003); but see (Hutcheson et al. 2004).

20. (Entman 2004). See also (Entman and Page 1994).

21. (Althaus et al. 1996).

22. The normative concerns that motivate this literature trace back to journalistic independence and the prerequisites of a free and open society. For political communication scholars, the indexing hypothesis is deeply troubling because it suggests that the press reflects, rather than challenges, ongoing discussions about the exercise of military power and the definition of the national interest. Rather than forcing political elites to answer hard questions, journalists permit them to say as much or as little as they prefer about topics of their choosing. The public may witness journalists grilling members of the administration; but for the most part, these journalists press arguments and issue challenges that come straight from the opposition ranks of Congress. Rather than formulating an independent judgment about the efficacy of a planned military venture, the press often cribs directly from the speeches of elected officials within the federal government. And when they do, the press hardly lives up to its billings as a "fourth branch of government," an outside and independent check on government powers (Carter 1959). To be sure, by parroting existing debates within Washington, the press serves an important public service—it is just that its contribution is quite circumscribed. The press conveys elected officials' arguments and evidence, but rarely questions either. Technically speaking, journalists may be free and independent. But as guardians of truth and champions of responsible government, they are more lapdogs than watchdogs.

23. (Mermin 1999, p. 151).

24. But see (Althaus et al. 1996), which presents evidence that the media occasionally distort aspects of congressional debate over the use of force.

25. (Brody 1991; Brody and Shapiro 1989; Brody 1994). See also (Larson 1996).

26. (Brody 1991, pp. 66–67).

27. (Berinsky 2005, pp. 1–2). See also (Russett 1990; Oneal and Bryan 1995; Baker and Oneal 2001; Zaller 1994a, 1994b; Zaller and Chiu 1996).

28. For a large-N empirical investigation supporting this claim as well as a review of this debate in the context of the international relations literature, see (Baker and Oneal 2001).

29. The exact functional form of this relationship is less clear. There is no reason to expect that the views expressed by each member of Congress will have an equivalent impact on media coverage of a planned use of force. If, for instance, the opinions of individual members of the majority party are given more weight

than the views of individual members of the minority party, then dramatic changes in media coverage may occur when switching from unified to divided government. In his survey of local newspaper coverage of Congress, Douglas Arnold finds some evidence that this may be the case, though the effects generally are rather small (2004, pp. 29–63). See also (Mayhew 2000).

30. Outside of the literature on indexing, Doug Arnold (2004) has surveyed an expansive sample of local media coverage of Congress. His data, however, are limited to local newspapers. In addition, Arnold focuses on how the media portray individual members of Congress, and not how (or whether) journalists take their cues from these members when they craft their coverage of proposed policies generally, and the use of military force in particular.

31. (Mermin 1999; Graber 1989). But see (Hallin and Gitlin 1994).

32. (Bennett 1990, p. 106).

33. (Gilliam and Iyengar 2000, p. 560).

34. With the one exception of online news sources, all of these figures have dropped markedly in the last decade. In 1993, 77 percent of Americans watched local news, 60 percent nightly network news, and 52 percent network television magazines; while 58 percent read a newspaper, 47 percent listened to the radio, and 2 percent went online. The online figure is from 1996; data for cable television news were not included in survey until 2002.

35. *Weekly Compilation of Presidential Documents,* 2002, pp. 1717–18.

36. Ibid., p. 1533.

37. Ibid., S10314.

38. Ibid., S10328.

39. Ibid., S10238.

40. Ibid., S10278-9.

41. PL 107-243.

42. By market rank, these include: New York; Los Angeles; Chicago; Philadelphia; San Francisco; Boston (including Manchester); Dallas; Washington, D.C.; Atlanta; Detroit; Houston; Seattle; Tampa; Minneapolis; Cleveland; Phoenix; Miami; Denver; Sacramento; Orlando; Pittsburgh; St. Louis; Portland (Oregon); Baltimore; Indianapolis; San Diego; Hartford; Charlotte; Raleigh-Durham; Nashville; Milwaukee; Cincinnati; Kansas City; Columbus; Greenville; Salt Lake City; San Antonio; Grand Rapids; West Palm Beach; Birmingham; Norfolk; New Orleans; Memphis; Buffalo; Oklahoma City; Greensboro; Harrisburg; Providence; Albuquerque; and Louisville.

43. The Wisconsin NewsLab at the University of Wisconsin captured these news stories. For a description of the technology Newslab uses for doing so, see appendix 2 of (Franklin et al. 2004).

44. This is perhaps the weakest possible test of the indexing hypothesis, as presidents and members of Congress surely can influence the content and scope of media coverage without actually appearing in the news.

45. Throughout this chapter, we treat the story as the unit of observation. When weighting stories by their length, measured in either time (for television news) or word-length (for print news), comparable findings emerge.

46. For more on this concept, see (Zaller 1992).

47. Arguments for the use of force include: the United Nations is inadequate to

address the threat posed by Iraq; Iraq has defied the United Nations and/or the world; Iraq has or is developing weapons of mass destruction; Iraq has links to terrorist groups; Iraq violates the human rights of its citizens; Iraq must be disarmed; the Bush administration has made a convincing case to attack Iraq; Iraq is a threat to American lives; Iraq is a threat to the region; Iraq is a threat to its own people; Iraq is a threat, no specific threat mentioned. Arguments in opposition to the use of force include: Iraq has not defied the world; Iraq has no or is not developing weapons of mass destruction; Iraq has no links to terrorist groups; Iraq does not violate human rights of its citizens; Iraq has disarmed; the Bush administration has not made a convincing case to attack Iraq; a military venture is likely to involve many casualties and high financial costs; Iraq is not a threat to American lives; Iraq is not a threat to the region; Iraq is not a threat to its own people; and Iraq is not a threat, no specific threat mentioned. The majority of arguments fell into the one of preceding categories. We coded the few remaining arguments as either "other positive" or "other negative."

48. This, of course, is a necessary but not a sufficient condition for the indexing hypothesis to hold. If the media present a very different set of arguments than those that appear within Congress, then the indexing hypothesis is obviously wrong. That they present similar arguments, however, does not establish, once and for all, the veracity of the indexing hypothesis. If, for instance, the terms of the debate are shaped entirely outside of the media and Congress—say, within the White House—then the observed relationship between arguments emanating from congressional speeches and television and print stories is spurious.

49. As one might expect, the president and members of his administration presented, on average, 1.97 arguments for the use of force and 0.03 arguments against.

50. Individually, Democrats tended to offer arguments either for or against the use of force. Among those Democrats who offered arguments against the use of force, 59 percent did not offer any countervailing argument on behalf of using force; and among those Democrats who offered arguments for using force, 21 percent did not offer any argument against using force.

51. The arguments that members of Congress presented in the media, for the most, track the arguments made on the floors on the House and Senate.

52. Neither party gave a disproportionate number of speeches on Iraq during this period. Indeed, on a daily basis, Democrats and Republicans contributed roughly equally to the *Congressional Record* page counts.

53. The scales across the media outlets are not comparable. For the local television news, the y-axis denotes the sum of arguments that appear across the four networks in 50 media markets; for national news, it denotes the sum of arguments that appear each evening in three networks; and for the *Times,* it denotes the sum of arguments that appear in the paper each day.

54. The *Times* evidence also supports our contention that, even in the midst of midterm elections, the Iraq issue remained highly salient, contrary to the perception given by local and national television news coverage.

55. We begin with a very simple model that takes the following form: Argument = f(Authorization, PostAuthorization, LocalNews, NationalNews), where the unit of observation is the story, and *Argument* intermittently denotes the total number of arguments on the use of force presented in a news story, including both

the number of arguments for the use of force and the number of arguments against. *Authorization* and *PostAuthorization* identify the periods October 2–16 and October 17–30, respectively; the preauthorization period, as such, is the reference category. *LocalNews* and *NationalNews* identify the type of media outlet presenting the news story; the *New York Times,* in this instance, represents the reference category. The indexing hypothesis does not generate clear predictions about the size or direction of the effects associated with *LocalNews* or *National-News.* Given what we know about Congress's activities, however, we should expect the effect of *Authorization* to be positive, and of *PostAuthorization* to be negative. We further note the possibility that observations in this model are not independent of one another. The trouble, though, comes in discerning the structure of the dependence—that is, whether observations are clustered by media market, by ownership group, by time of airing, or by some combination of the three. We note, though, that corrections for correlations across observations should affect only the standard errors; and as these are quite small relative to the estimated coefficients, we do not expect that models that explicitly account for lack of observational independence will change the substantive conclusions drawn.

55a. Because our theoretical priors about the relationship between Congress and the media are more diffuse, all statistical tests in this chapter are two-tailed.

56. None of the results presented depend on this decision. We have estimated all of the models in this chapter using poissons and negative binomials (treating the dependent variable as an event count) and ordered probits (treating the dependent variable as a measure of different thresholds of argumentation) and the estimated impacts are virtually identical to those presented.

57. When estimating models that include the number of *Congressional Record* pages devoted to Iraq, rather than separate indicator variables for Congress's schedule, significant and positive effects are regularly observed. When adding a quadratic, impacts again appear significant, though of different signs, suggesting a nonlinear relationship between congressional and media activity.

58. The models in table 6.3 assume that congressional activity influences the news coverage of all media outlets equivalently—the only allowance for media sources is an indicator variable that permits the constant term to shift upwards or downwards. On reflection, however, there is good reason to believe that some outlets will be more sensitive to changes in congressional activity than others, if only because different outlets have access to different levels of independent information about foreign policy. To enhance flexibility, we reestimate the previous regressions, this time interacting each media with every period of congressional activity, thereby allowing us to gauge the variable production of arguments within local television, national television, and *Times* stories over time. Specifically, we estimate the following model: Argument = f(LocalNews*PreAuthorization, Local-News*Authorization, LocalNews*PostAuthorization, NatlNews*PreAuthorization, NatlNews*Authorization, NatlNews*PostAuthorization, Times*Authorization, Times*PostAuthorization). The reference category is the number of arguments in *Times* stories issued before Congress formally considered the authorization. And as before, models were estimated using least squares. Again, local news follows the expected trajectory: slightly fewer arguments before the authorization, a moderate bump up during debate, and then a massive decline. A Wald test that

$\beta_1 = \beta_2 = \beta_3$ is rejected at $p < 0.01$, indicating that the observed shifts across the period under consideration are not due to chance alone. Evidence of indexing is weaker in national news reporting trends. While the coefficients for national news retain the expected signs, they never approach standard thresholds for statistical significance. Moreover, we can never reject the hypothesis that $\beta_4 = \beta_5 = \beta_6$, indicating that a steady flow of arguments (total, for, and against) were aired in the national news, even though Congress's involvement in the issue varied dramatically. The number of arguments published in *Times* stories on Iraq did appear to increase during the authorization debate. Curiously, though, the effect is insignificant in models of the number of arguments against the use of force, perhaps because the newspaper had already taken a relatively critical stance against the Iraq War. Wald tests regularly reject the null hypothesis that the production of arguments across the three periods is constant, albeit not at the levels of significance observed for local news.

59. Specifically, we estimate the following model: Argument = f(Authorization, PostAuthorization, Fox, NBC, ABC, Saturday, Sunday, MARKETDEMO-GRAPHICS), where *Fox, NBC,* and *ABC* are indicator variables for the affiliate that aired the story (CBS being the reference category); *Saturday* and *Sunday* identify the day that the story aired (weekdays being the reference category); and *MARKETDEMOGRAPHICS* is an assembly of variables that characterize the population that resides within each media market. Models that include fixed effects for the 50 media markets where local stories aired generated virtually identical results. Because the national news and the *Times* distribute their stories nationwide, equivalent models obviously cannot be estimated for these media outlets.

60. Ordered probit models that assess whether the overall slant of coverage within a story tends negative, neutral, or positive toward Bush generate comparable results.

61. (Mayhew 2000).

CHAPTER 7

1. For reviews, see (Kinder 1998; Sniderman 1993).

2. (Converse 1964).

3. (Green, Palmquist, and Schickler 2003).

4. (Fiorina 1981).

5. (Mendelberg 2001).

6. (Popkin 1991; Sniderman, Brody, and Tetlock 1991; Hurwitz and Peffley 1987).

7. (Almond 1950; Zaller 1992; Lippmann 1992).

8. Although this position has become known as the "Almond-Lippmann thesis," many others have pointed to the tendency of the American public to be fickle concerning foreign policy. See (Kennan 1951; Morganthau 1985).

9. It is true that a number of studies now suggest that public opinion regarding foreign policy is not as fickle or unstable as suggested by the Almond-Lippmann thesis. Yet, even advocates of this new "revisionist" position concede that the public still lacks basic knowledge and experience of foreign affairs, which is im-

portant for our argument. Indeed, Holsti (1992, p. 447) outlines this as a central puzzle in foreign affairs public opinion research. See also (Jentleson 1992; Peffley and Hurwitz 1992; Page and Shapiro 1988).

10. See, for example (Druckman 2001a, 2001b; Druckman and Nelson 2003).

11. (Capella and Jamieson 1997; Iyengar 1991; Cohen 1963; Baum 2003; Mutz and Martin 2001).

12. (Iyengar and Kinder 1987, p. 2).

13. Balanced news, however, may affect public opinion in other ways, such as by priming respondents about national priorities and establishing criteria for how to think about them.

14. (Zaller 1992, 1996).

15. (Kinder 1998, p. 178).

16. (Goldstein and Ridout 2004).

17. The October 10, 2002 report was entitled "Americans Thinking about Iraq, But Focused on the Economy; Midterm Election Preview." The October 30 survey was entitled, "Support for Potential Military Action Slips to 55%; Party Images Unchanged with a Week to Go." Both reports, and the data on which they are based, are available at: http://people-press.org/dataarchive/#2002.

18. Approximately two-thirds of the observations—roughly 1,000 of 1,500 adults—in the two Pew surveys resided in one of the 50 largest media markets. The analyses conducted below are restricted to this subsample.

19. (Zaller 1992, p. 1).

20. Little hinges on the decision to characterize local news coverage by the proportion of negative arguments. We also calculated the total number of anti-use-of-force arguments that were presented in the local news of each media market, as well as the average number of arguments against the use of force that each local news story on Iraq presented. For the most part, findings from tests that used these alternative specifications compared favorably to those presented below.

21. Specifically, we estimate the following model: Support = f(News), where *Support* denotes a respondent's willingness to back military action and *News* identifies the proportion of arguments against the use of force that were aired on all four local news affiliates in the respondent's media market during the prior three weeks. For the early October survey, *News* includes stories from September 17 to October 5. Using a slightly later end date does not affect the findings at all. We estimate the model using least squares; to account for the fact that observations are not independent within media markets, we allow for clustering of the standard errors within media markets.

21a. Because our theoretical priors about the relationship between the media and public opinion are more diffuse, all statistical tests in this chapter are two-tailed.

22. Specifically, we estimate the following model: Support = f(News, IDEOLOGY, Educ, Age, Male, Parent), where *IDEOLOGY* identifies conservative Republicans, moderate Republicans, moderate Democrats, and liberal Democrats, with independents and third parties as the reference category; and *Educ, Age, Male,* and *Parent* identify each respondent's education level, age (measured in tens), gender, and parental status, respectively. In models not reported, we also included quadratic terms for education and age, as well as splines for different intervals. We did not find any evidence of nonlinear effects. Again, the model is estimated using least squares, and standard errors allow for clustering on media markets.

23. We thank Ken Goldstein and Travis Ridout for compiling and sharing these data.

24. The model, as estimated, is Support = f(News, IDEOLOGY, Educ, Age, Male, Parent, PctDem, PctMin, PctBornUS, PctColl, Pop, South, CapInc), where *PctDem* identifies the percentage of registered voters who voted for Gore in the 2000 presidential election; *PctMin* and *PctBornUS* identify the percentage of residents who are non-white and the percentage of residents who were born in the United States; *PctColl, Pop, South,* and *CapInc* identify the percentage of residents who had graduated from college, the population (measured in millions), an indicator variable for residents living in the South, and the average per capita income (measured in ten thousands). Demographic characteristics are measured at the level of counties, which are subsections of media markets. When aggregating up to the media markets, most estimates associated with *News* remain unchanged; in a couple of instances, the point estimates fall just below standard thresholds for statistical significance.

In this model, data are collected at different levels of aggregation (individual, county, media market), each of which is nested within its successor. For at least three reasons, however, it does not make sense to estimate a hierarchical model in lieu of least squares, as is occasionally done under these circumstances. First, hierarchical models are typically used in instances where large numbers of subjects (e.g., students) are divided into a smaller number of well-defined and self-contained settings (classrooms or schools). Here, the number of settings (media markets) is more than double the average number of subjects (survey respondents) within them; and the boundaries of media markets are both porous and ill-defined. Second, these hierarchical models typically assume that both individuals within settings and the settings themselves are randomly selected. In our case, individuals are randomly drawn, but the settings (media markets) are not. Finally, we are less interested in the explicit macro- and micro-level relationships between variables measured at the individual, county, or media market level.

25. When weighting each observation by the population of the media market, the main results for the early October survey remain unchanged. The only discernible differences concern *African American* (which is no longer statistically significant) and *Population* and *South* (which are).

26. For the main effect of *News*, it again does not matter whether or not we weight observations by media market size. Some of the background controls, however, are sensitive to this modeling specification. In particular, when weights are used *Hispanic, Pct College Graduate,* and *South* become statistically significant, while *Liberal Democrat, African American, Male, Parent, Pct Vote Democratic in 2000,* and *Per Capita Income* no longer are.

27. It bears mentioning that the *News* variable for the late October survey analysis aggregates coverage over the entire period of observation, that is, from September 17 to October 31. The selection of the end-date proved immaterial; virtually identical results are observed when one considers the proportion of negative arguments that aired in local news through October 31, 25, or 20. The start-date, however, matters greatly. If one considers only the local news that aired during the three weeks before the survey, as done for the early October survey, the estimated effects for *News* disappear entirely. Recall, though, that during this period, the volume of local news plummeted (see figure 6.2). Local newscasts

occasionally gave airtime to a member of Congress interested in explaining her authorization vote to her constituents, just as they occasionally noted the administration's ongoing planning for war. Judging from the decline of coverage, however, local arguments about whether the president ought to intervene, for all intents and purposes, were resolved the moment that the president signed the authorization vote. With the virtual evaporation of elite and media discussion of the issue came the decline in public attention to the prospect of war against Iraq. Within the survey, 64 percent of respondents in the early survey claimed to follow the debate closely, whereas just 54 percent claimed to do so in the latter survey. It is not surprising, therefore, that the coverage that aired in late September and early October—when debates within the media and Washington were vibrant and the public was attuned—appeared most informative and influential.

28. Katherine Seelye, "How to Sell a Candidate to a Porsche-Driving, Leno-Loving Nascar Fan," *New York Times*, December 6, 2004, p. 18.

29. We also estimated the effect of *News* on the opinions of respondents who claimed to pay more and less attention to the debate over Iraq. In the early October survey, the results for less attentive respondents are slightly larger than those observed for more attentive respondents. The effects, however, are not statistically significantly different from either zero or from each other. In the late October survey, however, the point estimates of *News* for less attentive respondents are fully three times as large as those observed for more attentive respondents. Moving from the minimum to the maximum sample values for *News* corresponds with a 22-percentage-point drop in the probability that less attentive respondents support the use of force; an equivalent move for more attentive respondents translates into just an 8-percentage-point decline. We admit that it is somewhat odd that the differences between more and less attentive respondents would appear most pronounced once media coverage of a prospective war with Iraq died down. Still, one substantive interpretation, admittedly post hoc, does come to mind: namely, the question used to distinguish more and less attentive respondents worked in different ways for the two surveys. In the early October survey, while public debate roiled, the question may have isolated those people who followed the specific news on Iraq; it makes sense, therefore, that they appeared most affected by the news that aired on local television. But by late October, almost everyone in the country had been exposed to the issue. Once public debate quieted, and once people's views settled, the attention question did more to distinguish more and less politically sophisticated respondents than it did to distinguish respondents who were more or less likely to follow this particular issue. As they watch more local television news, and they are more easily persuaded by new information, less politically sophisticated respondents are more likely to be affected by the kinds of information that *News* captures.

30. Due to the structure of the dependent variable, we estimated these regressions as ordered probits.

31. See, for example, (Zaller 1992; Brody 1991). In an exhaustive analysis of "legislative speech," Kevin Quinn and his colleagues show that public views on "the most important problems" facing the United States tend to track congressional discourse in matters involving international affairs, the use of force, and intelligence. As they note, "its seems very likely that the public calls for attention to defense/international issues *after* elites are already paying attention to them" (Quinn et al. 2006, p. 24, emphasis in original). Interestingly, though, the authors

do not find any evidence that congressional speech on such domestic policies as social security, employment, taxes, or employment precede public opinion. Analyzing trends in public support for the president during World War I, Adam Berinsky also finds that "patterns of elite discourse determine the nature of opinion toward war"—and not, presumably, the other way around (2005, p. 1).

32. See, for example, (Iyengar and Kinder 1987).

33. We thank Sunshine Hillygus, Todd Shields, and the Diana D. Blair Center of Southern Politics and Society at the University of Arkansas for including these questions in their survey and making the data available for analysis.

34. Random assignment appears to have worked. When considering a wide range of family background characteristics, differences between populations assigned to different question types are not observed.

35. A chi-square test of differences between responses in columns 2 and 3 is statistically significant at p < 0.05, two-tailed tests.

36. Possible agreement (support) scores range from 0 to 4, where 0 indicates complete disagreement (opposition) and 4 indicates complete agreement (support). Here we report average levels of agreement and support.

37. A t-test for difference in means in columns 2 and 3 is statistically significant at p < 0.01, two-tailed test.

38. We also examined the results for groups defined by their ethnicity, educational attainment, age, gender, and parental status. Again, comparable differences were observed across the three experimental conditions. It is true that for some groups, congressional opposition (or support) appeared to matter more than congressional support (or opposition). Congressional opposition registered little impact on the willingness of parents and younger respondents to believe the president's claims about Eritrea and on the willingness of parents to back the use of military force. Meanwhile, congressional affirmation of the president did not enhance the levels of belief among Hispanics or older residents nor did it buoy support for military action among Hispanics, older residents, or men. Among all these groups, though, where congressional opposition did not appear to matter, congressional support did, and vice versa. No population completely disregards congressional claims. Though different information composites elicit different levels of belief and support, they almost always follow Congress's decision to back or oppose the president.

39. Question reads: "Some people believe the United States should solve international problems by using diplomacy and economic sanctions and only use military force when absolutely necessary. Other people believe diplomacy and sanctions often fail and the U.S. must be ready to use military force. Still others have opinions somewhere in between. Where would you place yourself on the scale below?"

40. Question reads: "People have different views on the best way to solve problems, such as terrorism and the environment, that are of a more international nature. Some people think it is better for the U.S. to work with other countries through international institutions. Other people think that international institutions are slow and bureaucratic, so the U.S. should be prepared to solve such problems on our own. Still others have opinions somewhere in between these two. Where would you place yourself on the scale below?"

41. Question reads: "Taking everything into account, do you agree or disagree that the war in Iraq has been worth the cost?"

42. The one exception to this pattern concerns those respondents who believe that "international institutions are slow and bureaucratic, so the U.S. should be prepared to solve [foreign policy] problems on our own." While congressional opposition to the president does depress these respondents' propensity to believe the president and support the use of force, congressional confirmation of presidential claims has no discernible effect on respondents' views. This, perhaps, should come as no surprise. Just as these individuals see no need to secure the endorsement of international institutions before exercising force abroad, they see little added value in checking that Congress confirms presidential claims and, in turn, backs the use of force.

43. We note one technical matter. When estimating the relationships between different variables, we follow the conventional practice of public opinion scholars and drop the survey weights that are used to adjust for nonresponse. Up until now, this decision has proved innocuous. Virtually identical regression results are observed whether or not we weight the data. In this instance, however, the weights seem to matter. When using the weights, the coefficients for congressional opposition are roughly twice the magnitude of those associated with congressional support—consistent with the summary statistics provided in previous tables. Moreover, the estimate for congressional support in column 3 is barely statistically significant, and it crosses standard thresholds in column 4. The evidence that congressional opposition hurts the president more than congressional support helps him appears contingent on one's views about whether weights should be used in standard regressions.

44. See, for example, (Berinsky and Kinder 2004; Berinsky 2005). In our own research (Howell and Kriner 2007), we find evidence that congressional influence over public opinion depends on the partisan orientation of the survey respondent and the member of Congress who either supports or opposes the presidential use of force. We also find evidence that when the president contemplates the exercise of military force in response to a terrorist threat, the views of members of Congress weigh more heavily in the minds of average citizens than do either the views of international organizations or interests groups. Interestingly, though, when it comes to humanitarian interventions, the views of members of the United Nations tend to hold slightly more sway than do those of members of Congress.

45. Moreover, recent work suggests that presidents' fear of Congress's public reaction to military operations as they unfold is well placed. Consistent with the literature on credible signals and the media (Baum 2002; Baum and Groeling 2005), Kriner (2006) finds that popular calls for deescalation or withdrawal of American forces abroad reported in the mass media decrease the expected duration of a military deployment, while support for staying the course among the president's partisan opponents yields valuable political cover and increases the expected duration of a foreign venture.

46. (Brody 1991, 1994; Brody and Shapiro 1989; Russett 1990; Oneal and Bryan 1995; Baker and Oneal 2001; Zaller 1994a, 1994b; Zaller and Chiu 1996).

47. See, for example, (Baum 2004b; Holsti 1996; Sobel 2001).

48. Fergal Keane, "President Bush Will Have to Shock the American People into War," *The Independent.* September 7, 2002, p. 18.

49. Elisabeth Bumiller, "War Public Relations Machine Is Put on Full Throttle," *New York Times,* February 9, 2003, p. 17.

50. Elisabeth Bumiller, "Traces of Terror: The Strategy; Bush Aids Set Strategy to Sell Policy on Iraq," *New York Times,* September 7, 2002, p. A1. Recall that Bush spent much of August 2002 at his ranch in Crawford, Texas, and during this period he said little about the looming threat in Iraq. According to White House Chief of Staff Andrew Card, who would orchestrate the public campaign on Iraq, this tactic was deliberate. "From a marketing point of view, you don't introduce new products in August."

51. See, for example, Judy Keen and William M. Welch, "Bush Takes Control of Debate on Iraq Attack," *USA Today,* September 5, 2002, p. 7A; Karen DeYoung, "U.S. Escalates Iraq Rhetoric," *Washington Post,* January 22, 2003, p. A1; Janice Tibbetts, "Bush Says He's Fighting for Peace: President Says War Can Turn Iraq into Beacon of Hope," *Ottawa Respondent,* February 27, 2003, p. A1; Marc Sandalow, "Iraq War Hangs over Bush Speech," *The San Francisco Chronicle,* January 28, 2003, p. A5.

52. These figures come from ABC News/*Washington Post* polls. Fox News reports slightly higher figures in August 2002. All polls available at http://people-press .org/otherpolls/. See also Richard Morin and Claudia Deane, "Poll: Americans Cautiously Favor War in Iraq: Public Not Prepared for Large Number of U.S. Casualties," *Washington Post,* August 13, 2002, p. A10.

53. Quotes from Bush and Doherty in David Westphal, "Public Opinion Pivotal in Iraq Policy; While Bush Says it Doesn't Matter, It's Already Influenced U.S. Actions and Will Continue Doing So," *Sacramento Bee,* March 12, 2003, p. A12.

54. Todd S. Purdum, "The Nation: Focus Groups? To Bush, The Crowd Was a Blur," *New York Times,* February 12, 2003, p. 5.

55. In the spring of 2005, the *Times of London* released a British memo indicating that the Bush Administration had intended to launch a military strike against Iraq as early as the summer of 2002. Though Bush would later dispute the authenticity of the memo, most political observers concede that his administration wanted to exercise force long before March 2003. According to Todd Purdum, "There has been ample evidence for many months, and even years, that top Bush administration figures saw war as inevitable by the summer of 2002. In the March 31, 2003, issue of *The New Yorker* magazine, with the invasion just under way, Richard Haass, then the U.S. State Department's director of policy planning, said that in early July 2002 he had talked to Condoleezza Rice, then the U.S. national security adviser, about invading Iraq "and she said, essentially, that that decision's been made." "Shedding Light on U.S. Thinking: British Memos in '02 on Iraq Cause a Stir," *New York Times,* June 15, 2005, p. 7.

56. See Bruce Schulman, "A Matter of Debate: Building National Resolve by Talking about It," *New York Times,* September 15, 2002, section 4, p. 5.

57. See chapter 3.

CHAPTER 8

1. (Rossiter 1956, p. 24).
2. (Schultz 1998; Smith 1998; Fearon 1994; Smith and Guisinger 2002).
3. Had we, we might have examined how congressional opposition to the Iraq

War—coupled with widespread opposition voiced by European allies—delayed the war's initiation and encouraged members of the Iraqi insurgency to resist the American occupation months after the war had ended.

4. For recent work on this topic, see (Fowler forthcoming).

5. See, for example, (Burke 1992, 2000; Hess 2002; Kumar and Sullivan 2003; Arnold 1998; Campbell 1986; Weko 1995; Walcott and Hult 1995; Pfiffner 1999).

6. See (Drezner 1999; Baldwin 1985; Pape 1997; Martin 1992).

7. For some preliminary efforts to address this concern, see (Howell and Kriner 2007).

8. This section borrows from (Howell and Kriner 2006).

9. In many policy arenas, presidents find the authority they need to act unilaterally in some vague statute or broad delegation of power. And when doing so, it is difficult to make the case that the president is merely fulfilling the expressed wishes of Congress. In this instance, it is worth noting that Congress refused to formally declare war against Afghanistan or Iraq. Rather, it passed authorizations in the fall of 2001 and of 2002 that gave the president broad discretion to use the military as he deemed appropriate in the nation's campaign against terrorism.

10. "Under Challenge," *Economist,* January 14, 2006, p. 38.

11. David Moberg, "An Imperial President," *In These Times,* February 2006, p. 4.

12. See, for example, (Fisher 2006).

13. "A Stumble a Day," *New York Times,* March 15, 2006, p. 26.

14. Tom Raum, "Both Sides Critical of Bush Pick," *Washington Post,* May 9, 2006, http://www.washingtonpost.com/wp-dyn/content/article/2006/05/09/AR 2006050900383.html. Site accessed May 30, 2006.

15. Robin Toner, "The Struggle for Iraq: Congress; House Rejects Timetable for Withdrawal from Iraq," *New York Times,* June 17, 2006, p. A1.

16. Kate Zernike, "Senate Rejects Calls to Begin Iraq Pullback," *New York Times,* June 23, 2006, p. A1.

17. Farhan Bokhari and Stephen Fidler, "Release of Pakistani Scientist Seen as Closing Khan Inquiry," *Financial Times,* May 3, 2006, p. 11.

18. Howard LaFranchi, "US Diplomacy Becomes More . . . Diplomatic," *Christian Science Monitor,* May 16, 2006, p. 1.

19. Melinda Smith, "US Senators Call for Direct Talks with Iran," *VOA News,* April 18, 2006. http://www.voanews.com/english/2006-04-18-voa40.cfm. Site accessed May 30, 2006.

20. "Senators Urge Direct Diplomacy with Iran," *USA Today,* April 16, 2006. Available at http://www.usatoday.com/news/washington/2003-04-16-senate-iran x.htm.?csp=15. Accessed November 10, 2006.

21. Glenn Kessler, "US Under Pressure to Talk to Tehran," *Washington Post,* May 11, 2006, p. A20.

22. Maggie Farley and Paul Richter, "White House Calls Letter a Ploy," *Los Angeles Times,* May 9, 2006, p. A1.

23. Much of the criticism grew not out of Iraq or Iran issues, but because Hayden, as director of the National Security Agency, reportedly oversaw a program to collect information on U.S. citizens in the aftermath of 9/11.

24. See Scott Shane, "CIA Leader Will Face Crucial Gaps in Iran Data," *New York Times,* May 7, 2006, p. 26.

25. PBS, OnLine NewsHour. Available at http://www.pbs.org/newshour/bb/politics/jan-june06/hayden-hearing_05-18.html. Accessed May 30, 2006.

26. Craig Gordon, "Mission Would Be a Tall Order," *Newsday,* May 15, 2006, p. A23.

27. Andrew Gowers, Krishna Guha, and Demetri Sevastopulo, "Republican Senator Signals Resistance to Using Force in Iran," *Financial Times,* January 29, 2005, p. 5.

28. Charles Kupchan and Ray Takeyh, "The Wrong Way to Fix Iran," *Los Angeles Times,* February 26, 2006, p. M5.

29. "How Your Lawmakers Voted," *Baltimore Sun,* May 3, 2006, p. G4.

30. Craig Gordon, "Divided on Iran," *Newsday,* April 13, 2006, p. A5.

31. Richard Sisk, "'Stay the Course' Is Axed by W. 'Milestone,' 'Benchmarks' Are New Iraq Catchphrases," *Daily News,* October 24, 2006, p. 19.

32. "Blowing in the Wind," *New York Times,* October 22, 2006, p. 11.

33. "Minimum Wage, War Top Dems' Victory Plans," MSNBC online. http://www.msnbc.msn.com/id/15390733/. Site accessed November 8, 2006.

34. "What Happens if the Democrats Win?" *Foreign Policy,* October 2006, www.foreignpolicy.com/story/cms.php?story_id=3622&print=1. Site accessed November 8, 2006.

35. Ibid.

36. As quoted in Sydney J. Freedberg, "Out Now? Not Likely," *National Journal,* September 9, 2006, p. 60.

37. Robert McMahon, "The Oversight Elections," Council on Foreign Relations Daily Analysis, November 6, 2006. Available online at www.cfr.org/publication/11920/oversight_elections.html. Accessed November 8, 2006.

38. David Brody, "How Would Dems Reshape Congress?" CBN News, October 31, 2006, www.cbn.com/CBNnews/48742.aspx?option=print. Site accessed November 8, 2006.

39. Sydney J. Freedberg, "Out Now? Not Likely," p. 61.

40. William Powers, "After the Fall," *National Journal,* September 9, 2006, p. 86.

41. David Sands, "Democratic Majority Ready to Go to War over Iraq," *Washington Times,* October 30, 2006, p. A1.

42. Eugene Robinson, "How Low Will Bush Go? President's Scare Tactics Demean Politics and Voters," *Washington Post,* November 3, 2006, p. A21.

43. "What Happens if the Democrats Win?"

44. Press Conference by the president, November 8, 2006, 1 PM. Full text available at: http://www.whitehouse.gov/news/releases/2006/11/20061108-2.html. Site accessed November 8, 2006.

45. Richard Schmitt and Richard Simon. "Democrats Are Set to Subpoena," *Los Angeles Times,* November 10, 2006, p. A16.

46. Barbara Slavin, "Democrats Offer to Help Steer New Course in Iraq," *USA Today,* November 9, 2006, p. 11A.

47. Glenn Kessler, "Democrats May Urge More Contact With U.S. Adversaries," *Washington Post,* November 10, 2006, p. A7.

48. As quoted in *Guardian* Comment and Debate pages, November 1, 2006, p. 35.

APPENDIX B

1. (Meernik 1994).
2. Meernik has since updated the data through 2000.
3. (Meernik 1994, p. 136).
4. Ibid., p. 124.
5. Ibid., p. 123.
6. (Fordham 1998b).
7. (King and Lowe 2003).
8. In addition to the criteria defined below, see chapter 4 for discussion on the exclusion of opportunities that run contemporaneously with the Korean, Vietnam, and Gulf War or an ongoing major or minor use of force; and on the omission of opportunities conducted by non-state actors.
9. Typically, values greater than 0.7—or, by some standards, 0.8—are considered acceptable.
10. So as to consistently identify the most important news items of the day, and to eliminate from the database legal notices, classifieds, letters to the editor, editorials, op-eds, reviews (books, movies, theater), advertisements, sports, television listings, travel logs, and such, we limited the search to front-page articles in the *Times*.
11. Specifically, we conducted 27 separate searches of the full text of news stories using the following library of terms: guerrilla*; insurgents; clash* and border* or shell* or battle* or fighting or skirmish*; fighting and heavy or battle* or siege or casualties; battle* and kill*; troops or soldiers or rebels and invade* or capture* or attack* or fighting; troops or soldiers or rebels and kill* or raid*; artillery or mortar* or rocket* and fire* or attack* or battle* or fighting; artillery and duel* or shell* or fighting; shell* and wounded or fighting or attack*; tank* and fighting or kill* or battle* or attack*; plane* or jet* and fighting or kill* or battle* or bomb* or strafe*; aircraft or helicopter* and fighting or kill* or battle* or bomb* or strafe*; plane* or jet* or aircraft or helicopter* and shot down or downed; aerial bombardment or air raid*; civil war and fighting or kill* or attack* or battle*; soldier* or seaman or seamen and American and kill* or wounded; military plot* or assassinate* and chief of state or head of state or president; coup and government or fighting or head of state; plot and government and overthrow or topple; martial law or state of emergency and military; frigate* or vessel* or navy boat* and ram* or fire*; warship* or navy or patrol boat* and blockade*; embassy or consulate and American and attack* or storm* or fire*; ambassador or consul and American and shot or kill* or assassinate*; territorial waters or military sea boundary or freedom of navigation. The " * " tells the search engine to pull all articles that contain the identified root and any extension to the word. Hence, "ram*" identifies any article with the words ram, rams, rammed, or ramming. Obviously, many stories were identified by multiple searches. We therefore wrote a computer program to automate the task of eliminating duplicate stories.
12. Almost all stories concerning qualifying events that occurred longer than one year before the story's publication consisted of anniversary reports, such as the tenth anniversary of Pearl Harbor or the fifth anniversary of the Six Day War. We therefore exclude them from the analysis.

References

Adler, David G. 1996. Court, Constitution, and Foreign Affairs. In *The Constitution and the Conduct of American Foreign Policy*, edited by David G. Adler and Larry N. George. Lawrence: University Press of Kansas.

Adler, David, and Larry George. 1996. *The Constitution and the Conduct of American Foreign Policy*. Lawrence: University of Kansas Press.

Aldrich, John, Christopher Gelpi, Peter Feaver, Jason Reifler, and Kristin Thompson Sharp. 2006. Foreign Policy and the Electoral Connection. *Annual Review of Political Science* 9: 477–502.

Almond, Gabriel. 1950. *The American People and Foreign Policy*. New York: Harcourt, Brace.

Althaus, Scott. 2003. When Norms Collide, Follow the Lead: New Evidence for Press Independence. *Political Communication* 20: 381–414.

Althaus, Scott, Jill Edy, Robert Entman, and Patricia Phalen. 1996. Revising the Indexing Hypothesis: Officials, Media, and the Libya Crisis. *Political Communication* 13 (4): 407–21.

Arnold, Douglas. 2004. *Congress, the Press, and Political Accountability*. Princeton: Princeton University Press.

Arnold, Peri E. 1998. *Making the Managerial Presidency: Comprehensive Reorganization Planning, 1905–1996*. Lawrence: University Press of Kansas.

Aronson, Cynthia. 1993. *Crossroads: Congress, the President, and Central America, 1974–1993*. 2d ed. University Park: Pennsylvania State University.

Auerswald, David, and Peter Cowhey. 1997. Ballotbox Diplomacy: The War Powers Resolution and the Use of Force. *International Studies Quarterly* 41 (3): 505–28.

Baker, William, and John Oneal. 2001. Patriotism or Opinion Leadership? The Nature and Origins of the "Rally 'round the Flag Effect." *Journal of Conflict Resolution* 45: 661–87.

Baldwin, David. 1985. *Economic Statecraft*. Princeton: Princeton University Press.

Barbieri, Katherine. 2002. *Liberal Illusion: Does Trade Promote Peace?* Ann Arbor: University of Michigan Press.

Barnett, Michael. 2003. *Eyewitness to a Genocide: The United Nations and Rwanda*. Ithaca: Cornell University Press.

Bartels, Larry. 1991. Constituency Opinion and Congressional Policy Making: The Reagan Defense Buildup. *American Political Science Review* 85: 457–74.

Baum, Matthew. 2002. The Constituent Foundations of the Rally-Round-the-Flag Phenomenon. *International Studies Quarterly* 46: 263–98.

———. 2003. *Soft News Goes to War: Public Opinion and American Foreign Policy in the New Media Age*. Princeton: Princeton University Press.

————. 2004a. Going Private: Public Opinion, Presidential Rhetoric, and the Domestic Politics of Audience Costs in U.S. Foreign Policy Crises. *Journal of Conflict Resolution* 48 (5): 603–31.

————. 2004b. How Public Opinion Constrains the Use of Force: The Case of Operation Restore Hope. *Presidential Studies Quarterly* 34 (2): 187–226.

Baum, Matthew, and Timothy Groeling. 2005. What Gets Covered? How Media Coverage of Elite Debate Drives the Rally-'Round-the-Flag Phenomenon, 1979–1998. In *In the Public Domain: Presidents and the Challenges of Public Leadership*, edited by L. Cox Han and D. Heith. Albany, NY: State University of New York Press.

Bennett, W. Lance. 1990. Toward a Theory of Press-State Relations in the United States. *Journal of Communication* 40: 103–25.

Berger, Raoul. 1974. *Executive Privilege: A Constitutional Myth*. Cambridge: Harvard University Press.

Berinsky, Adam. 2005. Assuming the Costs of War: Events, Elites, and American Public Support for Military Conflict. Paper read at Annual Meetings of the Midwest Political Science Association, at Chicago.

Berinsky, Adam, and Donald Kinder. 2004. Making Sense of Issues through Frames: Understanding the Kosovo Crisis. Paper read at the Political Psychology Workshop, Harvard University.

Berman, Larry. 2001. *No Peace, No Honor: Nixon, Kissinger, and Betrayal in Vietnam*. New York: Free Press.

Bianco, William T. 2005. Last Post for the Greatest Generation: The Decline of Military Experience in the U.S. Senate. *Legislative Studies Quarterly* 30 (1): 85–102.

Billings-Yun, Melanie. 1988. *Decision against War*. New York: Columbia University Press.

Binder, Sarah. 1999. The Dynamics of Legislative Gridlock, 1947–96. *American Political Science Review* 93 (3): 519–34.

————. 2003. *Stalemate: Causes and Consequences of Legislative Gridlock*. Washington, D.C.: Brookings Institution Press.

Blainey, Geoffrey. 1988. *The Causes of War*. 3d ed. London: Macmillan Press.

Blechman, Barry. 1990. *The Politics of National Security*. New York: Oxford University Press.

Blechman, Barry, and Stephen Kaplan. 1978. *Force without War: U.S. Armed Forces as a Political Instrument*. Washington, D.C.: Brookings Institution Press.

Bond, Jon, and Richard Fleisher. 1990. *The President in the Legislative Arena*. Chicago: University of Chicago Press.

————. 2000. *Polarized Politics: Congress and the President in a Partisan Era*. Washington, D.C.: Congressional Quarterly Press.

Box-Steffensmeier, Janet M., and Bradford Jones. 2004. *Event History Modeling: A Guide for Social Scientists*. New York: Cambridge University Press.

Brady, David, Joseph Cooper, and Patricia Hurley. 1979. The Decline of Party in the U.S. House of Representatives, 1887–1968. *Legislative Studies Quarterly* 4 (3):381–407.

Brody, Richard. 1991. *Assessing the President: The Media, Elite Opinion, and Public Support*. Stanford: Stanford University Press.

———. 1994. Crisis, War and Public Opinion. In *Taken by Storm: Media, Public Opinion, and U.S. Foreign Policy in the Gulf War,* edited by W. L. Bennett and D. Paletz. Chicago: University of Chicago Press.

Brody, Richard, and Catherine Shapiro. 1989. A Reconsideration of the Rally Phenomenon in Public Opinion. In *Political Behavior Annual,* edited by S. Long. Boulder: Westview.

Brown, Alan W. 2003. *U.S. Armed Forces Abroad: Selected Congressional Roll Call Votes since 1982.* Washington, DC: Congressional Research Service.

Burke, John. 1992. *The Institutional Presidency.* Baltimore: John Hopkins University Press.

———. 2000. *The Institutional Presidency: Organizing and Managing the White House from FDR to Bill Clinton.* Baltimore: Johns Hopkins University Press.

Buzzanco, Robert. 1996. *Masters of War: Military Dissent and Politics in the Vietnam Era.* New York: Cambridge University Press.

Campbell, Angus, Phillip Converse, Warren Miller, and Donald Stokes. 1964. *The American Voter: An Abridgement.* New York: John Wiley and Sons.

Campbell, Colin. 1986. *Managing the Presidency: Carter, Reagan, and the Search for Executive Harmony.* Pittsburgh: University of Pittsburgh Press.

Campbell, James, and Joe Sumners. 1990. Presidential Coattails in Senate Elections. *American Political Science Review* 84 (2): 513–24.

Canes-Wrone, Brandice. 2005. *Who Leads Whom?: Presidents, Policy, and the Public.* Chicago: University of Chicago Press.

Canes-Wrone, Brandice, William Howell, and David Lewis. Forthcoming. Toward a Broader Understanding of Presidential Power: A Re-Evaluation of the Two Presidencies Thesis. *Journal of Politics.*

Capella, Joseph, and Kathleen Hall Jamieson. 1997. *Spiral of Cynicism: The Press and the Public Good.* New York: Oxford University Press.

Carter, Douglass. 1959. *The Fourth Branch of Government.* Boston: Houghton Mifflin.

Chang, Steve. 1997. In Search of Democratic Peace: Problems and Promise. *Mershon International Studies Review* 41 (May): 59–91.

Churchill, Winston. 1996 (1930). *My Early Life.* New York: Charles Scribner's Sons.

Clark, David. 2000. Agreeing to Disagree: Domestic Institutional Congruence and U.S. Dispute Behavior. *Political Research Quarterly* 53 (2): 375–400.

———. 2003. Can Strategic Interaction Divert Diversionary Behavior? A Model of U.S. Conflict Propensity. *Journal of Politics* 65 (4): 1013–39.

Clinton, Bill. 2004. *My Life.* New York: Alfred A. Knopf.

Cohen, Bernard. 1963. *The Press and Foreign Policy.* Princeton: Princeton University Press.

Converse, Phillip. 1964. The Nature of Belief Systems in Mass Publics. In *Ideology and Discontent,* edited by D. Apter. New York: Free Press.

Cooper, Phillip. 2002. *By Order of the President: The Use and Abuse of Executive Direct Action.* Lawrence: University Press of Kansas.

Corwin, Edward. 1948. *The President, Office and Powers, 1787–1948: History and Analysis of Practice and Opinion.* New York: New York University Press.

Cotton, Timothy. 1986. War and American Democracy: Electoral Costs of the Last Five Wars. *Journal of Conflict Resolution* 30 (4): 616–35.

Cox, Gary, and Matthew McCubbins. 1993. *Legislative Leviathan.* Berkeley: University of California Press.

Crawford, Vincent, and Joel Sobel. 1982. Strategic Information Transmission. *Econometrica* 50: 1431–51.

Dahl, Robert. 1950. *Congress and Foreign Policy.* New York: Harcourt, Brace.

Davison, W. P. 1974. New Media and International Negotiation. *Public Opinion Quarterly* 38: 174–91.

Deering, Christopher, and Forrest Maltzman. 1999. The Politics of Executive Orders: Legislative Constraints on Presidential Power. *Political Research Quarterly* 52 (4): 767–83.

Dennis, Everette, and Arnold Ismach. 1981. *Reporting Processes and Practices.* Belmont: Wadsworth.

DeRouen, Karl. 1995. The Indirect Link: Politics, the Economy, and the Use of Force. *Journal of Conflict Resolution* 39 (4): 671–95.

———. 2000. Presidents and the Diversionary Use of Force: A Research Note. *International Studies Quarterly* 44 (2): 317–28.

Deuth, Karl, and David Singer. 1964. Multipolar Power Systems and International Stability. *World Politics* 16: 390–406.

Doherty, Carroll. 1990. Consultation on the Gulf Crisis Is Hit or Miss for Congress. *Congressional Quarterly Weekly Report:* 3441.

Draper, Theodore. 1991. *A Very Thin Line: The Iran-Contra Affair.* New York: Hill and Wang.

Drezner, Daniel. 1999. *The Sanctions Paradox.* New York: Cambridge University Press.

Druckman, James. 2001a. The Implications of Framing Effects for Citizen Competence. *Political Behavior* 23: 225–56.

———. 2001b. On the Limits of Framing Effects: Who Can Frame? *Journal of Politics* 63: 1041–66.

Druckman, James, and Kjersten Nelson. 2003. Framing and Deliberation: How Citizens' Conversations Limit Elite Influence. *American Journal of Political Science* 47: 729–45.

Duiker, William. 1994. *U.S. Containment Policy and the Conflict in Indochina.* Stanford: Stanford University Press.

Eagleton, Thomas. 1974. *War and Presidential Power: A Chronicle of Congressional Surrender.* New York: Liveright.

Edwards, George C. 1986. The Two Presidencies: A Reevaluation. *American Politics Quarterly* 14 (3): 247–63.

———. 2003. *On Deaf Ears: The Limits of the Bully Pulpit.* New Haven: Yale University Press.

Eisenhower, Dwight. 1963. *Mandate for Change, 1953–1961.* Garden City, NY: Doubleday.

Ely, John Hart. 1993. *War and Responsibility: Constitutional Lessons of Vietnam and Its Aftermath.* Princeton: Princeton University Press.

Entman, Robert. 2004. *Projections of Power: Framing News, Public Opinion, and U.S. Foreign Policy.* Chicago: University of Chicago Press.

Entman, Robert, and Benjamin Page. 1994. The Iraq War Debate and the Limits to Media Independence. In *Taken by Storm: Media, Public Opinion, and U.S. Foreign Policy in the Gulf War,* edited by W. L. Bennett. Chicago: University of Chicago Press.

Epstein, David, and Sharyn O'Halloran. 1999. *Delegating Powers: A Transaction Cost Politics Approach to Policy Making under Separate Powers.* New York: Cambridge University Press.

Epstein, Lee, and Jack Knight. 1997. *The Choices Justices Make.* Washington, DC: Congressional Quarterly Press.

Epstein, Lee, and Jeffrey A. Segal. 2000. Measuring Issue Salience. *American Journal of Political Science* 44 (1): 66–83.

Everts, Philip, and Pierangelo Isernia, eds. 2001. *Public Opinion and the International Use of Force.* New York: Routledge/ECPR Studies in European Political Science.

Fearon, James. 1994. Domestic Political Audiences and the Escalation of International Disputes. *American Political Science Review* 88: 577–92.

———. 1995. Rationalist Explanations for War. *International Organization* 49 (3): 379–414.

———. 1998. Domestic Politics, Foreign Policy, and Theories of International Relations. *Annual Review of Political Science* 1: 289–313.

Feaver, Peter, and Christopher Gelpi. 2005. *Choosing Your Battles: American Civil-Military Relations and the Use of Force.* Princeton: Princeton University Press.

Ferejohn, John, and Frances McCall Rosenbluth. 2005. Warlike Democracies. Yale University, typescript.

Fiorina, Morris. 1981. *Retrospective Voting in American National Elections.* New Haven: Yale University Press.

Fisher, Louis. 2000. *Congressional Abdication on War and Spending.* College Station: Texas A&M University Press.

———. 2002. A Dose of Law and Realism for Presidential Studies. *Presidential Studies Quarterly* 32 (4): 672–92.

———. 2004. *Presidential War Power.* 2d ed. Lawrence: University Press of Kansas.

———. 2005. Judicial Review of the War Power. *Presidential Studies Quarterly* 35 (3): 466–95.

———. 2006. The Scope of Inherent Powers. Paper read at Politics and Polarization: The George W. Bush Presidency, at Oxford, England.

Fordham, Benjamin. 1998a. Partisanship, Macroeconomic Policy, and U.S. Uses of Force, 1949–1994. *Journal of Conflict Resolution* 42 (4): 418–39.

———. 1998b. The Politics of Threat Perception and the Use of Force: A Political Economy Model of U.S. Uses of Force, 1949–1994. *International Studies Quarterly* 42: 567–90.

———. 2002. Another Look at "Parties, Voters, and the Use of Force Abroad." *Journal of Conflict Resolution* 46 (4): 572–96.

———. 2005. Strategic Conflict Avoidance and the Diversionary Use of Force. *Journal of Politics* 67 (1): 132–53.

Fordham, Benjamin, and Christopher Sarver. 2001. Militarized Interstate Disputes and United States Uses of Force Abroad. *International Studies Quarterly* 45: 455–66.

Fowler, Linda. Forthcoming. *Dangerous Currents: Party Conflict at the Water's Edge*. Book manuscript, Dartmouth College.

Fowler, Linda, and Richard Law. 2005. Declining Fortunes: The Senate Foreign Relations Committee from 1946–2004. Paper read at Annual Meeting of the American Political Science Association, at Washington, D.C.

Foyle, Douglas. 1999. *Counting the Public In: Presidents, Public Opinion, and Foreign Policy*. New York: Columbia University Press.

Franklin, Charles, Erika Fowler, Ken Goldstein, and Daniel Stevens. 2004. Political Information Flows and their Effects in the 2002 Elections. Chicago: American Political Science Association Annual Meeting.

Gandy, Oscar. 1982. *Beyond Agenda Setting: Information Subsidies and Public Policy*. Norwood, NJ: Ablex Publishers.

Gans, Herbert. 1979. *Deciding What's News: A Study of CBS Evening News, NBC Nightly News, Newsweek, and Time*. New York: Vintage.

Gartzke, Eric, Quan Li, and Charles Boehmer. 2001. Investing in the Peace: Economic Interdependence and International Conflict. *International Organization* 55: 391–438.

Gaubatz, Kurt. 1991. Election Cycles and War. *Journal of Conflict Resolution* 35: 212–44.

Gelb, Leslie. 1979. *The Irony of Vietnam: The System Worked*. Washington, DC: Brookings Institution Press.

Gelpi, Christopher, and Peter Feaver. 2002. Speak Softly and Carry a Big Stick? Veterans in the Political Elite and the American Use of Force. *American Political Science Review* 96 (4): 779–93.

Ghosn, Faten, and Glenn Palmer. 2003. *Codebook for the Militarized Interstate Dispute Data, Version 3.4*. University Park: Pennsylvania State University.

Gibler, Douglas, and Meredith Sarkees. 2004. Measuring Alliances: The Correlates of War Formal Interstate Alliance Data Set, 1816–2000. *Journal of Peace Research* 41 (2): 211–22.

Gilliam, Frank, and Shanto Iyengar. 2000. Prime Suspects: The Influence of Local Television News on the Viewing Public. *American Journal of Political Science* 44: 560–73.

Gilligan, Thomas, and Keith Krehbiel. 1990. Organization of Informative Committees by a Rational Legislature. *American Journal of Political Science* 34: 531–64.

Gleditsch, Kristian. 2002. Expanded Trade and GDP Data. *Journal of Conflict Resolution* 46 (5): 712–24.

Goldstein, Judith. 1996. International Law and Domestic Institutions: Reconciling North American "Unfair" Trade Laws. *International Organization* 50 (4): 541–64.

Goldstein, Kenneth, and Travis Ridout. 2004. Measuring the Effects of Televised Political Advertising in the United States. *Annual Review of Political Science* 7: 205–26.

Gowa, Joanne. 1998. Politics at the Water's Edge: Parties, Voters and the Use of Force Abroad. *International Organization* 52 (2): 307–24.

———. 1999. *Ballots and Bullets*. Princeton: Princeton University Press.

Graber, Doris. 1984. *Processing the News: How People Tame the Information Tide*. New York: Longman.

———. 1989. *Mass Media and American Politics*. Washington, DC: Congressional Quarterly Press.

———. 2001. *Mass Media and American Politics*. 6th ed. Washington, DC: Congressional Quarterly Press.

Graubard, Stephen. 2004. *Command of Office: How War, Secrecy, and Deception Transformed the Presidency, From Theodore Roosevelt to George W. Bush*. New York: Basic Books.

Green, Donald P., Bradley Palmquist, and Eric Schickler. 2003. *Partisan Hearts and Minds*. New Haven: Yale University Press.

Grimmet, Richard. 2001. *Congressional Use of Funding Cutoffs since 1970 Involving U.S. Military Forces and Overseas Deployments*. Washington, DC: Congressional Research Service.

———. 2004. *The War Powers Resolution: After 30 Years*. Washington, DC: Congressional Research Service.

Gullick, Edward. 1955. *Europe's Classical Balance of Power*. New York: Norton.

Haas, Richard. 1999. What to Do with American Primacy. *Foreign Affairs* 78 (5): 37–49.

Haig, Alexander. 1984. *Caveat: Realism, Reagan, and Foreign Policy*. New York: Macmillan.

Hall, David Locke. 1991. *The Reagan Wars: A Constitutional Perspective on War Powers and the Presidency*. Boulder, CO: Westview Press.

Hallin, Daniel. 1986. *The "Uncensored War": The Media and Vietnam*. New York: Oxford University Press.

———. 1992. The Media, the War in Vietnam, and Political Support: A Critique of the Theory of Oppositional Media. In *Media Voices: An Historical Perspective*, edited by J. Folkerts. New York: Macmillan.

Hallin, Daniel, and Todd Gitlin. 1994. The Gulf War as Popular Culture and Television Drama. In *Taken by Storm: Media, Public Opinion, and U.S. Foreign Policy in the Gulf War*, edited by W. L. Bennett. Chicago: University of Chicago Press.

Hartley, Thomas, and Bruce Russett. 1992. Public Opinion and the Common Defense: Who Governs Military Spending in the United States. *American Political Science Review* 86: 905–15.

Heckman, James. 1979. Sample Selection Bias as a Specification Error. *Econometrica* 47 (1): 153–61.

Hendrickson, Ryan. 1998. War Powers, Bosnia, and the 104th Congress. *Political Science Quarterly* 113 (2): 241–58.

———. 2002. *The Clinton Wars: The Constitution, Congress, and War Powers*. Nashville: Vanderbilt University Press.

Herman, Edward, and Noam Chomsky. 1988. *Manufacturing Consent: The Political Economy of the Mass Media*. New York: Pantheon.

Hess, Gary. 2001. *Presidential Decisions for War: Korea, Vietnam, and the Persian Gulf*. Baltimore: Johns Hopkins University Press.

Hess, Stephen. 2002. *Organizing the Presidency*. 3d ed. Washington, DC: Brookings Institution.

Hinckley, Barbara. 1994. *Less Than Meets the Eye: Foreign Policy Making and the Myth of the Assertive Congress*. Chicago: University of Chicago Press.

Hinckley, Ronald. 1988. Public Attitudes toward Key Foreign Policy Events. *Journal of Conflict Resolution* 32: 295–318.

———. 1992. *People, Polls, and Policy-Makers: American Public Opinion and National Security.* New York: Lexington.

Holsti, Ole. 1992. Public Opinion and Foreign Policy: Challenges to the Almond-Lippmann Consensus. *International Studies Quarterly* 36 (4): 439–66.

———. 1996. *Public Opinion and American Foreign Policy.* Ann Arbor: University of Michigan Press.

Howell, William. 2003. *Power without Persuasion: The Politics of Direct Presidential Action.* Princeton: Princeton University Press.

———. 2005a. Unilateral Powers: A Brief Overview. *Presidential Studies Quarterly* 35 (3): 417–39.

Howell, William. 2005b. Power without Persuasion: Rethinking Foundations of Executive Influence. In *Readings in Presidential Politics,* edited by G. Edwards. Belmont, CA: Wadsworth.

Howell, William, Scott Adler, Charles Cameron, and Charles Riemann. 2000. Divided Government and the Legislative Productivity of Congress, 1945–1994. *Legislative Studies Quarterly* 25: 285–312.

Howell, William, and David Lewis. 2002. Agencies by Presidential Design. *Journal of Politics* 64 (4): 1095–1114.

Howell, William, and Douglas Kriner. 2006. Bending So as Not to Break: What the Bush Presidency Reveals about the Politics of Unilateral Action. Paper read at Politics and Polarization: The George W. Bush Presidency, at Oxford University.

———. 2007. Political Elites and Public Support for War. University of Chicago, typescript.

Howell, William, and Jon Pevehouse. 2005. Presidents, Congress, and the Use of Force. *International Organization* 59 (1): 209–32.

Howland, Charles P. 1928. *Survey of American Foreign Relations.* New Haven: Yale University Press.

Huntington, Samuel. 1999. The Lonely Superpower. *Foreign Affairs* 78 (2): 35–49.

Hurwitz, Jon, and Mark Peffley. 1987. How Are Foreign Policy Attitudes Structured? A Hierarchical Model. *American Political Science Review* 81: 1099–1120.

Hutcheson, John, David Domke, Andre Billeaudeaux, and Phillip Garland. 2004. U.S. National Identity, Political Elites, and a Patriotic Press Following September 11. *Political Communication* 21: 27–50.

Huth, Paul. 1988. *Extended Deterrence and the Prevention of War.* New Haven: Yale University Press.

———. 1999. Deterrence and International Conflict: Empirical Findings and Theoretical Debates. *Annual Review of Political Science* 2: 25–48.

Huth, Paul, and Bruce Russett. 1984. What Makes Deterrence Work: Cases from 1900 to 1980. *World Politics* 36 (4): 496–526.

Irons, Peter. 2005. *War Powers: How the Imperial Presidency Hijacked the Constitution.* New York: Metropolitan Books/Henry Holt.

Iyengar, Shanto. 1991. *Is Anyone Responsible? How Television Frames Political Issues.* Chicago: University of Chicago Press.

Iyengar, Shanto, and Donald Kinder. 1987. *News that Matters: Television and American Opinion*. Chicago: University of Chicago Press.

Jacobs, Lawrence, and Benjamin Page. 2005. Who Influences U.S. Foreign Policy. *American Political Science Review* 99 (1): 107–24.

Jacobs, Lawrence, and Robert Shapiro. 2000. *Politicians Don't Pander: Political Manipulation and the Loss of Democratic Responsiveness*. Chicago: University of Chicago Press.

Jaggers, Keith, and Ted Robert Gurr. 1995. Tracking Democracy's Third Wave with the Polity III Data. *Journal of Peace Research* 32 (4): 469–82.

James, Patrick. 2002. *International Relations and Scientific Progress*. Columbus: Ohio State University Press.

James, Patrick, and John Oneal. 1991. The Influence of Domestic and International Politics on the President's Use of Force. *Journal of Conflict Resolution* 35 (2): 307–32.

Jentleson, Bruce. 1992. The Pretty Prudent Public: Post Post-Vietnam American Opinion on the Use of Military Force. *International Studies Quarterly* 36: 49–74.

Johnson, Robert David. 2006. *Congress and the Cold War*. New York: Cambridge University Press.

Jones, Daniel, Stuart Bremer, and David Singer. 1996. Militarized Interstate Disputes, 1816–1992: Rationale, Coding Rules, and Empirical Patterns. *Conflict Management and Peace Science* 15 (2): 163–213.

Kaplan, Morton. 1957. *System and Process in International Politics*. New York: Wiley.

Katyal, Neal Kumar. 2006. Internal Separation of Powers: Checking Today's Most Dangerous Branch from Within. *Yale Law Journal* 115: 2314–2349.

Katzmann, Robert. 1990. War Powers: Toward a New Accommodation. In *A Question of Balance: The President, the Congress, and Foreign Policy*, edited by T. Mann. Washington, DC: Brookings Institution Press.

Kennan, George. 1951. *American Diplomacy: 1900–1950*. Chicago: University of Chicago Press.

Kennedy, David M. 1999. *Freedom from Fear: The American People in Depression and War, 1929–1945*. New York: Oxford University Press.

Keynes, Edward. 1982. *Undeclared War: Twilight Zone of Constitutional Power*. University Park: Pennsylvania State University Press.

Kinder, Donald. 1998. Communication and Opinion. *Annual Review of Political Science* 1: 167–97.

King, Gary. 1998. *Unifying Political Methodology: The Likelihood Theory of Statistical Inference*. Ann Arbor: University of Michigan Press.

King, Gary, and Will Lowe. 2003. An Automated Information Extraction Tool for International Conflict Data with Performance as Good as Human Coders: A Rare Events Evaluation Design. *International Organization* 57 (summer): 617–42.

King, Gary, and Langche Zeng. 2001. Explaining Rare Events in International Relations. *International Organization* 55 (3): 693–715.

Kissinger, Henry. 1979. *White House Year*. Boston: Little, Brown.

Krause, George, and David Cohen. 1997. Presidential Use of Executive Orders, 1953–1994. *American Politics Quarterly* 25 (October): 458–81.

Krause, George, and Jeffrey Cohen. 2000. Opportunity, Constraints, and the Development of the Institutional Presidency: The Case of Executive Order Issuance, 1939–1996. *Journal of Politics* 62: 88–114.

Krauthammer, Charles. 1991. The Unipolar Moment. *Foreign Affairs* 70 (1): 23–33.

Krehbiel, Keith. 1992. *Information and Legislative Organization.* Ann Arbor: University of Michigan Press.

———. 1998. *Pivotal Politics: A Theory of U.S. Lawmaking.* Chicago: University of Chicago Press.

Kriner, Douglas. 2006. Taming the Imperial Presidency: Congress, Presidents and the Conduct of Military Action. A PhD Dissertation presented to the Government Department, Harvard University, Cambridge, MA.

Kugler, Jacek, and Douglas Lemke, eds. 1996. *Parity and War.* Ann Arbor: University of Michigan Press.

Kull, Steven, and I. M. Destler. 1999. *Misreading the Public: The Myth of a New Isolationism.* Washington, DC: Brookings Institution Press.

Kumar, Martha, and Terry Sullivan, eds. 2003. *The White House World: Transitions, Organization, and Office Operations.* College Station: Texas A&M Press.

Larson, Eric. 1996. *Casualties and Consensus: The Historical Role of Casualties in Domestic Support for U.S. Military Operations.* Santa Monica, CA: Rand.

Leeds, Brett. 2003. Do Military Alliances Deter Aggression? The Influence of Military Alliances on the Initiation of Militarized Interstate Disputes. *American Journal of Political Science* 47 (3): 427–39.

Leeds, Brett Ashley, and David R. Davis. 1997. Domestic Political Vulnerability and International Disputes. *Journal of Conflict Resolution* 41 (6): 814–34.

LeoGrande, William. 1993. The Controversy over Contra Aid, 1981–1990: An Historical Narrative. In *Public Opinion in U.S. Foreign Policy: The Controversy over Contra Aid,* edited by R. Sobel. Lanham, MD: Rowman and Littlefield.

Levy, Jack. 1981. Alliance Formation and War Behavior: An Analysis of the Great Powers, 1496–1975. *Journal of Conflict Resolution* 25: 581–613.

———. 1985. The Polarity of the System and International Stability. In *Polarity and War,* edited by A. N. Sabrosky. Boulder: Westview Press.

———. 1989. The Diversionary Theory of War. In *The Handbook of War Studies,* edited by M. Midlarksy. Boston: Unwin Hyman.

Levy, Jack, and Lily Vakili. 1992. Diversionary Action by Authoritarian Regimes: Argentina in the Falklands/Malvina Case. In *The Internationalization of Communal Strife,* edited by M. Midlarsky. London: Routledge.

Lian, Brian, and John Oneal. 1993. Presidents, the Use of Military Force, and Public Opinion. *Journal of Conflict Resolution* 37 (2): 277–300.

Lindsay, James M. 1995. Congress and the Use of Force in the Post–Cold War Era. In *The United States and the Use of Force in the Post–Cold War Era,* edited by T. A. S. Group. Queenstown: Aspen Institute.

———. 1999. Congress, War, and the Military. In *The Oxford Companion to*

American Military History, edited by J. W. Chambers. New York: Oxford University Press.

Lippmann, Walter. 1992. *Public Opinion.* New York: Free Press.

Livingston, Steven, and W. Lance Bennett. 2003. Gatekeeping, Indexing, and Live-Event News: Is Technology Altering the Construction of News? *Political Communication* 20: 363–80.

Livingston, Steven, and Steven Eachus. 1996. Indexing News after the Cold War: Reporting U.S. Ties to Latin American Paramilitary Organizations. *Political Communication* 13: 423–36.

Lupia, Arthur, and Mathew McCubbins. 1994. Who Controls? Information and the Structure of Legislative Decision Making. *Legislative Studies Quarterly* 19 (3): 361–84.

MacKuen, Michael. 1983. Political Drama, Economic Conditions, and the Dynamics of Presidential Popularity. *American Journal of Political Science* 27: 165–92.

Manheim, J. B. 1994. *Strategic Public Diplomacy and American Foreign Policy: The Evolution of Influence.* New York: Oxford University Press.

Mansfield, Edward. 1994. *Power, Trade, and War.* Princeton: Princeton University Press.

Mansfield, Edward, and Jon Pevehouse. 2005. Preferential Trade Agreements and the Duration of Interstate Conflict. Typescript. University of Pennsylvania.

Mansfield, Edward, and Brian Pollins. 2001. The Study of Interdependence and Conflict: Recent Advances, Open Questions, and Directions for Future Research. *Journal of Conflict Resolution* 45 (6): 834–59.

Mansfield, Edward, and Jack Snyder. 2002. Democratic Transitions, Institutional Strength, and War. *International Organization* 56 (2): 297–337.

Markel, Lester, ed. 1949. *Public Opinion and Foreign Policy.* New York: Harper and Brothers.

Marshall, Bryan, and Richard Pacelle. 2005. Revisiting the Two Presidencies: The Strategic Use of Executive Orders. *American Politics Research* 33 (1): 81–105.

Marshall, Monty. 2005. *Polity IV Dataset.* College Station: CIDM, University of Maryland.

Martin, Lisa. 1992. *Coercive Cooperation: Explaining Multilateral Economic Sanctions.* Princeton: Princeton University Press.

Mayer, Kenneth. 1999. Executive Orders and Presidential Power. *Journal of Politics* 61 (2): 445–66.

———. 2001. *With the Stroke of a Pen: Executive Orders and Presidential Power.* Princeton: Princeton University Press.

Mayer, Kenneth, and Kevin Price. 2002. Unilateral Presidential Powers: Significant Executive Orders, 1949–99. *Presidential Studies Quarterly* 32 (2): 367–86.

Mayhew, David R. 1974. *Congress: The Electoral Connection.* New Haven: Yale University Press.

———. 1991. *Divided We Govern: Party Control, Lawmaking, and Investigations, 1946–1990.* New Haven: Yale University Press.

———. 2000. *America's Congress: Actions in the Public Sphere, James Madison through Newt Gingrich.* New Haven: Yale University Press.

McCormick, James, and Eugene Wittkopf. 1990. Bipartisanship, Partisanship, and Ideology in Congressional-Executive Foreign Policy Relations, 1947–1988. *Journal of Politics* 52 (4): 1077–1100.

McCubbins, Mathew, Roger Noll, and Barry Weingast. 1989. Structure and Process, Politics and Policy: Administrative Arrangements and the Political Control of Agencies. *Virginia Law Review* 75 (2): 431–82.

McCubbins, Mathew, and Thomas Schwartz. 1984. Congressional Oversight Overlooked: Police Patrols versus Fire Alarms. *American Journal of Political Science* 28 (1): 165–79.

Meernik, James. 1993. Presidential Support in Congress: Conflict and Consensus on Foreign and Defense Policy. *Journal of Politics* 55 (3): 569–87.

———. 1994. Presidential Decision Making and the Political Use of Force. *International Studies Quarterly* 38: 121–38.

———. 1995. Congress, the President, and the Commitment of the U.S. Military. *Legislative Studies Quarterly* 20 (3): 377–92.

———. 2000. Modeling International Crises and the Political Use of Military Force by the USA. *Journal of Peace Research* 37 (5): 547–62.

Meernik, James, and Peter Waterman. 1996. The Myth of the Diversionary Use of Force by American Presidents. *Political Research Quarterly* 49 (3): 573–90.

Melvern, Linda. 2004. *Conspiracy to Murder: The Rwanda Genocide and the International Community.* London: Verso Books.

Mendelberg, Tali. 2001. *The Race Card: Campaign Strategy, Implicit Messages, and the Norm of Equality.* Princeton: Princeton University Press.

Mermin, Jonathan. 1999. *Debating War and Peace: Media Coverage of U.S. Intervention in the Post-Vietnam Era.* Princeton: Princeton University Press.

Miller, Ross A. 1999. Regime Type, Strategic Interaction, and the Diversionary Use of Force. *Journal of Conflict Resolution* 43 (3): 388–402.

Mitchell, Sarah, and Will Moore. 2002. Presidential Uses of Force during the Cold War: Aggregation, Truncation, and Temporal Dynamics. *American Journal of Political Science* 46 (2): 438–53.

Moe, Terry. 1999. *The Presidency and the Bureaucracy: The Presidential Advantage.* Edited by M. Nelson, *The Presidency and the Political System.* Washington, DC: Congressional Quarterly Press.

Moe, Terry, and William Howell. 1999a. Unilateral Action and Presidential Power: A Theory. *Presidential Studies Quarterly* 29 (4): 850–72.

Moe, Terry M., and William Howell. 1999b. The Presidential Power of Unilateral Action. *Journal of Law, Economics, and Organization* 15 (1): 132–79.

Moore, Will, and David Lanoue. 2003. Domestic Politics and U.S. Foreign Policy: A Study of Cold War Conflict Behavior. *Journal of Politics* 65 (2): 376–96.

Morgan, T. Clifton, and Sally Campbell. 1991. Domestic Structure, Decisional Constraint, and War: So Why Kant Democracies Fight? *Journal of Conflict Resolution* 35 (2): 187–211.

Morgan, T. Clifton, and Kenneth Bickers. 1992. Domestic Discontent and the External Use of Force. *Journal of Conflict Resolution* 36: 25–52.

Morganthau, Hans. 1985. *Politics among Nations.* 6th ed. Revised and edited by Kenneth Thompson. New York: Alfred Knopf.

———. 1967. *Politics among Nations.* 4th ed. New York: Wiley.

Morrow, James. 1994. Modeling the Forms of International Cooperation: Distribution versus Information. *International Organization* 48 (3): 387–423.

———. 2003. Assessing the Role of Trade as a Source of Costly Signals. In *Economic Interdependence and International Conflict: New Perspectives on an Enduring Debate,* edited by E. Mansfield and B. Pollins. Ann Arbor: University of Michigan Press.

Mueller, John. 1973. *War, Presidents and Public Opinion.* New York: Wiley.

Mutz, Diana, and Paul Martin. 2001. Facilitating Communication across Lines of Political Difference: The Role of Mass Media. *American Political Science Review* 95 (1): 97–114.

Nzelibe, Jide. 2005. A Positive Theory of the War Powers Constitution. Evanston, IL: Northwestern University Law and Economics Research Paper.

Oneal, John, and A. L. Bryan. 1995. The Rally 'Round the Flag Effect in U.S. Foreign Policy Crises, 1950–1985. *Political Behavior* 17: 379–401.

Organski, A.F.K., and Jacek Kugler. 1980. *The War Ledger.* Chicago: University of Chicago Press.

Ornstein, Norman and Thomas Mann. 2006a. "When Congress Checks Out." *Foreign Affairs.* 85(6): 67–82.

———. 2006b. *The Broken Branch: How Congress is Failing America and How to Get It Back on Track.* New York: Oxford University Press.

Ostrom, Charles, and Brian Job. 1986. The President and the Political Use of Force. *American Political Science Review* 80 (2): 541–66.

Ostrom, Charles, and Dennis Simon. 1985. Promise and Performance: A Dynamic Model of Presidential Popularity. *American Political Science Review* 79: 334–58.

Page, Benjamin, and Robert Shapiro. 1988. Foreign Policy and the Rational Public. *Journal of Conflict Resolution* 32: 211–47.

———. 1992. *The Rational Public: Fifty Years of Trends in Americans' Policy Preferences.* Chicago: University of Chicago Press.

Pape, Robert. 1997. Why Economic Sanctions Do Not Work. *International Security* 22 (2): 90–136.

Peake, Jeffrey. 2001. Congressional Responses. In *Historical Encyclopedia of U.S. Presidential Use of Force, 1789–2000,* edited by K. DeRouen. Westport: Greenwood Press.

Peffley, Mark, and Jon Hurwitz. 1992. International Events and Foreign Policy Briefs: Public Responses to Changing Soviet-American Relations. *American Journal of Political Science* 36: 431–61.

Peterson, Mark. 1990. *Legislating Together: The White House and Capitol Hill from Eisenhower to Reagan.* Cambridge: Harvard University Press.

Peterson, Paul E. 1994. The President's Dominance in Foreign Policy Making. *Political Science Quarterly* 109 (2): 215–34.

Pevehouse, Jon. 2004. Interdependence Theory and the Measurement of International Conflict. *Journal of Politics* 66 (1): 247–66.

Pfiffner, James, ed. 1999. *The Managerial Presidency.* 2d ed. College Station: Texas A&M Press.

Pious, Richard. 1991. Prerogative Power and the Reagan Presidency. *Political Science Quarterly* 106 (fall): 499–510.

Popkin, Samuel. 1991. *The Reasoning Voter.* Chicago: University of Chicago Press.

Power, Samantha. 2002. *A Problem from Hell: America and the Age of Genocide.* New York: Basic Books.

Powlick, Phillip. 1995. The Sources of Public Opinion for American Foreign Policy Officials. *International Studies Quarterly* 39 (4): 427–52.

Quinn, Kevin, Burt Monroe, Michael Colaresi, Michael Crespin, and Dragomir Radev. 2006. An Automated Method of Topic-Coding Legislative Speech over Time with Application to the 105th-108th U.S. Congress. Paper read at Annual Meeting of the Midwest Political Science Association, at Chicago, IL.

Richards, Diana, T. Clifton Morgan, Rick Wilson, Valerie Schwebach, and Garry Young. 1993. Good Times, Bad Times, and the Diversionary Use of Force. *Journal of Conflict Resolution* 37 (3): 504–36.

Rosenau, James. 1961. *Public Opinion and Foreign Policy.* New York: Random House.

———, ed. 1967. *Domestic Sources of Foreign Policy.* New York: The Free Press.

Rosencrance, Richard. 1966. Bipolarity, Multipolarity, and the Future. *Journal of Conflict Resolution* 10: 314–27.

Rossiter, Clinton. 1956. *The American Presidency.* 2d ed. New York: Harcourt, Brace.

Rudalevige, Andrew. 2002. *Managing the President's Program: Presidential Leadership and Legislative Policy Formation.* Princeton: Princeton University Press.

Russett, Bruce. 1990. Economic Decline, Electoral Pressure, and the Initiation of Interstate Conflict. In *Prisoners of War? Nation-States in the Modern Era,* edited by C. Gochman and N. A. Sabrosky. Lexington: Lexington Books.

Russett, Bruce, and John Oneal. 2001. *Triangulating Peace: Democracy, Interdependence, and International Organizations.* New York: W. W. Norton.

Schlesinger, Arthur. 1973. *The Imperial Presidency.* Boston: Houghton Mifflin.

Schultz, Kenneth. 1998. Domestic Opposition and Signaling in International Crises. *American Political Science Review* 92 (4): 829–44.

Shepsle, Kenneth. 1992. Congress Is a "They," Not an "It": Legislative Intent as Oxymoron. *International Review of Law and Economics* 12: 239–57.

Sigal, Leon. 1973. *Reporters and Officials: The Organization and Politics of Newsmaking.* Lexington: D. C. Heath.

Singer, David, and Melvin Small. 1994. *Correlates of War Project: International and Civil War Data, 1816–1992.* Ann Arbor, MI: Inter-University Consortium for Political and Social Research.

Siverson, Randy, and Michael Sullivan. 1984. Alliances and War: A New Examination of an Old Problem. *Conflict Management and Peace Science* 8 (1): 1–15.

Small, Melvin, and David Singer. 1990. *National Material Capabilities Dataset.* Ann Arbor: University of Michigan.

Smith, Alastair. 1995. Alliance Formation and War. *International Studies Quarterly* 39 (4): 405–25.

———. 1996. Diversionary Foreign Policy in Democratic Systems. *International Studies Quarterly* 43 (4): 1254–83.

————. 1998. International Crises and Domestic Politics. *American Political Science Review* 92: 623–38.

Smith, Alastair, and Alexandra Guisinger. 2002. Honest Threats: The Interaction of Reputation and Political Institutions in International Crises. *Journal of Conflict Resolution* 46 (2): 175–200.

Smyrl, Marc. 1988. *Conflict or Codetermination? Congress, the President, and the Power to Make War*. Cambridge: Ballinger.

Sniderman, Paul. 1993. The New Look in Public Opinion Research. In *The State of the Discipline II,* edited by A. Finifter. Cambridge, UK: Cambridge University Press.

Sniderman, Paul, Richard Brody, and Phillip Tetlock. 1991. *Reasoning and Choice: Exploration in Political Psychology*. Cambridge, UK: Cambridge University Press.

Sobel, Richard. 1989. A Report: Public Opinion about United States Intervention in El Salvador and Nicaragua. *Public Opinion Quarterly* 53: 114–28.

————, ed. 1993. *Public Opinion in U.S. Foreign Policy: The Controversy over Contra Aid*. Lanham: Rowman and Littlefield.

————. 2001. *The Impact of Public Opinion on U.S. Foreign Policy since Vietnam*. New York: Oxford University Press.

Sobel, Richard, and Eric Shiraev. 2003. *International Public Opinion and the Bosnia Crisis*. Lexington: Lexington Books.

Stoll, Richard. 1984. The Guns of November: Presidential Reelections and the Use of Force. *Journal of Conflict Resolution* 28: 231–46.

————. 1987. The Sound of the Guns: Is There a Congressional Rally Effect after US Military Action? *American Politics Quarterly* 15 (2): 223–37.

Thucydides. 1972. *History of the Peloponnesian War*. Translated by R. Warner. New York: Penguin.

Tuchman, Gaye. 1978. *Making News: A Study in the Construction of Reality*. New York: Free Press.

Vasquez, John. 1987. The Steps to War: Toward a Scientific Explanation of Correlates of War Findings. *World Politics* 40: 108–45.

Wagner, R. Harrison. 1986. The Theory of Games and the Balance of Power. *World Politics* 38: 546–76.

Walcott, Charles, and Karen Hult. 1995. *Governing the White House: From Hoover through LBJ*. Lawrence: University of Kansas Press.

Wallerstein, Immanuel. 1974. *The Modern World System: Capitalist Agriculture and the Origins of the European World-Economy in the Sixteenth Century*. New York: Academic Press.

Walsh, Lawrence. 1998. *Firewall: The Iran-Contra Conspiracy and Cover-up*. New York: W. W. Norton.

Waltz, Kenneth. 1967. *Foreign Policy and Democratic Politics: The American and British Experience*. Boston: Little, Brown.

————. 1979. *Theory of International Politics*. New York: McGraw-Hill.

Weingast, Barry, and William Marshall. 1988. The Industrial Organization of Congress. *Journal of Political Economy* 96: 132–63.

Weissman, Stephen. 1995. *A Culture of Deference: Congress's Failure of Leadership in Foreign Policy*. New York: Basic Books.

Weko, Thomas. 1995. *The Politicizing Presidency: The White House Personnel Office.* Lawrence: University Press of Kansas.

Wildavsky, Aaron. 1989. The Two Presidencies Thesis Revisited at a Time of Political Dissensus. *Society* 26 (5): 53–59.

Wittkopf, Eugene. 1990. *Faces of Internationalism: Public Opinion and American Foreign Policy.* Durham: Duke University Press.

Wittkopf, Eugene, and Mark Dehaven. 1987. Soviet Behavior, Presidential Popularity, and the Penetration of Open Political Systems. In *New Directions in the Study of Foreign Policy,* edited by C. Hermann, C. Kegley, and J. Rosenau. Boston: Unwin Hyman.

Zaller, John. 1992. *The Nature and Origins of Mass Opinion.* Cambridge, UK: Cambridge University Press.

———. 1994a. Elite Leadership of Mass Opinion: New Evidence from the Gulf War. In *Taken by Storm: Media, Public Opinion, and U.S. Foreign Policy in the Gulf War,* edited by W. L. Bennett and D. Paletz. Chicago: University of Chicago Press.

———. 1994b. Strategic Politicians, Public Opinion, and the Gulf Crisis. In *Taken by Storm: Media, Public Opinion, and U.S. Foreign Policy in the Gulf War,* edited by W. L. Bennett and D. Paletz. Chicago: University of Chicago Press.

———. 1996. The Myth of Massive Media Impact Revived: New Support for a Discredited Idea. In *Political Persuasion and Attitude Change,* edited by D. Mutz, P. Sniderman, and R. Brody. Ann Arbor: University of Michigan Press.

Zaller, John, and Dennis Chiu. 1996. Government's Little Helper: U.S. Press Coverage of Foreign Policy Crises, 1945–1991. *Political Communication* 13: 385–405.

Zelikow, Phillip. 1987. The United States and the Use of Force: A Historical Summary. In *Democracy, Strategy, and Vietnam,* edited by G. Osborn. Lexington: Lexington Books.

Index

Abu Ghraib, 229
Adams, Sherman, 120
Adler, David, 265n.13
Afghanistan, 228
Africa, opportunities to use force in, 85–87
Ahmadinejad, Mahmoud, 233
Aideed, Mahommed Farah, 16
Aiken, George D., 117
Aksai Chin, 83
Albania, 144
Albright, Madeleine, 145
Aldrich, John, 30
Algerian War, 83, 93
alliances, 44–45, 94–95
al-Qaeda, 87, 168, 207, 228
Americas, opportunities to use force in, 84, 86
Angola, 14–15, 86–87
appropriations as tool for congressional influence, 10, 14, 16–17, 21. *See also* case studies: Bosnia, Indochina (1954), Kosovo, Lebanon, Nicaragua, Panama
Aquino, Benigno, 253
Arab-Israeli War (1948), 81, 87
Argentina, 83, 86, 88
Argov, Shlomo, 126
Aristide, Jean-Bertrand, 26, 285n.56
Arnold, Douglas, 161, 294n.29–30
Aronson, Cynthia, 125–26
Asia, opportunities to use force in, 84–86
Aspin, Les, 132
Auerswald, David, 42
Authorization for Use of Military Force (2002), xvi

Baker, Howard, 131
Bangladesh, 86
Barnes, Michael, 123
Barone, Michael, 22
Bas v. Tingy, 265n.13
Baum, Matthew, 31, 302n.45
Baumgartner, Frank, 268n.63
Bayh, Evan, 169, 235
Begin, Menachem, 127

Belgium, 86
Bennett, W. Lance, 159–61, 166, 171, 184
Bentsen, Lloyd, 130
Berger, Sandy, 145
Berinsky, Adam, 149, 164–65, 301n.31
Biden, Joseph, 140, 169
Billings-Yun, Melanie, 24, 117, 119
bin Laden, Osama, 228
Birnbaum, Jeff, 239
Blackstone, William, xi
Blechman, Barry, xxii, 53–54, 58, 67–69, 274n.3, 280n.4
Boer War, 21–22
Boland, Edward, 122
Boland Amendment(s), 122–24, 287n.23
Bonior, David, 169
Boren, David, 137–38
Bosnia, 31, 39, 86, 139–44, 290n.106
Boutros-Ghali, Boutros, 139
Brady, David, 60
Breyer, Stephen, xvi–xvii
Britain. *See* United Kingdom
Brody, Richard, 164, 216
Brown, Hank, 140
budget, federal, appropriations as tool for congressional influence, 10, 14, 16–17, 21. *See also* case studies: Bosnia, Indochina (1954), Kosovo, Lebanon, Nicaragua, Panama
Bueno de Mesquita, Bruce, 46
Burns, Robert, 22
Bush, George H. W.: Bosnia, actions regarding, 139, 141; Panama, actions regarding, 135–38; Somalia, mission in, 39
Bush, George W.: Iran, actions regarding, 234; Iraq, impact of the insurgents' bombs on, 270n.78; Iraq, refusal to establish timetable for withdrawal from, 29; Iraq, visit to, 231; Iraq War, actions preceding, xviii, 28, 73, 157–58, 167–71, 180, 302n.50; Iraq War, the 2006 elections and, 238, 240–42;

Bush, George W. (*continued*): Iraq War, treatment received from Congress regarding, 269n.64; Military Commissions Act, remarks regarding, xvii; public opinion a matter of concern for, 219–20; public skepticism about undocumented claims by, 210; rally-around-the-flag effects experienced by, 57; unilateral powers, congressional responses to exercise of, 230–32; unilateral powers, exercise of, 48, 227–29; unilateral powers, factors supporting the exercise of, 229; "war on terror" pursued by (*see* "war on terror")

Bush administration: Democratic Congress after 2006 elections, fears regarding, 238–39; Iran, actions regarding, 73–74, 233–37; Iraq War, early decision on, 303n.55; Iraq War, media coverage during the run-up to, 157–58; Syria, flirtations with confronting, 73–74; United Nations support for actions in Iraq, efforts to acquire, xviii; "war on terror" pursued by (*see* "war on terror")

Buzzanco, Robert, xv

Byrd, Robert, 16, 131, 169–70, 242

Campbell, Angus, 279n.77

Campbell, S., 274n.18

Campbell v. Clinton, 267n.49

Card, Andrew, 303n.50

Carter, Jimmy, 121

cascading activation model, 162

Central Intelligence Agency (CIA), 122, 158

Chafee, John, 139

checks and balances, constitutional authority regarding war and, 3, 5–6

checks on presidential war powers: the courts, xv–xvii; interbranch dynamics regarding, 17–23; international organizations and alliances, xvii–xviii; legislation/appropriations, congressional opposition through, 10–23; limits on the analysis of, xiv–xxi; the military, xiv–xv; politics preceding military action, focus on, xix–xxi; public appeals/dissent, congressional opposition through, 23–26; public opinion (*see* public opinion). *See also* congressional dissent; opportunities to use military force; use-of-force politics

Cheney, Richard, 137–38

China, People's Republic of: fall of Indochina and, U.S. concerns regarding, 119–20; India, conflict with over Aksai Chin, 83; intervention in Pakistan-India conflict, threat of, 85; Iranian nuclear activity, response to, 234; opportunities to use force relating to, 89

Christopher, Warren, 141

Churchill, Winston, 11, 21–22

CIA. *See* Central Intelligence Agency

citizens: political views of, 193–95. *See also* public opinion

Clark, David, 69–70, 274n.21, 279n.76

Clinton, Bill: Bosnia, actions regarding, 139–41, 143–44, 290n.106, 290n.112; foreign affairs, initial lack of attention to, 19; Haiti, policy regarding, 7, 25–26, 285n.56; Kosovo, actions regarding, xvii, 36–37; Republican mistrust of, 36–37; Rwanda, failure to intervene in, 16–17; Somalia, military operation in, 31, 39; unilateral powers, exercise of, 48

Cohen, William, 137–38, 145

Cold War, the, 45, 62, 94

collective action problems, 34

Congo, Democratic Republic of, 86, 93

Congress, United States: agendas pursued by members of, 40–41; beyond partisanship, considerations for future research that go, 224–25; characteristics of, 34–36; dissent, expressing (*see* congressional dissent); Framers' (of the Constitution) views on war powers of, 264–65n.13; hearings held by, 268–69n.63; impact/actions by before and during a military action, distinction between, xix–xxi; impotence of assumed in the use-of-force literature, 56–58; influence by, distinction between possibility and realization of, 33; influence over the media and public opinion, considerations for future research regarding, 227; information about foreign affairs, lack of, 19–20; Iraq War, debate and authorization preceding, 167–71 (*see also* Iraq War); the media and (*see* indexing hypothesis; media, the; news stories on Iraq); military tribunals/commissions, actions regarding the Bush administration's, xvii; military veterans among congressional representatives and senators, impact of, 70–72, 110; partisanship in (*see* partisanship); presidential war powers, interbranch dynamics regarding, 6, 17–23, 222–23; public opinion, influence over through local news, 192, 214–17 (*see also* media, the; public opinion); reporting requirements imposed on the president by, 266–67n.40; unilateral powers exercised by Bush, responses to, 230–32; the War Powers Resolution and, 5 (*see also* War Powers Resolution of 1973)

congressional dissent: case studies of (*see* Bosnia; Indochina (1954); Kosovo; Lebanon; Nicaragua; Panama); domestic irresolution, signaling of, 27–29; the indexing hypothesis and, 164 (*see also* indexing hypothesis; media, the); international variables as factors mediating, 42–47; Iran, potential use of force in, 234–37; legislation/appropriations in opposition to presidential war powers, 10–17; partisanship as a factor in, 34–40 (*see also* partisanship); public appeals in opposition to presidential war powers, 23–26; public opinion, influence on, 29–32 (*see also* public opinion); size and duration of military deployment as a factor in, 40–42; volition in use of force and, 43. *See also* opportunities to use military force; use-of-force politics

Constitution of the United States, Article II, xvi

Contact Group, the, 145

contras, 121–26

Converse, Philip, 193

Cooper, Joseph, 60

Corwin, Edward, xi, 265n.21, 267n.55

Costa Rica, 86

Coughlin, Charles, 11

courts, actions regarding presidential war powers by, xv–xvii

Cowhey, Peter, 42

Cranston, Alan, 131

Croatia, 139

Cuba, xvi, 13, 60, 86, 93

Cuban Missile Crisis, 83

Cyprus, 86

Dahl, Robert, 9

D'Amato, Alfonse, 136–37

Daschle, Tom, 170

data. *See* methods/methodology and data

deployments, military. *See* military deployments

Derrick, Butler, 136

Detainee Treatment Act (2005), xvi

Dien Bien Phu, 116, 118–21

dissent, congressional. *See* congressional dissent

diversionary war hypothesis, 56–57, 62, 101, 107

Dodd, Christopher, 128, 234, 236

Doherty, Carroll, 219

Dole, Robert, 25, 36, 139–40, 142–44, 147–48

Dulles, Allen, 119

Dulles, John Foster, 118–19, 121

Durbin, Richard, 136

economics and the economy: interstate relations and the domestic politics of military action, 45–46; opportunities to use military force and, 87–88; presidential willingness to exercise force abroad and, 54, 56–57, 62; strategic avoidance behavior and, 90–92

Economist, The, 228

Edwards, George, 40

Egypt, 60, 83, 87

Einaudi, Luigi, 122

Eisenhower, Dwight: electoral victory of 1952, 12; Indochina, policy regarding, 20, 23–24, 116–21; Korean War's impact on the foreign policy of, 150; legislative success rate on foreign policy of, 67; opportunities to exercise military force faced by, number of, 245

Eisentrager, Johnson v., 263n.8

ElBaradei, Mohammed, 233

elections and electoral behavior: of 2006, impact on discussion of the Iraq War, 238–42; partisanship in foreign policy and, 37–38; presidential willingness to exercise force abroad and, 54, 62 (*see also* rally-around-the-flag effects)

El Salvador, 86, 121–22, 125

Ely, John Hart, 5

Ely, Paul, 116

Ensign, John, 168

Entman, Robert, 162

Eritrea, 207

Ethiopia, 86, 207

ethnic cleansing, 146
EU. *See* European Union
Europe, opportunities to use force in, 84, 86
European Union (EU), 233–34

Falkland/Malvinas Islands, 83
Fearon, James, 47
Feaver, Peter, 70–71, 110, 278n.72–73, 279n.74–75
Feingold, Russ, 229
Feinstein, Diane, 234–35
Ferejohn, John, 18
Financial Times, 236
Fisher, Louis, 5, 143–44, 264–65n.13
Force Without War (Blechman/Kaplan), 53–54
Ford, Gerald, 14–15, 228
Fordham, Benjamin, 54, 58, 69, 90, 247, 276n.45, 278n.69, 279n.76
foreign policy: citizens' knowledge of and views about, 193; international factors mediating congressional influence regarding, 42–47; isolationism, 11–12, 286n.5; party affiliation of the president and, 72–73, 99; public opinion and, 30–32. *See also* international relations; military deployments; opportunities to use military force
France: the Contact Group regarding Kosovo, membership in, 145; in Indochina, 23–24, 116, 120–21; Iranian nuclear activity, response to, 234; opportunities to use military force related to, 86; trade with the United States, amount of, 88
Friedman, Thomas, 141
Frist, Bill, 263n.12
Frost, Martin, 17

Gaddis, John Lewis, xi
game theory, 27, 37
Gelpi, Christopher, 70–71, 110, 278n.72–73, 279n.74–75
Gemayel, Bashir, 128
Geneva Conventions, xvi–xvii
George, Walter, 117
Gephardt, Richard, 169
Germany, 60, 145
Gilliam, Frank, 166
Ginsburg, Ruth Bader, xvi
Giroldi, Moises, 135
Gleditsch, Kristian, 281n.18

Glenn, John, 124–25
Goldwater, Barry, 13
Gonzalez, Henry, 125, 129–30
Gorbachev, Mikhail, 86
Goss, Porter, 25–26
Gowa, Joanne, 5, 55–56, 69–70, 72, 278n.69
Graber, Doris, 166
Graham, Lindsey, 263n.12
Graubard, Stephen, 228–29
Great Britain. *See* United Kingdom
Greece, 60
Greek Civil War, 86
Grenada, 39
Grimmet, Richard, 265n.22
Groeling, Timothy, 302n.45
Guantanamo Bay, Cuba, xvi
Guatemala, 86
Gulf of Tonkin Resolution, 14

Haass, Richard, 303n.55
Habib, Philip, 127–28
Hagel, Chuck, 145, 235, 237
Haig, Alexander, 124–26
Haiti, 7, 25–26, 39
Hall, Fawn, 124
Hamdan v. Rumsfeld, xvi
Hamdi v. Rumsfeld, xvi
Hamilton, Alexander, 220
Hamilton, Lee, 132
Hastert, Dennis, 147, 170
Hayden, Michael, 235
hearings, congressional, 268–69n.63
Heckman, James, 284n.46
Heckman selection models, 100
hegemony, 62–63
Helms, Jesse, 136
Hendrickson, Ryan, 142
Hess, Gary, 269n.64
Hill, Christopher, 145
Hinckley, Barbara, 5, 57, 287n.23
Hitler, Adolf, 11
Hoagland, Jim, 19
Hobson, John, 273n.42
Holbrooke, Richard, 145–46
Hollings, Fritz, 135
Holsti, Ole, 30, 271n.87
Howland, Charles, xi
Hungary, 86
Hurley, Patricia, 60
Hussein, Saddam, xviii, 27, 157, 167–68, 180, 218–19

imperial presidency, 4
impotence thesis, 30
indexing hypothesis, 156–66; evidence
   supporting, 174–87; local news and,
   166–67; normative concerns arising
   from, 293n.22; summary of support for,
   187–91; two ways Congress may affect
   media coverage, 171
India, 83, 85–86
Indochina (1954), 23–24, 115–21. See
   also Vietnam War
information: asymmetry of congressional
   and presidential regarding foreign affairs, 36; congressional lack of regarding
   foreign affairs, 19–20; lack of accurate
   during the run-up to the Iraq War, 158;
   the media's lack of, the indexing hypothesis and, 157; partisanship and the credibility of, 36–37; quantity and quality of
   exchange of and incentives to fight, relationship between, 45; reporting requirements imposed on the president by Congress, 266–67n.40. See also signaling
Institute for Science and International
   Security, 158
interbranch relations: dynamics of, 17–23;
   primary function of theory of, 33
International Atomic Energy Agency
   (IAEA), 233
international organizations: presidential
   war powers and, xvii–xviii. See also
   names of organizations
international relations: citizens' knowledge
   of and views about, 193; decisions to deploy and, 108; future research, avenues
   for, 225–27; hypotheses regarding systemic impact on presidential decisions,
   78; International System hypothesis, evidence supporting, 108, 112; rational theory, war explanations of, 46; structural
   conditions shaping military deployments, 42–47, 55, 62–63; structural/
   systemic theory and the balance of
   power, 42–44, 272–73n.33
international trade, 46, 87–88, 273n.40
Iran, 232–38
Iran-Contra scandal, 123–24, 126
Iran-Iraq war, 24–25
Iraq: impact of the insurgents' bombs on,
   270n.78; impact of the war in, 228;
   Iran, impact of ongoing military intervention on policy towards, 237; recent

events in, 231; trade with the United
   States, amount of, 88
Iraq War: Bush administration decision to
   go forward with, 303n.55; congressional
   authorization of the use of force in, 28,
   38–39, 167–71; media coverage during
   the run-up to (see news stories on Iraq);
   the midterm elections of 2006 and,
   238–42; partisan composition of Congress, significance of, 134; presidential
   concerns with public opinion before
   launching, 219–20; public support for
   based on experimental data, 205–13;
   public support for based on survey data,
   196–205; public support for influenced
   by Congress, summary of evidence regarding, 213–17; signaling of resolve in,
   importance of, 28–29; the United Nations and U.S. actions in, xviii. See also
   Bush, George W.
Irons, Peter, 5
isolationism, 11–12, 286n.5
Israel: Lebanon and, 126–28, 133; opportunities database, coding of conflict with
   Palestinians in, 252–53; opportunities to
   use force, examples of, 83, 87; opportunities to use force, number of, 81; trade
   with the United States, amount of, 88;
   use of force in, 60
Italy, 145
Iyengar, Shanto, 166, 194

Jackson, Jesse, 132
Jacobs, John, 137
Jacobs, Lawrence, 31–32
James, Patrick, 54
Javits, Jacob, 4
Job, Brian, 54, 62, 66
Johnson, Lyndon, xvii, 18, 20, 22, 230–31
Johnson v. Eisentrager., 263n.8
Jones, Bryan, 268n.63
Jordan, 60

Kamber, Victor, 239
Kant, Immanuel, xi
Kaplan, Stephen, xxii, 53–54, 58, 68–69,
   274n.3, 280n.4
Kashmir, 85–86
Kasich, John, 146
Katyal, Neal, 5
Katzman, Robert, 4–5
Keane, Fergal, 218

Keating, Kenneth, 13
Kempthorne, Dirk, 16
Kennedy, Anthony, xvi–xvii
Kennedy, John, 13, 20
Kenya, 87
Kerry, John, 264n.20, 269n.64
Keynes, Edward, xv
Khatami, Mohammed, 233
Kinder, Donald, 194
King, Larry, 290n.112
Kissinger, Henry, 14
KLA. *See* Kosovo Liberation Army
Knowland, William, 118, 120
Korea, Democratic People's Republic of, 60
Korea, Republic of, 60
Korean War, xv, 12–13, 230
Kosovo, 17, 36–38, 86, 144–49
Kosovo Liberation Army (KLA), 144–46
Kosovo Verification Mission (KVM), 146
Kriner, Douglas, 265n.17, 268n.56,
    272n.17, 278n.65, 302n.45
Kuwait, 24–25
Kyl, Jon, 263n.12

Lanoue, David, 55
Lantos, Tom, 25
Laos, 85
Laxalt, Paul, 132
Leach, Jim, 123
Leahy, Patrick, 140
Lebanon: case study of interbranch dynam-
    ics over deployments between 1982 and
    1984, 126–34; civil war as opportunity
    for military action, 83, 87; in 1982–
    1983, 15–16; partisanship in congres-
    sional reaction to military action in, 39
Lebanon Emergency Assistance Act
    (LEAA), 130
Leeds, Brett, 45
Lend-Lease Act, 12
Lenin, V. I., 273n.42
Levin, Carl, 128, 139, 169, 239
Lewinsky, Monica, 148
Lewis, Anthony, 141
Lieberman, Joseph, 169–70
Lincoln, Abraham, 3
Lindbergh, Charles, 11
Lindsay, James, 7, 10, 265n.22
Lippmann, Walter, 156–57
Los Angeles Times, 235, 241
Lott, Trent, 146, 170
Lugar, Richard, 125, 139, 146, 235, 237

MacArthur, Douglas, xv, 12
Madison, James, 268n.57
Marcos, Ferdinand, 253
Mayhew, David, 18, 155, 190
McCain, John, 139–40, 145–46, 235–37
McConnell, Mitch, 146, 168–69
McDermott, Jim, 169
media, the: citizens' views, potential to
    shape, 194–95; Congress and, 160–
    66; Congress's influence over, consid-
    erations for future research regarding,
    227; Democratic Congress after 2006,
    impact of, 240; descriptive statistics re-
    garding, 259; experimental data on the
    relationship of local news and support
    for the Iraq War, 205–13; government
    officials, dependence on, 157–60; the
    indexing hypothesis (*see* indexing hy-
    pothesis); the information problem
    preceding a deployment, 157–59; jour-
    nalists, role of, 293n.22; local news,
    166–67; news, preferences among
    sources of, 167; news and public opin-
    ion, scholarship on, 192–95; news
    stories on Iraq, local and national
    (*see* news stories on Iraq); observational
    data on the relationship of local news
    and support for the Iraq War, 196–205;
    summary of evidence on the relationship
    of local news and support for the Iraq
    War, 213–17
Meernik, James, 55–56, 245–47, 249,
    274n.14, 275n.22, 280n.1
Mermin, Jonathan, 159–61, 163, 166
methods/methodology and data: Blechman/
    Kaplan and Militarized Interstate Dis-
    pute data, relative consideration of,
    68–69; case studies, 114–15; endogene-
    ity, problem of, 205–6; event-count
    models, limitations of, 75; event-history
    models, advantages of, 103–4; Heck-
    man selection models, 100; impact of
    television news on citizens' views, chal-
    lenges of quantitative research on, 195;
    opportunities database, construction
    of, 78–81, 245–55; right-censoring,
    103–4; strategic avoidance as a selection
    effect, 99–100; use-of-force statistical
    data/models, limitation of extant, 55
Michel, Robert, 132
MID. *See* Militarized Interstate Dispute
    data

Middle East, opportunities to use force in, 81, 83, 85, 87
Militarized Interstate Dispute (MID) data (MID), 69–72
military alliances, 44–45, 94–95
Military Commissions Act of 2006, xvii
military deployments: avoidance behavior by potential targets to avert, 89–93; descriptive statistics regarding, 243; military veterans in the House and cabinet, impact of, 70–72, 110; modeling decisions to deploy, 93–95; modeling decisions to deploy with an adjustment for strategic avoidance, 99–103; modeling the frequency of to ascertain congressional effects on, 58–63; opportunities for (*see* opportunities to use military force); party affiliation of the president and propensity toward, 72–73; politics preceding (*see* use-of-force politics); results from modeling the frequency of to ascertain the congressional effects on, 63–67, 244; results of modeling decisions to deploy, 95–99; robustness of congressional effects on, 67–70; size and scope of (*see* size/scope of military deployments); timing of decisions to deploy (*see* timing of decisions to deploy). *See also* opportunities to use military force; use-of-force politics
military tribunal system, xvi–xvii
Milosevic, Slobodan, 144–48
Mitchell, George, 136, 139–40
Moberg, David, 228
Montesquieu, Charles-Louis Secondat, Baron de, xi
Moore, John Bassett, xi
Moore, Will, 55
Morgan, C., 274n.18
Morgan, T. Clifton, 275n.26
Morocco, 60
Multinational Force in Lebanon Resolution (MFLR), 131
Murtha, John, 229, 241

Nasser, Gamal Abdel, 83
national will, 29–30
NATO. *See* North Atlantic Treaty Organization
Navarre, Henri, 116
Nelson, Bill, 235

neorealist international relations theory, 42–44, 54–55
Neutrality Acts, 11–12, 20–21
news stories on Iraq: content of individual stories, analysis of, 182–87; findings supporting the indexing hypothesis, 174–82; *New York Times* coverage of the Bush administration's case for war, 157–58, 171, 181; summary of evidence supporting the indexing hypothesis, 187–91; testing the indexing hypothesis, assembling a sample for, 171–72; who appears in, 172–74
New York Times: Bush administration, coverage of during lead-up to Iraq War, 157–58; on Bush's Iraq policy prior to the 2006 elections, 238; construction of the opportunities database and, 250–51; indexing hypothesis, use in database for testing, 171, 181; opportunities database, use in constructing, 78–80
Nicaragua: case study of interbranch dynamics regarding, 121–26; congressional foreign policy agenda, significance in, 15, 287n.23; media coverage of U.S. policy regarding, 160; opportunities to use military force in, 86; public opinion and the formulation of policy regarding, 31
Nickles, Don, 36, 146
Nixon, Richard, 4, 119–21
Non-Proliferation Treaty (NPT) of 1968, 233
Noriega, Manuel, 134–38
North, Oliver, 124
North Atlantic Treaty Organization (NATO), xvii, 17, 142, 145–48
North Korea, 60
nuclear weapons in Iran, 232–38
Nunn, Samuel, 132
Nzelibe, Jide, 133

October War (1973), 87
Ogaden War (1978), 86
Oneal, John, 45, 54, 216
O'Neill, Thomas, Jr., 123, 127, 132
opportunities to use military force: case studies of (*see* Bosnia; Indochina (1954); Kosovo; Lebanon; Nicaragua; Panama); chronological distribution of, 81, 83; country list of, 256; database, construction of, 78–81, 245–55;

opportunities to use military force (*continued*): descriptive statistics regarding, 257; economic and political relations with target countries, 87–89; geographic distribution of, 81–82, 84–87; the international system and, 108; modeling deployment decisions, 93–95; modeling deployment decisions with an adjustment for strategic avoidance, 99–103; party affiliation of the president and the decision to deploy, 111; probability of a deployment, modeling the, 76–78; results of modeling deployment decisions, 95–99, 258; strategic avoidance behavior and, 89–93, 99–103; timing of deployments, 103–8; veterans in Congress and the decision to deploy, 110; the War Powers Resolution and the effects of congressional partisan composition on the decision to deploy, 108–10. *See also* military deployments; use-of-force politics
opportunity costs, 41
Ornstein, Norman, 239
Ortega, Daniel, 123
Ostrom, Charles, 54, 62, 66
Owen, David, 290n.106

Page, Benjamin, 31–32
Pahlavi, Shah Reza, 232
Pakistan, 85–86
Palestine Liberation Organization (PLO), 87, 127–28, 133
Palestinian National Authority (PNA), 252–53
Panama, 39, 60, 134–38
partisanship: Bush as beneficiary of, 229; citizen views on Iraq and, 200, 202–3, 214; congressional responses to presidential use of force and, 35–40, 222–23, 229–32; congress members' support for a president of the same party, reasons for, 36–38; in the debate preceding the Iraq War, 177–78, 181; hypotheses regarding, 58, 78; the indexing hypothesis and, 166 (*see also* media, the); interbranch relations, as the most salient dimension of, 149, 217; Iran, in the congressional response to potential military action against, 236–37; modeling the frequency of troop deployments to ascertain congressional effects, 58–63; the president's decision to deploy

and, 94–98, 101–2; results from modeling the frequency of troop deployments to ascertain congressional effects, 63–67; robustness of congressional effects, 63–67; timing of the president's decision to deploy and, 104–6; the War Powers Resolution and decisions to deploy influenced by, 108–10
Peake, Jeffrey, 57–58
Pell, Claiborne, 139
Pelosi, Nancy, 241
Peron, Juan, 86
Persian Gulf: the Iraq War (*see* Iraq War); the "tanker war" between Iran and Iraq in, 24–25; unscheduled exercises in (1974), 60
Persian Gulf War (1991), 31, 38
Peterson, Paul, 9
Pew Research Center for the People and the Press, 196
Pletka, Danielle, 240
PLO. *See* Palestine Liberation Organization
Poindexter, John, 124
Poland, 60, 86
politics, use-of-force. *See* use-of-force politics
Polk, James, 3
Powell, Colin, xviii, 219
Powers, William, 240
"power without persuasion," 7
presidency/the president: case studies of use-of-force decisions by (*see* Bosnia; Indochina (1954); Kosovo; Lebanon; Nicaragua; Panama); foreign policy, reasons for dominance in making, 6–10, 162–63; imperial, 4; military veterans in the cabinet, impact of, 70–72; as a nonunitary actor, considerations for future research emphasizing the Executive Office, 225; opportunities for use of military force by (*see* opportunities to use military force); partisan reasons for supporting, 36–38; party affiliation of, foreign policy and, 72–73, 99, 111; public opinion, concerns regarding, 217–20; reporting requirements imposed by Congress on, 266–67n.40; "two presidencies" thesis, 67; unilateral powers of, 7–9, 47–48. *See also* names of presidents
Presidential Decision Directive (PDD) 25, 17

presidential war powers: Bush's exercise of, 227–29 (*see also* Bush, George W.; Iraq War); checks on (*see* checks on presidential war powers); congressional dissent regarding (*see* congressional dissent); domestic politics and, 54, 56–57; evolution of, 3–5; Framers of the Constitution regarding, views of the, 264–65n.13; interbranch dynamics regarding, 17–23; international factors and, 42–47, 55; public opinion and (*see* public opinion); signaling resolve, domestic opposition as impediment to, 27–29; strength of, 222–23; as unilateral power, reasons for, 6–10; War Powers Resolution of 1973 and (*see* War Powers Resolution of 1973)

public opinion: congressional appeals to, 23–26; congressional dissent and the shaping of, 29–30; Congress's influence over, considerations for future research regarding, 227; descriptive statistics of citizen's positions on Iraq, 260–61; drugs, concern regarding, 134; experimental data on the relationship of local news and support for the Iraq War, 205–13; foreign policy impact of, 30–32; on intervention in Central America, 125; Iran, level of support for taking military action against, 236; Kosovo, opinions regarding action in, 147; news and, scholarship on, 192–95; observational data on the relationship of local news and support for the Iraq War, 196–205; presidential concerns regarding, 217–20; summary of evidence on the relationship of local news and support for the Iraq War, 213–17

public sphere, definition of, 155

Purdum, Todd, 303n.55

Quinn, Kevin, 300n.31

Rabin, Yitzhak, 253

Radford, Arthur, 119, 121

Raines, Howell, 157–58

rally-around-the-flag effects: congressional impact on, 29, 165; presidential approval ratings and, 37, 56–57; presidential incentives to use force due to, 62

Rasul v. Bush, xvi

Reagan, Ronald: Lebanon, intervention in, 16, 126–29, 132–34, 149–50, 230–31; Libya, air strikes against, 7; media coverage of the administration of, 160; Nicaragua, actions regarding, 15, 121–26; opportunities to exercise military force faced by, number of, 245; the "tanker war" in the Persian Gulf, actions regarding, 24–25; Tripoli, media coverage of bombing of, 161

realist international relations theory, 42–44, 54–55

Reid, Harry, 241

reporting requirements, 266–67n.40

resolve, signaling, 27–29, 236

Rice, Condoleeza, 230, 303n.55

Ridgway, Matthew, 119

Riegle, Donald, 131–32

right-censoring, 103–4

risk propensity, 46

Roberts, John, xvi

Roberts, Pat, 235

Roosevelt, Franklin, 11–12, 266n.23

Roosevelt, Theodore, 137

Rosenbluth, Frances, 18

Rossiter, Clinton, 222

Rumsfeld, Donald, 219, 230, 235, 241

Rumsfeld v. Padilla, xvi

Russell, Richard, 117

Russett, Bruce, xix, 45, 216

Russia, 87, 145, 234. *See also* Union of Soviet Socialist Republics

Rwanda, 16–17, 87

Sandinista National Liberation Front (FSLN/Sandinistas), 121–22

Sarver, Christopher, 69

Saudi Arabia, 60

Schlesinger, Arthur, Jr., xi, 4

Schroeder, Patricia, 135

Schultz, George, 130, 133

Schultz, Kenneth, 27

Schumer, Charles, 134

Scowcroft, Brent, 137

Seiberling, John, 128

separation of powers: constitutional authority regarding war and, 3, 5; the indexing hypothesis and, 163

Serbia and the Serbs, 139–48, 289n.103

signaling: information exchanged through and the propensity to fight, relationship of, 45; international trade as mechanism for, 46; partisanship and the content/credibility of, 36–37; resolve, 27–29, 236. *See also* information

Simon, Paul, 137
Sinai Peninsula, 83, 87
Six Day War, 83, 87
size/scope of military deployments: congressional attentiveness to military actions and, 41–42; hypothesis regarding, 58; the president's decision to deploy, as a factor in, 99
Skelton, Ike, 239, 241
Smith, Gordon, 145
Sobel, Richard, 31, 125
Somalia, 16, 31, 39, 87
Somoza Debayle, Antonio, 121
Souter, David, xvi
South Africa, 88
Southeast Asia Treaty Organization, xvii
South Korea, 60
Soviet Union. *See* Union of Soviet Socialist Republics
Stassen, Harold, 119–20
steel mills, Truman's seizure of, 13
Stennis, John, 117
Stevens, John Paul, xvi
Stoll, Richard, 54
strategic avoidance behavior, 89–93, 99–103
structural theory, 42–44
Studds, Gerry, 122
Suez, Gulf of, 60
Suez crisis (1956), 83, 87
Sununu, John, 137–38
supranational institutions. *See* international organizations
Supreme Court, United States, xv–xvii
Syria, 126–27, 133
systemic theory, 42–44

Taft, Robert, 12, 117
Tanzania, 87
terrorism, war on. *See* "war on terror"
Thucydides, 22
Thurmond, Strom, 127
Times of London, 303n.55
timing of decisions to deploy: Bosnia as a case study of congressional influence on, 139–44; modeling, 103–5; partisanship and, 104–6; results from modeling, 105–8
trade, 46, 87–88, 273n.40
transaction costs, 34–35
Truman, Harry: congressional opposition to, 12–13; Indochina, policy regarding,

116; Korea, deployment in, xvii, 230–31; Korea, treatment from Congress regarding, 269n.64; MacArthur, struggle with, xv; political cost of military action experienced by, 22; precedence for presidential war powers established by, 3, 12
"two presidencies" thesis, 67

Uniform Code of Military Justice (UCMJ), xvi
unilateral action, theory of, 7–9, 47–48
Union of Soviet Socialist Republics, 44–45, 86–88, 94, 101. *See also* Russia
United Kingdom, 83, 86, 88, 145, 234
United Nations: Bosnia, actions regarding, 140; Iranian nuclear activity, response to, 234; Iraq, actions regarding, xviii, 168, 170, 180; Korea, justification for U.S. action in, xvii; Kosovo, actions regarding, 145; Somalia, action in, 16
use-of-force politics: case studies of (*see* Bosnia; Indochina (1954); Kosovo; Lebanon; Nicaragua; Panama); lessons from the case studies about, 133–34, 148–49; the media and Congress, relationship of (*see* indexing hypothesis; media, the); by the military, xv; military veterans in the House and cabinet, impact of, 70–72; modeling the frequency of military deployments to ascertain congressional effects on, 58–63; opportunities to use military force, responses to (*see* opportunities to use military force); party affiliation of the president and, 72–73; political economy of, 62; preceding and during military action, distinction between, xix; quantitative literature regarding, 53–58, 73; relationship of experiences to each other, 150; results from modeling the frequency of military deployments to ascertain congressional effects on, 63–67; robustness of congressional effects on, 67–70; unilateral actions by the president and, constraints regarding, 48–49 (*see also* unilateral action, theory of)
U-2 spy plane incident, 86, 93

Vance, Cyrus, 290n.106
Vietnam, 60, 85–86

Vietnam War, xvi, 13–14, 18, 20. *See also* Indochina (1954)

Waltz, Kenneth, 43–44, 47, 54
Warner, John, 139–40, 146, 235
War of 1812, 268n.57
"war on terror": authorization of military action in, 304n.9; expansion of to Iraq, 167 (*see also* Iraq War); Supreme Court actions regarding, xvi–xvii
war powers. *See* presidential war powers
War Powers Resolution of 1973: congressional effects following passage of, 67–68; decisions to deploy before and after, congressional partisan composition and, 108–10; enactment of, 4; failings of, 4–5; invocation of regarding Lebanon, 15; Supreme Court actions regarding, xv–xvi

Weinberger, Casper, 29–30
Weissman, Stephen, 5
Wellstone, Paul, 169
Wilson, Charles, 118
Wise, Robert, 135
Wolfowitz, Paul, 219
World War II, events preceding American entry into, 10–12
Wright, Jim, 121

Yom Kippur War, 83
Yugoslavia, disintegration of, 139. *See also* Bosnia; Kosovo

Zablocki, Clement, 128
Zaire, 86, 93
Zaller, John, 161, 196, 216, 271n.93
al-Zarqawi, Abu Musab, 231